CURRENT ISSUES IN THEOLOGY

There is a need among upper-undergraduate and graduate students of theology, as well as among Christian teachers and church professionals, for a series of short, focused studies of particular key topics in theology written by prominent theologians. *Current Issues in Theology* meets this need.

The books in the series are designed to provide a "state-of-the-art" statement on the topic in question, engaging with contemporary thinking as well as providing original insights. The aim is to publish books that stand between the static monograph genre and the more immediate statement of a journal article, by authors who are questioning existing paradigms or rethinking perspectives.

Other titles in the series:

Human Anguish and God's Power

The power of God and its relevance to human suffering has always been a deeply contested subject. David H. Kelsey is one of the most thoughtful and distinguished theological writers in English, and is well known for his innovative work with George Lindbeck and Hans Frei in pioneering a distinctive 'postliberal' way of doing theology. In this long-awaited new book, he brings a lifetime's learning to bear on one of the most difficult questions that there is: namely, how can we speak meaningfully and authentically to those in anguish while at the same time maintaining plausible talk of divine potency? Kelsey shows that some pastoral approaches to people's distress so often undermine the very case they are making. His nuanced and subtle argument about the paradoxical power/ powerlessness of the divine, which includes a path-breaking account of transcendence, transforms our understanding of God's relationship to the world and its creatures.

DAVID H. KELSEY is the Weigle Professor Emeritus of Theology at Yale Divinity School. He is the author of *Proving Doctrine* (1999), *Imagining Redemption* (2005), and *Eccentric Existence* (2 vols., 2009).

DAVID H. KELSEY
Yale University

Human Anguish and God's Power

CAMBRIDGE
UNIVERSITY PRESS

University Printing House, Cambridge CB2 8BS, United Kingdom

One Liberty Plaza, 20th Floor, New York, NY 10006, USA

477 Williamstown Road, Port Melbourne, VIC 3207, Australia

314–321, 3rd Floor, Plot 3, Splendor Forum, Jasola District Centre, New Delhi – 110025, India

79 Anson Road, #06–04/06, Singapore 079906

Cambridge University Press is part of the University of Cambridge.

It furthers the University's mission by disseminating knowledge in the pursuit of education, learning, and research at the highest international levels of excellence.

www.cambridge.org
Information on this title: www.cambridge.org/9781108836975
DOI: 10.1017/9781108873246

First published 2021

Printed in the United Kingdom by TJ Books Limited, Padstow Cornwall

A catalogue record for this publication is available from the British Library.

ISBN 978-1-108-83697-5 Hardback

For J. V. K.,
and all those, whatever their roles,
who find themselves called to pastor the anguished.

Contents

The Echternach Procession: A Preface

This book is based on my 2011 Warfield Lectures at Princeton Theological Seminary. In those lectures, I reflected on some implications for Christian doctrine of God of a hermeneutical and exegetical move that is central to the theological anthropological project worked out at considerable (some would understandably say "excessive"!) length in *Eccentric Existence*.[1] That "move" turns on the claim that what makes the diverse writings assembled in the Christian bible construed as "canon" a certain sort of "whole" is not, as is usually assumed, a single extended narrative. That narrative, which runs through the canon, tells of God's relating to all that is not God to create it, to reconcile it to God when it is self-estranged from God, and to consummate it eschatologically. Rather, my claim is, it is a braid of three inseparable but irreducibly different sorts of narrative: respectively, God actively relating in importantly different concrete ways to create, to reconcile estranged creatures, and to draw creatures to eschatological consummation. The patterns of inter-relations among the three ways in which God concretely goes about relating to all that is not God, I argue, serve to rule and shape what may be said on the basis of each of them about God and about all else in relation to God. *Eccentric Existence* explored how those patterns shape what can be said on their basis about human creatures; the Warfield Lectures suggested how those patterns should shape aspects of what is said about God's glory, kingdom, and power.

---

[1] *Eccentric Existence* (Louisville, KY: Westminster John Knox Press, 2009).

This book's emergence from those lectures has been a slow process, five pages forward daily followed by three deleted, daily. I lamented about this to a friend. "It sounds like the Echternach Procession," he said. "Check it out." I consulted Wikipedia. Sure enough, a religious dancing procession is held every Whit Tuesday in Echternach in eastern Luxembourg. It is held in honor of St. Willibrord the Patron Saint of Luxembourg who established the Abbey of Echternach in the seventh century. Over a distance of about a mile, pilgrims in rows of four or five abreast, sometimes with arms linked, "'dance" or "jump" from left to right and thus slowly move forward to the basilica. It has taken other forms in the past. At one time, "pilgrims would take 3 steps forward and 2 steps backwards thus taking five steps in order to advance one." Uplifting as the Echternach Procession may be as an expression of the piety of a public liturgy, it is – at least in my case – a depressingly apt image for the experience of writing theology. At the same time, it is also an apt image for several features of this project for which I can be grateful.

The pilgrims' linked arms in the Echternach Procession is an apt image for the way in which theological projects in progress are always directly or indirectly collaborative. I am deeply grateful to Iain Torrance, the President of Princeton Theological Seminary at the time, to Daniel Migliore my faculty host, and to Professor George Hunsinger for the invitation to deliver the Warfield Lectures and for their generous hospitality while I was there; to students and faculty colleagues at Princeton for their engagement with the lectures; and especially to the lively groups of students who invited me to theological discussion over lunch and coffee during the days of the lecture series.

Parts of Chapter 11 are based on a lecture, "Picturing God in a Fragmented World," delivered at the meeting of the *Societas Homileticus* at Yale Divinity School in August of 2010. An early version of Chapter 6 was presented as a lecture at the University of Tuebingen in June, 2012, and versions of Chapters 5 and 9 were the basis of discussion in theology seminars there led by Professor Christoph Schwoebel. I am deeply grateful to the Protestant Theology Faculty of the University of Tuebingen for the invitation to lecture and to our hosts, Professor and Mrs. Schwoebel, for their most thoughtful and generous hospitality to my wife, Julie, and me. In each of these settings, questions and discussion have made collaborators even out of people who were at best dubious about the proposals developed here.

My Echternach Procession might never have come to an end had I not been invited to present my effort to "develop" the Warfield Lectures into a book to the 2014 Graduate Theological Seminar in the Yale Department of Religious Studies. Participants in the seminar (you know who you are!) patiently worked their way through over-long chunks of a "work in process," gently and most firmly identifying innumerable places where the line of thought disappeared down conceptual rabbit's holes, weakening the argument and pointlessly inflating length of the manuscript. I abandoned the entire project in the distorted form it had taken up to that point, and I started over. I and my readers owe the members of the seminar deep thanks.

The final steps in the preparation of this text owe a large debt to Ed Watson. I am deeply grateful to him for creating the book's index and, more broadly, his meticulous spotting of innumerable typos.

Which brings us to a second way in which the Echternach Procession is an apt image for this project. At less than a mile, the procession is a modest pilgrimage, no matter how frustratingly slow its three-steps-forward two-steps-back process may be. Its modesty is an apt image for the central topic of this project, namely, the relation and distinction between God's sovereignty and God's power, which are frequently conflated under the name of "God's Lordship." That is a modest topic, a subtopic of a subtopic of Christian Trinitarian doctrine of God which is itself only one "place" or "locus" in the whole body of Christian Divinity. This book's topic is a subtopic of the larger topic of the intrinsic or "metaphysical perfections" of the Triune God, in contradistinction to God's "relational perfections." That, in turn, is a subtopic of the even more complex topic "divine nature" or "divinity-as-such" in contradistinction to the topic "divine triunity," both of which are subtopics of Christian Trinitarian doctrine of God. Full-ledged Trinitarian doctrines of God must address a huge agenda. This project is far more modest. To keep that clear, it is best if kept (relatively!) brief. As pilgrimage processions go, after all, the Echternach Procession is relatively short.

1 | Introduction: Consoling Anguish and Making It Worse

Despite the title of this Introduction, this book is about the concept of God's power. It does not focus directly on the dynamics of anguish or how best to console it. In the division of intellectual labor in contemporary Christian academic theology, it falls into the area of "doctrinal theology" rather than the area of "pastoral theology." However, behind it is the conviction that much talk by Christians who seek to console those who anguish about others' horrific suffering is itself problematic from the perspective of central Christian theological beliefs. It is problematic because it mischaracterizes the Triune God. Its mischaracterization, in turn, implies a picture of the nature of God's power that, rather than consoling anguish, simply makes it worse. That conviction defines the focus and shapes the approach of these proposals concerning how to talk about the power of God in ways that are faithful to the ways in which God relates to us.

The sort of anguish I have in mind here is often evoked, not just by terrible things that have happened to us, but by terrible things that happen to other people. They may be people we know well and love; they may equally well be passing acquaintances or complete strangers we know about only through the news. Such anguish is a complicated tangle of feelings: horror at the circumstances that cause others' suffering; outrage that such circumstances can occur; fear at the abrupt reminder that such things could suddenly happen to us; an intense desire that such circumstances be taken away from our common world, i.e., from both them and us; and an overwhelming feeling of helplessness in the face of those circumstances and the suffering they cause. It is a bone-deep emotional ache that suffuses the core of one's being, burdening every moment the way an intense headache does, weighing one down. The problematic ways of talking about God's power that focus the proposals in this book are addressed for the most part to console both people who are themselves undergoing horrific suffering and those who anguish about what is happening to others.

The problematic forms of would-be consolation that I have in mind use variations on a few conventional themes. For example, anguished persons are often consoled by being told that the circumstance evoking horrific suffering are "God's will," "have a reason," "are sent by God for a purpose," or that "God has a plan in this," or "God never sends more suffering than you can bear." They are platitudes of conventional wisdom. In *Everything Happens for a Reason, and Other Lies I've Loved,*[1] Kate Bowler's theologically wise and moving book about being on the receiving end of such comments, she notes in these sentiments the "trite cruelty in the logic of the perfectly certain."[2] Maybe most people who use them would identify themselves as "people of faith." In any case, those ways of speaking remain commonplace in our culture, even as it becomes increasingly secularized. Well-intentioned would-be consolers need not necessarily be themselves devoutly religious or deeply spiritual people. Not knowing what to say to those in anguish, we easily slip into using familiar clichés about God's power whether we "believe in God" or not.

One sign that such efforts to console the anguished are problematic is that, rather than easing anguish, such words of "consolation" often make the anguish worse; they evoke an entirely understandable outrage at God in particular. "Don't talk to me about a loving God!" our friend raged. "A God of love would not have let him

---

[1] Kate Bowler, *Everything Happens for a Reason, and Other Lies I've Loved* (New York: Random House, 2018).
[2] Ibid., p. 119.

suffer the way he did." Her husband had died after enduring days of intense pain from bone cancer, pain that sophisticated palliative care could not ease. "And don't tell me that God knows better what is good for us than we do ourselves, or that God sent this whole thing for a reason, or that God never gives more than you can handle. I could only hate a God like that."

Rare and intensely painful disease is not the only sort of circumstance that evokes anguish in others. Natural catastrophes do also. As I write this chapter, Mexico City has endured two earthquakes and three hurricanes in one month. Today a small army of volunteers attempts to remove the debris of an earthquake-collapsed school building in which a dozen children were trapped, some of whom may still live and others who suffocated to death. It is not difficult to imagine the outrage with which their parents might greet the "consoling" suggestion that God had a "purpose" in "sending" that earthquake. One does not even need to "believe in God" to be angered by the suggestion that God, whom we should praise and love with all our hearts, minds and souls, is a God who has the power to cause such circumstances for some "purpose" or as a part of some "plan." Even if one does not believe in the reality of God, one can understandably rage at the very hypothesis that a supposedly loving God would exercise God's power intentionally to do such things. Anger at the reality of such a God, or only at the concept of such a God, makes the burden of anguish worse. It does not ease any of the inter-braided feelings that make up the anguish. It only complexifies and intensifies that tangle of feelings even more than they already are. Well-intentioned efforts to console the anguished by invoking the power of God have the unintended consequence of making the anguish even worse, simply by evoking anger at the God portrayed in those efforts.

Such horrific suffering does not always evoke anger at God. Especially in believers, it leads to a deeply anguished on-going struggle with many conventional Christian spiritual practices. Writing about her young adult daughter's multiply diagnosed problems – "Oppositional defiance. High-functioning Asperger's. Clinical depression. Generalized anxiety. Social anxiety. Obsessive compulsive disorder," – Debie Thomas writes "My daughter's limitations block her from accessing the effective benefits of religion: a sense of belonging, inner peace, the joys of worship, deliverance from existential despair." "On my worst days," Thomas writes, "or on my daughter's – I have thrown the words of Scripture right back in God's face. 'The peace that passes understanding? Abundant life? An easy yoke and a light burden? Daughter, your faith has made you well – go in peace'? Are you kidding me?" As a preteen, her daughter referred to her problem as "a wall." About herself Thomas says, "I've inherited a Christian vocabulary that is rich and beautiful – but also impoverished when it comes to deep psychological anguish." "So now I simply sit next to the wall" – i.e., next to the limitations that wall her daughter from a "normal" life.

> I face it and endure it. I live each day in its shadow, hoping my daughter will decide to keep on living too, even in that chilly darkness – and hoping that my presence at the wall shows her something of God's steady presence in its shadow too... I read about Jesus at Gethsemane, deserted and afraid. I read bout manna – mysterious substance for one day at a time. And I read bout the lost lamb the shepherd follows into the treacherous night, the little one who can't help but wander. The exhausted, endangered one who needs so badly to come home but just can't find the way.[3]

There are several ways in which trying to console those who anguish by speaking of God in this fashion is problematic. In the chapters that follow, I focus on only one: Assumptions about what the phrase "the power of God" means in a Christian context. They are assumptions that are symbolized by the common, unqualified

[3] 'My Daughter's Wall,' *The Christian Century*, August 1, 2018, p. 35.

use of the adjective "almighty" to describe God, as though what makes God "God" is that God has "all might or power" or that God has "absolute and unqualified" might or power.

Those assumptions, I suggest, lie deep in the theological and cultural background of such exchanges between those who anguish and those who would console them. They lie implicit in the exchanges' theological *background* because, in the exchanges themselves, nobody is explicitly engaged in reflection on theological concepts. Nor should they be. No one can be consoled by being argued with about theological questions or by being subjected to an informal lecture on relevant theological topics. No one can be placated in the heat of their anger at God by being shown that the anger is "irrational" or "inconsistent with other ideas you do hold dear." Not only would the psychological obtuseness of such efforts count as pastoral care malpractice but the very idea of trying to console someone by talking to them that way is laughable on the face of it.

The assumptions about God's power on which the rest of this book focuses lie also in the broader cultural background of such exchanges. They are so deeply entrenched in North American culture, at least, and reinforced by conventional ways of talking about the God in whom one either does not or does "believe," ways of talking in both the culture generally and in communities of Christian faith particularly, that everyone whose identity is formed by that culture is so deeply shaped by those assumptions that their appropriateness is rarely questioned.

There are, of course, other ways in which it is problematic to try to console those who anguish by reminding them that God has the power to control all things. Some of the ways that it is problematic are more immediately present up front in such exchanges and not in the background. They are both *psychologically* problematic and, from a "spiritual" point of view, *pastorally* problematic. Those aspects of the problematic character of such efforts to console the anguished are certainly important, because they directly distort the effort to console. However, many of the questions they raise are different than the conceptual questions that are raised in the examination of how such efforts are also theologically problematic. What is *theologically* problematic about them only indirectly distorts their effort to console. This book does not directly address ways in which efforts to console the anguished are psychologically and pastorally problematic. It focuses only on theologically problematic ways of talking about God's power that lie in the background of those inadequacies. All the same, as the book progresses, I aim to exhibit how an examination of the concept of the power of God in a Christian conceptual context cumulatively has, over the long haul, practical relevance to the reshaping of ways to address in God's name people's anguish at others' suffering that are less problematic. That is one way in which the focus of the book is narrowed.

Theological Goals

A second way in which the book's focus is narrowed lies in its aspiration. Theological writings may have any of several goals they aspire to realize. Many of them share the aim to explain some theological concept, as this one aims to clarify the claim that God is powerful.

Of those works that aim to explain the concept of God's power, many also aim to defend the claim that God is "almighty" in the face of "the problem of evil." Their explanations of God's power are exercises in "theodicy" i.e., exercises in justifying claims about the power of a loving and just God in the face of the reality of evil that seems to be scattered randomly and unjustly in the lives of humankind. Affirmation of (a) the reality of evil seems to bring with it strong reasons to deny the reality of a God who is at once, (b) loving, (c) just, and (d) "almighty" or "omnipotent." The four are inconsistent – if evil is real, then either God cannot prevent it

despite God's love for creatures and therefore is not "almighty";
or God could prevent it but does not and therefore is not "just";
or God is incapable of preventing it although in love God wants
to, and therefore is not "almighty." Hence, the argument against
God's existence concludes, such a God cannot exist. Indeed,
the objection goes, such a God cannot even be coherently conceived. Just that objection seems to be what is going on in the
angry responses of many who are anguished by others' horrific
suffering to conventional efforts to console them. Hence, in
addition to aiming to clarify the claim that God is powerful,
the theological projects engaged in theodicy also aim to engage
in "apologetics." They offer arguments to show how affirmation
of God's reality can cohere with affirmations of God's love,
justice and power.

There is nothing novel in modern theology about a theological
project like this book that proposes to analyze what it means to
characterize God as "almighty" or "omnipotent."

In contemporary theology, many such projects also aim to be an
"apologetic theology." They offer a justification for affirming the
reality of a God of power (in some sense of the word "power"), who
is also loving and just, in the face of the undeniable reality of
horrendous suffering that evokes anguish. Their "apologias" are
one sort or another of theodicy. They have often been formulated
on the basis of a systematic metaphysics, such as the process
metaphysics of Charles Hartshorne or Alfred North Whitehead,[4]
or on the basis of an ontology, such as the one developed by Paul
Tillich and modified by Kyle Pasewark.[5] Or, like Edward Farley, the

---

[4] Cf. John B. Cobb, *A Christian Natural Theology* (Philadelphia, Westminster Press,
1964); John B. Cobb and David Ray Griffin, *Process Theology: An Introductory
Exposition;* (Philadelphia, Westminster Press, 1976); Anna Case-Winters, *God's Power:
Traditional Understandings and Contemporary Challenges* (Louisville: Westminster
John Knox, 1990).

[5] *A Theology of Power: Being Beyond Domination* (Minneapolis, MN: Fortress
Press, 1993).

challenge can be formulated on the basis of a phenomenological analysis of the conditions of the possibility of human consciousness and free agency.[6]

This book's focus limits itself to the single aim of analyzing the Christian theological concept of the power of God. The "logic" of anyone's coming to trust in and "believe" the reality of God is another and quite separate question. An exploration of the "logic" or "grammar" of Christian beliefs is not necessarily an exploration of the "logic" of "coming to Christian belief." It does not aim to be an apologetics. It is self-limited to exploring what is often referred to as the informal "logic" or the "generative grammar" of Christian talk about God – in this case talk about God's power. In such contexts, "logic" and "grammar" are both used analogically. The analogy with "logic" suggests that the essay aims to explore how the concept of "power" is related to other key theological concepts: Some are "more basic" than others, some necessarily imply others, some may imply others but not necessarily, some are incoherent with others, etc. The analogy with grammar suggests that the essay aims to explore something like "grammatical rules" in Christian discourse about God, and discourse about all else in relation to God, in virtue of which what is said grammatically is intelligible to any one who has learned to speak that language or dialect. However, the rules do not dictate the content of what one says. Instead, such grammatical rules are the condition of the possibility of intelligible communication. They are socially constructed and can change. However, logic and grammar are only analogies for the sort of analysis this essay aims to realize. The success of the analysis has to be assessed on the basis of what it manages to show about the concept of God's power and not on the basis of how closely it approximates an essay in either logic or grammar. Nor can it be assessed on how successful it is in "solving the problem of evil."

[6] Cf. Edward Farley, *Divine Empathy* (Minneapolis, MN: Fortress Press, 1996).

It does not even try to do that, although it may contribute to dissolving it in the form in which it is usually posed.

What Makes It "Christian"?

I have already signaled that the focus of this essay is also limited in a third way. As a reflection on the concept of the power of God, it is specifically a "Christian" theology. It is not a proposal about the sense in which power might be ascribed to generic "transcendence," "holy mystery," or "sacredness." What makes it more narrowly and particularly "Christian"? I suggest that, put in a concise formula, the answer is that this essay counts as Christian insofar as (a) it is grounded in the ways in which God actively relates to all that is not God, (b) those ways of relating as told in Christian canonical scripture as (c) that scripture is read through the lens of the life-trajectory of Jesus Christ as it is variously narrated in the canonical Gospels and, in very brief accounts, in other New Testament texts (mostly letters). These supplementary texts comment on the significance of Jesus and what he did and underwent. Put broadly, it counts as Christian insofar as it is in that fashion "Christocentric."[7] It proceeds in that way without attempting to defend the decision to do so.

It needs to be noted that that decision does not necessarily imply that proceeding in this fashion is the only procedure that entitles a theological proposal to count as "truly Christian." It merely claims that it is one way in which a theological project may count as Christian, and it is the one adopted here.

In doing so, it is obvious that this book, whose theological focus is explicitly Christian, proceeds on the basis of a number of

---

[7] In this approach, it follows the basic approach that Daniel Migliore's adopts in his important book *The Power of God and the Gods of Power* (Louisville: Westminster John Knox, 2008), although it may develop it in ways Migliore would find problematic.

background theological assumptions that it does not pretend to have defended. It may be useful to identify five of them at the outset.

First, I assume that a Christian understanding of God is based on the ways in which God goes about actively relating to all that is not God. The traditional name for God's ways of relating is "God's economy."

Second, I assume that there are communities that are self-described as "Christian" that acknowledge canonical Christian scripture as an authoritative collection of texts. These texts tell of the concrete ways in which God goes about relating to all else and these communities seek to shape their common and individual lives in ways that are appropriate responses to the ways in which God has related to them.

I assume, third, that those same communities affirm that what Jesus does and undergoes – through his ministry of proclaiming the immanence of the in-breaking of God's eschatological kingdom by teaching and healing, his trial, arrest, suffering, crucifixion, and resurrection, as narrated in the canonical Gospels – is definitive of the way God goes about relating to all else. This is not to assume that the entire content of what can be said about how God relates to all else can and must be derived from scripture's accounts of what Jesus does and undergoes. "Definitive" does not entail "exhaustive." It does, however, set a negative standard by which any effort to characterize God, including God's power, must meet: It cannot be incoherent with the way in which God relates to all else in and through what Jesus does and undergoes.

Fourth, I assume that the literary structure of canonical New Testament accounts of Jesus warrants the judgment that what is said on the basis of those accounts about the ways in which God relates to all that is not God is most felicitously expressed in Trinitarian accounts of God. Regularly those narratives have three focal characters: Jesus, the One He calls "Father," and the Spirit. That is a structure of the concrete way in which God is said to relate to all else in and through what Jesus does and undergoes. This

Trinitarian structure of their narratives is part of the way in which the Gospels' accounts of how God relates to all else in Jesus is definitive for what can be said about God, including God's power. It is not that God, who is powerful, happens also to be triune. It is intrinsic to the triune God *as Triune* that God is powerful.

Fifth, I assume that the way scripture's accounts of God's relating to what is not God are written warrants the judgment that the most apt analogies for God's active relating are human intentional actions and interactions. Such analogies entail markedly "personal" accounts of God that suggest that God is in some respects analogous to what moderns consider to be a "personal" being. The proviso has to be that a characterization of God's ways of relating in "personal" terms uses those terms analogously and not univocally. Here "analogy" entails that the differences between the two things being compared are greater in important ways than their similarities. That proviso opens the door to placing important blocks against drawing certain inferences from the use of "personal" terms to describe God that might, in strictly interhuman personal actions, be entirely warranted.

Given these five assumptions, what the communities mentioned in the first assumption say about God, including "God's power," should comport with scripture's accounts of how God relates to all else. The argument developed in this book appeals to those self-commitments by such communities of faith: Because you affirm these things, should not your way of talking about God's power be shaped by what is proposed here?

Implications for Where to Begin This Proposal

Together, those five assumptions have an important implication about where this proposal about the power of God should begin. If what we say about the power of God must be guided by God's economy, as it is rendered in Christian Scripture's accounts of how God relates to all that is not God, then the concepts that are key to the explication of each of those accounts of how God actively relates are more "basic" than the concept of the power that is properly ascribed to God. So we cannot begin an account of God's power by simply assuming that we already know what "power" *really* means in general and then proceed to ascribe that analogically to God. Rather, the power that is ascribed to God must be understood in the context of other theological concepts that are more basic logically than the relevant concept of power. As the context in which "God's power" must be understood, the concepts that are key to explication of the basic ways in which God relates to all else serve to nuance in important ways the sense in which "power" should be understood as ascribed to God. They serve to block certain inferences that might otherwise reasonably be drawn from ascription of "power" to God on the assumption that there is some generic concept of power that we already understand and is, so to speak, "free standing" and not defined by a larger conceptual context.

Thus, read canonically, Christian Scripture tells of God relating to create all else, with its entailment that in so doing God is self-committed to relate to creatures in providential care. It also tells of God relating to creatures to draw them to an eschatological consummation. Finally, it tells of God relating to creatures to reconcile them to God when they are estranged from God. Scriptural accounts of each of those ways in which God relates uses a distinctive set of terms analogically to characterize the way in which God concretely goes about relating in that particular way. For example, in regard to God's relating to create: "creating," "bringing to be from nothing," "making," "shaping," "sustaining," "ordering," and "providing"; in regard to God's relating to consummate eschatologically: "glorifying," "redeeming," "re-creating," "transforming," "transfiguring," "destining for glory," and "sanctifying"; and in regard to God's relating to reconcile the estranged: "reconciling," "justifying," "judging," and "forgiving." Many of those images are drawn from forms of intentional action and interaction that are particularly characteristic of human "personal" action. Concepts that are central to theological explanations of "God creates creatures," "God eschatologically consummates creatures" and "God reconciles estranged creatures" are more basic in Christian theology than the concept of God's power. And they are the conceptual context within which an explanation of the concept of God's power should be laid out.

Furthermore, if what we say about the power of God must be guided by God's economy as rendered in Christian Scripture's accounts of how God relates to all that is not God, and if God is understood in Trinitarian terms, then it is the one self-same Triune[8] God who relates, respectively, to create, consummate creatures eschatologically, and reconcile estranged creatures. It is not that one "Person" of the triune God relates alone to create, another relates alone to draw creatures to eschatological consummation, and a third relates alone to reconcile the estranged. Nonetheless, canonical accounts of how God goes about relating in each of these ways generally give pride of place as the "lead" "person" of the Trinity in each way of relating to a different "person": "God the Father" in creating; "God the Holy Spirit" in drawing to eschatological consummation; and "God the Son" in reconciling. Accordingly, I argue that, when we try to explain the sense in which the Triune God *as such* is powerful in the ways God relates to all else, it is proper to frame the explanation by using the set of images typically used analogically in Scripture to characterize the way the

---

[8] Because, in ordinary English usage, the word "person" means something very different than what traditional theological use of the word means in the context of accounts of the Triunity of God (as a translation of the Latin *persona* and the Greek *hypostasis*), I shall regularly capitalize it and enclose it quotes when discussing the Trinity to remind readers that it is a technical term into which modern concepts of "personhood" must not be read. I do that at grave risk of annoying readers. The annoyance, however, gets the reader's attention every time as a warning: Be wary what you read *into* this term.

"lead Person" of the Trinity in each of the three ways in which the triune God relates to creatures.

It follows that, if God, whose power is in question, is understood as the Triune God, then an account of God's power must begin with some reflections on the implications of a Trinitarian understanding of God for what must be said in response the questions: "*what* is it to be God?" and "*who* is God?" I suggest that it is not possible to make either one of those two questions the "basic" question from whose answer we can derive an answer to the other question. Instead, the two questions are interdependent. I argue that the interdependence of those two questions is particularly clear when we focus on the concept of the *glory* of God as the concept that sums up all of God's perfections or attributes, including power.

Against the background of reflection on the glory of God, we can then see that two distinguishable but inseparable senses in which God is characterized as *sovereign* are grounded, respectively, in canonical accounts of God relating creatively and accounts of God relating to consummate creatures eschatologically. It is only in the context of that bifocal concept of God's sovereignty, itself understood in the context of the concept of the Triune God's glory, that an analysis can be offered of the sense in which *power* may be properly ascribed to God. The Triune God's "power," it is argued, is the power of God's sovereignty, and different senses of "sovereign" entail different senses in which God is "powerful."

The Overall Movement of the Argument

So the argument takes the three following major steps: Following this Introduction, Part I (i.e., Chapter 2) outlines three sorts of reference that the expression "the glory of God" has in canonical Scriptural texts. It then focuses on the way in which "glory" is ascribed to God intrinsically. It explores the suggestion that "glory" be understood as the ensemble of all the qualities that may be ascribed to the Triune God as qualities of the dynamics of the Triune God's intrinsic and utterly singular life. Part II then sorts out different senses in which the Triune God may be said to be "sovereign" or, in another image, "kingly." These ways are nuanced and ruled by the senses in which God is "glorious," in regard to, respectively, God's intrinsic reality (Chapter 3), God's relating to all else in creative blessing and providential care (Chapter 4), and God's relating to all else in providential care and to reconcile the estranged (Chapter 5), followed by a brief excursus defending this book's departure from traditional theological accounts of God's sovereignty. Part III reflects critically on theologically problematic assumptions about power that underlie and warrant theologically problematic remarks offered in the pastoral care of those who anguish (Chapter 7). It then turns to sort out different senses in which "power" may appropriately be ascribed to God's intrinsic sovereignty (Chapter 8) and to God's sovereignty in relating to creatures to bless them eschatologically. It continues to discuss God's sovereignty in reconciling them when they are estranged from God (Chapter 9). Part IV reflects on the reasons why our praise of the Triune God, which itself is the third reference of the phrase "the glory of God," must necessarily stammer. Chapter 10 roots that necessity in the irony that praise of the Triune God *for God's own sake* is necessarily praise of an intrinsically inexplicable and "useless" God. Chapter 11 explores how that "inexplicability" locates those whose acts of pastoral care of the anguished praise God in an "anomic" context that, ruling out "explanations" of evil and suffering, makes stammering unavoidable.

Part I | Glory

2 | The Glory of the Triune God: What and Who the Powerful God Is

A hymn sung in both synagogues and churches urges:[1]

> The God of Abraham praise,
> Who reigns enthroned above;
> Ancient of everlasting days, and God of love;
> the Lord, the great I AM, by earth and heaven confessed;
> we bow and bless the sacred Name for ever blest.

The injunction to praise God raises two questions: Why *praise* God? and, second, Why focus on praise of God in connection with this book's examination of efforts to console those anguished by others' deep suffering?

Why praise God? Why not first of all thank God, or confess our unworthiness to God, or beseech God to aid us? The short answer to the first question, I suggest, is this: Because praise is not identical to any of those other ways of addressing God. It lies at the heart of appropriate human response to what and who God is intrinsically, in and of Godself, quite apart from what God has done, could do, or will do for us.

Appropriate human response to God does, of course, include many other kinds of expressions of subjective states: expressions of thanks for gifts God has given to us; intercessions for gifts to others

---

[1] The Hymnbook 1982 (Episcopal Church in the USA). The Hymnal, 1933 (Presbyterian Church in the USA) ascribes the text to "Daniel ben Judah, fourteenth century. The English version is an eighteenth-century translation credited to Thomas Olivers (1725–1799) of an ancient and well-known Jewish Hymn.

now; confession of wrong done to others, ourselves, and God; expressions of acknowledgement of hopes and longings for what God might do in future; expressions of trust in God's love for us; expressions of love for God that is inseparable from gratitude for God's love for us; expressions of anguished lament at others' terrible sufferings; and expressions of angry demands for explanation by God of how those sufferings can occur in the context of God's powerful justice and love.

Praise of God for God's Sake as the Basis of Worship

Used in that way, "praising" God is the basis of worship of God. Worship is enacted in a large variety of communal and individual practices: prayer, song, instrumental music, rituals of various sorts, reading and expositing Scripture, delivering and listening to sermons, etc. As acts of worship, however, they are all done to the same end. Although etymology can only get us a little way toward clarifying a word's meaning, it may be sufficient here: "Worship" comes from Old English "worthscipe," which might be modernized to "worth-ship." It is a human response that is appropriate to something's *intrinsic* worth, i.e., a response to its worthiness of, precisely, worship. The practices in which worship is enacted have the single end of expressing appropriate response to the *intrinsic* value of God's reality. Praise to God for God's own sake is the proper response to God's intrinsic value, in contradistinction to responses to God's "worth-*for-us*" in freely blessing us, freely granting our petitions, freely forgiving our sins while we are yet sinners, freely proving to be trustworthy to us, freely guiding our lives morally, freely teaching us an appropriate conceptual grasp of the world as related-to by God, freely sustaining and comforting us in the midst of affliction, and so on.

This brings us to the nub of issue raised by the questions, "Why first of all praise God rather than, say, thanking God?" The short answer: Because our acts of praise of God for God's own sake are the *basis* of appropriate expressions of our thanks, confession, trust, hope, and love to God in response to all the ways in which God freely relates to us. All of the above are indeed expressions in response to God's "worth" or value for us. However, God's "worth *for* us" is not the basis of praise of God. Praise is the "basis" of those expressions because it is response first of all to God for God's own sake, the response to God for "who" and "what" God intrinsically is, whether or not God freely actively relates to all that is not God.

Praise of God for God's Sake as Acknowledgment of Grace

The distinction between praise of "what" and "who" God is intrinsically, i.e., praise of God's "worth" for *its own sake*, and praise of God for God's "worth" for *us* is critically important. If God's "worth for us" were simply identical with "what" and "who" God intrinsically is, then God's ways of being of "worth for us," i.e., God's ways of relating to us, would not be "grace" in any sense of the term. That is, they would not be ways of lovingly relating to us that are free. God would *necessarily* relate in those ways just by being God.

"Free" is a quality ascribed (rightly or wrongly) to some human in at least three senses. (a) A human agent may be said to be free in the sense that, in her intentional actions, she acts whole-heartedly in relation to God and to fellow creatures. St. Augustine argued that, more particularly, one only acts fully freely when one wholeheartedly relates to God and to one's neighbors in unqualified love. Accordingly, he argued, one is only truly free in this sense in fully actualized eschatological life in heaven when one is incapable of *not* loving God and neighbor. Acting in a self-divided way is not, in this sense, a free action. (b) A human agent may be said to be free in the sense that he can self-regulate his identity, either in ways that are coherent with what he essentially is or in ways incoherent and cross-grained to what and who he essentially is. This is sometimes characterized as the freedom of "self-transcendence," in which all human subjects can "stand outside" themselves and relate to themselves in ways that constitute "how" they are set into their lived worlds.

(c) A human agent may be said to free in a particular intentional action "if she could have done otherwise." Only actions that are enactments of intentions, i.e., actions that "intend" to actualize a certain goal that has been deliberately selected for reasons that the actor can supply if requested, can be free or unfree. Because "doing otherwise" assumes that there were other courses of action she might have chosen instead; this sense of "free" can also be characterized as "freedom of choice." Therefore, attribution of this sense of "free" to a human intentional action depends on the action's circumstances. If in those circumstances there is in fact no alternative course of action to actualize her goal, she is said have been "unfree," to have had "no choice" or to have faced a "forced choice."

One thing all these senses of "free" have in common is that they are senses of "finite freedom." That is, the resources, capacities, and concrete situations of each and every human agent are limited both internally and externally. Their intentional actions are "free" within the limits of capacities, powers, and circumstances in their kinds.

Perhaps only two of those senses of "free" can be attributed to God. Given that Creator God is not a creaturely item within the complex networks of interactive, inter-related, and mutually limiting creatures that comprise the created cosmos, but rather is at once radically "other" than it and radically "close" to it, the Triune God is not "finite." Accordingly, "finite freedom" can only be attributed to God analogically. This attribution may be made both in the sense that, in each of the ways in which the Triune God relates to all else, God relates "whole-heartedly," and in the sense that each way in which the Triune God relates to all else faithfully expresses some aspect of the ways in which in God's self-relating God constitutes ("generates") and, thus, in a manner self-regulates, "who" God is.

However, it is more debatable whether "free" in the sense of "could have done otherwise" may be attributed to God analogically to God. It is difficult to conceptualize God "choosing" among alternative courses of action across time and in differences circumstances without invoking the premise that such "choosing" is a discursive activity. There is a long and strong theological tradition arguing that God's "act of knowing" cannot be rightly conceived as discursive. The issue largely turns on whether the claim that God is "eternal" is best interpreted as the claim that God is "timeless." If God is absolutely a-temporal, then God's knowing cannot take time to go through the cognitive steps that constitute discursive thinking. If God cannot be said to "know" discursively, God may perhaps be said to "know" everything by absolutely comprehensive, all-at-once "sight." But, in that case, it is difficult to know what would count as "choosing" among possible courses of action that are presented to the knower as the logical precondition of the knower's "choosing" one of them.

Because, as rendered in canonical Christian scriptural accounts, God's ways of relating to us *are* grace (in one sense of the term or another; we sort out some of those senses elsewhere in this work), precisely *because* they are free, praise of the Triune God who relates graciously must be praise of who and what God is intrinsically, whether or not God also relates at all in gracious love to all that is not God.

If, conversely, response to God's worth for us in the ways in which God relates to us were the context within which "praise" of God is understood, then expressions of praise become distorted in at least two ways.

The first distortion is that "what and who God is" comes to be identified with the ways in which God relates to us. In canonical Christian Scripture, the ways in which God relates are told as freely enacted. But when they are taken to be constitutive of what and who God is intrinsically they are taken to be that which makes God to be *God*. It follows that God cannot be "God" without actively relating to us in just those ways.

Characterizations of God's ways of relating to us – sustaining, blessing, judging, illumining, explaining, nurturing, etc. – largely rely on analogies from human intentional actions. Internal to those analogies is a "grammatical rule": intentional actions, i.e., teleologically ordered actions, are either (a) contingent on the agent's freely and "mindfully" or "responsibly chosen" intentions, or (b) they are necessary and unavoidable expressions of the agent's predetermined "nature." If God's ways of relating to us are assumed to *constitute* God's intrinsic reality, i.e., to constitute "what" and "who" God is, they cannot any more be considered as ways of relating that God "freely" enacts. They are logically and ontologically necessary, rather than contingent. However, it is precisely as contingent and "freely enacted" that they are rendered in the canonical scriptural accounts of God's ways of relating, which theological accounts of God's power supposedly aim to explicate.

Furthermore, if God's ways of relating are not enacted freely, then it seems odd to be thankful for them or to petition for them, for God will necessarily enact them anyway. But just such pointless expressions are what are enacted when praise of who God is and what it is to be God are done in the context of expressions of various sorts of response to the ways God relates to us.

The second distortion of praise to God is the trivialization of praise. When praise is enacted on the basis of expressions of responses to ways in which God relates to all else – rather than the latter being enacted on the basis of and in the context of praise of God for God's own sake – the language of worship drifts toward trivialization. Praise of God slides toward paying complements to God for how well God has done what God must do anyway just because God is God: "Thank you that I healed so quickly; you are truly mighty O God! I confess my sin and beg your forgiveness; you are so endlessly merciful O God!" The classic instance of such trivialization is the remark often attributed to Voltaire, "God will forgive me. That's His job." This kind of God-talk in the language of worship moves as a kind of undertow toward ritualized solemn

patting of God on the head, or at least on the shoulder. It threatens
to become a riptide toward "worship" that sounds absurdly like the
patronizing of God.

To avoid both sorts of distortion an account of God should begin
with praise of the of God for its own sake and not for the sake of
what God can "do" for us. Only so will an account of the glory, the
sovereignty, or the power of God begin with praise of the *grace*, not
only of God's intrinsic reality, but of God's ways of relating to us in
the economy.

Praise of God for God's Sake as Praise of God's Intrinsic Glory

The proposal being developed in this chapter is that *glory* is the
most adequate comprehensive characterization of the Triune God's
intrinsic reality, because it is a relational term that expresses the
dynamics of "what" it is to be God and "who" God is, the dynamics
that constitute God's intrinsic reality. Ascribed to God, "glory"
connotes that the Triune God dynamically self-relates in ways that
have qualities, aspects of which are also freely and faithfully
expressed in qualities of God's ways of relating to all that is
not God.

That is, the Triune God "does" (in the ways in which God relates
to all else in the economy) *as* God intrinsically "is"; and the Triune
God "is" as God "does." The qualities of the ways in which God
goes about relating to all else, i.e., the qualities of God's "doings," do
not exhaust the qualities of God's "manner of existing," i.e., the
qualities of how God intrinsically "is"; but as far as they go, they
faithfully express aspect of those intrinsic qualities. It is because
God "does" as God "is" that we are warranted to ascribe to God
qualities of God's ways of relating to all else, because those qualities
are rendered in canonical Christian Scripture read through the lens
of Scripture's accounts of how God and Jesus of Nazareth relate to
each other. Because God "does" as God "is," we are warranted in

judging that some ways of relating to all else that are attributed to God cannot be correct because, given "what" and "who" God is, God would not do things like that.

But why privilege God's quality of "glory" as the most apt characterization of the entire ensemble of qualities that are intrinsic to God's intrinsic reality, i.e., God's "attributes" independent of God's relating to all else? After all, glory has traditionally been considered just one of many qualities that we are warranted to attribute to God. In accounts of God's "attributes," the central point traditionally has been to emphasize that God's attributes do not name various discrete "parts" or "pieces" of which God is composed. Although "justice," "mercy," and "ubiquity" do not mean the same thing, in God they are not different realities that God might develop and might lose, as though they were so many different talents or competencies an agent might or might not have while remaining one and the same agent. Rather, they are distinguishable ways of naming God's one reality. As such, they are substitutable for one another. Hence, the argument goes, no one of them can be privileged as the attribute that "most" adequately characterizes what and who God is. Each of them could be said to encompass all of the rest of them in its own fashion.

Granting all of the above, the proposal here is that "glory" does nonetheless most adequately characterize God's intrinsic reality, because it most clearly and richly maps onto classical Trinitarian doctrine of God. A full-fledged doctrine of God would exhibit how the dynamics that are together the Triune God's glory generate all of God's attributes or, as Karl Barth names them, all of the "perfections" of God. I shall refer to them as the Triune God's "qualities." This book has a much narrower scope. It is limited to discussion of senses in which the qualities of "sovereignty" and "power" may rightly be ascribed to the Triune God. The rest of this chapter is devoted to making a case for the proposal that "glory" is an apt characterization of "what" and "who" the Triune God intrinsically is, and as such is the conceptual context within which other intrinsic qualities of God, especially "sovereignty" and "power," are best explained.

Why Focus on Praise of God in Connection with Efforts to Console the Anguished?

An answer to the second question raised by the injunction to praise the God of Abraham grows out of the explanation given above of why we should praise God for God's own sake, rather than praise God for what God has done, is doing, or could in the future do for us. As the appropriate human response to God's intrinsic gracious glory, praise of God for God's sake is the basis of all practices of worship, practices acknowledging that the *intrinsic* "worth-ship" or, in Old English, "worthscipe," of God is the basis of the gracious freedom of God's ways of relating to us.

Efforts to comfort and console those who are anguished by other's horrendous suffering are among an array of practices in the common life of communities of Christian faith that are commonly called "pastoral care." They are an important part of the practices that comprise, in the broad sense of the term, those communities' worship of God. As such, they are done to the same end as are all the other practices that comprise worship of the Triune God: to praise God's intrinsic glory for its own sake. Most acts of comforting the anguished only praise God's intrinsic glory implicitly.

The crucial point here is that such enactments of practices of pastoral care do implicitly praise God's intrinsic glory for its own sake only when they make *theologically nonproblematic* assumptions about the nature of God's power. That is because problematic assumptions about God's power warrant attribution to God of senses of "the glory of God" that do not comport with "what" and "who" the Triune God intrinsically is. They distort what it is that is "glorious" about God. The "glory" of the God they praise, however

27

implicitly, is not the intrinsic "glory" of the Triune God that is expressed in the three strands of God's economy, as they are rendered in canonical Christian Scripture.

If the Triune God is powerful, God is powerful in God's own way. A theological account of what is meant by "God is powerful" should be laid out in the context of a more basic account of "what" and "who" this powerful God is intrinsically. In the nature of the case, of course, no account of what and who God is can be more than very partial and easily distorting. I suggest that one fruitful way in which to lay out what can be said, however partially and however easily open to distortion it may be, is to focus on the sense in which the Triune God is intrinsically glorious, i.e., is intrinsically worthy of praise and worship.

Some Assumed Reality Claims about God

An account of the sense in which the Triune God is intrinsically glorious can begin at a very general level with three reality claims about who God is and what it is to be God. These claims are rooted in Christian scriptural accounts of how God relates to all that is not God and are affirmed to be true by many communities of Christian faith. They are that God is intrinsically glorious, God relates to all else freely, and God is triune. The argument that follows takes these three reality claims for granted and does not attempt to justify them.

God Is Intrinsically Glorious

One of those reality claims has already been in play: The Triune God is intrinsically glorious. The primary appropriate response to God's intrinsic glory is silence. As Rowan Williams points out,[2] it is

[2] Cf. Rowan Williams, *Being Human: Bodies, Minds, Persons* (Grand Rapids, MI: Wm. B. Eerdmans Publishing, 2018), pp. 88–91.

the sort of silence that follows our experience of something that challenges "our urge to get on top of situations, to control." We have a strong urge to tame a "wild" experience that we cannot control, an urge to "domesticate" it. One way to try to domesticate an experience we cannot control is to talk about it. In contrast, Williams goes on to say, silence is the wholly appropriate acknowledgement that "'I cannot domesticate, I cannot get on top of this.'" A glimpse of God's intrinsic glory is a "wild" experience of this sort, one we cannot control. God's intrinsic glory just is *what* it is to be God and the full richness of *who* God is. It cannot be domesticated. Silence is the appropriate initial acknowledgement of that reality.

In English translations of the Old Testament, "glory" is most frequently used to translate the Hebrew *kabod*, which connotes honor, weight, and heaviness. We might say it connotes "gravitas." "Glory" is also used to translate Hebrew terms meaning adornment (*hadar*, e.g., in Ps. 90:6) and beauty (*hod*, e.g., in Ps. 8:1, and *tiphereth*, e.g., in Isa. 46:13). The Septuagint's Greek translation of the Old Testament rendered *kabod* as *doxa*, the Greek term New Testament writers frequently use. English translations of the New Testament regularly translate *doxa* as "glory." *Doxa* is usually characterized in Scripture by images such as an attention getting and attractive shining, radiance, brilliance, or resplendence.

One thing all those connotations of "glory" have in common is their relationality. "Glory" is a relational concept. It denotes not just God's gravitas, but also the essential *self-expressiveness* of such gravitas, its resplendence or radiance or brilliance or beauty that attracts an "other." More exactly, in its "glory," an intrinsic gravitas expresses itself faithfully in such a way that it attracts another simply by being self-expressively what it fundamentally is. Hence, when ascribed to God, "glory" is God relating to an "other" in self-expressiveness that is faithful to what and who God intrinsically is. Thus, God's glory is also God relating in a way that attracts an "other" to relate responsively back to God, on analogy with the way in which beauty not only attracts attention, as radiance and brilliance do, but also attracts an "other" to relate responsively to that which is beautiful.

This brief word study serves to orient our decision to use "glory" as the most apt term for that about God to which we respond most appropriately by praising God for God's own sake. However, "relationality" is too abstract. We can explain it a bit more concretely by noting that, in canonical Christian Scripture, the phrase "the glory of God" is used of three different referents. Each uses "glory" as a relational term, as outlined. The three are related to one another in a certain pattern.[3]

We have seen, first, that "the glory of God" is said in reference to *ways in which human beings relate to God in praise* of what and who God intrinsically is for God's own sake. Such praise glorifying God is itself called the "glory of God" in this use of the term. That is the sense of the term we have discussed most extensively thus far.

"The glory of God" refers, second, to particular places (e.g., holy ground), things (e.g., a burning bush), events (e.g., an escape from the Egyptian army; a crucifixion), or persons (e.g., prophets, saints, Jesus of Nazareth) in whom God's intrinsic glory is self-expressed in space and time. They are the *concretely particular contents* of what is traditionally called God's "economy." We have already noted in passing that human expressions of thanks to God, trust in God, acknowledgement to God of guilt, petitions to God, hope in God, and love to God are responses to such concrete events, persons, and things that are God's faithful self-expression of God's glory in space and time.

A third referent of the phrase is, we have noted, *what and who God is intrinsically,* whether or not God relates to what is not God. Each of these sorts of reference for the phrase "the glory of God" is "relational" insofar as each of them is a way in which God is faithfully self-expressive in a fashion that attracts the attention and

---

[3] The following very brief analysis is heavily indebted to Donald Evans' *The Logic of Self-Involvement* (London: SCM Press, 1963), ch. 5.

evokes the response of an "other." However, the third referent of the phrase is "relational" in an importantly different way than are the other two. That different sense of "relational" is the primary subject of this chapter.

The three sorts of referents of canonical uses of "the glory of God" are related to one another in a pattern that is the reverse of the order in which they have been identified. It is an order of conceptual and ontological dependence. The conceptually basic referent of the phrase is God's intrinsic glory. God's intrinsic glory is inherently relational in ways that are faithfully self-expressive and attractive to an "other." Insofar as God's intrinsic glory is faithfully self-expressed to an "other-than-God," such self-expression characterizes God's economy and is itself "the glory of God" in a secondary reference. It is "secondary" both conceptually and in the order of being because it is expressive of something else and dependent on something logically and ontologically prior, viz. God's intrinsic glory, i.e., the first and basic referent of the phrase "the glory of God." Insofar as God's self-expression of God's intrinsic glory attracts "others" and evokes from them a response that is appropriate to the concrete way in which God faithfully self-expressed God's intrinsic glory in relating to them, their response consists of praise. That is itself an aspect of God's glory (in its third reference), just because it serves to glorify God in a particular set of circumstances. It is dependent both on the order of conceptual meaning and on the order of being on two realities that are before and basic to it, viz., the concrete contents of God's economy to which it is the appropriate response, which itself is dependent on something before and basic to it, viz., God's intrinsic glory.

All three referents of scriptural use of the phrase "the glory of God" are important to this discussion of the power of God. The third sort of referent – human glorification of God in acts of praise of God's glory for its own sake – is important for the topic of this book: how to overcome distortions of efforts to console those anguished by other's terrible sufferings by invocation of misleading concepts of God's power. The second sort of referent, i.e., strands of God's economy as God's self-expression of God's intrinsic glory, is the proper immediate conceptual context for discussion of the concept of God's power. But the first sort of referent of the phrase "the glory of God" – God's intrinsic glory – must be taken up first because it is basic to the other two.

God Relates to All Else Freely

We have already seen that a second, highly general reality claim typically affirmed by many communities of Christian faith is that the powerful Triune God relates to all else freely in ways which, if only partially, express aspects of God's intrinsic glory. They are enacted "freely" in the sense that God does not need to relate in those ways – or in any other ways for that matter – to be God. The human response they invite is praise that celebrates in speech and action God's ways of relating to all that is not God. Such celebratory praise is a rejoicing in God's glory for its own sake.

It is, I am suggesting, against the background of reflection on the concept of God's glory that an account of God's power is properly laid out. Doing so ultimately nuances the concept of God's power by locating it as the power of God's gracious (i.e., freely loving and lovingly free) intrinsic glory that is faithfully self-expressive in the ways in which God empowers realities other than God in their own right and for their own sakes.

God Is Triune

A third reality claim typically affirmed by many communities of Christian faith is that the intrinsically glorious and free powerful God is Triune. I stipulated in the Introduction that, for the purposes of this work, a doctrine of God that comports with the Nicene–Constantinopolitan Creed of 381 AD counts as a "Trinitarian" doctrine of God. Like Christian creeds generally, the Nicene–

Constantinopolitan Creed does not explain the terms it uses in making its claims. Nor does it explore how the claims it makes relate to one another. For example, it does not explain how the relations "begetter of," "begotten of," and "proceeds from" are different from each other and how they are related to each other. It does not explain whether the three "Persons" of the Trinity are three instances of some one kind of reality. It does not explain how to understand the relation between the different identities each of the three is, on one hand, and on the other hand their unity as "divine" or eternally "of one substance." It does not explain how to understand the relation between the two kinds of identity description that it gives in each article. They are conventionally distinguished respectively as the "immanent" Trinity and the "economic" Trinity. It seems clear they cannot be separated as though they were two different "trinities," but just how they are related is left open.

However, the creed's silences do open up conceptual space for various doctrinal theological proposals of ways in which to explain such things. Doctrines of the Trinity are efforts to do just that. In particular the structure, internal movement, and imagery of the creed create space for further theological explanations in regard to how each of the three "Persons" of the Trinity are to be identified and related to one another. Such doctrines purport to explain more fully what is merely affirmed by the creed. This essay does not aim to develop a Doctrine of the Trinity. It does not attempt to explain all of the creed's unexplained terms and claims. What is decisive for my proposal here are some features of the overall structure, movement, and imagery of the creed and some of its explicit affirmations.

The Nicene Creed's Structure

The creed is structured in three roughly parallel articles, each beginning "We (or I) believe in. . .." Each article then names one of the "Persons" of the Trinity – Father, Son, and Holy Spirit in that order.

Each article makes claims about the "Person" it begins by naming. Those claims concern both the eternal relations of the three "Persons" of the Trinity with each another and their roles in the ways in which the Triune God relates to all that is not God.

The creed thus serves as a short summary of canonical Christian Scripture's accounts of various ways in which God relates to all that is not God. More exactly, the creed's three-fold structure is rooted in an analysis of how the four canonical Gospels' narratives render God's relation to Jesus of Nazareth, Jesus' relations to God and to fellow human creatures, and the Holy Spirit's relation to both of them and each of their relations to the Spirit. Thus, the creed serves as a very broad guide how to read those Gospel narratives in relation to accounts in Christian Scripture of ways in which God relates to all else without explicit reference to God's relation either to both Jesus and the Spirit or to one of them alone.

That is to say, the creed is a hermeneutical guide to reading the Christian canon as a kind of whole. It is a "whole" in virtue of its various books being read as accounts of different ways in which the one self-same Triune God relates to all else. Early Christian writers brought at least three assumptions to those analyses. First, that canonical writings rendered those relationships faithfully; second, that in those ways of relating God is faithful to Godself (i.e., that God reliably is as God does, and faithfully does as God is); and third that, for Jesus to accomplish what the canonical Gospels' narratives in particular seem to say Jesus accomplished, God must have had an especially close, indeed unique, relationship to Jesus.

That last assumption entails a certain privileging of the Gospels' accounts of Jesus' overall life trajectory, treating them as definitive for Christian accounts of who and what the one God is that relates to all else and how that God goes about relating to all else. Accordingly, the Gospels' accounts are at least negatively definitive in that they block proposed claims about who and what God is that conflict with the implications of the Gospels' accounts of God's ways of relating to Jesus and to all else in and through him, even though those inferences might otherwise seem to be plausibly inferred from other scriptural accounts of God's relating to all else.

It did not escape the attention of early Christian writers that (a) in addition to the canonical Gospels, the Christian Bible contains many accounts of other and different ways in which God relates to all else besides relating in and through the life-trajectory of Jesus, and (b) the narratives of the four Gospels in particular (not to mention the very brief narratives in some of the Epistles) differed from one another. Nonetheless, despite their differences, one thing the Gospels' narratives do have in common is a certain three-fold structure or pattern of relationships among three central "agents" in the Gospels' narratives: Jesus, the One Jesus often calls "Father," and the Holy Spirit. Broadly speaking, most theological controversies through the first five centuries can be seen as controversies about the most adequate way in which to characterize the relationships among those three "agents." Given that the core theological issues in interpreting the canonical Gospels' narratives of Jesus Christ are how most adequately to characterize what God accomplishes in and through Jesus Christ and what that implies about God's relation to Jesus and Jesus' relation to God, those controversies focused principally on Christological issues.

That focus – given the conviction that God is self-consistent, faithful to Godself in the way in which God relates to Jesus Christ in the economy – determines the three-article structure of the Nicene Creed. The creed's lack of explanations of its key terms "Person," "Father," "Son," "Spirit," etc., leaves it open to controversies about the implications of the three-fold structure of canonical narratives for theological characterizations of how God as somehow intrinsically and eternally three-fold and not merely three-fold in the "economy." Nonetheless, the structure of the Creed does lay it down that intrinsic three-foldness – however it is to be understood – characterizes one self-same God that relates to all else in three sorts of ways that the Creed identifies in each of its three articles.

The Nicene Creed's Interior Movement

One thing that makes the three articles roughly parallel in the creed's structure is a *movement* that is the same within each of the articles. It is a movement through two different kinds of identity description of the "Person" it begins by naming.

One kind of identity description given in each article of the creed provides a uniquely identifying description of the "Person" named at its beginning ("Father,"[4] or "Son," or Holy Spirit) expressed in terms of the relation each has to realities other than God in time and space. "Father" is identified as "maker of heaven and earth, and of all things visible and invisible"; "Son" is identified as one "by whom all things were made," and who "for us and for our salvation came down from heaven and was made incarnate by the Holy Spirit of the Virgin Mary and was made man" and was crucified, suffered, buried, risen on the third day, ascended into heaven and will come in glory to judge the living and the dead; the Holy Spirit is identified as the "Lord and giver of life," who spoke by the prophets, and in the holy, catholic and apostolic church.[5] Each identifies "who" one of the three "Persons" of the Trinity is in terms of strands of God's economy, as that is told by Christian canonical Scripture. Taken together, the three identity descriptions of this kind are identity descriptions of what is traditionally called the "economic Trinity," i.e., the Trinity in the economy.

---

[4] As with "Person" so too with "Father" and "Son," I will risk annoying the reader by regularly placing the terms in quotes as a reminder that, although the words' use is traditional, they are used as quasi-technical terms and nothing based on their conventional use in ordinary English is to be read into their use in the context of discussion of Doctrines of the Trinity. What their use connotes in any particular discussion of the creed must be limited to what is explicitly proposed in that particular doctrinal explanation of the creed.

[5] Plausibly, the Spirit is also identified in terms of its role in three following affirmations: we acknowledge one baptism for the remission of sins; we look for the resurrection of the dead; and the life of the world to come.

A second kind of identity description of one of the "Persons" of the Trinity is given in each article of the creed *before* it offers the kind of identity description that is framed in terms of a strand of the economy. This is expressed in terms of eternal relations between the "Persons," relations that are generative of the individual reality of each of the "Persons" of the Trinity. For example, the "Father" is first identified as "one God, the Father almighty"; the "Son" is first identified as "only begotten Son of God, begotten of the Father before all worlds, Light of light, very God of very God, begotten not made, being of one substance with the Father"; and the Holy Spirit is first identified as one that "proceeds from the Father"[6] and "with the Father and the Son is worshiped and glorified."

Here, the second "Person" of the Trinity is identified in terms of an eternal dynamic relation to the first "Person," viz. the relation of being eternally "begotten" of the Father ("begotten of the "Father" before all worlds, ... begotten not made"), a generative relation. Correlatively, the first "Person" of the Trinity is identified in terms of an eternal relation to the second "Person" of the Trinity, that of "eternal-begetter-of." It is far from clear how best to characterize those eternal relations, and far from clear what analogies are most apt and illuminating. Whatever the eternal relations of "being begotten" and "begetter of" may be, we may let them stand as place holders for some sort of dynamic eternal relation that is generative of the distinguishable reality, i.e., the unique identity, of each of the terms of the relation, namely "Father" and "Son." It is important to note that, in the context of this sort of identity description, charac-terization of the first "Person's" identity as that of "Father" is not warranted by the way it is related to spatiotemporal reality other

---

[6] In the eighth century, the Western Church unilaterally added the *filioque*, affirming that the Holy Spirit proceeded not only from the "Father" but also "from the Son," which has ever since been a point of profound controversy with Eastern Orthodoxy. For our purposes, we need not try to adjudicate the issue and can be content with the original wording.

than God. Rather, it is warranted by some sort of dynamic, ontologically generative relation between it and the second "Person" and
obtains "eternally" whether or not God relates to realities other
than God.

Similarly, in this sort of identity description the third "Person" is
identified in terms of its eternal dynamic relation of eternally
"proceeding from" the first "Person." This identification strongly
implies that, correlatively, the first "Person" is identified in terms of
its eternally relating in a dynamically generative fashion to the third
"Person" as one "from-which-the-third-proceeds." This property
holds no matter what such a relation of "eternal processing" may
be. It is sometimes added (although not in the original text of the
Creed of Nicea) that the third "Person," the Spirit, "proceeds from
the 'Father'" "*and the* Son" or "*with the 'Son',*" which strongly
implies that, correlatively, the second "Person" is identified in
terms of its eternally relating in a dynamically generative fashion
to the third "Person" as one "from-which-the-third-proceeds" or as
one "through-which-the-third-proceeds." Here, too, it is far from
clear what analogies would most aptly and illuminatingly characterize them. Nonetheless, as identity descriptions, each of these
ways of relating eternally describes "who" one of the "Persons" of
the Trinity is.

In addition, the relations of "begetter" and "begotten of" are
explicitly qualified as relations in which first and second
"Persons" are "of one being." Although it is not quite explicitly
affirmed in the creed, it is strongly implied and (after a period of
controversy) traditionally inferred that the relation "proceeds from"
is to be qualified the same way: Father and Spirit and the "Son" and
Spirit are all traditionally deemed to be "of one substance." As
identity descriptions, each of these ways of eternally relating affirms
that "what" each of the "Persons" of the Trinity is is identical in
concrete actuality with "what" the other two are, viz., "God." Taken
together, the three identity descriptions of this kind comprise an
identity description of what is traditionally called the "immanent

Trinity," i.e., God's intrinsic Triunity. "What" all three "Persons" identically are is constituted by nothing other than the eternal dynamics of their inter-relations.

The movement within each article of the creed, then, is from an identity description of one of the "Persons" of the Trinity framed in terms of eternal dynamic relations among them (i.e., from accounts of the "immanent Trinity") to an identity description of that "Person." It is framed in terms of a dynamic relation it has to reality other than God (i.e., to an account of the "economic Trinity").

Taken seriously, that repeated sequence implies that the Triune One identified in terms of a particular role or roles in the economy is identically the self-same Triune One already identified in terms an of eternally dynamic relation among the three "Persons" of the Trinity. The "Triune One" identified in terms of an eternally dynamic relation among the three "Persons" of the Trinity constitutes "who" and "what" it is that is the "Triune One" is, as identified in terms of a particular role or roles in the economy. The "immanent Trinity" and the "economic Trinity" are not two different Trinities. They just are the Triune God considered in two different contexts: with regard, respectively, to what and who the Triune God is, apart from the economy, and to what and who the Triune God is as engaged in the economy.

Given that accounts of the Triune God as "immanent Trinity" and as "economic Trinity" are accounts of one and the same reality, two important grammar-like "rules" follow that should govern appropriate descriptions of the Triune God's engagement in strands of the economy.

One "rule" is: Always keep it clear in the description that it is the self-same intrinsically *Triune* God that is engaged in every strand of God's economy. No one "Person" engages in any strand of the economy apart from the other two "Persons." The three "Persons" of the Triune God are eternally indivisible and inseparable in the economy (*opera ad extra indivisa sunt*). That inseparability in the economy is a faithful expression of their intrinsic inseparability.

A traditional technical term for this is *perichoresis*, translated into Latin as *circuminsessio* (the Greek word *perichoreo* means "to encompass" or "to indwell"; the Latin translation means "to sit around one another," *circum-in-sedere*). Hence, when each article of the creed identifies the "Person" it names in its second sort of identity description by relating that "Person" to a particular strand or strands of God's economy (e.g., "Father" with creation, "Son" with reconciliation, and Holy Spirit with eschatological life), it cannot be interpreted as implying that only that "Person" of the Trinity relates in that fashion to all that is not God. The creed's identification of each "Person," by tying it to one strand of the economy, helps to pick out or identify that "Person" in contradistinction to the other two. At most, it suggests that, when we try to characterize how the Triune God relates to all else in that strand of the economy, we privilege images canonical Scripture tends most frequently to use in its accounts of the "Person" being identified in that article of the creed.

A second important rule is: Always keep it clear in accounts of "who" and "what" God is that the Triune God is concretely actual. It is not an "ideal" possibility or "archetype." Nor is "Triune God" a cipher for a transcendental structure or dynamic that objectively orders reality-as-a-whole. Nor is it a cipher for a transcendental structure of consciousness that is the condition of the possibility of subjective experience having the features it has.

The Nicene Creed's Imagery

The imagery the creed uses to characterize the eternal relations among the "Persons" of the Trinity, and the "Persons'" relations to all that is not God, clearly connotes that those relations are dynamic and generative. "Begetter of," "begotten of," and "proceeds from" are dynamic metaphors for, respectively, the relation of "Father" to the "Son," the "Son" to the "Father," and the Holy Spirit to the "Father." Those relations are characterized by those metaphors as dynamically generative relations. They do not just modify each of the three "Persons"; those generative relations *constitute* the unique identity of each of the three "Persons" as the "Person" it is. That is, those relations generate the concrete *reality* of identities that are genuinely "other" than the "Father," who is, reciprocally, "other" than each of them.

However, the creed's images work in that way only in the context of a second affirmation about those eternal relations between the triune "Persons": In regard to the "divinity" of the "Persons," the relations between them is a relation of "identity of being." They are "of one substance," "very God from very God" (the "Son"); and regarding the Holy Spirit along with the "Father" and the "Son," the only reality that is worthy to be "worshiped and glorified."

What is constituted by the dynamic relations "begotten of" and "proceeding from" *expresses* that from which it is begotten or proceeds. In the case of the "only begotten Son," given that the phrase is a quotation from the prologue to the Gospel of John, it is fair to identify "Son" with "Word of God." He is the "Father's" explicit *self*-expression. What are constituted by those dynamic relations are different "identities" that are such perfectly faithful expressions of the "Father" that the two expressions ("Son" and Holy Spirit) are one and the same concrete actuality as that of which they are expressions (the "Father"). They are all one "substance."

God is intrinsically glorious, God relates freely, and the intrinsically glorious God that relates to all else freely is Triune: given these three reality claims as background beliefs, we set out to outline a somewhat more concrete account of several of the qualities of the intrinsic glory of the Triune God.

The Triune God Is Self-Relating

The imagery the Nicene Creed uses in its identity descriptions of each of the eternal relations that constitute each of the three

"Persons" of the Trinity privilege abstractly dynamic concepts of the Triune God's concrete actuality. Two in particular are important: the Triune God is generatively self-relating and is self-expressively self-relating. The self-relating is active. The Triune God's concrete actuality is constituted by God's dynamic *self*-relating, not by God's dynamic relating to other realities. That warrants analogical use of "dynamic" concepts in an account of "what" and "who" it is to be God.

The images used in the Nicene Creed characterize that dynamic as in some way "generative." As we have seen, the creed characterizes the "Son's" relation to the "Father" as "begotten of," and the "Father's" relation to the "Son" as "begetter of." So, too, it characterizes the Spirit's relation to the "Father" as "proceeding from" – sometimes "proceeding from the 'Father' with the 'Son'" or "proceeding from the 'Father' through the 'Son'" – and the "Father's" relation to the Spirit as One "from-which-the-Spirit-proceeds." The dynamic of the Triune God's different ways of self-relating "generate" the eternal concretely actual unique identity of each of three "Persons" of the Trinity.

At the same time, we saw that the creed's imagery for those generative dynamics characterizes them as perfectly self-expressive. What are constituted by those dynamic relations as different "identities" are perfectly faithful expressions of the "Father." This concept is brought out explicitly when the creed's use of "Son" is associated with the image "Word of God" to characterize the second "Person's" dynamic relating to the first "Person" (as it is in the Gospel of John, from which the creed takes its image of an eternally "begotten Son"). As God's "Word," the "Son" is God's perfect *self*-expression. The creed is traditionally interpreted as entailing that the generative dynamic of the Spirit's relating to the "Father" and the "Father" relating to the Spirit, "with" or "through" the "Son," is perfectly self-expressive as well.

The Triune God's dynamic generative self-relating is so completely self-expressive that it is a fully *generous self-giving*.

In dynamic self-relating that is generative of concretely actual genuine "others" the Triune God is so generously self-giving in perfect self-expression that the three "Persons" are, in the creed's language, "of one substance" (*homoousios*). In this dynamic self-relating, God is so fully self-giving in self-expression that the "others" – the "Persons" – constituted by that self-relating just are one and the same God. Their "unicity" is the *eternal* inseparability of the "self-givings" that constitute the three "Persons."

The Triune God's unicity is traditionally expressed by saying "God is One." In English, that statement can be misleading, because it suggests that there is a "kind" of being that is a "divine being" but, as it happens, there is only one instance of it. That notion is ruled out because what is expressed by affirmation of the Triune God's "oneness" is not that the three "Persons" of the Triune God are concretely actual instances, a "kind" or "class" of "being" or "substance" (call it "divinity," "divine nature," "divine essence," "divine substance," or "God-ness") of which there might be one, more than one, or no instances. To construe the "oneness" of the Triune God in that way would be to affirm that the three "Persons" are three Gods. But that is precisely what is being denied by the creed's images' emphasis on the dynamic character of God's concrete actuality. Rather, what is expressed by "oneness" is that the Triune God's intrinsic integral unity is such that the Triune God's dynamically self-relating, generously self-giving, and perfectly self-expressive reality is not subject to dis-integration. It is an *integral*, eternal, and dynamic self-relating.

The integral unicity of the Triune God's intrinsic self-relating requires a major qualification of the sense in which the three "Persons" can be said to be genuinely "other" than one another (as outlined in these last four paragraphs). That qualification can be brought out by contrasting three senses of "other."

The term "other" is often used in contemporary discourse to refer to categories of human beings that are culturally at once denigrated as inferior versions of humankind, and feared (at least unconsciously) as threats to "normal" or "standard" human beings (e.g., women, people of color, the "disabled," "savages," and the "uncivilized"). A culture's classification of certain populations as "other," in this sense of the term, at once manifests and implicitly justifies the culture's unjust distribution of various sorts of social, political, and economic power. This naming marginalizes the "other," indeed makes them "invisible." That sense of "other" is a quasi-technical term in critical cultural analysis and social theory. It is not the sense of "other" in play here.

"Other" is used in a second and more positive sense in discussions of the dynamics of emotionally fulfilling interpersonal relations. Human beings are said to be "relational" beings in that their emotional well-being is a function of their relating to other human beings, and being related to by other human beings, in mutual and reciprocal ways that acknowledge that each is a "genuine other." In those ways of relating, one treats the other, and is treated by the other, as a person in one's own right and not an adjunct to, an extension of, or an instrument of the "other." Correlatively, one does not seek in the relationship to lose oneself somehow "in" the other. Accordingly, in such relations each party at once relates in ways that honor and nurture the "other's" particular individual identity and in ways that insist on and strengthen one's own particular individual identity. Relations between "genuinely other" partners are only apparently paradoxical in simultaneously deepening "closeness" and nurturing the "otherness" of each personal identity, because the two are dialectically interdependent, each the condition of the possibility of the other.

It is a necessary precondition of such analysis of emotionally fulfilling interpersonal relations that each party to the relation comes to it as already an "other." No particular interpersonal relation constitutes either party as an "other." Each has been already been constituted as the particular individual "other" that it is upon entering into the relation by its having been born, by its previous history of relationships and interactions with fellow human beings, and – in a theological account – by being created by the Triune God through processes that are part of what God creates ex nihilo. Because it is created by God ex nihilo each creaturely genuine "other" is finite, inherently limited in its powers, vulnerable to harm, and radically contingent on God's creative blessing for its concrete actuality; it is, in short, subject to disintegration.

The imagery privileged by the Nicene Creed to characterize the Triune God's intrinsic dynamics ties the genuine "otherness" of three "Persons" to the dynamic of God's *self*-relating, and not to the dynamics of the ways in which God relates to creatures. This invokes a third sense of "other." It also pushes the theological use of "Person" to the very edge of articulate intelligibility because the "self-relating" on which that "otherness" is based can only be characterized by analogies to human self-relating that are so distant and thin as to be on the edge of vacuity.

Grammatically speaking, the "self" in "*self*-relating" is reflexive. It does not connote a relation between two "parties" that come into the relation with already concretely actual identities, say "me" and something "other" called "myself." Acts of human self-relating only go on within individual concretely actual human creatures. They may contribute over time to changes in that individual's personal identity. However, they do not constitute something concretely actual other than that particular human creature itself. However, when used analogically to characterize the dynamic that just is the Triune God's concrete actuality, "self-relating" *is* used to connote a relation between irreducibly different – i.e., "other" – identities that are each reciprocally "generated" by that active self-relating: "Father to Son" and "Son to Father"; "Father to Spirit" and "Spirit to Father"; and "Son to Spirit" and "Spirit to Son." They are not "other" than one another in the second sense of "other" noted, because they are not concretely actual independent of their relations to each other and then enter into a relation analogous to "self-relating." Rather, they are eternally "generated" by the dynamic of God's self-relating. They can be called "three 'Persons.'" However, when we ask what they are three "of," the analogy to "self-relating" fails us. They are each constituted by the dynamic of the Triune God's generative, self-expressive, and generously self-giving self-relating. However, we lack analogies by which to characterize any of the three that is thus generated. As we have seen, they cannot be characterized as three concretely actual instances of "divine essence," for that would mean they are three Gods. Nor can they be characterized as three different "modes" in which God's concrete actuality is self-expressed, for in that case they would be merely "modifications" of God's underlying concrete actuality and hence not be irreducibly different identities. Nor can the claim that the dynamic self-relating that is the Triune God's concrete actuality intrinsically is an eternal generating of three irreducibly different identities simply be abandoned. It cannot be set aside because it identified the quality of the concrete actuality of God that is the condition of the possibility of the free *grace* that characterizes the three-character structure ("Father," "Son," and Spirit) of each of the three ways in which God goes about relating to all else in the economy. At this point, analogy gives way to verbal gestures: the Triune God's generous self-giving and perfectly self-expressive self-relating generates three "somethings," we "know-not-whats," for which the quasi-technical and abstract term "Person" and the slightly more concrete analogies "Father," "Son," and Spirit are place holders.

Assuming the validity in Christian theology of Trinitarian accounts of God, I have thus far urged that the Triune God's concrete actuality is most aptly characterized in a highly general way as a dynamic eternal "self-relating." Left at that, it would be both an extremely abstract and a very vague account of God's concrete actuality. I have offered warrants from the language of the Nicene Cred for characterizing that self-relating in two ways: it has the qualities of being (a) generously self-giving and (b) perfectly self-expressive. Qualification of God's dynamic self-relating in those two ways offers a somewhat less abstract account of the Triune

God's concretely actual manner of existence than mere "dynamic self-relating." We turn now to warrant a third quality to that self-relating, which will make our account of God's concrete actuality still more concrete. We have warrant for characterizing the Triune God's concrete actuality as a communion in love among the three "Persons" of the Trinity.

The Triune God's Concrete Actuality Is a Communion in Love

It is a traditional move in Christian theology to identify the dominant quality of the eternal relations among the three "Persons" of the Triune God as "love." The warrant for doing so lies in canonical Christian Scripture's accounts of how God goes about relating to all else in the three strands of God's economy. They lie especially in the four canonical Gospels, and particularly in the Gospel of John. They render with narrative thickness what is needed to warrant analogical ascription of qualities of the triune God's loving in the economy to God's intrinsic reality. They do so inasmuch as the concrete particularities of their narratives of how Jesus of Nazareth goes about relating to those with whom he interacts during his ministry, arrest, trial, torture, crucifixion, and resurrection appearances render the way in which God concretely goes about relating to creatures. This relating serves both to draw those with whom he interacts to their eschatological consummation and to reconcile them to God when they are estranged from God. Those "concrete ways of relating" define God's particular way of loving human creatures in those strands of the economy. That said, however, it is striking how little textual basis there is in canonical Christian scripture for characterizing the dynamic of God's intrinsic self-relating as love.

It is important to distinguish among different contexts in canonical Christian Scripture in which "love" is used: our love for fellow people of faith, for neighbors, for enemies, and for God as commanded by God; love as the fundamental quality of God's ways of relating to all else in God's economy; and love as the fundamental quality of God's intrinsic self-expressive self-relating that constitutes God's own life and makes it intrinsically glorious. Each expression is relevant to this discussion in some way, but only the third is directly relevant to the central theme of this chapter: God's intrinsic glory.

Love as a Moral Norm Commanded by God

There are, of course, plenty of scriptural texts that use "love" in the first context, exhorting human creatures to love one another, their enemies, and God. For the most part in those contexts the Greek New Testament uses the verb *agapao*, meaning to feel and exhibit esteem and goodwill to a person and to prize and delight in a thing, or the noun *agape*, i.e., goodwill and esteem. Matthew, Luke,[7] and John also use a second Greek word for love, the verb *phileo* (the noun is *philia*). Where *agapao* connotes love based on esteem for someone, for which reasons can be given and so can be commanded, *phileo* connotes spontaneous natural affection and friendship for someone, emotional and unreasoned.[8] Both sorts of love are love of which human creatures are capable.

Like all human qualities that may be ascribed to God, such love can be ascribed to God only analogically. When a human quality is attributed to God analogically, the quality ascribed to God is understood partly to overlap in some respects with a quality of human creatures, but also to be quite different from any human quality. For Christians, the definitive clue to how God's "love" for creatures differs from human love for fellow creatures lies in the concrete way that God goes about relating to all that is not God in and through

---

[7] Matthew four times (6:5, 6:10, and 6:37 twice; 23:6); Luke once (20:46).

[8] That, at least, is the distinction that G. Abbott-Smith somewhat tentatively draws between *agapao* and *phileo* in his old standby, *Manual Greek Lexicon of the New Testament* (Edinburgh: T & T Clark, 1937), pp. 3, 4.

the life-trajectory of Jesus of Nazareth as portrayed in the New Testament.

Love as a Quality of God's Ways of Relating to All Else in the Economy

That brings us to the second kind of context in which "love" is used in canonical Scripture: contexts in which "love" is ascribed to God as the fundamental quality of God's ways of relating to all else in God's economy.

Outside the four Gospels, there are New Testament texts that refer to God's love for human creatures in a generalized connection with the economy, using either the verb *agapao* or the noun *agape*.[9] For example: Ephesians 2:4, "But God, ... out of the great love [*agapao*] with which he loved us even when we were dead through our trespasses, made us alive together with Christ"; Romans 5:8, "But God proves his love [*agape*] for us in that while we were still sinners Christ dies for us"; 1 John 4:10, "In this is love [*agape*]. Not that we loved God but that he loved us and sent his only Son to be the atoning sacrifice or our sins"; and the unqualified ontological claim in 1 John 4:8, "Whoever does not love does not know God, for God is love [*agape*]."[10] These texts' connection to the economy is general, in that they seem to assume, allude to, or cite Christ' death (and sometimes his resurrection), but do so through an absolute minimum of narrative that gives no account of the concrete particulars of the way in which God goes about "loving" us in the economy.

The Synoptic Gospels provide such narratives. The narrative thickness of accounts of how Jesus goes about relating to others

---

[9] I set aside here New Testament texts that speak of Jesus Christ loving us. They might or might not also warrant the claim that in Jesus Christ loving us it is none other than God who loves us, depending on what one takes a text's Christology to be.

[10] See also Romans 5:5, "God's love [*agape*] has been poured into our hearts through the Holy Spirit that has been given to us," – if what the Holy Spirit pours is God's love for us, not our love for God.

in the course of his life-trajectory nuances the sense in which we are to love our neighbors and, in particular, neighbors who are our enemies. However, whereas Matthew, Mark, and Luke use Greek words for love in presentations of Jesus' teaching about the importance of human love to God, neighbors, and enemies, they never use them to characterize *God's* ways of relating to any "other." Three of the four Gospels never write about God loving either creatures or Jesus Christ. Only John's Gospel does that.

What the thickness of the Synoptics' narratives does do is show, rather than tell, how God concretely goes about relating in love to sinful creatures who have estranged themselves from God. Their narratives of Jesus' life-trajectory implicitly show God relating in love to reconcile estranged creatures to God on *account of*, and *in spite of*, creatures' sinful estrangement from God *while they are still estranged.* Thus, the way the Canonical Gospels define God's love in that strand of the economy is precisely the same as the way the minimally narratival texts in various New Testament Epistles also define it.

However, the sense of "love" that the narrative "thickness" of the Gospels' accounts of how God goes about relating in love to estranged human creatures to reconcile them to God cannot be ascribed to the Triune God as a quality of the dynamic self-relating that is God's concrete actuality. It is exactly *not* an apt analogy for the love that characterize the generative and self-expressive self-relating that is the *intrinsic* dynamic of the relations among "Father," "Son," and Holy Spirit. That love cannot be conceived as a love among the three "Persons" of the Triune God on account of and despite *their* sin! How can sin be attributed to them?

Love as a Quality of the Triune God's Intrinsic Reality

This leaves us with the third sort of context in which "love" is ascribed to God in canonical New Testament texts when we look to them to warrant ascribing "love" to the Triune God's own intrinsic dynamic self-relating. It is to be found above all in the Gospel of John. It is perhaps for that reason that John has been the Gospel privileged in traditional Christian theological accounts of both the significance of Jesus and the Triunity of God. It has been privileged in the sense that, as the basis of traditional Christology and Trinitarian doctrine, the other three Gospels have tended to be interpreted through the lens of John. Showing that John does indeed characterize the sense in which love is a quality of God's intrinsic reality requires a longer exposition.

Although John, like the Synoptic Gospels, most frequently uses Greek words for love to name how Jesus commands his followers to relate to God, their fellow disciples, their neighbors, and their enemies, John alone also uses "love" to characterize God's way of relating to Jesus' followers, God's relation to Jesus, and God's relation to the "world." Some examples: regarding the Father's way of relating to the "Son," using *agapao*: "The Father loves the Son" (3:35; also 10:17, 15:9, and 17:26); by using *phileo*: "The Father loves the Son" (5:20); and by using *agape*: "I [Jesus] have kept the Father's commandments and abide in his love" [15:10]). Regarding God's relation to Jesus' followers, using *agapao*: "and he who loves me [Jesus] will be loved by my father: (14:21; also 14:23 and 17:23), and using *phileo*, "the Father himself loves you" (16:27). Regarding God's relation to all that is not God, using *agapao*: "God so loved the world that he gave his only Son, so that everyone who believes in him may not perish but may have eternal life" (3:16). John uses words for love to characterize what God is doing in and through what Jesus does and undergoes, as the latter is narrated in the Gospel. Repeatedly, that love by God for Jesus, Jesus' followers, and the "world" is identified with God's glory in the narrative.

At the same time, John's narrative of what Jesus does and undergoes has two strands that move toward different goals or ends that, in turn, nuance the meaning of "love" in different ways when the term is ascribed to God and God's ways of relating to all that is not God.

The two different goals or ends toward which John's overall narrative moves are set by two themes in the Prologue to the Gospel (John 1:1–18) that serve as the embracing context of the narrative that follows.

The First Theme in the Prologue: Eschatological Blessing

The first theme in the prologue identifies who Jesus Christ is in terms of his "eternal" relation with God. That is, it identifies him in terms of the relation between him and God that is, in the order of being, "prior" to ("prior" in the order of being, not in the temporal order) and independent of the "coming into being" of reality other than God. Jesus is identified as the "Word" of God that "became flesh and lived among us" (John 1:14a). The Gospel's use of "Word" certainly echoes Greco-Roman philosophical theorizing about the cosmos' "first principle," but the way in which it is used in the prologue probably is based on the way the word "Wisdom" is used in canonical Proverbs chapter 8, mapped onto Genesis 1:1. The "Word" that became flesh is characterized in terms of its role in the cosmos. The prologue, probably echoing Genesis 1, identifies the "Word" of God, who was "in the beginning" and through whom "all things came into being" (John 1:2, 3), as one that "was with God" (John 1:1) and indeed "was God" (John 1:1). The prologue then uses a sequence of images to characterize that cosmic role: what comes into being *in* him is "life'" (John 1:3c, 4a). It is not just that the Word brings "life" into being; the Word is himself concretely "life." Later in the Gospel, it is imaged as "eternal life." That life is then characterized by the image "light," "the light of all people" (John 1:4b). The way in which the Word is life giving is by enlightening others. The concrete way in which he enlightens others is by becoming flesh and living among us. What we are enlightened about is the reality and nature of God's "glory": in the Word become flesh. "[w]e have seen his *glory* [in the flesh!], the glory of father's only son, full of grace and truth" (John 1:14b).

The prologue ends by characterizing the Word's intrinsic cosmic relation to God independent of "all things coming into being" through him, the relation which is faithfully expressed or "made known" when the Word is enfleshed, in a familial image: "No one has ever seen God. It is God the only Son [i.e., the Word], who is close to the Father's heart, who has made him known" (John 1:18). "Close to the Father's heart": their eternal relation is characterized as "love."

One overall goal of what God is doing in and through what Jesus does and undergoes, as rendered by the narrative that follows John's Prologue, is identified by this theme in the prologue. It is the actualization of "eternal life" or the "eschatological glorification" of creatures who "came into being through him" (1:3a). Although it has often been argued that, in contrast with the Synoptic Gospels, John promotes a "fully actualized" or "realized" eschatology, there are many places in John's text that imply that the eschaton is not yet fully actualized. It is nonetheless evident that John stresses more than the Synoptic Gospels do that God has indeed decisively inaugurated the *beginning* of God's fulfillment of a long-standing promise of creation's eschatological consummation. John's narrative renders the life-trajectory of Jesus that culminates in his resurrection from the dead and ascension as the concrete way in which God goes about starting to keep that promise in the eschatological glorification of the enfleshed Word of God's human life.[11]

John's Gospel renders the movement toward the goal of God's ultimate full actualization of creatures' eschatological consummation as a circular flow of the glorious intrinsic love between God and Word, "Father" and "Son," eternally; to Jesus Christ enfleshed; and in God's economy through him to Jesus' followers and to the world; and back to God in creatures' glorification of God. For

---

[11] See the account of Mary Magdalene's encounter with the risen Jesus (John 20:17).

example, the "Father" loves the "Son" who, apparently (given that the text's context is Jesus' conversation with Nicodemus), "comes from above" (John 3:16, 35); indeed, "the Father loves me [Jesus] because I lay down my life in order to take it up again" (John 10:17); the Son in turn loves the Father (cf. John 14:38); the Son also loves his followers: "As the Father has loved me, so have I loved you; abide in my love" (John 15:9) – i.e., live in the love I have to God and God has to me. Jesus commands his followers to love one another: "This is my commandment, that you love one another as I have loved you" (John 15:12). And Jesus explicitly ties the "flow" together: "If you keep my commandments, you will abide in my love, just as I have kept my father's commandments and abide in his love" (John 15:10).

Thus, it is the flow of God's love that, in John's account, ties together God's intrinsic love, Jesus' love for God, God's love for Jesus, God's love for Jesus' followers, and their responsive love to God and one another.

It is not that the "Father's" love is an example that Jesus followed, and his love is an example that his followers are to follow. Rather, the reality of the "Son's" life is his participation in the love that is God's concrete actuality; and the reality of the "Son's" followers' lives is their participation in Jesus' participation in God's love, which makes Jesus the life-giving light. The upshot of the Johannine narrative's overall movement is a union of creatures, the "Son" as Word, and the "Father" in God's intrinsic love: "On that day you will know that I am in my Father, and you in me, and I in you" (John 14:20). "That day" is the full actualization of "eternal life." It is the full actualization of God's promise to consummate creatures' eschatological glorification in the love that expresses the attractiveness of God's intrinsic glory.

As expressed in scenes of Jesus' "signs" and teachings in John's narrative, climaxing in his resurrection, God's intrinsic reality is loving, and the attractiveness of that love evokes the human response of glorifying God in their love to God and to one another. To live in that responsive love is eternal life for human creatures, their eschatological glorification, beginning now and fully actualized in their ultimate resurrections. Their living in love to God and to one another is not just an imitation of Jesus' living in love to God and to them; John represents it as participation by them in Jesus' own life in love to God and to others. In itself, it is a perfectly faithful expression of the Word's intrinsic eternal life in mutual love with God.

Such participation in God's glory is by grace because, according to the prologue, it is a free gift: "But to all who received him, who believed in his name, believe he [the Word] gave power to become children of God, who were born, not of blood or of the will of man, but of God" (John 1:12–13).

Such participation in God's glory by participating in Jesus' eschatologically glorified life is also "truth," not as grasping the truth of Jesus' "teaching," or of his "wisdom," or of his "spiritual insight," or of his "experience of God," but simply as participation in what God's love is doing in and through what Jesus does and undergoes in his concrete bodily life. Jesus draws creatures to their own eschatological glorification, which the Gospel then proceeds to narrate in a certain way. It is just Jesus' bodily life that is the "glory" of God in the economy. Such participation in God's glory is truth, not the "truth" of Jesus' "teachings," or his "wisdom," or his "spiritual insight," or his "experience of God." Rather, it is that truth simply is what Jesus does and undergoes in his concrete bodily life, which is the "glory" of God lived among us.

The movement of the circular "flow" of God's love in the economy, and therewith the movement of John's narrative of that flow through the life-trajectory of Jesus, is, as "grace and truth," simply God's blessing on creatures. Its movement is not driven by any conflict or by neediness on the part either of creatures or of God. The flow is instead God's steady-state blessing on creatures consisting of the temporally extended fulfillment of a long-promised eschatological consummation. What moves it is nothing but

God's faithfulness in loving creatures in this particular, i.e., "Incarnational," way.

Fundamentally, the flow is moved by God's self-faithfulness: rooted in the dynamism of God's intrinsic life, God's love just is God's intrinsic glory. It is God being "who" and "what" God is. If, in addition, God relates in the economy to reality other than God, the flow of God's love there faithfully expresses the Triune God's intrinsic dynamic of loving self-relating. As the faithful expression of "who" and "what" God is, the flow moves in the economy in delight and joy in ways ordered to the good of the beloved. It is the movement of a strand of John's narrative whose goal is set by the theme of eternal life in John's Prologue.

The Second Theme in the Prologue

There is, however, a second theme in John's Prologue that sets the goal of a second strand in John's narrative of what God is doing in and through what Jesus does and undergoes. This theme nuances the sense in which a "love" for reality other than God is ascribed to God that is different from that of the strand just discussed. It is different in a way that raises the question of whether the Gospel of John really does provide any more basis for ascribing love to God than do the Synoptic Gospels.

This second theme in the Prologue of John's Gospel is framed as a characterization of the "world" into which the Word "became flesh" in the economy and "lived among us." The image it uses to characterize that world is "darkness." Although the Word through whom the world came to be (John 1:10) is the life-giving "light" of that world, that very world into which the Word "became flesh" had become dark. So, although the Word-become-flesh was "in the world, and the world came into being through him, ... the world did not know him" (John 1:10). Indeed, "his own people did not accept him" (John 1:11). Accordingly, in consequence of having become flesh, "the light shines in the darkness, and the darkness did not overcome it" (John 1:5). The darkening of a world that came into being through the Word is not explained. It is not identified as the "reason" why the Word "became flesh." It is merely acknowledged as the dominant characteristic of the context in which the things Jesus does and undergoes take place.

It is this theme that sets a second goal of what God is doing in and through what Jesus does and undergoes, as rendered by the narrative that follows in John. The world's darkness signifies its estrangement from God, who brings it into being and is its life-giving "light." The goal of what God is doing in and through Jesus' life-trajectory is to overcome that estrangement and reconcile it to God. The Word's becoming flesh is not only God's way of inaugurating, but not fully actualizing, the blessing of "eternal life" in the world; it is also God's way of bringing the "light" that will reconcile estranged creatures to God by overcoming the "darkness" of their estrangement from God. That narrative of how God goes about relating to make eternal life possible for human creatures by pouring God's love into their lives through God's love for the Son, who in turns loves his followers, leads into John's version of the Passion story, the goal of which is not the blessing of eschatological consummation, but rather God's overcoming that which estranges creatures from God. Throughout the text of John, the two narratives are mapped onto each other.

In particular, the Gospel of John maps a narrative of Passion Week that is largely shared with the Synoptics onto John's account of the circular flow of God's intrinsic love "outward" in the Word's enfleshment to Jesus' followers and back to God in their love for one another, for their enemies, and for God.

Here are some examples of how John's narrative of how God relates to make eternal life possible for human creatures (i.e., by pouring God's love into their lives through God's love for the Son, who in turns loves his followers) is mapped onto a version of the Passion story that is remarkably close to the Synoptic Gospels' Passion story:

- In Jesus' conversation with Nicodemus, John has Jesus say, "No one has ascended into heaven except the one who descended from heaven, the Son of Man. And just as Moses lifted up the serpent in the wilderness, so must the Son of Man be lifted up" (3:13–14). The "lifting up" of the Son of Man is commonly understood to be an allusion at once to Jesus' crucifixion and to his glorification by being raised and ascending to the "Father." Similarly, in the course of a controversy with the Pharisees (8:13), Jesus follows up the claim that he is "from above" (in the context set by the prologue, an allusion to the ontological status of the Word) by saying, "When you have lifted up the Son of Man, then you will realize that I am he and that I do nothing on my own, but speak these things as the Father instructed me" (8:28). What he speaks is the truth, whose light reconciles a darkened world to God.

- Before turning to its account of the Jesus' act of washing the disciples feet and Jesus' "high priestly prayer," the Fourth Gospel maps both the last judgment and the "Father's" "glorification" of Jesus onto Jesus' crucifixion: Jesus says,

> Now my soul is troubled. And what should I say – 'Father save me from this hour? No, it is for this reason that I have come to this hour. Father, glorify your name.' Then a voice came from heaven, 'I have glorified it and I will glorify it again.' . . . Jesus answered, 'Now is the judgment of this world; . . . And I, when I am lifted up from the earth, will draw all people to myself.' He said this to indicate the kind of death he was to die. (12:27–28, 30–33)

- That is, crucifixion, which is itself Jesus' "glorification," is the particular way in which his death faithfully expresses the quality of God's glory. It is a scandalous expression of God's glory in that, as a way to be executed, crucifixion was commonly seen as a curse and a disgrace.

- John begins his account of the disciples' final night with Jesus just before the festival of the Passover, which replaces the Synoptic's account of the Last Supper with an account of Jesus washing the disciples' feet. John maps Jesus' betrayal and the beginning of his final weekend onto his account of Jesus' role in the circular movement of God's love: "Having loved his own who were in the world, he loved them to the end. The devil had already put it into the heart of Judas son of Simon Iscariot to betray him: (13:1–2). The concrete way in which that love is enacted is in a servant's role, washing the guests feet. Its outcome is Jesus' betrayal into the hands of his enemies and his unjust and cruel execution by crucifixion.

Mapping its account of Jesus' arrest, trial, torture, and crucifixion onto its narrative of the movement of a circular flow of God's intrinsic love that draws creatures into the "eternal life" of eschatological consummation has the effect, however, of ordering John's overall narrative toward a different goal. It frames the narrative as moving toward a decisive event that will be God's victorious overcoming of the darkness that estranges creatures from God. That decisive event is Jesus' death by crucifixion: likening his own death to that of a shepherd who gives his life for his sheep, Jesus is represented as saying, "I lay down my life in order to take it up again. No one takes it from me, but I lay it down of my own accord. I have power to lay it down and I have power to take it up again" (10:18).

That the overall point of the entire narrative is the singular event of God's giving "his only Son" is already announced in the third chapter's account of Jesus' conversation with Nicodemus: "God so loved the world that he gave his only Son . . ." (3:16). The mode of "giving," which is unspecified there, is more explicitly identified much later in John's account of Jesus' "triumphal" entry into Jerusalem at the beginning of his last week. Immediately after that procession, when even some gentile Greeks ask to see Jesus, the

Gospel reports that Jesus sees it as a decisive turning point: Jesus says, "Now is the judgment of this world; . . . And I, when I am lifted up from the earth, will draw all people to myself. He said this to indicate the kind of death he was to die" (12:31–33), i.e., crucifixion. It is on the cross, and not yet at his resurrection and ascension, that Jesus is "lifted up" and is "glorified."

The Gospel does not offer much by way of metaphor for or analogy of Jesus' crucifixion to suggest how his death on a cross decisively effects God's overcoming the darkness of creatures' estrangement from God. Nonetheless, it is the crucifixion that is the end to which the entire Gospel narrative has been moving, when John's entire narrative of Jesus' life-trajectory is read as an account of what God is doing in and through it in the context of the "darkness" that has (inexplicably) overcome that which God brought into being through God's Word, the "Son."

Because the two themes in John's Prologue set two different ends or goals for its subsequent narrative, the Gospel's overall narrative embraces two strands that cannot be conflated with each other. Neither strand can be read as a subordinate part, a subplot as it were, of the other, because they are fundamentally different sorts of narrative. They have irreducibly different narrative "logics." We have noted that, read as a narrative of how – in and through what Jesus does and undergoes – God goes about relating to creatures to begin to keep a promise that they will be drawn into an eschatological consummation the Gospel of John is an account of a steady-state relation in which God is blessing creatures. Read that way, the narrative is moved by the "logic" of God's self-faithfulness: the movement of the narrative is the movement of the way God goes about keeping a promise. In contrast, read as a narrative of how – in and through what Jesus does and undergoes – God goes about relating to creatures to overcome creatures' estrangement from God, reconcile them to God, and free them from the consequences to them of their estrangement from God, the Gospel of John moves inexorably toward a punctiliar event, the crucifixion of Jesus, that decisively accomplishes God's reconciling goal. The movement of the narrative is driven – as is the movement of all three of the Synoptic Gospels' overall narratives – by a conflict between Jesus and religious and political authorities that builds in intensity as the narrative progresses and comes to its inevitable narrative climax in Jesus' arrest, unjust trial, and execution by crucifixion as a disgraced criminal.

Each of the two strands in John's narrative renders a different way in which God relates to all else in love in the economy. However, each strand renders love that is enacted in a different way that it is irreducible to the other. Each strand characterizes a way in which God concretely goes about relating to all else in a different sense of "love" than the other.

The second strand of John's narrative shows God's love in the economy moving toward the reconciliation of creatures estranged from God by the world's "darkness" by way of an Incarnation of the Word into that darkness that, in conflict with the darkened world, leads to crucifixion. It shows that love to be love of creatures on account of and despite their estrangement from God. In doing so, God is shown to be relating to all else in the economy in a way that faithfully expresses an aspect of the Triune God's intrinsic concrete actuality. God is self-faithful in relating in that way, and therefore is trustworthy in the relation. Nonetheless, that sense of "love" can no more be aptly used analogically to characterize the Triune God's intrinsic love than can the sense of "love" by God to creatures that is rendered in the Synoptic Gospels. And, for the same reason, "love" by God *defined* as being both on "account of" and "despite" creatures' sinful estrangement is exactly *not* an apt analogy for the love that characterizes the dynamics of the self-expressive self-relating that is the common life of the "Father," "Son," and Holy Spirit. They cannot be said to "love" one another on account of and in spite of their estrangement from one another. They are not estranged. On the contrary, they are so united in their love as to be "of one substance."

However, the first strand of John's narrative shows God's love in the economy moving in the circular flow of eschatological blessing on creatures of the gift of the eternal love between God and the "Word," which by becoming flesh, lives that love in the life of Jesus of Nazareth, draws Jesus' followers into that love so that they are transformed to begin living an eternal, eschatologically blessed life; share that love with one another; and are empowered to love God rightly. In the first strand of John's narrative, God's loving creatures by beginning to keep God's promise of eschatological blessing does not presuppose that they live in a darkened world – although in fact they do. The concrete way God goes about loving in eschatological blessing, i.e., by way of Incarnation, is ordered both to glorification of the Word's flesh in his resurrection and ascension and the glorification of those human creatures who abide in his love and love him and the "Father."

The communion in love between Jesus and the one he calls "Father," as rendered in John's account of the economy, is the apt analogue for the dynamic of the Triune God's intrinsic self-relating. The ways in which Jesus enacts his love for the "Father," and the "Father" for Jesus, in John's account of the economy can best be characterized as a communion in love. It is the "love" of friendship. It is rooted in and faithfully expressive of the way in which the Triunity of God is eternally generated in God's generously self-giving and perfectly self-expressive self-relating. That self-relating is a self-giving love that not only "generates" the unique identity of the beloved "other," but does so in a way that at once seeks "closeness" to the beloved and the full "otherness" of the other in its own right and for its own sake.

Accordingly, we are warranted in using the phrase "communion in love" analogically to name a quality of the Triune God's intrinsic dynamic: God's intrinsic self-relating in generative self-*giving* is a *self*-giving in love so radically generous as to constitute genuine "others" that are "of the same substance"; the Triune God's *self*-expressive self-relating is a self-*expression* in love is so radically perfect as to constitute genuine "others" that are "of the same substance." The Triune God's intrinsic dynamic of self-relating is the dynamic of a communion in love among three irreducibly "other" identities that are one integral concrete actuality.

The Triune God Lives

Inasmuch as the dynamic self-relating that consists of a communion in love just *is* the Triune God's concrete actuality, we are warranted is saying that "communion in love" is a quality of "what" and "who" it is to be the Triune God. If we can ascribe communion in love to the Triune God's intrinsic reality, then we are also warranted to ascribe "life" to God analogically. It is apt to characterize the dynamics of "what" and "who" the loving Triune God intrinsically is as the dynamics of "life," because there is a certain amount of overlap between those dynamics and what ascription of "life" to loving human creatures ordinarily means. It can only be an analogical ascription, because the difference between the two is much greater than the similarities.

In this case, for example, the forms of "life" with which we are familiar, both vegetable and animal life, are bodied. They are based in organic matter and, it is generally thought, depend on that basis for their continued existence across time. The Triune God, however, is not an item on the inventory list of the material cosmos' material entities. God's immateriality makes God's manner of existing so radically different than the manner of existence of any forms of life with which we are familiar that the sense in which God can be said to "live" must be extremely different than the sense in which we say any kind of material creature lives.

Nonetheless, there is a certain similarity between, on one side, the dynamic of the Triune God self-relating in ways that are exercises and expresses of "love," and on the other side the "life" of creatures complex enough to be self-consciously aware of their contexts and relate to one another in "love" as friendship. Human beings are the kind of creatures with which we are most familiar whose forms of life include relating to one another in love as friendship.

That similarity is reflected in the common use of "agentic" terms to characterize love as friendship when it is ascribed to both human creatures and, analogically, to the Triune God. Human "love" as friendship is typically described, not simply as an emotion, but more complexly as a certain array of "intentional acts" of relating to other human creatures. As friendship, human love is lived out in "mindful" intentional acts, that is, acts that attend *to* and intend the fulfillment *of* the beloved in its concrete particularity in delight and joy at the beloved's sheer actuality. They are "mindful" acts, in contradistinction to "caused" behaviors, in that reasons rather than causes can be identified to explain why one did them, as opposed to explaining why they happened. They are actions that one not only acknowledges were done by oneself but one "owns" as enactments of one's conscious intensions. In enactments of love as friendship, a human lover freely "wills" the beloved's full reality as the particular "other" that it is.

If one is to love in that way, such love also requires that the lover "knows" the beloved in his concrete particularity so as to enact her intention in ways that are appropriate to the particularities of the beloved's situation. Further, if the lover is to know the beloved in this way and will the enactment of an appropriate intention for the well-being of the beloved, such that the lover can give the reason for the loving action, the lover must have capacities for conceptual thought. All of that is fundamental to one kind of creaturely "life."

God's active self-relating was characterized as the "love" each of the "Persons" bears to the other two "Persons" of the Trinity for their own sakes, for what each of them is in and of itself, drawn by the attractive radiant intrinsic glory of each of them. The love among the "Persons" of the Trinity is characterized as a self-giving that at once seeks "closeness" to the beloved and seeks the full "otherness" of the other in its own right. The concrete actuality of the Triune God is described above as an intrinsic dynamic of "love" that "knows" the beloved, "fosters" or "freely wills" the beloved's reality in its particularity for its own sake, "delights" in its beauty, and "rejoices" in its concrete actuality. It is the "love" of friendship. In that case, it is appropriate also analogically to ascribe to the Triune God the "agentic" sense in which "life" is ascribed to human creaturely agents.

The "life" that is the Triune God's concrete actuality is nothing other than the dynamic among the three "Persons" that is intrinsically integral. The *perichoresis* of the "Persons" is inseparable. This life is not a function of the intersection or confluence of three otherwise independent "dynamics" that have come to be "integrated." If it were, it would be reasonable to assume that they might also "dis-integrate" from one another. Rather, each one of them is what it is in virtue of the other two actively relating to it eternally. It is "one" life in the sense that it is an indivisible unity. The Triune God is a living God.

The Intrinsic Glory of the Triune God

We have noted that, as ascribed to God in canonical Christian Scripture, "glory" is a relational term used in regard to three referents: enactments of practices of praise to God are in one sense the "glory" of God. They are responses to some of the qualities of the concrete particularities of God's ways of relating to all else in God's economy, which are themselves a second sense of the "glory" of God. Third, those qualities of how God concretely goes about relating to all else are rooted in, and are faithfully expressive of, aspects of qualities intrinsic to God's reality, whether or not God relates to anything other than God. Those intrinsic qualities of God are the "glory" of God in the most fundamental sense of the term. It is only that third sense of "glory" that we examine in this chapter.

We also have noted that, as ascribed to God in its most funda-mental sense, "glory" has a distinctive dynamic. It connotes some-thing like an intrinsic "gravitas" that is described in Scripture by images of shining, radiance, brilliance, or resplendence. In short, it is the quality of attention getting from "others" and attractiveness to "others." As such, it is an inherently actively relational term con-noting the "glorious" One's intrinsic self-expressiveness that attracts "others" to it simply for its own sake and not for the sake of what it might do or does do for those who are attracted by it.

That dynamic maps well onto the dynamic that, as analyzed, is the intrinsic concrete actuality of the Triune God as that is outlined in the internal movement and imagery of the Nicene Creed: The Triune God's concrete actuality is best characterized in dynamic terms as an active self-relating that "generates" the irreducibly different identities of three "Persons." That "generating" can be characterized slightly more exactly: it is perfectly self-expressive and generously self-giving, such that each of the three "Persons" is of the same being as the other two. They are integrally one in the self-expressive and self-giving dynamic of the self-relating that "generates" the differences of their respective identities. In that relating each of the three "Persons" relating to each of the other two is correlatively so radically "other" than they as to be irredu-cibly "other" and so radically "close" as to be the same reality.

Thus far, the self-expressiveness of "glory" maps onto the dynamic "self-relating" that is the concrete actuality of the Triune God. However it is essential to the relational character of "glory" that its self-relating be attractive, and the characterization given thus far of the Triune God's "self-relating" is too abstract to count as "attractive." There is warrant (mostly from the Gospel of John) for further characterizing the Triune God's self-relating even more concretely as a self-relating in a communion-in-love among the three "Persons" of the Trinity in which each of them is (a) "gener-ated" as the unique "identity" it is and (b) the three are together one in the integral dynamic that is their concrete actuality. The combination of a dynamic self-relating that is generously self-giving of, and perfectly self-expressed in, three "identities," on the one hand, and on the other the attractive integral communion-in-love that *is* that self-relating, warrant another more concrete character-ization of the Triune God's intrinsic glory: it is a living glory, a glorious life.

These remarks about "what" and "who" the glorious Triune God is intrinsically, apart from God's ways of actively relating to all else in the economy, bring with them implications for how to talk – and not talk – about God's concrete actuality. We turn to them in Chapter 3.

Part II | Kingdom

3 | God's Intrinsic "Sovereignty"

If God is powerful, God is powerful in God's own way. In Chapter 2, I urged that an account of the sense in which God is powerful should be conceptually nested in a more basic account of what and who God is, independent of whether or not God "powerfully" relates to anything other than God. It proposed that we begin to identify "God's own way" of being powerful in an account of God's intrinsic glory. It is the glorious God who is powerful. "Intrinsic glory" was understood as the dynamic self-relating that, by its perfect self-expressiveness, constitutes God's Triunity and, by the attractiveness of its self-expression, constitutes the communion of genuine "others" that just is the integral unicity of God's glorious Triune life.

In Part II of this book, I urge that, although indeed an account of God's power ought to be conceptually nested in that account of God's more basic quality of intrinsic glory, it ought to be so "nested" only indirectly. That is, an account of God's power ought to be explained in the conceptual context of an account of another quality of God's intrinsic glory – sovereignty – which is itself explicated in the context of an account of God's intrinsic glory. The claim that is defended here is that, in as much as God is powerful in God's own way, what "power" means when attributed to God needs to be explained in terms of an account of what "sovereignty" means when attributed to God, an account that itself explains "sovereignty" in terms of an even more basic concept of what "glory" means when attributed to God. Part I outlined the basics of the relevant explanation of "glory" as attributed to God.

Part II aims to outline the basics of the relevant explanation of "sovereignty" as attributed to God.

The central theme of this explanation of sovereignty is that, rather than basing an account of God's sovereignty on the assumption that what constitutes God's "divinity," i.e., it is what makes God "God," is God's way of being powerful (thus construing God's sovereignty in terms of prior assumptions about what God's power is), God's "power" ought to be construed in terms of what we know to say about God's sovereignty on the basis of different ways in which God goes about being sovereign. Part II thus sets the stage for Part III's outline of an explanation of "power" when attributed to God framed in terms provided by Part II's account of senses in which "sovereignty" may be attributed to God.

This chapter moves through three stages. The first is to explain what theological basis we have for attributing any qualities to God at all, sovereignty and power in particular. The second is to address well-grounded objection to attributing "sovereignty" to God, naming what makes it problematic both in general and in theology. Finally, because God does as God is, to outline a sense in which the God may be said to be intrinsically sovereign in God's own Triune life, independent of whether or not God relates to reality other than God.

Why Praise the God of Abraham in Particular?

To get hold of the concept of God's glory in Chapter 2, we asked why we should praise the God of Abraham, as the hymn exhorts us, rather than thank God or petition God to help us in our need. The answer was that, after silence, praise is the appropriate human response to the intrinsic glory of God. That tenet still leaves open the question of why we should praise the God of Abraham *in particular*. The answer has to do with what justifies or warrants our attributing any qualities at all to God, including glory, sovereignty, and power. I propose that, insofar as the ways in which God relates to all else in the economy, as rendered in canonical Scriptural narratives, do faithfully express qualities of God's intrinsic self-relating, it is some of the concrete *particularities* of the ways in which God goes about relating to all else that express God's intrinsic qualities and warrant our ascribing them to God as intrinsic qualities.

Granted that human praise is the response evoked by God's intrinsic glory, why praise the God of Abraham *in particular*? Why not praise generic "divinity" or "transcendence" or "mystery" or "the holy"? The short answer is this: because of the particularity of the self-expression of God's own intrinsic glory that occurs in the distinguishable ways God goes about relating to reality other than God according to Christian canonical scriptural witness. In each of the ways that God relates to something else, God's intrinsic glory is faithfully, if partially, self-expressed in a different way. Those "different ways" in which God's glory is self-expressed just *are* the differences among the ways in which God concretely goes about relating, say, to create, or to reconcile the estranged, or to consummate creatures eschatologically. There are no accounts of the "self-expression of God in general." Nor are there accounts of divine "creativity," "reconciling," or "eschatologically consummating" in general.

For Christians, one of the roles of canonical biblical writings, read as Christian Holy Scripture, is to testify to the ways God goes about relating to all else, including us. It is especially the narrative character of much of that testimony that conveys the particularity of the ways in which God goes about relating to us. That is what Christian communities of faith have to go on when they seek guidance about how to characterize God. So, why praise the God of Abraham in particular? Because two distinct kinds of canonical scriptural narratives about Abraham and the particular ways in which God related to him entail two different ways in which God's sovereignty in relating to Abraham is nuanced. The two are these: narratives of how God goes about relating to Abraham in liberative promise making and promise keeping, and narratives of how God goes about relating to Abraham in creative blessing.

Maker and Keeper of Liberative Promises

According to Genesis 12:1–25:11, God is One who relates as a trustworthy and liberative promise maker and promise keeper to Abram (who after a later name change is called Abraham [Genesis 17:5]). Genesis tells of several events of God relating to Abram in that fashion. In one complexly structured narrative, for example, God is said to make a promise to Abram in a vision (15:1) while Abram is passive "in a deep sleep"" "[A] deep and terrifying darkness descended upon him" (15:12). But in the same story, God's promise making is conjoined with Abram's physical action of making a ritual sacrifice (15: 7–11, 17–21) that becomes a numinous moment. Nowhere in the narrative is God's promise making rendered simply as an event in Abram's private subjective interiority. God's relating to him by making promises is narrated as occurring in public, in the context of the rough and tumble of extended family and clan conflicts and of battles among kings and city-states.

The content of what is promised to Abram sounds grand but is relatively vague: eventual possession of Canaan (Genesis 12:7, 13:14; 15:18–21), whose extent varies from one episode of promise making to another, and a host of descendants variously estimated to be greater in number than the stars in the sky (15:5; 22:17), or the dust of the earth (13:16), or the sand by the sea (22:17). Overarching all these promises is the promise that, through their fulfillment, Abram will be a "blessing" in whom "all the families of the earth shall be blessed" (Genesis 12:3). It remains unspecified just how all the families of the earth will be blessed "in Abram," except that, after his name change to Abraham ("ancestor of a multitude"; Genesis 17:15), the promise will be fulfilled through the offspring of

Abraham's son Isaac with whom God's covenant will be "everlasting" (17:19). The time frame for the fulfillment of the promises is utterly open ended. However, the birth of Sarah and Abraham's only son Isaac marks the inauguration of God's making good on these covenant-establishing promises.

What makes God's promises to Abraham radically generous is not so much their content as the fact that they are utterly unconditional. They do not depend on anything Abraham has previously done, and their fulfillment does not depend on conditions Abraham must satisfy in future. They invite in response only a trust in the faithfulness of the promise maker. The Scriptural narratives render Abraham's way of living out that trust as an ongoing discourse with God, sometimes questioning (15:1–3), sometimes incredulous (17:15–17; 18:9–15), and sometimes contentious (18:22–33), but always reciprocal.

In all of this, the reference to Abraham is short hand. The One we are to praise is not the God only of Abraham. According to the narratives in Genesis 12:1–25:11 that One is explicitly the God of Sarah also, and beyond them the God of Rebekah as well, and Isaac, Rachel, Leah, and Jacob and, given Jacob's name change to "Israel," the God of all the daughters and sons of Israel. And among them, as the generations unfold, the God of Jesus of Nazareth.[1]

The description of God given by canonical narratives of God's relating to Abraham is that of a trustworthy and radically generous promise maker. But that is not all. The description is of a trustworthy and radically generous *liberative* promise maker. This nature is brought out, not by the content of the narratives, but by analysis of the narratives' role in their larger literary context, the

---

[1] Hence, the God Christians are exhorted to praise is the God they must acknowledge is praised also by Jews. By the same token, the One who is to be praised is the God of Hagar and Abraham and, therefore, the God also of their son Ishmael, whose descendants Muslims understand to be the people among whom the prophet Muhammad was inspired by God. The God Christians are to praise is the God they must acknowledge is praised also by Muslims.

Pentateuch as a whole. In his commentary on Genesis 1-11, Claus Westermann[2] affirms the near consensus scholarly judgment that the literary center of the Pentateuch is its narrative of God's liberation of the children of Israel from bondage in Egypt. He also affirms that at the heart of Old Testament theology lie such confessions of faith as Deuteronomy 26:5-9 ("a wandering Aramean was my ancestor," etc.)[3] that testify to deliverance at the Red Sea, liberating the children of Israel from bondage in Egypt, as part of the fulfillment of God's promise to their ancestor Abraham. That is the heart of the Pentateuch.

According to Westermann, Genesis 12-50 serves as an introduction to the rest of the Pentateuch that centers on an account of the event of Israel's liberation from Egypt. Genesis' narratives of the ways in which God relates to each of the patriarchs "present the history of Israel before it became a people."[4] Those stories about the patriarchs serve to establish a backstory to the longer and theologically central narrative of Israel's deliverance from Egypt. The backstory serves to show that the event of deliverance at the Red Sea was not an arbitrary interruption by God of the course of human affairs, but was rather the fulfillment of a promise made by God long before to Israel's progenitor, Abraham. Accordingly, the canonical narratives in Genesis 12:1-25:11 of God's promise making to Abraham are already implicitly narratives of a *liberative* promise making. God's faithfulness in keeping promises entails God's capacity to transform circumstances that might seem to militate against fulfillment of those promises, that is, against God's capacities for liberating deeds of deliverance.

---

[2] Westermann, C. *Genesis 1-11: A Commentary* (Minneapolis: Augsburg, 1984).

[3] Cf. Joshua 24:2-4, "Thus says the Lord, the God of Israel: Long ago your ancestors – Tereh and his sons Abraham and Nahor – lived beyond the Euphrates and served other gods. Then I took your father Abraham from beyond the River and led him through all the land of Canaan and made his offspring many."

[4] Ibid., p. 2.

What makes canonical narratives of God's relating to Abraham theologically important is their very narrativity. That narrativity conveys the utter singularity of who God is in relating to others. It is easy enough to characterize God as One who relates by making generous and inherently liberative promises to nurture humanity's general well-being and then faithfully makes good on them. That would reduce the narrative to a few abstract ideals – generosity, beneficence, trustworthiness – of which God is the un-surpassably excellent exemplification. But God's ways of relating to all else are not illustrations of abstract qualities. Scriptural narratives of God relating to Abraham in particular require theological inquiry about God to focus on *who* God is in the singular manner in which God *goes about* making promises to Abraham, and then fulfills them.

In the canonical narratives, God goes about relating to Abraham by making and keeping promises with a particularly complex faithfulness. First, God's faithfulness means God can be trusted to fulfill what is promised. God's faithfulness in promise making is rendered in canonical narratives as God's act of self-commitment to which God is faithful. God thereby defines who God is: One faithful to God's own self-binding by just these particular promises.

Second, in promise making God is faithful to the well-being of those to whom the promises are made. God's faithfulness means that God makes good on the promises in ways that are good for the promisees in the particularities of their own personal identities and circumstances. Such faithfulness to creatures in their kinds makes it appropriate to characterize this way in which God goes about relating as a "covenantal" faithfulness. This faithfulness entails that, if those circumstances involve bondage in personal distortion and oppression, God will fulfill the promises in ways that liberate them from such bondage.

Thus, third, as canonically narrated, in promise making God is faithful to Godself. God is as God promises. God does not betray or contradict Godself in making just these promises to just these people. God's promise making faithfully expresses God's own intrinsic glory.

The combination of God's faithful self-commitment in promise making and God's faithfulness to the well-being of the promisees makes it appropriate to characterize this covenantal way in which God goes about relating as "covenant love." It is an attractive love in which God faithfully expresses God's intrinsic attractive glory.

As canonically narrated, God's faithfulness in promise making to Abraham is gift making. In an act of utterly free faithfulness, God gives to Abraham and his descendants a covenant relationship with God and, through them, a blessing on all people. Correlatively, God is free in regard to how God will concretely go about fulfilling the promises, free in how God will do so in ways that make for the well-being of the promisees, free in how God will be concretely self-determined in making promises, and free in how God will be concretely self-consistent and self-expressive in fulfilling the promises.

We are exhorted to praise the God of Abraham in particular because the canonical narratives of God relating to Abraham give a description of "who" God is: One radically free as the generous and faithful maker of just these promises in just these concrete ways. They also imply some claims about "what" the God of Abraham is: One capable of freely self-relating in ways that are self-determining, self-committing, and consistently faithful to God's commitments, faithful to those to whom the commitments are made, and faithful to Godself.

Promise Maker as Creator

In one of the stories of Abraham's military adventures (Genesis 14:1–7, 21–24), he identifies God as "the Lord, God most high, maker of heaven and earth." The One who is the freely generous maker and keeper of liberative promises is the Creator of all that is not God. Hence, any description of the particularity of the singular God ("the God of Abraham") must also stress that it is nonetheless the particularity of the universal God, the God of all that is not God.

Of course, in Genesis 12:1–25:11 there is no narrative of God relating to Abraham to create him. That is a way in which God relates that is narrated elsewhere. Given the literary placement of the Abraham stories within Genesis, it has been traditional in Christian theology to associate Abraham's reference to the "maker of heaven and earth" in Genesis 14 with the narratives of God creating in Genesis 1 and 2. Thus, canonical narratives in Genesis 1–2 of God relating creatively to all that is not God (including Abraham) are read as the first episode, as it were, in the story of God's promise making and promise keeping to Abram/Abraham.

If Claus Westermann's analysis of the literary structure of Genesis is correct, such conflation of the Genesis 1 and 2 creation stories with narratives of Abraham and other patriarchs is problematic. The association of the narratives of Abraham's identification of God as the promise maker and keeper as well as "maker of heaven and earth" with the creation narrative in Genesis 1 and 2 links two very different kinds of narrative of God's relating to reality other than God. Westermann[5] argues that the difference between the two kinds of narrative lies in the way each relation is experienced. As narrated in the Pentateuch, God's promising and then keeping the promise of liberation or deliverance is experienced as a particular event (or set of events), i.e., God's act to deliver and to liberate. But, as narrated in Genesis 1 and 2, God relating creatively is God relating in a steady-state creative blessing. That is not a punctiliar event, but rather a continuously ongoing relating by God that can no more be experienced as a punctiliar event than can progressive growth or decline of strength. Genesis' account of God's relating in creative blessing is an ongoing, steady-state relating to creatures. Moreover, it is not a narrative of an event in which God delivers or liberates creatures *from* anything. Rather, God's creative ongoing blessing on creatures grounds and constantly

---

[5] Cf. Claus Westermann, 1972, 1974, 1978.

undergirds creation's "forward-thrusting, ever pregnant power of becoming."[6] That power of becoming is the necessary background condition for any history and, therefore, for any particular divine acts of liberation in history. God may relate to Abraham by making a liberative promise, but the precondition of God's liberative relating is God's relating in a quite different way: in creative blessing. Canonical narratives of God relating to create and God relating to liberate have different narrative logics. They are two irreducibly different strands of God's economy.

These two strands can be associated with each other because it is the same God who relates in each. Narratives in Genesis of God's liberative promise making to Abraham can consistently allude to God's also relating to Abraham in creative blessing. However, narratives of God relating by making and keeping promises are not suited to rendering how God goes about relating in creative blessing, and vice versa. If either narrative is absorbed into the other as though it were the story of some one moment or episode in a larger narrative, then its own narrative logic is distorted. The longer narrative made by synthesizing them will have an incoherent narrative logic because it attempts to conflate two sorts of narrative with irreducibly different narrative logics. That is an abstract way of saying that it will not be possible for a reader to follow the conflated narrative.

God's intrinsic glory is self-expressed in each of the two sorts of narrative in "glory's" secondary reference. That is, places, or events, or persons, etc., in each sort of narrative expresses in one way or another some aspect or aspects of God's intrinsic "glory." This is the case because each narrative strand is a different way in which the intrinsically glorious God goes about self-expressing Godself such that it evokes from creatures praise of God's glory. The concrete particularities of each sort of narrative are different. Accordingly,

---

[6] Westermann, 1978, 55; cf. 4–8.

those particularities may express different qualities of the richness of God's intrinsic glory. When they express the same quality, they nonetheless express it with importantly different nuances. The quality of God's intrinsic glory we focus on in this part of the book is "sovereignty." I argue that it is expressed in a different way in the secondary "glory" of each strand of God's economy, in each way in which God goes about relating to all else.

Objections to Attributing "Sovereignty" to God

Before we can go further, we must acknowledge objections to attribution of "sovereignty" to God. There are two broad sorts of objection. Both seem to me to be well-founded. The first sort of objection is culturally general. The second is internal, although not necessarily unique, to Christian theology.

"Sovereign" and "sovereignty" are generally associated in most cultures with the political authority to rule and with attendant powers of certain sorts. Used to name a quality of God, they function, along with "Lord" and "Master," as images for active relations God enters into. Such images are often judged to be deeply problematic on the general nontheological grounds that properly understood human beings' free and morally responsible agency gives them a dignity that must be honored by relating to them as ends in themselves and not as only means to further ends. However, "sovereign" and related terms represent God's priority to creatures, in regard to both their reality and their intrinsic value, on analogy with a human ruler's hierarchical relation to her or his subjects in regard to power, of which the ruler by definition has more power than her or his subjects. Thus, they represent God's priority to creatures in relating to them actively as a zero-sum game, a game in which the more power the ruler has, the less the ruler's subjects have. As an image for God's ways of actively relating to what is not God, "sovereignty" would then seem necessarily to imply a

81

competitive relating in regard to power. If God's active relating to human creatures is aptly represented by such images, then God's active relating would be undeniably oppressive of human beings. This has problematic implications for human beings' well-being as free and responsible agents in their own right.

The specifically theological objection to use of "sovereignty," "Sovereign," "Lord," and "Master" as images for the Triune God's way of going about active relating to creatures requires a somewhat longer explanation. That is because a theological argument in defense of the allegedly problematic use of such images to attribute a quality to God is itself an argument that claims to be rooted in the canonical narratives of how God concretely goes about relating to creatures to create them ex nihilo. In this section, I outline the major theological argument in support of the use of the allegedly problematic terms to attribute "sovereignty" to God.

A theological defense of the allegedly problematic use of "sovereignty" to image a quality of God is based on a conventional and traditional reading of canonical Genesis' narrative in Chapter 1 of how God goes about relating to create reality other than God. It is not an incorrect reading, but it does not warrant some theological inferences conventionally drawn from it.

God's creative relating ex nihilo is traditionally represented as a radically free decision on God's part that is intelligently ordered to the good. It is radically "free" in that it is unconstrained either by anything other than God (part of the import of creation ex nihilo is that, apart from God's relating to create, there is nothing "there" that might require or limit God's creative relating) or by God's own "nature" (creating reality other than God is not essential to being God). The account of how God goes about creating in Genesis 1 seems to make the point that God need only "speak" and reality other than God comes into being ("God says 'Let there be . . . x,' and there was x."). Clearly, God's relating to create in that fashion makes a cosmic difference: the entire cosmos comes into concretely actual reality. It is hugely powerful.

It has been conventional to infer from that account of God's active relating to create that it implies that God's power in relating to create is absolutely unconditioned power. It is assumed to define *the* sense, i.e., the only sense, in which "power" may be attributed to God. Because God's relating to create ex nihilo is understood to be free and ordered to the good, that power is not to be conceived as an "impersonal" force. "Free" and "ordered to the good" are construed as "personal" qualities and are used analogically to characterize God's creative relating. Nonetheless, the power of that relating is absolutely unrestricted, except in two purely conceptual ways: it would be self-contradictory to say that, in such relating, God "could" relate in ways ordered to evil or in ways that are essentially conditioned by realities other than God. Given the legitimacy of that inference from the account in Genesis 1 of how God goes about relating to create ex nihilo, it is entirely reasonable to attribute "sovereignty" or "kingly rule" to God in precisely the sense in which it is now often held to be problematic.

Two further inferences are traditionally drawn from this reading of the account of God's relating to create in Genesis 1. The first is that "power," understood as "absolute," is then transferred to two other ways in which God relates to all else in the economy: to reconcile estranged creatures to God and to fully actualize eschatological consummation of creatures. God's power to reconcile, enacted through Jesus' crucifixion, is construed as one more exercise of power in the same sense of "power" as in exercised in God's creating. God's actualizing the consummation of creatures eschatologically in a "new creation" is construed as yet another exercise of power in the same sense of "power" as God's creating ex nihilo. Thus, both reconciliation and eschatological consummation are traditionally explained in a conceptual framework that construes each of them as an instance God's relating to create. In each, God exercises "power" in the same sense of the term as God is said to do in creative blessing ex nihilo: absolute power-as-such. This reasoning is the basis of conventional explanations of the claim that God is "omnipotent." Rebuttal of that inference must wait until Chapter 9 in Part III, where reasons are given why the theological concept of God's "power' should also be analyzed in two other registers of the economy (God relating in eschatological blessing and God relating to reconcile the estranged), rather than in the single register of God relating in creative blessing.

The second additional inference is that such power is conventionally assumed to constitute God's very reality, as though being absolute power just *is* being God. As Karl Barth points out, "the earliest creeds obviously thought it was sufficient to ascribe only this one attribute [omnipotence] to God. *Credo in Deum patrem omnipotem, pantakratora.* Clearly they saw in this attribute that which embraced all the others; what might be called a compendium of them."[7] Because the Creeds do not offer any further explicit characterization of that "power," the assumption that "power" "embraces all the other divine attributes" is open to the inference that "power" is God's *defining* attribute. Rebuttal of that inference must wait until Part III, where reasons are given why the theological concept of God's "power" should be explained in terms of an account of God's intrinsic reality, understood in terms of the intrinsic glory that constituted "what" God is, instead of explaining God's intrinsic "glory" in term of God's intrinsic and constituting "power."

That entire set of inferences from the Genesis 1 account of how God concretely relates to create, construed as an account of God creating ex nihilo, is the theological home of the pastoral issue with which the Introduction began this book: pastorally problematic efforts to comfort and console those who are anguished and angry at God on account of the horrendous suffering of others. Those efforts invoke the unconditioned and unrestricted power of God in

---

[7] He has the Nicene–Constantinopolitan Creed in mind. *Church Dogmatics* Vol. 11/1, edited by G. W. Bromiley and T. F. Torrance. Translated by T. H. L. Parker et al. (Edinburgh: T. & T. Clark, 1957), p. 522.

creating all else "from nothing." If that power defines what it is to be God, then it can be inferred that God's creative power also explains the existence of horrific suffering. And if God's creative power is inherently ordered intelligently and to the good, then it can be inferred that such suffering is "sent" by God "for a good purpose" and that, ultimately, it will turn out to have been "for the good" of the sufferer and, presumably, of those who are anguished on the sufferer's behalf. However, if that chain of inferences is sound, and if God's creative power is also utterly free, unconditioned, and unrestricted, then it is equally sound to infer that God could just as freely have not "sent" the suffering or could just as freely have prevented it and freely did not do so. And that inference deepens anguish by quite reasonably eliciting profound anger at God, so understood.

I urge that those inferences are blocked if an account of the Triune God's *intrinsic* sovereignty, based as it ought to be on the way in which God goes about relating in creative blessing (as that, in turn, is canonically narrated), is explained in the context of an account of the Triune God' intrinsic glory rather than in the context of an account of God's intrinsic power, as it has been conventionally.

The Triune God's Sovereignty in Creative Blessing

The Triune God's concrete ways of self-expressively relating in the economy to all that is not God both by creating and by making and keeping promises to creatures are traditionally characterized as "sovereign" or "kingly." The argument in this chapter is restricted to examination of the sense in which "sovereignty" or "kingly rule" is a quality of the Triune God as expressed in God's relating in creative blessing. We turn in Chapter 4 to examine how that sense of God's "sovereignty" is further nuanced when it is understood in two quite different registers based on the quite different ways in which the Triune God also relates, respectively, to draw creature into an eschatological blessing and to reconcile estranged creatures to God.

It may seem odd to begin an essay purporting to qualify power as an attribute of God in such a way that it does not invite problematic inferences about God precisely by proposing that use of the term "power" be governed or "ruled" by a concept of sovereignty that is ascribed to God independent of and logically prior to ascribing "power" to God. After all, the conventional attribution of "sovereignty" to God has been as problematic as attribution of "absolute power" to God.

Indeed, as we have just seen, a key reason why conventional attribution of power to God is so deeply problematic is the underlying assumption that what makes God "God," what fundamentally constitutes God's reality as "God," is infinite or unbounded and unrestricted power. That idea is regularly expressed by using the phrase "almighty God" when beginning a prayer, when referring to God in sermons, and in all manner of informal jocular or blasphemous secular talk. The implicit assumption in the use of "almighty" is that what makes God "God" is above all that God's power is unrestricted, that God has all power.

If that were basically "what" and "who" God is, then God's sovereignty would rightly be understood, in turn, as God's exercise of such power in all the ways God actively relates to particular creaturely contexts in the economy. In that case, it would be a licit and reasonable inference that God's sovereignty is also in principle unrestricted. In that case, to ascribe "sovereignty" to God is to characterizes God's way of relating to realities other than God as ordered to a divine monopoly on power that would be oppressive of creatures' efforts to exercise freely their own creaturely powers. If God's priority in relating to what is not God entails a monopoly on power, then any sense that we have our own powers would be a delusion. Further, any effort we might make to exercise our creaturely powers would be sinful resistance of God. So also any effort we might make to change the God-given status quo to right wrongs and make it more just would be rebellion against God. Only God would be permitted to exercise power to make any changes in and between creatures. So, whatever it means to be God's "creature," it could *not* mean having or exercising power of one's own. Any sense that we have power to exercise would be a delusion. The reality would be that God has it all.

Such a construal of God's sovereignty is theologically problematic for the obvious reason that it contradicts important implications of the claim that the Triune God relates to all else in creative blessing. Namely, it contradicts the claim expressed in the traditional doctrine of creation that, in creating human creatures in particular, God creates realities genuinely "other" than God that nonetheless do have powers of their own, such as powers of intellect, will, free choice, and free action, which they can and should exercise in glorifying God by responding to God (using "glory" in its third sort of reference). If the Triune God's sovereignty means that God controls everything that happens, it would be reasonable to construe God's exercise of sovereignty as dominating creatures oppressively, legitimated by exercise of violence against creatures, and having an authority that is unchallengeable by creatures.

However, when ascribing to God some particular qualities that characterize God's ways of relating to creatures it is important to assess their appropriateness by the way they cohere with "what" and "who" God is intrinsically, i.e., their coherence with the singular "identity" of the One to whom they are being attributed. In regard to our limited topic here, I suggest that if we attribute "sovereignty" to God in ways that define "sovereignty" in terms of how it expresses God's intrinsic glory, and only in that context explain the sense in which "power" may be attributed to God in terms of those senses of "sovereignty," it will ease the problematic features of conventional attribution of both "sovereignty" and "power" to God.

So, we begin by considering "sovereignty" as an aspect of "who" and "what" God is before we try to get clear what it means to attribute "power" to God. Here we consider "sovereignty" as a quality in the economy of the Triune God's relating specifically in creative blessing as expressive of God's intrinsic sovereignty. I follow that by noting its implications regarding the Triune God's intrinsic quality of "sovereignty."

I noted in Chapter 2 that, in addition to its primary Scriptural use in reference to God's intrinsic reality, the word "glory" is also used in Scripture in reference to particular things, persons, and events involved in the ways in which God relates to realities other than God. Those ways in which God relates to others are strands of what is traditionally called God's "economy." In them, God is consistent, faithful to God's self, so that the particular, concrete ways in which God is said to relate to all else, according to Scriptural witness, are faithfully – although not exhaustively – self-expressive of aspects of who and what God is. Hence, the concrete particulars of the ways in which God relates to all else are a secondary sort of reference of "glory" as used in canonical Scripture. "God is as God does"; and "what God does God does in God's own way." The strands of the economy in their particularity serve to guide theological judgments about what are and are not apt ways in which to characterize "what" and "who" God is. Accordingly, the way in which God is "sovereign" needs to be explained in the context of an account of how God's "glory" is expressed in the ways in which God relates to all else.

It was pointed out in Chapter 2 that, according to Westermann's reading of Genesis 1, God's way of relating in creative blessing is fundamentally different from God's way of relating by making and keeping liberative promises in that it is a steady-state, on-going relating to creatures rather than a punctiliar event. We noted also that, as canonically narrated, the concrete particularities of the way in which God goes about such ongoing steady-state creative blessing express the glory of God (in its secondary sort of reference) in four ways: as unconditioned and unrestricted, it is free; it is the transcendental condition of the possibility of there being events at all and is not just one event among many, not even the "first" one; it is ordered to the good; and it is nonviolent. I urged that, taken together, those qualities of the economy of God's of relating in creative blessing express a general quality of God's glory in the economy: the Triune God's radical prevenience in relating to all else, God's absolute priority in being and doing. It is a prevenience in active relating such that God is correlatively radically "close" to creatures and radically "other" than creatures. The two are not mutually exclusive; rather, each is the condition of the possibility of the other.

We now add that the Triunity of God, who relates in this fashion in creative blessing on all that is not God, nuances in several ways theological accounts of both the prevenience of God's relating and its correlative "radical closeness to" and "radical otherness than" creatures. Those nuances can be brought out by a Trinitarian formula for the pattern of relationships among the three "Persons" of the Trinity in creative blessing: "The 'Father' creates through the 'Son' in the power of the Spirit." That is the pattern or *taxis* of the Trinity's relating in creative blessing.

Placing the "Father" in the lead position in God's relating in creative blessing underscores that God's creating ex nihilo faithfully expresses (in a relationship to creaturely reality that is not God) the generative self-relating that constitutes the common life of the Trinity that is God's intrinsic glory. That intrinsic self-relating of God underscores both the generosity and the utterly unconstrained freedom of God's generative relating in creative blessing. It is an active relating *to* creatures that simultaneously (a), as the condition of the possibility of their concrete actuality, is more radically "interior" or "close" to each creature than it can be to itself, and (b) constitutes each as a concretely actual being "other" than God, thus, establishing the basic ontological distinction between creatures and Creator. In the dynamics constituting the intrinsic life of the Trinity, the "Father's" generous, eternal, self-regulated self-giving in perfectly self-expressive self-relating constitutes the reality of the other two "Persons" of the Triune God. Placing the "Father" in the lead position in the Trinitarian formula for the pattern in which the triune God relates in creative blessing underscores that God's absolute priority in the order of reality, God's "ontological prevenience" relative to all creatures, faithfully expresses God's intrinsic eternal dynamic of perfectly expressive self-giving in self-relating.

Adding that, in creative blessing, the "Father" creates "*through the Son*" qualifies God's free and generous generative relating in three ways when the "Son" is understood to be the subject characterized in the prologue to the Gospel of John as God's "Word" (*Logos*), and when John's use of "Word" is understood as an allusion to "Wisdom," personified as "Lady Wisdom" in Proverbs 8.

Most fundamentally, the one referred to in John as "Son" and "Word," understood to have "become flesh" in the life-trajectory of Jesus of Nazareth, is understood to be the definitive self-expression of God in the economy. So, although placing the "Father" in the lead position in the formula for the Trinity's relating in creative blessing underscores God the "Father's" priority in the order of reality, adding that creative blessing comes through the "Son," who, "taking on flesh," is the Triune God's definitive self-expression, underscores Jesus Christ's priority in the order of human coming to understand and speak of God – to the extent that they can. Indeed, as variously narrated in the four canonical Gospels, it is the very structure of Jesus' life-trajectory that warrants framing an account of what and who God is in Trinitarian terms. Thus, the Triune God's relating in creative blessing involves God relating, not only ontologically transcendentally *to* all that is not God, but also relating self-expressively as one who can be *one among many* that are not God.

Second, adding that creative blessing comes "through the Son," understood in terms of Proverbs 8's description of "Lady Wisdom's" role in creation, underscores that, although the Triune God's way of relating in creative blessing is in some sense "rational," ("logical," as suggested by *Logos*), it is more analogous to "wisdom" as "practical reason" than it is to "rational" as "theoretical reason." It underscores that God's creative blessing is a wise relating that is ordered to the reality and value of creatures as genuine "others" to the Triune God. To say that it is "wise" embraces both the note that it is a cognitive relating, God's knowing creatures, and the note that it is more like an ad hoc relating that works cannily toward its ends in ways that take into account and honor the integrity of creatures' concrete particularities.[8]

Third, adding that creative blessing comes "through the Son" understood in terms "Lady Wisdom's" role in creation underscores a note found only in Proverbs 8: that in creative blessing God relates delightedly to that which is not God. The note struck there is not only that blessing creatively – to the end that realities other than God be both real and intrinsically valuable – is a sort of love for

---

[8] In *The Kingdom and the Glory*, Giorgio Agamben underscores this point from a different direction. The Greek word that is translated by the English word "economy" is *oikonomia*. *Oikos* means "household," usually a quite large set of members of an extended family, clients, servants, and slaves. *Oikonomia* names "management of a household." Agamben holds that, whereas in the Classical period there was a sharp distinction in political thought between "politics" as the power arrangement in a city or *polis* and "economy" as the management of a household or *oikos*, beginning in the Hellenistic period the two are conflated (2011, p. 24). Agamben argues that New Testament writers (he is mostly thinking of Paul) follow suite and characterize "the messianic community ... in terms of an *oikonomia* – and not in terms of politics" (2011, p. 25). Such management by creatures is "equivalent to 'task assigned by God.'" It is simply human "activity ordered to a purpose" (2011, p. 26), a purpose that is God's. Although God's "purpose" may be eternal, its enactment is not framed as the enactment of a timeless "plan." Agamben stresses that such management is not the ordering of the particulars of any given situation according to a timeless plan grounded in the ontological structure of the cosmos, but rather an ad hoc, practical wisdom about how best to order the givens of particular situation in the interests of the well-being of the household. That is what is analogous to how God concretely goes about exercising "sovereignty." It is in some sense a "rational" exercise of sovereignty, ordered to the good. However, the "rationality" of God's sovereignty, like God's creation through the *Logos,* is more like the rationality of Wisdom's ad hoc, situation-dependent, and situation-specific practical wisdom than it is like timeless theoretical rationality.

creatures by God, but furthermore that it is on God's part a playful, perhaps improvisational, relating.

Adding to all that, the claim that in creative blessing "through the Son" the "Father" creates "*in the power of the Spirit*," the Trinitarian formula for the Triune God's relating in creative blessing underscores that God's relating in creative blessing is particularly ordered to the concrete reality and value of living creatures and that such "ordering" circumambiently attends to them in love of their concrete particularity in such fashion so as not to violate their creaturely integrity in their kinds. Inasmuch as the Trinity's creative blessing constitutes the fundamental ontological distinction between Creator and creatures, it is fitting that the "Father's" radically "other than" way of relating *to* creatures be given pride of place in the Trinitarian formula for creative blessing ex nihilo. However, it does not warrant the inference that the unqualified and radically free priority of God's generative creative blessing by itself exhaustively *defines* either God's "power," or the sense in which God is "sovereign." Even in regard to creative blessing, an account of the Triune God's "sovereignty" requires that implications that might be drawn from what is expressed by saying the "Father" relates *to* creatures must cohere with implications that might be drawn from what is expressed by saying that the "Father" creates "through the Son" who, incarnate, relates to creatures as *one among them* and "in the power of the Spirit" that relates to creatures *circumambiently*.

Building on those points, what I want to note here is that, in relating in that fashion, the Triune God is self-committed in several ways by the act of creative blessing ex nihilo. Those self-commitments regulate how God concretely goes about relating in an on-going, steady-state, creative blessing that constitutes the reality of all that is not God, i.e., that creates ex nihilo. The Triune God's self-regulation of how God goes about creative blessing just *is* God's "sovereignty" in, or "kingly rule" of, God's relating in creative blessing. The Triune God takes the initiative in creative blessing. God is in a certain way "in charge"; but, being "in charge," has a definite profile that is set by the self-commitments God makes in relating in creative blessing.

The unique profile of the Triune God's intrinsic sovereignty in creative blessing is defined by two sorts of self-commitment that God makes in the act of creative blessing. As such, they are intrinsic to creative blessing ex nihilo. They are (a) the Triune God's self-commitment to Godself, and (b) the Triune God's self-commitment to the creaturely recipients of creative blessing. Those self-commitments faithfully express the Trinity's intrinsic glory, God's *intrinsic* self-commitment to Godself always to be faithfully self-expressive in all relating to "others." Hence, God's ways of relating to all else in creative blessing are self-regulated faithfully to express aspects of God's intrinsic identity, "who" and "what" the Triune God is in the dynamic generative, self-expressive self-relating that constitutes its life.

Accordingly, on one hand, the Triune God's relating in creative blessing is free – unconstrained and unconditioned by any other reality. God's relating in this way is transcendental of all creaturely actions and interactions. It is the ultimate condition of the possibility of their being and acting. It is a relating to all else that God "regulates," i.e., in which God exercises "sovereignty," in such a way that in it God always takes the initiative, is always freely prevenient in such relating. God is self-committed to relate in creative blessing in a way that is faithful to God's intrinsic glory, i.e., faithful to "what" and "who" God intrinsically is, whether or not God freely does relate in creative blessing.

Accordingly, on the other hand, in creative blessing God is self-committed to go about relating in creative blessing in ways that are faithful to the integrity of creatures in their kinds, faithful not merely to their well-being, but more fundamentally faithful to their reality and value as genuine "others" to God having their own creaturely powers. God is self-bound not to relate in ways that would violate what creatures are in their kinds and in their concrete, particular circumstances. We have noted that nonviolence is among the qualities intrinsic to God's glory.

Moreover, in relating in creative blessing, the Triune God is self-committed to relate in ways that are ordered to creatures' good in their kinds. This implies that God's relating in creative blessing is ordered to the particularities of creatures, which, in turn, has several further particularly important implications about some qualities of the intrinsic glory of God that are expressed in God's relating in creative blessing. First, it implies that, in the economy of creative blessing, God can in some sense know creatures not simply in general as "creaturely," but in their concrete particularities, and know what makes for their "good" in their particular circumstances. Second, it implies that in creatively blessing God attends to creatures in their particularity and to their needs in their particularity. Third, it implies that in creative blessing God is wise about how to relate to creatures in ways that make for their good in their particular situations without violating their integrity as genuinely "other" realities. Taken together, to know an "other" in its particularity, to attend to that other in its particularity in ways ordered to its good, and to seek wisely to actualize that good without violating the "other's" integrity as a creature is, all taken together, to love that other. The Triune God's "sovereignty" in God's way of going about relating in creative blessing is a self-regulating of that relating in concrete circumstances that is intrinsically ordered by a delighted love for what God creates.

Together, these qualities of the concrete particularities of how the Triune God relates in creative blessing are themselves qualities of the glory of God in its secondary reference. They mark the way in which God's relating in creative blessing is regulated by self-commitments that are intrinsic to that relating. Inasmuch as God's self-regulation in blessing creatively is God's sovereignty in that strand of the economy, such sovereignty has a particular and distinct profile. Here "sovereignty" is not the name of the exercise of absolute, unconditioned, unrestrained power over other powers.

It names, rather, the distinctive way in which God self-regulates how God goes about relating in creative blessing.

The Triune God binds Godself to realities other than God in the commitments God makes to them in relating to them. In those ways of relating to all else, God's free self-relating is a free self-binding. That self-binding is the basis for part of an answer to the questions, "Who is the Triune God? If God does as God is, who is God?" God's self-binding does not constitute God's reality as God. It does not answer the question, "What is it to be God?" However, God's self-binding in the economy does define God's concrete identity, "who" God is. In regard to God's self-relating in relating to all else in creative blessing, the strand of the economy that has been in view in most of this chapter, God's identity is self-defined as, "One who is wisely (with all of the facets of 'wisdom' noted above: free, transcendental, ordered to the good, nonviolent) and lovingly self-binding to creatures in blessing them creatively."

Such prevenient self-binding by God in the creative blessing strand of the economy does not, however, compromise God's intrinsic sovereignty. It does not, for example, subject God's sovereignty to regulation by actions of other agents that are enacted before and independent of God's relating to them. Rather, the qualities of God's self-binding in creative blessing are the qualities of God's sovereignty in that strand of the economy that faithfully express God's intrinsic glory (in "glory's" primary sort of reference) and are aspects of the glory of God (in its secondary sort of reference).

The Triune God's Intrinsic Sovereignty

I noted in Chapter 1 that, according to Genesis' narrative, the God of Abraham relates to Abram/Abraham in highly particular ways to create reality other than God and to make and keep liberative promises. The particular ways in which God's relating to realities other than God that are rendered in Genesis' narratives, irreducibly different from one another as they are, nonetheless share a common pattern: God's ways of concretely relating to what is not God all consistently entail faithful expression of aspects of how God is intrinsically self-related. Particularly important is that God's ways of relating to all else always entails God's self-regulation by self-commitments. God does as God is: that the Triune God is self-regulating in the ways God goes about relating to all else faithfully expresses that God is also self-regulating in the generative self-relating in love that is God's attractively glorious intrinsic life. That intrinsic self-regulating is the sense in which the Triune God is "sovereign" in God's own life. Aspects of that intrinsic sovereignty are faithfully expressed in qualities of God's sovereignty in the economy.

It is important to keep in mind that the term "self" as used in hyphenated expressions like "self-related," "self-expressive," and "self-regulating" only has the force of a reflexive and does not connote "personhood" as "subjectivity" or "self-hood."

We have a very limited basis on which to give content to the "sovereignty" we attribute to God's intrinsic life. The language that is ordinarily used to characterize the Triune God's life is largely drawn from what we consider to be human ways of relating "interpersonally" in faithful self-commitments to others and to shared projects, such as the covenants, marriages, societies, and commercial transactions that are constituted by explicit and implicit promise making to which the promise makers commit themselves. Insofar as the dynamics and structures of such interpersonal relations entail dynamics and structures of *intra*personal "self-relating," they may also be used to characterize not only how God relates to all else but how God "self-relates" in self-commitments. Such human interpersonal ways of relating and intrapersonal ways of self-relating share such qualities as intentionality, faithfulness, a certain limited knowledge of the "other" in her or his concrete particularity, orderedness to the good of the "other," love for the other, etc.

Such language must be used analogically when attributed to God's intrinsic dynamic self-relating. We may be able to offer warrants for using such language. However, we have no way to know just how such language means in relation to God's intrinsic reality. We use language that is appropriate to use in characterizing properly interpersonal and intrapersonal relations because we have warrant for believing that there is some overlap between how such language means when used to characterize human relationships and how it means when used to characterize how God actively relates. However, we use it with the proviso that the differences between the two sorts of active relating (interpersonal and intra-personal on one side and God self-relating relating) are far greater than the similarities. We have little grasp of the definition of those qualities thus named when used in reference to God, little grasp of their boundaries and the limits to the range of further qualities that may be inferred from them when their attribution to God is accepted.

So we attribute a quality to God (say, "love") and then qualify the attribution radically in regard to ways in which it is misleading or inept and then attribute another quality analogically (say "free" or "just") to "balance" the inadequacies of the first attribution, and so on. Accordingly, when we attempt here to explicate how the Triune God's self-regulating sovereignty in the economy express God's intrinsic "sovereignty" in the self-regulated self-relating that consti-tutes the Triune God's life, we inevitably stammer.

Then, let us stammer boldly about the Triune God's intrinsic quality of sovereignty that is independent of whether or not God relates to any other realities.

I noted in Chapter 1 that, as formulated in the Nicene–Constantinopolitan Creed, the Triune God's intrinsic generative self-relating is a perfect self-giving that constitutes the reality of each of the three divine "Persons" of the Trinity. Each "Person" has its own distinctive eternal identity in virtue of the character of the self-relating-by-self-giving that constitutes it as the "Person" it is.

Furthermore, it is a self-relating in which "what" the three identically are (i.e., "divinity," "God's nature") is faithfully and fully expressed in each of them.

We now add that it is implicit in those claims about the Triune God's generative self-expressive self-relating that, in them, God is also intrinsically *self-regulating*. That self-regulating is aptly characterized by several qualities.

For example, as "generative," the Triune God's eternal self-relating constitutes the reality of each of the "Persons" of the Trinity as genuinely "other" than one another. Such self-relating, I urged in Chapter 1, is a self-giving ordered to the full reality of the other as the identifiable particular "Person" it is. Self-giving ordered to the "other's" good as the particular "Person" it is, is a way of loving the "other." So, God's own life may be characterized by the quality "love." God's way of generatively self-relating is self-regulated as a loving self-relating that excludes attribution to God of any form of self-relating that is not love.

Further, as "generative," the Triune God' eternal self-relating is an unrestricted self-giving, a giving of itself, i.e., "divinity," to an "other." There is nothing that could be given that is not given. Such self-relating is maximally *generous* love. So, God's life may be characterized by the quality of "generosity." The generosity of God's eternal self-relating entails an intrinsic *negative freedom*. The generosity of God's intrinsic self-relating is not contingent on or limited by any reality other than God or by any commitment God has to any reality other than God. However, the generosity of God's self-relating is not positively "free," as though God could regulate God's self-relating by being more or less generous in self-giving. There is no self-relating by the Triune God that lies somehow "behind" God's self-relating that regulates it by "deciding" that it be unrestrictedly generous. Rather, God's way of generatively self-relating is self-regulated as an unrestrictedly generous self-relating that is so perfectly "whole-hearted" that it excludes attribution to God of any form of self-relating that is not generous. That is its intrinsic freedom. The Triune God just *is* that unrestrictedly generous and loving generative self-relating.

As "generative," the Triune God's eternal self-relating constitutes the reality of each of the "Persons" of the Trinity as genuinely "other" than one another. Inasmuch as that self-relating is ordered to the "other's" good, it *intends* that "other." God's intrinsic self-relating has the quality of "intentionality." Thus ordered, the Triune God's intrinsic self-relating is cognizant of the particularities of the good of the "other" relative to its concrete particularity.

In such self-giving self-relating, each "Person" *knows* an "other" (the "given-to") in its particular identity. Indeed, given that each of the three "knowers" is at once terminally irreducible to and radically close to the two "others" that it "knows," nothing about the "known" is unknowable or unintelligible to the "knower." The Triune God is unqualifiedly transparent to Godself. Call it God's "self-knowledge." This is not the "self-regulating" of a thermostat. It is God's intrinsic "self-omniscience." God's life, constituted by generative self-relating in self-giving, is *intelligently* self-regulating.

The cognitive transparency and "self-omniscience" of such generous self-giving entails that the Triune God's intrinsic love for the "other" is self-commitment to communion with the beloved, in which the lover intrinsically knows any suffering or joy that the beloved has. It entails that the God's intrinsic self-relating has a quality we might call "com-passibility." That is, the transparent "self-omniscience" of the Triune God's intrinsic self-relating entails that each "Person" of the Trinity's knowledge of the other two "Persons" includes complete knowledge of their "affects" or "passions." That rules out ascription to the Triune God of an absolute intrinsic "impassibility," i.e., the unqualified incapacity to suffer any "passion." In short, the concrete way in which God goes about relating in creative blessing and the concrete way God goes about relating in liberative promise making and promise keeping warrant ascription to the Triune God's intrinsic self-relating of unlimitedly *generous* love, including love's vulnerability to "com-passible" suffering as well as joy.[9]

In sum, the Triune God's reality is a life with distinguishable qualities: an eternally generative self-relating–in–self-regulation that is loving, unrestrictedly generous, free, intentionally ordered to the good, intelligent, and in principle prevenient, prior to any way in which it relates to realities other than God, and wise. In its wise self-relating the Trinity's life is singularly "in charge" of itself. It is, in that sense, intrinsically "sovereign," whether or not it is also related to reality other than God.

* * * * *

We are to praise the God of Abraham in particular because the two particular ways in which God goes about relating to him, as testified by canonical Scriptural narratives, are in a secondary sense the glory of God in which the intrinsic glory of God in and for Godself is faithfully self-expressed. This justifies a further claim about God.

The narrative logics of canonical accounts of God relating to Abraham in both liberative promise making and in creative blessing make narrative sense only if God is understood to be, in a way, a concrete singularity and not an abstract object. Abstract objects, such as justice itself, or being itself, or perfectly unconditional love, or the sacred, neither promise nor bless. Concretely actual agents do.

Consequently, the aim of any theological description of God is to characterize One who has the ontological status of a concrete singular reality that is not on the inventory of creaturely beings and to which the only appropriate human response is praise for what God is in and of Godself. Theological reflection is rooted in such praise.

---

[9] Paul L. Gavrilyuk argues persuasively in *The Suffering of the Impassible God: The Dialectics of Patristic Thought* (Oxford: Oxford University Press, 2004) that many of the Fathers do not ascribe absolute impassibility to God.

4 | Creation, Providence, and Theologically Problematic Pastoral Consolation

Three things are important in assessing the appropriateness of "sovereignty" and similar words as analogical characterizations of God's way of relating to creatures in the economy. They are (a) "what" and "who" the One who exercises "sovereignty" is; (b) the ends to which that "sovereignty" is exercised; and (c) the way, as canonically narrated, in which God goes about concretely relating to what is not God to actualize those goals.

I propose that oppressive explanations of the Triune God's "sovereignty" would be ruled out if God's sovereignty were not understood in terms of an already and independently defined concept of God's intrinsic power. Rather, I explore in this Part II of the book the proposal that God's sovereignty is best understood in the context of a logically prior account of God as One who is intrinsically glorious, such as the account outlined in Part I. There God's intrinsic glory was explained in terms of the dynamics of God's intrinsic triune life and not, be it noted, in terms either of God's intrinsic power or of displays of God's power. Part II then argues that God's power is best explained in the context of a logically prior account of God's sovereignty, such as the one outlined in this and Chapter 5 of Part II. In this approach, God's sovereignty would be rightly understood, not as a function of the qualities of God's power. Rather, the qualities of God's power are best understood in terms of God's sovereignty. For its part, God's sovereignty is best interpreted in the context of an understanding of the glory of God.

Chapter 6 holds that a theologically adequate account of God's sovereignty should not be developed solely on the basis of some one strand of the economy, say, only on the basis of God relating to create ex nihilo. Rather, what can be said about the character of God's sovereignty on the basis of canonical accounts of God relating in creative blessing must be nuanced by what must be said about it on the basis of canonical accounts of God relating in two additional ways: in providential care and in eschatological blessing. Each is a different register in which "sovereignty" is understood when attributed to God. Chapter 6 explores these two registers and their inter-relations in the economy. Each strand of the economy expresses an aspect of the "glory of God" in the secondary reference of that phrase. In each strand, God is faithfully self-expressive of God's own intrinsic glory. They define two different but coherent senses of "sovereignty" when the word is used in reference to the Triune God.

Before we turn to that, however, we need to take note here of some features of the relation between God's providential care of creatures, on one side, and, on the other, the strand of the economy discussed in Chapter 3, God's active relating to all that is not God in creative blessing.

Creative Blessing and Providential Care

"Providence" is short-hand for the claim that God "provides" for creatures what they need in their kinds for their well-being for their own sakes. Canonical narratives of God relating to all else in providential care are extensions of canonical narratives of God relating in creative blessing. They are "extended" on the basis of a well-warranted inference from the logically more basic claim that God relates to all that is not God to create it ex nihilo. The inference is this: God's creative "utterance," "Let there be ...," is a self-involving act by which God is necessarily self-committed to sustain creatures in reality and to foster their well-being in their kinds for as long as they last. In creating ex nihilo, God is self-committed to care "providentially" for the creatures that are created.

The observation that theological claims about the nature of God's providential care are in some way "extensions" of claims about the nature of God's relating to create ex nihilo immediately and rightly raises a red flag warning that they might underwrite theologically problematic explications of God's sovereignty. This possibility is fully realized in much conventional theological talk about how God's providence "means" that whatever happens within human creatures, and whatever happens to them in their interactions with each other, is "sent" or "caused" by God, who is entirely "in control," according to God's plan for how to achieve God's purposes for each creature. That is precisely the sort of theologically and pastorally problematic talk that we identified in Chapter 1.

Here we need to distinguish between currently "conventional" theological talk about God's providence and "traditional" theistic explications of God's providence, pre-modern as well as modern. To avoid the problematic character of much conventional affirmation of God's providential care, traditional theistic interpretations regularly nuanced their explanations of God's sovereignty in providential care by a more careful analysis of the complexity of the relation between accounts of God's providential relating to all else and God's creative relating ex nihilo. Whether traditional explications of God's providential care of creation finally prove adequate to invalidate and block pastorally and theologically problematic remarks about providence is another question. However that may be, it is obvious at this point that clarity about the relation between God's way of going about relating in providential care and God's way of going about relating in creative blessing is critical to a pastorally and theologically unproblematic account of providential care.

I have already acknowledged that the Triune God's relating to all else in providential care is necessarily entailed by God's self-involving self-commitment to the "good" of what God creates ex nihilo. Hence, God's way of relating in providential care has much in common with God's relating to all else in creative blessing. It is like God's way of relating in creative blessing in being an ongoing, steady-state relating to all that is not God. Like creative blessing, it is best expressed by saying that God providentially relates "to" creatures (in contradistinction to saying, e.g., that God relates to all else "circumambiently" or "as one among many"). Hence, God's *sovereignty* in providential care is rooted in God's sovereignty in the steady-state "on-goingness" of creative blessing. Chapter 3 suggested that God's "sovereignty" in creative blessing is best understood as God's prevenient "self-regulating" of how God concretely goes about relating in creative blessing. For their part, the "on-goingness" and "continuousness" of God's providential relating faithfully enact both God's self-commitment to what God creatively sustains in its reality other than and "over-against" God and also God's self-commitment to sustain its intrinsic value.

What I have dubbed "conventional" pastoral and theological talk about God's providential care seems to assume implicitly that acknowledging those points necessarily also entails acknowledging that the narrative "logic" of canonical accounts of God's providential care is identical with the narrative logic of canonical accounts of how God goes about creative blessing. "Conventional" talk about providence is tacitly considered to be simply a subtopic of the more basic topic "creation ex nihilo." God's acts of providential care are implicitly understood as nothing other than subsequent instances of God's exercise of creative absolute power "subsequent," as it were, to God's creating creatures in the first place.

However, the relation between theological claims about the Triune God's providence and claims about God's creative blessing ex nihilo is more complex than any simple identity of the two claims. The two are distinct and asymmetrically related. That is true first of all in the order of reality (i.e., true ontologically). On one hand, God's radically free creative blessing ex nihilo is prevenient, i.e., it "comes logically before" God's providential care in the order of reality. God's relating in creative blessing necessarily entails that God also relates in providential care. However, it does not presuppose that there already are realities other than God. Indeed, as creation "from nothing," it implies that, absent God's creative blessing, there is no reality whatsoever other than God. On the other hand, providential care of creatures presupposes not only the reality of God, but also that there are creatures to be cared for. It presupposes that God relates to all that is not God in creative blessing. Furthermore, although God's self-commitment to provide for creatures is thus contingent on the Trinity's radically free and logically prior relating in creative blessing, the claim that God exercises providential care of creatures does not of itself necessarily entail that God logically "must" also relate creatively simply because God is "God." Given that God freely blesses creatively, neither relating in creative blessing nor in providential care "makes" God "God." God would be "God" were it the case, contrary to fact, that God did not bless creatively and there were nothing to care for providentially.[1]

---

[1] In *The Kingdom and the Glory*, Giorgio Agamben argues that a fundamental problem in modern political thought, viz., that government (or perhaps "governance") is theorized without any basis in the way sovereignty is theorized (he credits the claim that this *is* a problem to Foucault; 2011, p. 113) has its roots in the role played by this stress on the freedom of God's providential action in the development of Christian Trinitarian doctrine of God. Christian doctrine of God built on, and claimed to preserve, Classical and Hellenistic philosophical theories of a single cosmic first principle or *arche*, sometimes characterized as the cosmos' "unmoved mover." Understood that way, God exercises something like providence in the cosmos by ontological necessity: that is what makes God "God." The activity of Divine providence (and by extension, human "governance") is rooted in the nature of Divine being. When Christians modified the received "pagan" view of God as cosmic *arche* to include the claim that God the "Father" is not only "providential" governor of the cosmos, but also its radically *free* creator ex nihilo "through the Son," (especially when the "Son" himself is affirmed, like the "Father," to have no *arche*, but to exist *a se*; cf., 2011 pp. 58–59), it severed that grounding of providence (and therewith, "governance") in the nature of (Divine) being. Agamben argues that Christian thought never found a way to show

The asymmetry of the relation between the two holds for a second reason: each has a different end or goal. What are asymmetrically related are the irreducibly different ways in which God relates to all else because each has a different end in its own right. God relates in creative blessing to the end that there *be* genuine "others" radically different than God in being and to the end that those "others" be intrinsically "*good*" in their kinds so that they are to be valued in their own right and not merely for some further end. On the other hand, God relates to creatures in providential care to the end that they have the "good" of the well-being appropriate to their kinds. Creatures' "well-being" is not identical with the creaturely "goodness" or "value" that constitutes a respect-demanding dignity, which is the end to which God blesses them creatively. A creature whose well-being is diminished, damaged, or violated, whether by other creatures or by its own actions, is nonetheless as intrinsically a "good" creature as any other creature. It has a dignity that demands the same respect in its own right. Neither goal, therefore, is simply the necessary means to the actualization of the other one. Providential care is not *that* sort of "extension" of creative blessing. Accordingly God's "sovereignty" in providential care must be nuanced in ways that are implied by the asymmetric way in which providential care is related to creative blessing.

What counts as creatures' "well-being" can be specified more exactly in terms of our account in Chapter 3 of the Triune God's creative blessing. What God creates are finite systems of various

how God's reality and God's providence (and therewith how "sovereignty" and "governance" in human politics) are related. The result is that providence (i.e., in Greek, *oikonomia*) and, in the resulting political theory, governance or administration, lack a "first principle." That is to say that they are anarchic ("without *arche*"). Nowhere in *The Kingdom and the Glory* does Agamben explore the most influential way in which Christian thinkers have proposed to connect the two: viz., through an analysis of the implications of the claim that God's intrinsic being is "perfect," in particular the way that analysis opens into theories of how creatures' realities in their kinds "participate" in "analogical" fashion in qualities of God's intrinsic reality (cf. esp. pp. 20–27; 53–59).

sorts of energy that are inter-related in complex networks of inter-actions, and are inherently fragile, vulnerable to violation by one another, and, finally, vulnerable to dis-integration. A creature's well-being is defined by the kind of creature it is. God's faithfulness to creatures entails that the way God goes about relating in providential rule must be variegated. It is conditioned by a respect for the particular powers and capacities, the particular array of types and degrees of "energy," a given creature of a given kind can exercise for as long as it lasts. Understood in this way, neither creatures' intrinsic, respect-commanding "goodness" or "value" as creatures nor the "good" of their well-being entails God's commitment to their lasting for ever. Creatures' demise is not necessarily contradictory to the goodness of God's relation to them either in creative blessing or in providential care. Nor do the respective ends of God's creative blessing or providential care point to some transfigured condition of creatures lying beyond what they are precisely as creatures. In God's creative blessing, creatures are valued and maintained in being for their own sakes, and by God's providence their well-being in their kinds is valued for its own sake, so that neither of those two ways in which God relates to all else has an end that allows creatures to be related to as disposable instruments used for the sake of a future condition of creation as a whole.

The asymmetry between God's creative blessing and God's providential care in their ontology and their respective ends entails that God's relating in providential care differs from God's relating in creative blessing in being constrained and conditioned by reality other than God. It is constrained by the nature and conditions of the creatures to which God is relating. Unlike God's creative blessing ex nihilo, God's providential care is shaped by God's faithfulness to the ontological integrity and particularity of already existing creatures. That is true at two levels.

The first level has to do with creatures' basic "creatureliness." Essential to their creatureliness is that creatures are centers of more or less organized but very limited energy, "centers" that are interactive and interdependent members of (depending on their degree of complexity) physical, biological, social, psychological, and cultural networks of relations. They come into being and, as long as they last, are fragile, vulnerable to damage, radically limited in their resources of various sorts of energy, moving toward extinction, and, if living, mortal. In its faithfulness to creatures' ontological integrity, God's providential care is not ordered to eliminating any of those essential features of creatureliness. In particular, although God's providential care is ordered to sustaining mortal creatures in their kinds for as long as they last, it is not itself necessarily ordered to sustaining their well-being everlastingly.

In providential care, God is self-committed at a second level by the particular way God goes about creative blessing to be faithful to creatures' own ontological integrity. God's end in providential care is not the actuality and goodness of creatures as genuine "others" to God (that is the goal of God's creative blessing), but rather the well-being of such creatures in their kinds. Accordingly God's ways of relating in providential care are different than God's way of relating in creative blessing. In creative blessing, as narrated in canonical Christian scripture, God relates un-mediatedly to creatures as One that is on-goingly at once "radically other than" and "radically close to" them in actively relating to them. In providential care, as an "extension" of creative blessing, God also relates in ways that are at once "radically other than" and "radically close to" creatures. But, unlike creative blessing, God's relating to creatures in providential care is at once in some aspects unmediated and in other aspects mediated through creatures' interactions with other creatures. Creatures fall into many different "kinds," each with its specific "nature." What counts as the "well-being" of a creature is a function of the kind of creature it is. That sets a limit to God's way of relating in providential care – whether it be immediate or mediated through other creatures' interactions with it. These are self-imposed limits that God does not have in relating in creative blessing. Where God's relating in creative blessing is uniform in regard to all creatures,

God's relating in providential care is differentiated. God is limited by God's self-commitment to respect the integrity of the specific nature of every given creature in relating to it providentially. God is not self-committed to nurture in squid those forms of well-being that are species-appropriate for tigers.

Nor does what counts as a creature's well-being in its kind consist in its being provided a superabundance of the resources its kind of life requires. In creative blessing, God either creates a creature or God does not. Creative blessing does not allow for "degrees" of "createdness." However, in being self-committed to providential care God is not self-committed to a cosmic prosperity gospel according to which every creature would necessarily be "wealthy" in resources appropriate to its kind. Rather, in creative blessing God is self-committed merely to provide what is sufficient for creatures' well-being in their kinds. In theological accounts of God providing such care, God cannot be characterized as relating in ways that violate *what* each kind of creature is.[2]

God's relating in providential care is differentiated in an even more particular way. Because creatures are essentially interdependent and intercontingent realities in a multitude of different ways, God's providential care of each creature is necessarily qualified by being appropriate to that creature's uniquely particular contingent situation and circumstances in relation to other creatures. Accordingly, an account of God's "sovereignty" in the providential care of creatures cannot be so framed as to imply that it is uniform and blanket, so to speak, relating to all creatures in an undifferentiated way that is indifferent to the particularity of the creature's concrete situation and circumstances.

In sum, an account of God's "sovereignty" in providential care framed on the basis of canonical accounts of God's relating in creative blessing ex nihilo must be nuanced in accord with these

---

[2] Except, perhaps, in the case of Balaam's ass; cf. Numbers 22.

ways in which God's relating in providential care are different from God's way of relating in creative blessing, even though relating in providential care is necessarily entailed by the way God goes about relating in creative blessing.

"Traditional" theistic explications of God's providence have typically drawn some distinctions that went a considerable distance toward nuancing accounts of God's "sovereignty" in providential care so as to be appropriate to the implications of the asymmetries in the relation between canonical narratives of God's creative blessing and God's providential care of creatures. Most fundamentally, given that an account of God's creative blessing ex nihilo makes the Creator/creature distinction the fundamental ontological distinction, traditional accounts of God's providence built on a distinction, based on the doctrine of creation, between two ontologically distinct orders of "causality": "primary causality" (i.e., God's causality) and "secondary causality" (i.e., creatures' causality). Primary causality is exercised in God's providential care of creatures. Secondary causality is exercised by creatures in their interactions with one another.

Obviously, framing an explanation of providence in terms of this distinction between two orders of causality makes the explanation depend on some concept of "cause." Traditional theistic explanations of providence generally have relied on a metaphysical theory of causality. It has sometimes been characterized as "substance" causality, in contradistinction to concepts of "event causality" that are customary in modern scientific "causal" explanations.[3] Given that they seek to honor the Creator/creature ontological distinction, however, traditional accounts of providence generally stress that, in

---

[3] That it is not, in the modern sense, "scientific" does not necessarily count against either its relevance or its intelligibility. It is arguable that, although inferential explanations of empirically available changes in the world that are framed in terms of event causality are both conceptually more economical and logically more persuasive, they are finally not conceptually transferrable to efforts to elucidate God's relating in providential care to empirically available creatures.

providential care of creatures, the Creator God is not to be thought of as just one more causal agent interacting with other creatures in a common field or plane of interaction.

Creaturely agents interact in a common plane or space in pursuit of their own ends, which may conflict. The "common plane" is a field in which conflict among agents is not only possible, but also probably necessary. Any given agent's achievement of the end toward which it acts depends on whether it can out-power those with whom it is in conflict. Were God's "causality" in providential care understood as that of just one more such agent, God's engagement with creatures would be a zero-sum game in which either God or creatures achieve the ends to which they act. Understood in that way, God's ends in providential care would be understood always to be achieved simply because God is ever so much more powerful than any one creature or all creatures taken together. God's sovereignty would be understood to be exercised in ways that include conflicts in which creatures' ontological integrity might be violated.

To block such a view, a metaphysical theory of causality is generally used in "traditional" accounts of providential care on the understanding that, although it is used straightforwardly to explain intercreature interaction and changes, that theory of causality can only be used analogically to explain God's engagement with creatures in providential care. In relating in providential care God is not conceived as one more "causal" agent on the inventory list of creaturely causal agents. Given the Creator/creature distinction, God's exercise of providential care cannot be explained as "caused" by God as one agent among many interacting within the creaturely field or on the creaturely plane. Rather, given that the Creator/creature distinction does not entail a Creator/creature separation of two incommensurate realities, God's sovereignty in providential care must be said to be expressed in God's relating in differentiated fashion "to" that entire set of networks of creaturely interactions. In relating differentially to creatures in providential care, God is thus at once radically other than (because not "acting" on the same plane) and radically close to (as the condition of the possibility of creatures' well-being) the entire creaturely plane or space.

The reason why the use of a metaphysical concept of cause to explain God's providential care of creatures can only be analogical comes into focus when we consider the intellectual context of the concept of the "first cause." That intellectual context is a received tradition of pre-Christian philosophical cosmology that was part of early Christian thinkers' cultural and intellectual formation. The central question of that cosmology was this: given the many and complex sorts of change that constantly go on in the world as we experience it, what keeps it from being a chaos and makes it instead an orderly and intelligible cosmos? The question was answered in different ways by different philosophical schools, but particularly persuasive and influential responses to the question argued that the multitude of changes were super-intended and ordered by a cosmic "first principle" or *arche*. The claim that the *arche* "orders" all the dynamic cause–effect relationships that would otherwise be chaotic into a coherent cosmos implies that it too is a certain kind of "cause." It is the cosmos' "first" or "primary" cause of all changes (or, as it was often put, "motion") in the cosmos.

Because it was generally assumed that the cosmos is eternal, the *arche* did not explain why there is a cosmos. It was not conceived as the cosmos' creator. Nor need "cause" necessarily be used analogically when it is attributed to the *arche*. Indeed, for example, in an Aristotelian version of this sort of cosmological argument, the first cause was arguably understood to be indeed just one more cause among the many causal substances that make up the cosmos, distinguished only by being the logically most basic cause in chains of explanations of the entire set of interconnected causal links that compose the cosmos.

When Christian thinkers adopted the distinction between primary and secondary causality in their theological accounts of providence, they located their concept of providence in the larger conceptual context of this sort of cosmology centered on the concept of a cosmic *arche*.

However, in adopting the concept of *arche*, Christian thinkers also adapted it, modifying it in two fundamental ways. Those two "adaptations" have had a theologically mixed legacy. In one way, they cut against accounts of the Triune God's providential care from which theologically and pastorally problematic inferences can be drawn. They could do that by stressing how the creator God's self-commitment to honor the ontological integrity of creaturely secondary causes in creatively blessing them entails that God's providential care of creatures is constrained in the same way. They also could reinforce the "blocking" of problematic inferences by underscoring the importance of stressing that God can be called the "cause" of providential care only in an analogical sense of "cause." Because we do not know how "causality" means when attributed to God analogically, we have to be agnostic about many possible inferences from attribution of "causality" to God's providential care that would be perfectly reasonable were "cause" and "causality" attributed univocally to God as the cosmic *arche*.

The first way in which they modified the concept of an *arche* was to attribute to it the creation of the cosmos ex nihilo. The thought had hardly occurred to pagan Greco- Roman philosophers. As we have seen, that modified use of *arche* inescapably introduces the Creator/creature distinction as the most fundamental ontological distinction. That distinction, in turn, shapes the traditional "theological" analysis of God's way of relating in providential care. Traditional doctrines of providence factor providence into three distinct aspects: maintenance (*conservatio*), *concursus* (which has no good English translation; "running along-side" may come close), and governance, i.e., sovereignty (*gubernatio*). *Concursus* acknowledges that, in providential care, God respects creatures' ontological reality as concretely actual and good "others" to God. *Conservatio* affirms that God's providential care is ordered to the maintenance of those "other" creatures in the well-being defined by their kinds as the particular creatures they are. However it may be that God's *gubernatio* toward creatures' well-being works (and that is not available to us), the sovereignty of God in providential care must be understood in ways that are within limits set by *conservatio* and *concursus*. That modification of *arche* moves in the direction of blocking inferences from affirmation of God's providence to theologically problematic pastoral remarks meant to console those who anguish about others' horrific suffering.

However, the "traditional" theological accounts of providence as sketched were also framed in ways that conflict with their blocking otherwise plausible but pastorally and theologically problematic inferences from those accounts. When Christian writers adapted their culturally received cosmological concept of a cosmological *arche* by identifying it as the cosmos' creator ex nihilo, they modified the ancient picture of the *arche* to understand it as absolute and alone. That change has had the effect of subverting the force of the implication of the Creator/creature distinction that all qualities ascribed to God are attributed analogically rather than univocally. Early Christian thinkers framed their concept of God in terms of the cosmological *arche* in part to help explain to their pagan neighbors what they meant by the phrase "one God": the creator is the cosmic "prime cause," the *arche*. Everyone agrees that, if there is to be one cosmos, there can only be one "first principle" absolute and alone, the *mon-arche* (in English, "monarchy").

Accordingly the sort of unrestricted causality that is attributed to God as the "prime" or first cause in creative blessing is also traditionally attributed to God as the "prime cause" of providential care, along with the codicil that, unlike God's creative blessing, God's providential "causality" relates to creatures both immediately *and* mediated through creaturely "secondary causes." This helps to explain what Trinitarian Christians meant by their affirmation of "one God." The Triune God's "oneness,' i.e., God's unity and singularity, is explained in terms of one strand of the economy: God's providential care of creation (which is entailed by God's creative blessing). God's "oneness" is the logically and ontologically necessary singularity of the cosmos' "prime cause," the *arche,* of providential care. In that singularity God is absolute and alone.

By that move, however, the "oneness" or singularity of the Triune God is not explained in terms of the further assertion of the singular God's *tri*-unity. It is not explained in terms provided by affirmation of God's three-foldness that is itself warranted by a different strand of the economy than creation–providence, viz., God's relating in making and keeping liberative promises, specifically in all that Jesus Christ does and undergoes. A Trinitarian doctrine of God plays little or no role in the traditional explication of God's providential care of creatures framed in terms of the cosmological *arche.* Instead, one element of a Trinitarian doctrine of God alone is framed in terms of the *arche*: the first "Person" of the Trinity, the "Father," to whom relating to creatures in providential rule is ascribed, is characterized in terms of the concept of a cosmic *arche.* "Father" is used analogically to characterize God's relation to the created cosmos, not to characterize the first "Person" of the Trinity's eternal relation to the second "Person," the "Son." The "Father" relates to all else as creator in the way the cosmic *arche* relates to all else. The "Father" is the cosmic *mon-arche,* absolute and alone.

Accordingly, what can be said of God's way of relating to all else in "traditional" accounts of providence and, especially, what can be said of God's sovereignty in providential care for creatures, must be framed in terms of the way the *arche* relates to the cosmos. And the latter includes no conceptual space for the claim that in creative blessing the "Father" can intelligibly be said to be "*self*-involvingly *self*-committed," and thus "*self*-qualified" or "*self*-conditioned," to care for creatures providentially in ways that necessarily respect their particular integrities as the kind of creatures they are. That move tends to cut against, indeed to undercut, the possibility that attribution of creation to God (even when God is understood as cosmic *arche*) could serve to help block explanations of the creator's relating to creatures in providential care that imply the theologically and pastorally problematic remarks about God on which Chapter 1 focused. It seems instead to endorse them.

The second major modification that early Christian thinkers made to the concept of a cosmic *arche* was to attribute certain "personal" qualities to the "*arche*." In Greco-Roman philosophical cosmologies, the *arche* was generally understood in impersonal terms. It might be characterized as "rational," but that was because it was itself the "first principle" of rationality, rationality-itself, rationality pure and simple. It was not thought to fill its role as "orderer" of the flux and change of the cosmos because it "cared" about the cosmos or had "ends" that it freely "caused" to be actualized within the cosmos for creatures' "good" or for the "well-being" of creaturely agents within the cosmos. On the contrary, it fills the role of *arche* quite "impersonally." Doing so simply constitutes what makes it the "*arche*." In attributing creation of the cosmos ex nihilo to the *arche*, however, the Christian thinkers modified the notion of *arche* by attributing personal qualities to it, using the terms for those qualities analogically: their identification of the *arche* as the creator ex nihilo and not just providential orderer of the cosmos entailed attributing to the *arche* "intentions" or "ends" for the creatures that it "wills" and for whose actualization it has "a plan." Moreover, the creator *arche*'s "intending," "willing," and "planning" is done "freely" in "love" for creatures.

That goes some way toward avoiding the problematic accounts of God's providential care of creatures that we have identified in Chapter 1. Given the Creator/creature distinction, all such characterizations of God as creation's providential *arche* attribute human personal qualities to the "first cause" only analogically. In principle, such "personalizing" of the notion of the cosmic *arche* could block attribution to it of a causality that is utterly unconditioned and absolute. It could block such attribution on the grounds that in providential care God's causality as *arche* is constrained by God's free and loving commitment to respect the integrity of creatures in their kinds and in their concrete particularities by relating in ways that wisely avoid violating the creatures. Whatever terms like "will" and "plan" mean in regard to how God relates to "others," they cannot mean that the creatures are "fated," "instrumentalized," "manipulated," "forced" or in some other way violated by God.

I began this chapter by identifying three things that are important in assessing the appropriateness of "sovereignty" and similar words as metaphors for God's way of relating to creatures in the economy. Thus far, our discussion of the asymmetrical relation between the Triune God's relating to all else in creative blessing and relating to all else in providential care has addressed two of them: the different ends to which that "sovereignty" is exercised in different strands of God's economy, and certain aspects of the ways, as canonically narrated, in which God goes about concretely relating to what is not God in actualizing those goals. The underlying analytic theme has been that the differences between the two and the reason for the asymmetry are rooted in the way the theological claim that the Trinity creates all else ex nihilo implies that the Creator/creature distinction is the fundamental ontological distinction in Christian thought.

We have largely addressed those two key points in the context of an assessment of the appropriateness of explanations of the sense in which God is "sovereign" through a critical analysis of both currently "conventional" and classically "traditional" accounts of God's providence. In "traditional" accounts, God's "sovereignty" is usually understood in terms of the accounts of providential care that have been examined thus far. I have argued that, although those "traditional" accounts of providence, as the context within which accounts of God's sovereignty, were developed, could in principle block inferences about God's sovereignty drawn from their explanations of providence that are theologically and pastorally problematic, they have not been clear enough about "who" and "what" the God is who is sovereign – viz., Triune – to firmly block such inferences. In response to theologically problematic pastoral efforts to console those who anguish at others' horrific suffering, they do not warrant clearly enough the rejoinder, "No, God would not do a thing like that."

We have not yet suggested a sense in which God can be said unproblematically to be "sovereign" in providential care. Before we turn in Chapter 5 to propose such an understanding of "sovereignty" as attributed to the Triune God, we need to address some aspects of the third point: what and who the One who exercises "sovereignty" is.

Some Reality Claims about What and Who God Is

We have already touched on "what" and "who" God is. It will be helpful to review those remarks and note some elements of the internal "grammar" of those reality claims about the Triune God.

On "What" It Is to Be God

As for "what" it is to be God, Chapter 2 proposed that claims about God's reality ought to be framed as claims about the dynamics constituting the "living" Triune God. "What" makes God "God" is God's living reality. Chapter 2 argued for that proposal on the basis of the imagery used in the Nicene Creed to characterize the dynamic relations that constitute the three "Persons" of the Triune God as the "Persons" they are. That imagery represents the Triune God's reality as constituted by a determinate dynamic: it is a self-relating that is generative of the "terms" of the relating ("Father," "Son," and Spirit are each dynamically constituted by the ways in which each relates to the other two). It is a self-relating in which each "Person" is perfectly self-expressive in helping to generate two genuine "others." That perfect self-expressiveness is in each case an unrestrictedly generous self-giving, in that the two "others" that it constitutes in each case are all identically "God." The Triune God's unrestrictedly generous self-giving of that self-relating is most aptly characterized as relating in love, which makes the dynamics constituting the Trinity's "life" unqualifiedly beautiful, intrinsically attractive. Chapter 3 added that the dynamic self-relating that is the Trinity's living reality is a self-regulating self-relating. Hence, God is intrinsically "sovereign" in God's own living self-relating whether or not God also relates to reality other than God. What makes the dynamic that is the Triune God's life "determinate" are just those qualities of self-regulating, self-expressive, and generous self-giving that are the communion of love in which the three "Persons" of the Triune God are One. Chapter 3 pointed out that to attribute to the Trinity those relatively abstract qualities of the dynamic that are the reality of the Triune life is to express a set of metaphysical beliefs and to make a set of metaphysical claims about some of God's "attributes" or "qualities."

In addition to an analysis of the some qualities of the dynamic that just *is* the Trinity's life, three "grammatical" remarks about talk about "what" it is to be God are in order. They are "grammatical" in that they are remarks about some boundaries of intelligible talk about God that follow from some of the qualities of the dynamics of God's life that are identified above.

First grammatical remark: God is singular. I had a religiously agnostic college classmate who claimed nonetheless to have a theological creed, viz., "There is at most one God." It is sly in that it affirms, not the reality of God, but the maximum possibility for God ("*at most* one God") while at the same time seeming to align the affirmer with something called "monotheism": "at most *one* God." However, there is something deeply wrong with this. Its surface intelligibility trades on a tacit assumption that the word "God" names an individual instance of one kind of reality, call it "divinity," of which there logically might be one instantiation, or more than one, or none, albeit according to "monotheism" only one. In that case, it would be appropriate to ask for an explanation of why there are not fewer or more instances than there are. What's wrong is this: as a revision of the Christian affirmation of the God of Abraham, my classmate's "creed" betrays a failure to grasp the grammar of the use of the word "God" in Trinitarian (and many non-Trinitarian) doctrines of God.

It is a theological commonplace to say that classical Christian Trinitarian affirmations use "one" in the formula "The Triune God is One" to underscore the Triune God's intrinsic unity and not to make a claim about the "number" of Gods. However, using "one" and "three" in English-language theological discussion of Trinitarian doctrine of God seems almost unavoidably to slide into the linguistic gravitational pull of the use of each word as cardinal numbers, despite explicit denials that that is the force of their use in reference to the Triune God.

I suggest it may be less misleading to speak, not of God's "oneness," but of God's "singularity." In this context, "singularity" brings with it two verbal resonances that are theologically helpful. A person, action, or event may be described as "singular" to draw attention to its extraordinary strangeness or oddness without necessarily ridiculing or dismissing it. To characterize "what" it is to be the Triune God as "singular" is to underscore that, in a Trinitarian doctrine of God, the sense in which God is "objectively real" or concretely actual (i.e., very roughly speaking, "real independent of our thinking, dreaming, or consciously imagining it") is so very different to any of the senses in which the creatures we know are said to be "objectively real" as to be downright odd if not, indeed, bizarre. Second, using "singular" to characterize "what" it is to be the Triune God is somewhat analogous to the way in which, in early versions of the Big Bang theory of the origin of the universe the "Bang" was described as a "singularity." Part of what that implies is that the originating Big Bang is not itself an event explainable in terms of the regularities and mathematically expressible laws that do explain the changes through which the universe "originated" by the Big Bang subsequently developed. Multiple changes within the universe can be explained by those regularities; the postulated Big Bang is "singular" in that it itself cannot be so explained. In a loosely analogous way, to describe "what" it is to be the Triune God as "singular" is to underscore that, in contradistinction to what we know about what it is to be a creature of any particular "kind" and how to explain changes that creatures cause and undergo, God's capacity to relate to them in creative blessing ex nihilo, and God's actually doing so, are not themselves additional instances of creaturely "kinds," "powers," or interactions that effect causally explainable changes in creatures. The important dis-analogy between the two uses of "singular" and "singularity" (i.e., as [i] "odd," and [ii] as "an instance of 'explainable' chains of creaturely causality") is that, unlike their use in reference to the Big Bang, used in reference to God's creative blessing and providential care, the two terms do not characterize a punctiliar event, but rather "what" it is to *be* the agent of that blessing and care.

Clearly, the singularity of "what" it is to be the Triune God is rooted in the way in which the claim that God relates to all else in creative blessing ex nihilo makes the Creator/creature *distinction* as the most basic ontological distinction without entailing that there is an ontological *separation* between the two. We have seen that God's way of relating in creative blessing cannot be likened to interactions among creatures on a common plane or within a common three-dimensional space. Creatures come in different kinds, of which they individually are particular instantiations. They have different powers or different degrees of the same sort of power, according to their kinds. Their interactions can be zero-sum exercises of those powers. Consequently, their interactions are in principle open to competition, conflict, and violation of one another. In creative blessing ex nihilo, however, God is not an instance of yet another "kind" of entity engaged in zero-sum interaction with creatures, but unqualifiedly more powerful than all of them. To the contrary, in God's ways of relating to creatures God is correlatively "radically other than" and "radically close to" them. God's way of relating in creative blessing ex nihilo excludes in principle competition and conflict with creatures and their exercise of their own powers.

Rather, God's creative blessing is the condition of the possibility of there even being creatures and their having interactions.

This is where my classmate's failure to grasp the grammar of the use of the word "God"[4] in Trinitarian (and many non-Trinitarian) doctrines of God becomes clear. The question of "How many gods are there or could there be?" assumes a distinction, like the one that is appropriate to thinking about creatures, between something that might be called God's "nature" or "divine essence," or "divine substance" on one side and, on the other side, concretely actual instantiations of that "nature" or "substance." That is precisely what is ruled out by stress on the unqualified unity of "what" it is to be the Triune God. Traditional use of "one" to characterize God does not claim that there is one and only one instantiation of the "kind" of reality that is "divine." "One" is used to stress that the very distinction between a "kind" or "essence" or "nature," on one side, and concretely actual instantiations of it on the other does not obtain in regard to "what" it is to be God. It is a valid distinction in regard to creatures because it makes acknowledgment of their finitude essential to any account of "what" each of them is: an entity that is an instantiation of a certain "kind" of creature whose nature we know does exist but of which it, as an instantiation, may very well cease to exist. To make just this point, for example, Thomas Aquinas argues[5] that God's "existence" is not just an instantiation of God's "essence" (call that "divinity," "divine being," or "deity"). Rather, God's "essence" just is "to exist." This claim is – rightly – likely to strike

---

[4] For the same reason, the expression "monotheism" is not very helpful as a way of classifying the Abrahamic faiths by contrasting them with "polytheists," as though what distinguished the first from the latter was a disagreement about the number of Gods.

[5] Thomas Aquinas, *Summa Theologica* I, Question 3 "On the Simplicity of God," articles 3–7 in *Basic Writings of Saint Thomas Aquinas*, edited and annotated by Anton C. Pegis (New York: Random House, 1945), Vol. 1, pp. 28–33. The English translation is Pegis' revised, corrected, and annotated edition of the English Dominican Translation of St. Thomas *Summa*.

us as exceedingly strange. The sense in which God is "objectively real" is indeed singular. In the traditional theological terminology used to make this point, God is not "in" or "an instance of" any "species" of "objectively real" entities. Moreover, God is not "in" or "an instance of" any genus of "objectively real" entities of which it is logically possible that there might be other instances. The singularity of the sense in which God is objectively "real" is that God's "manner of existence" simply *is* God's "essence," in contradistinction to being an "instance" of that "essence."

According to this concept of God, the unity of "what" it is to be God is so absolute that it is a sign that one has not grasped the grammar of use of the word "God" in Trinitarian doctrine of God if one asks how many Gods there are or can be. However, there are different senses of "absolute unity" that need to be sorted here. The "unity" of what it is to be the Triune God is the unity of God's intrinsic life. Hence, it cannot be likened to the unity of a monad, the unity of absolute abstract undifferentiated numerical self-identity. Rather, it is the intrinsic unity of the inseparable "radical closeness" of "Father," "Son," and Holy Spirit that is dialectically correlative with their "terminally irreducible otherness" to one another in the dynamic divine self-relating that constitutes the "life" of the Triune God.

So, too, the Triune God's "unity" cannot be likened to the unity of a single integral process that moves through several necessary stages to the ultimate end or *telos* of full self-actualization that is required by an initial self-alienation or estrangement, which is overcome in final self-reconciliation. "What" it is to be the Triune God just *is* the communion in love of three "Persons" constituted by unrestrictedly generous self-giving. The concept opens no space for a self-estrangement that must be overcome before the communion can begin.

Nor can the Triune God's unity be grounded in an account of "divine substance" that is conceptually independent of, and logically antecedent to, the dynamics of unrestricted self-giving in generative self-relating that constitutes the living Tri-unity. That is why it is misleading to develop a Trinitarian doctrine of God on the basis of a logically prior "monotheistic" account of "what" it is to be "divine" and only after that turn to discuss God's Triunity as though it were one (of perhaps many?) logically possible variants of a monotheistic concept of God.

So, to characterize the Triune God's divinity as "singular" is at least to note certain limits to our capacity to make intelligible truth claims characterizing "divinity." It can be expressed in three negative grammatical rules governing talk about "what" it is to be the Triune God: (i) never speak of the Triune God in a way that implies that "divinity" is a property that is divisible, somehow "parceled out," or "shared"; (ii) never speak of the Triune God in a way that implies that God is one concrete instance of a reality-kind called "divinity," of which there is the logical possibility of more or no instances; and (iii) never speak of the "Father," "Son," and Holy Spirit in a way that implies that they are three concretely actual instances of a common reality-kind called "divinity" or "divine substance."

I do not know whether it is possible to show that it is "irrational" or "self-contradictory" *not* to acknowledge the reality of the Triune God or *not* to talk about what is not God in terms of the Trinity's ways of relating to it. One may very well elect never to think or talk about either subject. However, if one does decide to query Christian Trinitarian reality claims about God, one must question it on its own terms, examining just *that* concept of God by focusing, among other things, on its own grammar and what it implies about the limits of what can and cannot be asked intelligibly and what can and cannot be said intelligibly about God.

Second grammatical remark: God is a se. The question of "Why does God exist?" also makes a grammatical mistake. The very framing of the question betrays a failure to grasp the way the word "God" is used in the context of the Trinitarian doctrine of God. Traditionally, this point has been made, perhaps unhelpfully, by invoking this contrast: all that is not God exists contingently; God exists necessarily, of Godself, *a se*. That, ontologically speaking, is "what" it is to "be God."

Affirmation of God's *aseity* is a rejection of every demand for an explanation of God's singular concrete reality ("How come there is a God?") on the grounds that the question involves a grammatical mistake. The issue turns on the notion of "explaining." We have noted (a) that the distinction between Creator and creature is the basic ontological distinction; (b) that God is singular in respect of God's reality in not being one actual instantiation of some logically possible nature or kind of reality, of which there might be other instantiations but, as it happens, there are not; and (c) that the way in which God goes about relating to creatures in various strands of the economy is always characterized by God's radical closeness and otherness to genuine "others." It follows that it is a mistake to picture creatures and God as sharing the same level of reality as a field on which creatures and Creator interact in zero-sum exercises of power.

Creatures do share such a common field with one another. In it they interact in a multitude of ways. It is appropriate to ask why their interactions have the consequences they do have. If creatures' interactions are to be understood, we require, among other things, a variety of explanations of their interactions. Among creatures' interactions are their coming into being and ceasing to be. It is appropriate to ask why they do. It is arguably appropriate to ask why the entire set of networks of creaturely interactions exists. All such explanations share categorical frameworks that specifies just what counts as an "explanation" of any of the ways in which creatures interact and affect one another. By definition, creatures are not *a se* and the need for explanations is a function of their creaturely finitude.

However, if God's radical closeness to creatures is correlative to God's radical otherness to that entire creaturely field of creaturely interactions, and is not just one more player on that field, then the entire project of "explaining" and its conceptual framework cannot apply to God. It is limited to the interactions among creatures. It is not that God's reality and identity are "inexplicable" (presumably God explains them to Godself). The problem is that the very project of explaining why something is "objectively real" does not apply to the Triune God (or, perhaps, to God in some non-Triune theistic doctrines of God). Therefore, the distinction between being "able to offer a metaphysical explanation why God is actual" and being "unable to offer a metaphysical explanation why God is actual" does not apply. It is a category mistake to ask for a metaphysical (or any other) causal "explanation" of God's reality. Hence, it has been traditional to stress that the claim "God is *a se*" is not an answer to the question, "Why is God real?" as though "God is *a se*" means "God *causes* God-self to be 'objectively real.'" The claim, "God is *a se*" is not an explanation of God's "objective reality" in terms of a metaphysical theory of causality. "God is *a se*" should be understood as, at least, a remark about the grammar of Christianly intelligible talk about God.

This project promotes an account of the "power of God" in the context of Trinitarian doctrine of God. It explains "what" it is to be the Triune God in terms of the dynamics that constitute the "life" of communion in love that constitutes the reality of the three "Persons" of the Trinity, which is the "objective reality" of God, i.e., what it is to *be* the Triune God. Any intelligible account of "what" it is to be the Triune God must be regulated by the internal "grammar" of Christian Trinitarian talk about God. In particular, that means that it must follow rules respecting the singularity and the *aseity* of God. Insofar as it does so, it will not explain "*aseity*" as a quality of a singular "divine substance" that Christians claim happens also to be Triune, but which can be discussed prior to and independent of discussion of God's Triunity. For the same reason, it will not agree to discuss the question, "Why is God Triune?" Given that God's "objective reality" just is the life of the Triune God whose whole ensemble of qualities is the "glory of God"

CREATION, PROVIDENCE, & PASTORAL CONSOLATION

(in its primary reference), it is as much a grammatical mistake to demand, and in response to offer, an explanation of "Why God is Triune" as it is to ask and answer the question "Why is God 'objectively real.?" It is not some underlying "divine" reality that is singular and *a se*. It is the Trinity that is singular and *a se*.

If that is "what" the Triune God is and correctly identifies some "grammatical" rules for talking about the Triune God, then, whatever it may mean to say that "God is powerful," God's power cannot be explained in ways that are inconsistent with these determinate features of the nature the One alleged to be powerful. God does as God is. Given "what" and "who" God is, we know a priori about some characterizations of God's relating to all else (such as "God sent that bone cancer") that "God would not do something like that."

On "Who" God Is

Comment on "who" the Triune God is tacitly assumes that God has qualities that are, in some distant way, analogous to qualities we think of as attributes of human persons. Traditionally, they have been classified as "personal attributes" of God, in contradistinction to "metaphysical" attributes that characterize "what" it is to be God. It will be helpful, I suggest, if we distinguish between qualities whose attribution to God suggests that God is intrinsically self-relating in ways that are analogous to certain qualities human persons sometimes exhibit, on one hand, and qualities whose attribution to God suggests that the Triune God is intrinsically analogous to *a* human person. Both sorts of attribution suggest descriptions of "who" God is, but each in a different way that has its own limitations.

As with the attribution of "metaphysical" qualities to God in our comments on "what" it is to be the Triune God, so too the attribution of both sorts of "personal" qualities to God in these comments are based on qualities that characterize the way in which God goes about relating to all else in various strands of the economy. Chapter 2 argued that the qualities marking the ways in which God goes about relating in the economy faithfully express some of the qualities of the dynamic self-giving and self-expressive self-relating that just is the Triune God's intrinsic life of communion in love. The ensemble of the qualities of God's intrinsic life is the intrinsic glory of God (in its primary reference) that is faithfully expressed in the way in which the concrete particulars of the economy are God's glory (in its secondary reference).

Chapter 3 noted that some of those qualities are most aptly characterized by likening them analogically to qualities moderns think of as, in varying degrees, especially characteristic of human creatures as persons: "intentionality" of both consciousness and action; knowledge of others; and self-consciousness and some degree of self-knowledge. Others are qualities most aptly character-ized by likening them analogically to qualities we ascribe in varying degrees to certain morally admirable human persons: (in no particular order) love, generosity, faithful self-commitments to interpersonal relationships, trustworthiness, unusual transparency of self-knowledge, delight in others, and openness to others' joy and suffering.

A second, different, and especially "slippery" sort of such intrin-sic "personal" qualities can also be attributed to the Triune God on the basis of their expression in the particularities of the ways in which God relates to all else in the economy according to canonical narratives. They are the intrinsic qualities of God characterized by likening them analogically to the distinctive qualities of human "personal identities." However, in requests for descriptions of a human person's identity, the word "identity" is notoriously ambiguous.

The requested description might be one that could be used to refer to identifying features of the person that would help one to identify them or pick them out of the midst of a group of persons: "Of all the people at this party, which one is Jane Austin?"

The answer might consist of a description of how tall she is, what color clothing she is wearing, where in the room she is standing, with whom she is talking, etc. Or, "Of all of Rome's emperors which one was Tiberius?" The answer might consist of the dates of his birth and death, how he came to be emperor, stories of famous deeds he performed, historians' general opinion of him, etc.

It is sometimes suggested that a request for a characterization of God's "identity" is of this sort and is best answered by naming or narrating God's "mighty deeds." "Who" is God? The answer might be, "God is the creator of all that is not God, who kept liberating promises to Abraham and his descendants by reconciling estranged human creatures to God by way of Incarnation in the life-trajectory of Jesus of Nazareth, and who draws creatures to eschatological consummation by the power of the Spirit."

A problem with that definition lies in the question and the agreement to answer it as it is worded: The question tacitly assumes that there may be a number of "Gods" from among whom the Triune God can be "identified" and "picked out." But, as noted, the "grammar" of the concept of God question here makes that assumption a grammatical mistake. The unwisely offered "answer" is at most a set of God's job descriptions that does not characterize "who" God intrinsically is.

In current North American culture, the description that is requested might be understood to be an account of how a given human person tacitly, or with some degree of self-awareness, understands "who" ze is. It would be answered in terms of zer understanding of zer gender, skin tone, class, place, and role in the dynamics of zer family, zer talents and competencies, ethnic heritage, and the ways in which their intersections shape zer sense of zer responsibilities, familial and social roles, self-esteem, expectations laid on zer by society, zer aspirations, sense of opportunities, or sense of helplessness in zer context. In part, zer sense of these matters will have been projected onto zer by the social and cultural context within which ze is nurtured as ze matures. In part, they will be formed by the way ze responds to those projections. The result is "who" ze is at the point where ze answers the question, and subsequently that "identity" may change. Whatever the answer, at the moment it is given it is certainly one type of "personal identity description."

It is sometimes suggested that a request of this sort for a characterization of "who" God is can be answered by saying things like: "God is the one who loves us even when we are unlovable. That is God's fundamental identity," or "God shares your joys and your sorrows. That is who God most fundamentally is," or "God is the fellow sufferer who understands. That is God's fundamental personal identity." There probably are analogical senses in which each of those characterizations is correct.

Once again, a problem lies in the question and the agreement to answer it as it is worded: this sort of identity question tacitly assumes that the identity being asked about is the way a human "subject," i.e., a human center of consciousness, is "formed" or "shaped" in response to its environing physical, emotional, cultural, and social contexts. When it is asked as a question about God, it implicitly attributes to God something analogous to human consciousness. But, whereas human centers of conscious always emerge in larger contexts that impinge on them, "forming" them and at the same time eliciting from them responses that also help "form" the ways in which they are being "formed," the dynamic that is the Triune God's life, I have urged, is always radically prior in reality and value to what is not God and prevenient in God's ways of relating in the "economy" to what is not God. The difference between God's living reality, "what" God is, and creaturely human conscious, so central to "what" a human person is, is so great that any "analogy" between them must be so distant as to be next to empty.

A third sense in which a description of personal "identity" might be requested asks not how some person would describe her own "identity," but rather how someone else would describe "who" a third person is in her singular and unsubstitutable identity that seems not to change across time, "who" she consistently is in all circumstances: "Tell me about your friend (your favorite aunt, your grandmother, etc.). What is she like?" There are two aspects of most attempts to answer such a request.

One aspect is to identify what have traditionally been called moral "virtues." They are deeply ingrained habits that reliably shape their behavior in certain morally admirable ways in all circumstances: truthfulness, fairness, integrity, love, generosity, etc. Such virtues are usually described in abstractions that would just as accurately and without modification be attributed to some other person in an identity description of him. "Honesty" is "honesty" no matter who exhibits it.

A second aspect of efforts to give an identity description of someone, in this sense of "identity," is to characterize what we might call a person's distinctive "style" or even "flair" in their actions and interactions. That is usually done by telling stories, anecdotes of her interactions with other people or her way of coping with challenging events, of which we say, "That was her at her best," "That was what she was really like all the time," "That was really captures *her*." The narrative character of such identity descriptions of human persons goes further toward capturing the unsubstitutable concrete singularity of a person's identity than can a collection of abstract moral adjectives no matter how clearly and precisely defined they are.

There is a temptation to suppose that, because God is both prevenient and always correlatively "radically other than" and "radically close to" what is not God, God has the sort of "personal identity" analogous to the one identified by this third sort of identity description of human persons. So it may be said, "I'll tell you what God most fundamentally is like by telling you this story about God's interactions with Abraham; or about God's interactions with Moses in the wilderness; or about God's interactions with Jeremiah; or about God's interactions with Jesus, especially from the time he entered Jerusalem to Easter morning. Those stories really capture who God is."

Here, too, the problem lies in the question and the agreement to answer it as it is worded: this sort of identity question tacitly assumes that the identity being asked about is that of a human person dealing consistently and "characteristically" with many different circumstances across time. But the analogy between what it is to be a human person, a human psychosomatic "thou," and "what" it is to be God is vanishingly small. Human "thous" are *essentially* social. To exist, they essentially require not only a physical context, but also a socially interactive context with other instances of the "kind" of creature called "human." Chapters 2 and 3 argued that the "communion-in-love" that is the life of the three "Persons" of the Trinity is not analogous to a society of three instances of one and the same "kind." Furthermore, given "what" the Triune God is, God does not "need" the society of realities other than God to "exist," i.e., to be God. Hence, requesting an identity description of "who" God is as though God were a "social being" analogous to human persons, and agreeing to answer such a question on its terms, both betray a failure to grasp the "singularity" of "what" and "who" the Triune God is.

In sum, we have warrant in canonical Scriptural accounts of how God goes about relating to all else in the economy for analogical attribution of various "personal" qualities to God. However, we are not warranted in the same way to analogically attribute to the Triune God a "personal identity." It is, I suggest, a "grammatical" mistake to ask for an identity description of God in this sense of "identity" (the third sense we have discussed), because it is a "grammatical" mistake to construe "who" God is as though "what" it is to be God were analogous to what it is to be a human "thou." Not only does the "grammar" of a Trinitarian doctrine of God rule out likening God analogously to a human person, but it also rules out likening analogously the three "Persons" of the Trinity who are identically "God" to human persons.

* * * * *

One upshot of the analysis so far is that if talk of God's "sovereignty" in providential care ignores the asymmetrical relation between providential care and creative blessing it will simply assume that God's sovereignty in providential care is flatly identical with the sense in which God is "sovereign" in creative blessing. That will necessarily imply that God's "sovereignty" in providential care consists of God's unqualified control of what "goes on" in creation. It is, of course, precisely that assumption of conceptual identity of providential care with creative blessing ex nihilo that makes much 'conventional' talk about God's providence problematic pastorally and theologically. In Chapter 5, I propose an alternative way of conceiving God's providential care.

5 | The Triune God's "Sovereignty" in Two Registers

One upshot of the analysis thus far is this: if an account of the Triune God's "sovereignty" in providential care ignores the asymmetrical relation between providential care and creative blessing it will, however unintentionally, underwrite and warrant the sort of conventional talk about God's providence that we have identified as pastorally and theologically problematic. It will do so because it simply assumes that God's sovereignty in providential care is flatly identical with the sense in which God is "sovereign" in creative blessing. That assumption, in turn, implies that, just as God's "sovereignty" in creative blessing is a way of relating that is absolutely unconditioned by any reality other than God, so too God's "sovereignty" in providential care consists of God's unqualified control of what "goes on" in creation. It is, of course, precisely that assumption that makes much conventional talk about God's providence theologically problematic.

This chapter argues that what can be said about the character of the Triune God's sovereignty in the economy on the basis of canonical accounts of God relating in creative blessing should be nuanced by what can be said about it on the basis of the interplay between canonical accounts of God relating in two distinguishable ways: providential care and eschatological blessing, each understood in terms of the Triune God's relating in a different pattern or *taxis*. Where God's relating to all else in providential care is canonically narrated as an modified extension of canonical accounts of God's relating in creative blessing, canonical accounts of the Triune God relating in eschatological blessing are narrated in a quite different way. Each is a different register in which "sovereignty" is understood when attributed to God. This chapter explores those two registers and their inter-relations in the economy. Each strand of the economy expresses an aspect of the "glory of the Triune God" (in the primary reference of the phrase). In each strand, God is faithfully self-expressive of God's own intrinsic glory. They define two different but analogous senses of "sovereignty" that cannot be reduced to mere variations of the sense in which the Triune God is "sover-eign" in creative blessing.

I use "ensemble," "register," and "changes in register" as musical metaphors for the way in which the term under discussion – "God's sovereignty" in this and the previous chapter (and "God's power" in Part III) – is nuanced in different ways by the differences in the narrative logic of canonical Christian Scripture's testimony to the ways in which God goes about relating to creatures. Part I suggested that the Triune God's intrinsic glory is the "ensemble" of all God's qualities. On that understanding "glory" does not name an aggre-gate of discrete "powers" or "talents" of God. Rather, it names an inter-related, interdependent, and harmonious set of nonetheless distinguishable qualities that we are warranted to abstract from the Triune God's one dynamic and surpassingly rich life. God faithfully expresses various of those qualities in different strands of the economy as those strands are narrated in canonical Scriptural accounts of how God goes about relating in each of them. Hence, the Triune God's intrinsic qualities, such as glory, sovereignty, and power, are self-expressed in different registers in different strands of the economy. Because each "register" is faithful to, although not exhaustively expressive of, some aspect of God's intrinsic qualities, they are all together inter-related, interdependent in various ways, and polyphonically harmonious although nonetheless different from each other.

The Triune God's "Sovereignty" in the Register of Providential Care

We begin with the sense in which God's providential care of creatures, as canonically narrated, expresses God's intrinsic "sovereignty." I focus the discussion by asking what question a Christian doctrine of providence addresses.

Building on early work of H. Richard Niebuhr, Charles Wood has suggested that the question addressed by the doctrine of providence is, "*How are we to understand theologically what goes on?*"[1] It is a question about how "to understand *theologically*" because it is a question about the way in which God is involved in "what goes on," both among creatures in their interactions with one another and within each of them.

Two inter-related features of this formulation of this question are important for the sense in which the Triune God is "sovereign" in providential care of creatures. First, it focuses on events, interactions, and changes that happen between, among, and within creatures. It frames providential care in terms of God's involvement in changes in dynamic and fluid relationships among creatures insofar as those changes can be ordered to creatures' *relative* well-being in their kinds and interdependencies. In doing so, it notably does not frame a doctrine of providential care as primarily addressing a cosmological question about *how* God "causes" the constantly changing creation to be an ordered and intelligible cosmos and not an unintelligible chaos. It does not call for an explanation of the causal mechanism by which God works within and through those changes toward creatures' well-being. Any such "explanation" would need to identify what Austin Farrer famously called the

---

[1] *The Question of Providence* (Louisville, KY: Westminster John Knox Press, 2008), p. 12 (emphasis in original).

"causal joint"[2] between God's action and the actions that constitute creatures' well-being, a "joint" that Farrer noted is cognitively unavailable to human minds.

Accordingly, an account of God's providential care of creatures should be framed as an account of God's involvement in "what is going on" in particular creaturely interactions that are ordered to nurturing creatures' well-being, and not as an account of the causal mechanism by means of which God accomplishes that end.

Second is the force of the preposition the question uses: "within." That preposition signals the unique relation that the Triune God has to creatures in providential care. In creative blessing ex nihilo, the Triune God by definition relates "to" all else preveniently: by definition, absent God's relating in creative blessing ex nihilo there is "nothing" there either to relate to or to relate "back" to God, possibly to resist being related to creatively. The "sovereignty" of God's creative blessing by definition cannot be conceived as God's "control *over*" creation for there is nothing, *nihil*, to "control." That "prevenience" is God's radical "otherness" to creatures. However, also by definition, God's relating in creative blessing ex nihilo is also correlatively God's radical "closeness" to creatures in being the condition of the possibility of their concrete actuality. God's sovereignty in relating to them in creative blessing is not exercised externally, from "outside" their concrete actuality, and imposed "over them." Rather, it is God's sovereignty in a way of relating "to" them that is also intrinsic to their actually existing. In relating to bless creatively, I have argued, the Triune God is self-committed to nurture the well-being in their kinds of what is created ex nihilo.

---

[2] *Faith and Speculation* (New York: New York University Press, 1967), p. 65. Unlike any creaturely interaction we know that has a "causal joint," which always takes place on a common ontological plane, a field of multiple interactions of identifiable types that have identifiable regularities, God's relating to creatures in creative (and eschatological) blessing does not have any such plane or field and is in principle unique and not an instance of a class of possible additional instances. Hence, as Farrer concluded, that "joint" in principle escapes human cognitive grasp.

Thus, God's relating to all else in providential care is in a certain way an "extension" of God's relating in creative blessing.

There is this difference between them, however: in exercising providential care of creatures in their kinds God is engaging with concretely actual "others" that are "already there"; and in the ways in which God goes about exercising providential care God is self-committed by the very act of creative blessing to honor their particular "othernesses." That makes two ways of framing an account of God's providential care inappropriate. On one hand, it rules out any suggestion that God's sovereignty in providential care lies in God's extrinsic "control over" creatures' interactions, possibly conflicting with creatures' own self-regulation of their actions and, thereby, violating their ontological integrities. On the other hand, it rules out any suggestion that God's sovereignty in providential care is identical with some dynamic that is an essential structural feature of "creatureliness-as-such" that inevitably moves the entire complex of networks of creatures' interactions across time toward increased nurture of creatures' well-being, so that overall history *intrinsically* bends in an arc toward, say, justice, or freedom, or prosperity, etc. It is more appropriate to frame an account of God's providential care in term of God's ad hoc "wise" involvement *within* "what is going on" among creatures in concrete particular circumstances than to frame it in terms of God's "control *over*" "what is going on" or in terms of an implicit "logic" to history seen as a single overall process that inherently drives in a certain direction.

Thus far, we have noted qualities of the Triune God's relating in creative blessing and qualities of God's relating in providential care that overlap, precisely because the latter is entailed by the former. In both, God is radically prevenient to that to which God relates, i.e., to creatures, in the order of being. And in both God is correlatively both "radically close to" and "radically other than" creatures, albeit to different ends: in creative blessing, God creates ex nihilo to the end that they actually exist and are intrinsically good; in providential care, to the end that they have well-being in their kinds. Hence, like accounts of God's creative relating to creatures, accounts of God's relating in providential care must not be framed in such a way as to suggest that, as One "radically other than" creatures, God intervenes as an extrinsic agent in ways that violate creatures' ontological integrity. In short, given the Triune God's correlative "radical otherness than" and "radical closeness to" creatures, providential "care" cannot be explained in ways that leave open the logical possibility that in it creatures' powers and God's power might be in competition and in zero-sum conflict.

Given those qualities of God's way of relating in providential care that overlap with qualities of God's relating in creative blessing, it follows that the senses in which God is "sovereign" in each of them also overlap in regard to just those qualities: prevenience and correlative "radical otherness than" and "radical closeness to" all that is not God. However, characterized in those terms they are very abstract qualities indeed. Because it is asymmetrically related to God's creative blessing and ordered to a different end, God's "sovereignty" in relating to all else in providential care must have qualities that are different than, and do not map on to, qualities of God's "sovereignty" in relating in creative blessing. Wood makes a fruitful suggestion about how to characterize that difference.

Building on Niebuhr's formulation of God's providence, Wood notes that when the Fathers characterize God's relating in providential care, they tend to frame it in terms of the Greek word *pantocrator*. He cites studies by Jean-Pierre Batut of the Father's use of the word *pantocrator*: it is "[c]oined from the Greek verb *kratein* ['to maintain']; and an accusative pronoun . . ." *Pantocrator* "designates a relation to the universe on God's part, and it could be translated as 'he who holds all things together.'"[3] Note that the expression *pantocrator* holds together the three traditionally

---

[3] Jean-Pierre Batut, "'God the Father Almighty': Thoughts on a Disputed Term," *Communio* 26 (1999): 278–294. Cf. Batut, *Dieu le père tout-puissant* (Paris: Parole et Silence, 1998). Cited by Wood, *The Question of Providence*, p. 105, fn. 20.

distinguished aspects of providence as interdependent aspects: maintenance (*conservatio*), *concursus* (there is no good English translation; "running along-side" may come close), and governance, i.e., sovereignty (*gubernatio*). It does so in such a way that "sovereignty" is nuanced in a particular way. It frames "sovereignty" in terms of maintenance of creatures' interconnectedness and interdependence in their irreducible differences from one another *without* invoking images of God's power as "absolute and unrestricted power over" or "absolute and unrestricted control over" what goes on within the interactions among creatures.

In further support of Wood's proposal, it is worth noting that there has been some disagreement among translators of the Greek Nicene–Constantinopolitan Creed into English about how to translate *pantocrator* in the first article of the Creed. Perhaps the most common translation is "omnipotent," following the Latin translation of the term into *omnipotem*. However, for example, in his classic collection of ancient Christian texts, *Documents of the Christian Church*, Henry Bettenson translates it as "All-sovereign."[4] That obviously comports well with Wood's suggestion.

In "holding all things together," the Triune God is "prior" or "prevenient" in that it is God who always takes the initiative. In being "prior," God "takes the lead" in providing for creatures' well-being by bringing and "holding" together the resources for their well-being available *within* the limits of the ways in which they are situated in their present circumstances. That priority in "holding together" is one sort of "sovereignty."

Conceiving God's providential sovereignty as God's "holding together" what goes on among creatures is quite different from conceiving God's "sovereignty" as God's "controlling" what goes on. "Control" is exercised extrinsically, from "outside" the creatures that are "controlled," by power that is externally applied to them to

---

[4] London: Oxford University Press, 1943, p. 36.

cause them to change and interact in ways determined by the agent that exercises the power. As we saw in Chapter 3, construed as analogies for providence as God's control of creatures, terms like "sovereign," "kingly," and "Lord," too easily allow for, even invite, inferences that are highly problematic. However, those inferences are blocked when God's "sovereignty" in providential care is understood as the sovereignty of God's "holding all things together" in ways ordered to creatures' well-being in both absolutely general and particularly differentiated ways.

The sense in which the Trinity is "sovereign" in providential care when the latter is characterized in terms of the *pantocrator* can be further nuanced by a more detailed reflection on the implications of the claim that it is none other than the *Triune* God that is the *pantocrator*. Here, we reverse a traditional pattern of theological reflection on God's providence. The traditional move was to explain providence first, often in terms of the concept of the cosmos' *arche*. Only after that had been accomplished did it introduce the doctrine of the Trinity. It, thus, introduced the doctrine of the Trinity as a theological topic entirely extrinsic to providence. It ascribed providence, already fully explicated without reference to the Trinity, to the first "Person" of the Trinity. It did so simply because creative blessing is also ascribed to the first "Person" (cf. the Nicene Creed's opening: "I believe in God the Father almighty, maker of heaven and earth"). I want to explore here, in contrast with that pattern of thought, how Trinitarian doctrine of God can serve as the context within which to nuance further the sense in which the Trinity's sovereignty in providential care is the Triune God's prevenience, God's taking the initiative in working for creatures' well-being in their kinds.

Analyzed in the context of Trinitarian doctrine of God, the overlap between God relating in creative blessing and God relating in providential care can be expressed in the same short-hand formula for the pattern or *taxis* in which the Triune God relates in providential care: "The 'Father' exercises providential care through the "Son" in the power of the Spirit." That is identical to the formula for the triune God's *taxis* in creative blessing discussed in Chapter 3, except that "exercises providential care" is substituted for "creates."

Placing the *"Father"* in the lead role in the formula for the Trinity as such relating in providential care underscores that in providence the Triune God relates to all else, not in absolutely unqualified ways, but in ways expressive of qualities intrinsic to "what" it is to *be* Triunely God. Several features of "what" it is to be God, as that is expressed in the creative blessing strand of the economy, are qualities of God's sovereignty specifically in providential care. In that way, God's providential care of creatures expresses the intrinsic glory of God (in the primary reference of "glory") and is thus itself the "glory" of God in the economy (in "glory's" secondary reference).

Two qualities of the Trinity's sovereignty in providential care are its radical priority to creatures and the inherently nonviolent character of its providential care of creatures. Placing the first "Person" of the Trinity in the lead position in this formula underscores that the Triune God's relating in creative blessing entails that the distinction between Creator and creature is the fundamental ontological distinction. Recognizing the "Father" in the lead role in the Trinity's active providential relating underscores that providence is located in the radically prevenient and nonviolent quality of the creative blessing strand of the economy. Hence, in providential care the Triune God is nonviolent and radically prior to creatures in the order of reality, just as it is in creative blessing. Because it is prior in the order of reality, this way in which the Triune God relates is best characterized in terms of the way the "Father's" creative blessing on all else is characterized: providence is an ongoing relating by God *"to"* all reality other than God.

However, because of the asymmetric relation between God's relating in creative blessing and God's relating in providential care, it is precisely in regard to this "relating *to*" that the fundamental difference emerges between the sense in which God is "sovereign" in creative blessing and is "sovereign" in providential care. The difference is rooted in the different end each has. Each is ordered to a good for the creature here and now. The difference is this: in creative blessing ex nihilo, the Triune God is "sovereignly" in charge of an absolutely unrestricted relating that is ordered to the good for creatures that they are concretely actually real and inherently valuable here and now; however, in providential care, the Triune God is "sovereignly" in charge of a relating that is ordered to the "good" that they enjoy well-being in their kinds here and now through the Trinity's "holding together" of creatures in what is "going on" in their particular circumstances.

That the Triune God's providential care of creatures is ordered to their "well being in their kinds" implies another quality of God's sovereignty in providential care: in providential care, God is self-regulating. God's ways of relating in providential care to the end that creatures enjoy well-being is self-regulated by God to be appropriate both to each creature's particular kind of creatureliness and to the concrete particularities of its ever-changing contexts. This follows from God's radical prevenience in taking the initiative in providential care: given that prevenience, God's relating in providential care is "sovereignly" regulated by God to be appropriate to each creature's particularities. Such self-regulation in radically prevenient and nonviolent relating to creaturely "others" ordered to their well-being in their kinds just is God's "sovereignty" in providential care that "holds all things together."

In short, placing the first "Person" of the Trinity in the lead position in the formula underscores that the sense in which the Triune God is "sovereign" or exercises "kingly rule" specifically in providential care is nuanced by the fact that, in providential care, God faithfully expresses aspects of "what" it is to be the Triune God: generously generative in a self-regulating self-relating that is, in prevenient and nonviolent ways, a "holding together" of creatures that is ordered specifically to the well-being (rather than to the actualization of their reality and value) of genuine "others" that are "other" to God and to each other as creatures in their kinds rather than as "Persons" of the Trinity. As such, providential care is itself an aspect of the "glory" of God in its secondary reference.

The sense in which the Triune God exercises "kingly rule" specifically in providential care is further nuanced in ways stressed by the second phrase of the Trinitarian formula for providential care: the "Father" exercises providential care *through the* "*Son.*" In this Trinitarian formula "Son," of course, names the Second "Person" of the Triune God incarnate in the life of Jesus of Nazareth. The importance of linking the "Father's" prevenience (i.e., taking the initiative in providential care) to the "Son" is brought out by the iconographic tradition that depicts the risen Christ as the *pantocrator.* This underscores the point that the Triune God's relating to all else in providential care, even though it is an entailment of God's unrestricted and hence absolute sovereignty in creative blessing, is "restricted" by God's own self-regulating commitment to honor creatures' ontological integrity in providential care. Even (especially!) in Incarnation, God honors the creaturely otherness of Jesus by gracing his undistorted human creatureliness. Here is another reason why it is most aptly characterized as "holding creation together" in all that is "going on" rather than as unrestrictedly "controlling" all that is "going on."

The name "Son" denotes the One characterized in the Prologue to the Gospel of John as the "Word" of God that "was with God," "was God," "was in the beginning with God," through whom "all things came into being" (1:1–3a), and "became flesh and lived among us, and we have seen his glory, the glory as of a Father's only son, full of grace and truth" (1:14). This nuances in an additional way the sense in which the Triune God is "sovereign" in providence. As the "Word" of God, the "Son" is God's definitive self-expression of God's intrinsic glory (in its primary reference) in God's glory in the economy (in "glory's" secondary reference). Hence God's "sovereignty" in providential care is nuanced by the distinctive sense in which the Trinity is "sovereign" in relating to creatures in and through all that the Incarnate "Son" does and undergoes to keep long-standing liberative promises (this will be discussed more fully in Part III). In the latter strand of the economy, as canonically narrated, the Triune God relates to estranged creatures in a way best characterized as a relating that is at once "other than" and "close to" them on analogy with the way one human creature may relate to others as "one among many," but with one qualification. The qualification is that the "Son's" way of relating interpersonally are concurrently incomparably more radically "other than" and "close to" other human creatures than are the interhuman relations with which we are otherwise familiar.

John's use of "Word," *logos*, to name the "Son" has two additional connotations that also nuance the sense in which God is "sovereign" in providential care. I urged in Chapter 4 that, in John, *Logos* ought to be interpreted through the picture of "Wisdom" in Proverbs, and especially through the trope of "Lady Wisdom" in Proverbs 8.[5] If "Word" connotes that the "Father" exercises providential care through the "Son" as divine "rationality" or "intelligence," and if "Word" is understood in terms of "Lady Wisdom," the Triune God's exercise of providential care must be characterized as "rational" or "intelligent" in a doubly nuanced way. There are, after all, several distinguishable sorts of human "intelligence." They are not necessarily all equally appropriate analogs for the "rationality" of the Triune God's providential care of creatures.

First, the wise "rationality" or "intelligence" of such "sovereignty" is inseparable from certain emotion-like qualities: delight in and joy about the creatures whose well-being is being cared for.

---

[5] In Proverbs 8:29b-31 "Lady Wisdom" speaks for herself:

> When he [God] marked out the foundations of the earth'
> Then I was beside him, like a master worker;
> And I was daily his delight,
> Rejoicing before him always,
> Rejoicing I his inhabited world and delighting in the human race.

Hence it is analogous in particular to a high degree of human "emotional intelligence."

Second, God's "sovereignty" as wise self-regulation in providential care, when understood in ways guided by Proverbs' account of Wisdom, is more analogous to human "practical" intelligence that is canny about working ad hoc in a particular context to actualize particular ends, cognizant of many factors "going on" in the context but not relying on any one "theory" about what is "fundamentally going on." To say that the "Father" relates in providential care "through the Word" understood as "Wisdom" is to say that, in providential care, the Triune God holds all things together through a *logos* analogous to "know-how," to a *phronesis,* that makes for creatures' well-being.

The sense in which the Triune God exercises "kingly rule" specifically in providential care is yet more nuanced in ways stressed by the third phrase of the Trinitarian formula for providential care: the "Father" exercises providential care through the "Son" *"in the power of the Spirit."* In the context of the Nicene Creed, the Spirit is identified as the "Lord and giver of life." The Triune God's relating in providential care "in the power of the Spirit" is particularly ordered to sustaining the well-being of living creatures by providing the conditions that are necessary for life of all degrees of complexity.

In the third section, I urge that it is particularly apt to characterize that way of relating to creatures as "circumambient." The Triune God is self-regulatingly "sovereign" in providential care as it relates to human creatures circumambiently. "Circumambience" suggests that the Triune God's "sovereignty" in providential care is, however distantly, analogous to the way some particular climate and patterns of weather-change constantly move around human creatures, shaping their cultures and their daily lives, even in a way moving "through" them in a fashion that shapes their moods and without being a "violation" of their integrity. So, too, "circumambience" suggests that the Triune God's way of relating in providential care is, however distantly, analogous to the way in which a constant "rain" of subatomic "particles" flows around, over, and through all creatures, not as violations of their creaturely integrities, but as aspects of the make-up of the material world of which they are integral parts and which is essential to their well-being. Analogously, the Spirit is the "Lord and giver" of life to human creatures in regard to their complex capacities, not only for awareness of their proximate physical and socially constructed environments, i.e., "consciousness," but for their self-aware consciousness, i.e., "self-conscious consciousness" or "inwardness" or "interiority." The Trinity's relating circumambiently in providential care "in the power of the Spirit" shapes the proximate social contexts of human creatures' lives and the communicative media (whether by bodily movement, vocalizing, music, speech, writing, drawing, painting, sculpting, etc.) by which they express themselves to one another, which is essential to their well-being in those contexts.[6] The phrase "in the power of the Spirit" stresses that the Triune God's "sovereignty" in providential care is the sovereignty of, in John Taylor's phrase,[7] the "go-between God." Thus, God's sovereignty in providential care is nuanced as ordered, not only to creatures' well-being in general, but particularly to the well-being of human creatures' social and cultural life in community.

A Third Way the Triune God Relates to All Else: Eschatological Blessing

Here a third type of canonical scriptural narrative comes into play. We have already distinguished between narratives of God relating

---

[6] Surely that claim is fundamental to any Christian "theology of culture" or "theological aesthetics."

[7] John V. Taylor, *The Go-Between God: The Holy Spirit and the Christian Mission* (Oxford: Oxford University Press, 1972).

in creative blessing (and its entailment, providential care of creatures) and God relating by making and keeping liberative promises. A third sort of narrative renders the concrete way in which God goes about relating in eschatological blessing to what is not God. It has its own distinct narrative "logic." That "logic" rules out its conflation with the other types of canonical narratives of God relating to what is not God. The case for that distinctiveness is based on Claus Westermann's textual analyses in his commentary on Genesis 1–11[8] and his studies *Blessing*[9] and *Beginning and End in the Bible*.[10]

We have already discussed Westermann's distinction between what I am calling the "narrative logic" of canonical accounts of God promising and then faithfully enacting events that liberate or "deliver from bondage" and canonical accounts of God blessing creatively: the first move according to a "logic" of eventful and episodic deeds, and the second move according to a "logic" of ongoing steady-state of active relating.[11] There are many accounts of deeds of deliverance throughout canonical Scripture. In them, God relates punctiliarly to persons and communities in particular events in particular cultural, social, and historical contexts. Christian writers sometimes refer to the entire sequence of such events as "salvation history." Such accounts presuppose that God has "already" (in logical, not chronological, order) related in creative blessing so that there is something "there" for God to liberate if necessary. By contrast, God's ongoing steady-state creative relating is the condition of the possibility of God's liberative deeds in space and time. It constitutes creatures that are radically contingent in their dependence on God both for their very reality as beings

---

[8] *Genesis 1-11: A Commentary*, translated by John J. Scullion, S.J. (Minneapolis: Augsburg Publishing House, 1984).

[9] *Blessing*, tr. by Keith Crim (Philadelphia: Fortress Press, 1974), 65.

[10] Philadelphia: Westminster Press, 1972.

[11] Chapter 3, especially pp. 10 ff. and 20 ff.

"other" than God and for their intrinsic value. God's creative relating constitutes creaturely existence as a blessing in itself. Westermann forcefully protests Gerhard von Rad's characterization of creation narratives as accounts of the first event in salvation history. Given these quite different narrative logics, I have argued, canonical narratives of God relating creatively cannot be conflated with canonical narratives of God relating by making liberative promises, as though the former told just the first moment in the latter narrative.

Westermann goes further to distinguish a third kind of Christian canonical narrative. It is the narrative of God relating to all else to draw it to a long-promised eschatological consummation. In his two studies, *Blessing and Beginning and End in the Bible,*[12] Westermann urges that such canonical Christian narratives tell of that consummation as a promised blessing on creation. Eschatological blessing is explicitly promised in Old Testament prophetic writings, especially Isaiah, Jeremiah, and Ezekiel. Moreover, Westermann urges, the end of the Priestly creation narrative in Genesis 2:1–3 makes God's promise of the blessing of eschatological consummation coeval with God relating in creative blessing: "And on the seventh day God finished the work that he had done, and he rested on the seventh day and hallowed it, because on it God rested from the work that he had done in creation." The "rest" that marks eschatologically consummated human life, Westermann urges, is the blessing of the "eternal rest ... [that] has been suggested in the rest of the seventh day."[13]

So canonical scriptural narratives of God relating to draw all else to eschatological consummation are in one way like canonical narratives of God relating creatively and unlike canonical narratives of God relating by making and fulfilling liberative promises. Canonical narratives of both creative blessing and eschatological

---

[12] Philadelphia: Westminster Press, 1972.
[13] *Blessing*, tr. by Keith Crim (Philadelphia: Fortress Press, 1974), p. 65.

blessing are narratives of God relating in on-going, steady-state ways, whereas narratives of God relating by making and keeping liberative promises are accounts of episodic deeds of deliverance.

God relating to draw all else to an eschatological consummation is not *as such* an episodic way in which God liberates creatures from bondage or to delivers them from oppression. It might be liberative, but only if creatures are, in fact, in bondage. However, God's eschatological blessing is not contingent on creatures being in bondage, for it is primarily God relating in a second kind of blessing that transfigures and enhances creative blessing without negating or violating it. It is blessing added to blessing.

In three other respects, however, the narrative logic of canonical Christian accounts of God relating in eschatological blessing are quite different from the narrative logic of God relating in creative blessing. First, canonical narratives of God's eschatological blessing presuppose that God has "already" (in the order of reality; not temporally) related to all else in creative blessing.

Second, God's creative blessing is not narrated as the fulfillment of any promise. Apart from God relating creatively, there is nothing to which a promise could be made. Canonical New Testament accounts of God's inauguration of eschatological blessing, however, *are* narrated as the story of the fulfillment of a promise. The promise is coeval with creative blessing, but presuppose it while not being entailed by it. God's promise of eschatological blessing is logically independent of God's creative blessing. An entailment of the promise is that creatures' proximate contexts are in some way "promising" of a future that is not necessarily entailed by God's relating to them in creative blessing.

Third, as rendered in canonical New Testament narratives, the concrete way in which God goes about drawing creatures into eschatological blessing has a distinctive dynamic. It combines the "on-going, steady-state relating" of the narrative "logic" of God's creative blessing and the "episodic event" narrative "logic" of God's relating in deeds of deliverance.

On one hand, the Trinity's eschatological blessing has the form of a promise of an eschatological consummation that will be so radical a transformation of what creatures are by God's creative blessing as to be described as a "new creation." Yet it will be so faithful to the ontological integrity of human creatures as to be described as the "resurrection" of both "what" they have been, i.e., creatures, and "who" they have been, i.e., creatures with concretely particular unique identities. The promise constitutes a steady-state, on-going aspect of the ultimate context in which creatures are located by God's relating to them in eschatological blessing (along with the two other aspects of their ultimate context: God's creative blessing on them and God's reconciling initiative among them). God has not yet fully actualized that promise. If full actualization of that promise is what constitutes creation's "redemption," then creation, while undergoing redemption, is not yet "redeemed." So creatures continue to live in the context of the steady state of a divine promise, to which the appropriate human response is hope for its full actualization soon.

On the other hand, the canonically narrated Gospels' accounts of the ministry, passion, crucifixion and resurrection of Jesus of Nazareth often use Apocalyptic rhetoric to make a point about how God goes about concretely keeping the promise of eschatological consummation. As Ernst Kasemann,[14] J. Christian Beker,[15] and J. Louis Martyn[16] have pointed out in very different ways,[17] the Apostle Paul's reflections on the risen Christ make a similar point: The central sign of the inauguration of God's "eschatological rule" is the event of the resurrection of the crucified Jesus of Nazareth, the "first fruits" of the "new creation," by the power of the Spirit

---

[14] *New Testament Questions for Today.* Translated by W. J. Montague (Philadelphia: Fortress Press, 1969), pp. 82–108 and 108–136.

[15] *The Triumph of God: The Essence of Paul's Thought.* Translated by Loren T. Stuckenbruck (Minneapolis: Fortress Press, 1990).

[16] *Theological Issues in the Letters of Paul*, Part II. (Nashville, TN: Abingdon, 1997).

[17] Cf. ibid., pp. 176–183.

(Romans 1:4), and the pouring out of that eschatological Spirit, not just on selected individuals for particular purposes, but upon God's people as a whole (Acts 3).

That particular event is only the beginning of God's way of keeping the long-standing promise of eschatological consummation., However it is the concrete actuality of the *inauguration* of that beginning. As such, it is the concrete actuality of the inauguration of the beginning in this third strand of the economy of the Triune God's sovereignty, in the sense in which the Triune God is "sovereign" in this eschatological third strand of the economy. Accordingly, one aspect of creatures' proximate contexts is a tension between God's sovereignty in the already concretely actualized *inauguration* of God's keeping of eschatological promise and the not-yet full *actualization* of that promise.

The Triune God's drawing of creatures to eschatological consummation takes place within that tension. It can be considered a "movement" in history toward full actualization of God's promise. However, it cannot be considered to be a movement driven by historical "forces" that, however slowly, unfold potentialities already independently resident in creaturely resources that are ordered specifically to that actualization. It is not to be construed as the reality of "historical progress." Historical progress of some sort in certain aspects of society and culture may indeed be going on, say toward the elimination of slavery, or in technology, or the near-eradication of certain deadly diseases, or increases in literacy, etc. But if there is such "progress," it does not provide "evidence" or "signs" of God's drawing creatures toward eschatological consummation. Grounds for hope of radical fundamental and absolute systemic transformation of our unjust and oppressive proximate contexts lie, not in possibilities that can be identified in the resources human beings have at hand, but in the actuality of God's inauguration of God's process of keeping the promise of eschatological consummation – an inauguration that concretely happens in the resurrection of Jesus of Nazareth.

Its "now-actually-inaugurated, but-not-yet-fully-actualized-keeping-of-a-promise" dynamic fundamentally distinguishes the way the Triune God relates in eschatological blessing from both the way God relates in creative blessing and the way God relates in deeds of deliverance. Nonetheless, it shares with them a common pattern: in both the resurrection of the crucified Jesus and the outpouring of the Spirit, God relates in "sovereign" rule in a way that is concurrently radically "other" and radically "close" to creatures, each as the condition of the possibility of the other.

For example, the focus of the canonical Gospels' narratives on the life, ministry, crucifixion, and resurrection of Jesus as the inauguration of eschatological consummation emphasizes that this inauguration causes a discontinuity in human creatures' histories. It is a focus on Jesus as proclaimer of the imminence of God's eschatological kingly rule or "sovereignty," and the judgment that brings with it. It comes to a narrative climax in the resurrection of the crucified Jesus as the event in which the in-breaking of that kingdom is inaugurated. That marks a crisis in human societies, a cultural break. The inauguration of the beginning of God's eschatological rule does not evolve out of resources that human creatures have developed incrementally through their social histories. It injects into their social and cultural contexts a tension between this now actual inauguration of eschatological blessing and its not-yet full actualization.

So too, The Acts of the Apostles' initial focus on the pouring out of the Spirit as part of the inauguration of God's eschatological rule introduces a discontinuity in human creatures' interiorities and histories, a break that is experienced as an "in-breaking." The changes in creatures' interiorities and their new social experiences do not evolve out of resources that they have developed incrementally through their social and psychological histories. Rather, the in-breaking of God's sovereignty in eschatological "kingly rule" places human creatures in proximate contexts marked by a double tension: a tension between the now actual inauguration of eschatological blessing and its not-yet full actualization; and a tension between, on one side, their creaturely dependence on God's creative blessing which, as a contingent matter of fact is profoundly disordered by alienation, injustice, and hostility in both its public social aspects and its private individual aspects, and on the other side new, if fragmentary, moments of eschatological community and consciousness characterized by a just and reconciling love. God's way of inaugurating fulfillment of the promise of eschatological blessing in both Jesus' resurrection and the gift of the Spirit is an in-breaking into human beings' lived worlds of the Triune God that is radically "other than" them in the "sovereignty" of its eschatological "kingly rule."

At the same time, New Testament narratives of the way God goes about inaugurating eschatological blessing render God's "sovereign" relating as radically close to the creatures that are blessed. Especially narratives of Jesus' ministry stress that, sharing their common lot in suffering and oppression, he was one among many, often directly knowing what they were thinking and feeling without being told, closer to them than they could be to themselves. So, too, the Spirit is rendered as circumambiently present, relating to creatures more closely than they can relate to themselves. The Spirit is the "Lord and giver" of organic creatures' life. For human creatures, "Lord and giver of life" extends to their peculiarly complex "interior life," the set of attitudes, dispositions, passions, and beliefs by which each of them is oriented to their shared worlds and to one another in distinctive ways. God's relating to them in this radically close way is the condition of the possibility of both their bodily life and their subjectivity in the context of the double tension noted above. This is not just a relating to human creatures individual interiorities. It is also a relating that engages human creatures' inherent sociality by nurturing among them fragmentary societies genuinely structured by just and reconciling love. Moreover, those societies do not violate their creaturely societies by displacing them. Rather, they are a foretaste of that eschatological community that is the full actual-ization of what is inaugurated by the gift of the Spirit.

Given its combination of similarities and dissimilarities with canonical narratives of God's ways of relating in creative blessing and in making and keeping liberative promises, this third sort of narrative of the Trinity relating "sovereignly" to what is not God in eschatological blessing cannot be synthesized with them into a single coherent narrative of "salvation history."

In summary, eschatological blessing is a third strand in the Triune God's economy, braided together with God's relating to what is not God in creative blessing and in deeds of liberation. Taken together, the three ways in which God relates to what is not God are inseparable, bound together by the fact that it is the same Triune God who relates to all else in each of them. That it is one and the same Trinity who relates to what is not God in each of these ways does not erase their distinctiveness as irreducibly different ways in which God goes about relating to what is not God. However, they are bound together in a certain asymmetrical order. The asymmetry among these three ways in which God relates grounds and preserves the irreducibility of their distinctiveness from one another. To review, the asymmetry looks something like this. In the order of reality (although not necessarily in the order of our coming to understand God in faith, hope, and love), the Triune God relating in creative blessing presupposes only God. God is freely and faithfully self-relating when relating in creative blessing. But the Triune God relating both in eschatological blessing and by making and keeping liberative promises presupposes not only the reality of God, but also the reality of creatures. Those latter two ways in which God relates presuppose that God also relates to bless creatively. If no creatures are constituted and preserved by God's creative blessing, then there is nothing either to consummate escha-tologically or to liberate or deliver if oppressed in bondage.

What I particularly want to urge here is that the Triune God's exercise of eschatological "sovereignty" is in no way logically necessitated by God relating in creative blessing. That can be brought out by noting the different ends to which each sort of relating is ordered. In creative blessing, God is freely and faithfully self-committed to the well-being of finite creatures so long as they exist. Hence, it entails their providential care. However, nothing about the freedom or the faithfulness of God' relating in creative blessing ordered to *finite* creatures' actual reality and goodness for their own sakes as finite creatures also necessarily entails that God's entire creative project must persist everlastingly. Nor does it necessarily entail that any particular creature will exist everlastingly. Nor does God's creative blessing necessarily entail creatures' participation in their own creaturely way in the communion-in-love that constitutes the Triune life. God blesses creatively solely to the end of their well-being for their own sakes as finite creatures. In relating in that way, God's intrinsic self-expressive glory is reflected in actual, concrete creatures in every here and now. However, that does not entail that God's creative blessing must in all self-consistency sustain an everlasting sequence of heres and nows. Realization of the goal of creatures' well-being in which they can be actualized reflections of God's intrinsic self-expressive glory is not necessarily deferred until the end of an extended cosmic process through which creation is ultimately "actualized." Rather, it is realized in the actual reality of finite creatures in their kinds here and now. Because that is the case, creative blessing cannot be said necessarily to entail an eschatological consummation as the future full actualization of creative blessing.

Indeed, it is seriously problematic to hold that the end to which God blesses creatively – God's "purpose" or "intent" in creating – just *is* creation's full actualization as "creation" in an eschatological consummation. If it were, of course, God relating in creative blessing would indeed entail God also relating in eschatological blessing. In all self-consistency, God would necessarily have to draw all that God creates to eschatological consummation. Creating would be no more than (and, to be sure, no less than) the promise of eschatological consummation. God relating in eschatological blessing would be just another way of characterizing God's relating in creative blessing. That thesis is problematic, however, because of what it implies about realities other than God, creatures whose history of interactions constitute the postulated process leading up to eschatological consummation. It implies that none of those realities – including ourselves – are fully actual creatures yet, for creation will not be actualized until its full eschatological consummation. It further implies an instrumentalist view of whatever it is we actually are in every here and now: disposable stages in a cosmic process in which whatever is actual now is simply the necessary preconditions for the following stages of the process, and ultimately the preconditions for the final full actualization of creation. We might be potential human creatures, but we are not yet actual human creatures. And if not yet actualized creatures, we would not have the dignity of which fully actualized creatures require an unqualified respect. That is morally very problematic.

The irreducible difference between the ends to which the Triune God relates, respectively, in creative blessing and in eschatological blessing can also be brought out from the side of God relating in eschatological blessing. The narrative logic of Christian canonical accounts of God relating in eschatological blessing turns on the point that, in actualizing eschatological blessing, God fulfills a promise to bless creatures in ways that go beyond the gifts God gives in creative blessing. In eschatological blessing, God is self-committed, not merely to the well-being of creatures as defined by their finite creaturely kinds (although God in creative blessing is concurrently *also* self-committed to those ends), but also to their eschatological flourishing in ways that exceed the goods that make for their creaturely well-being. Consequently, God's eschatological blessing cannot be construed simply as the goal of God's relating in creative blessing. If it were, the "blessing" of eschatological blessing would not be an "excess" beyond the gifts of already actualized creaturely blessing, but rather simply the final actualization of creaturely blessing.

Hence, considered both from the perspective of God's way of relating in creative blessing and from the perspective of God's way of relating in eschatological blessing, as each of them is rendered in the canonical narratives, it is appropriate to stress that God's eschatological blessing is a second free self-commitment above and beyond God's free self-commitment to creatures in creative blessing. God's eschatological blessing may be construed as equi-primordial with God's free self-commitment in creative blessing. It may be construed as a gift in which God is faithful not to violate the finite creatureliness of the recipients of the gift. All the same, it is a gift above and beyond the gift of creaturely reality. Such is the asymmetry among the God's three particular and irreducibly distinct ways of relating to all that is not God, as narrated in canonical Christian narratives.

The Triune God's "Sovereignty" in the Register of Eschatological Blessing

The Triune God's way of relating to all else in eschatological blessing can be expressed in a short-hand formula for the *taxis* in which the Triune God relates to draw creatures into eschatological consummation: "The Spirit sent by the 'Father' through the 'Son'' draws creation toward its eschatological consummation." The particular *taxis* or pattern of relations among the "Persons" of the Trinity in that formula privileges a specific vocabulary for the qualities of the glory of God (in the phrase's second reference) self-expressed in God's sovereignty in eschatological blessing.

Placing the "Spirit" in the lead position stresses two points about that vocabulary. For one, placing the "Spirit" in the lead position in discussion of the sovereignty of God's rule in God's "eschatological kingdom" calls for a vocabulary that is consonant with the Spirit's noncoercive and nonviolating way of relating both freely and "interiorly" to self-consciously conscious creatures such as human agents. The Spirit is said to "blow" freely like the wind to "inspire," "instruct," "enlighten," and "empower" human creatures to be courageous, to be joyous, to be wise, to be creative, to be knit into communities. The common life of these communities aims to be shaped as an appropriate response to the way God has related to them in and through the life-trajectory of Jesus, and above all to love both God and fellow human creatures, especially their enemies, as their neighbors.

Second, where the "Father's" way of relating in the economy is perhaps best expressed with the preposition "to" and the incarnate "Son's" way of relating is best expressed with the preposition "among" (as in "one among many"), the Spirit's way of relating in the economy is best expressed with the adjective "circumambient." Placing the "Spirit" in the lead position calls for a vocabulary in discussion of the sovereignty of God's rule in God's "eschatological kingdom" that is consonant with the way the Spirit's "radiating" circumambience is rendered in Scriptural accounts of the Spirit's presence.

That is particularly important as a block to use of an alternative vocabulary that would characterize the Triune God's "sovereignty" in eschatological blessing as just one more instance of God's exercise of absolutely unconditioned "sovereignty" in blessing creatively ex nihilo. We have seen that even that sovereignty cannot be construed as the sovereignty of sheer impersonal force because it is a nonviolating power exercised by the "Father" wisely (through the "Son") and ordered to the goods of creatures' lives in their kinds for as long as they last ("in the power of the Spirit"). In creative blessing, the Triune God's relating to reality other than God is ordered to two creaturely "goods": creatures' concrete actuality and their goodness in their own right as creatures. As we have seen, God's creative blessing and its entailment, providence, are ordered to that end in a way that is faithful to the fundamental Creator/

creature distinction in virtue of which God is absolutely unrestricted by any other reality in creative blessing ex nihilo. The Triune God relating in eschatological blessing, on the other hand, is ordered to a different end, viz., creatures' eschatological flourishing. That difference in ends privileges use of a different vocabulary (one associated with narratives of the third "Person" and its ways of relating to creatures) to characterize distinctive sense in which God is "sovereign" in the ways God goes about blessing eschatologically.

Placing "Spirit" in the lead position in the Trinitarian formula for God's relating in eschatological blessing also blocks any suggestion that God's sovereignty in such relating may be characterized as analogous to God's "sovereignty" in the interpersonal relation of an "I" to "Thous" among whom the "I" has come to be present as one among many. That "I–Thou" rhetoric is consonant with characterization of the incarnate "Son's" way of relating as "one among many" in the Trinity's relating by way of Incarnation to reconcile estranged creatures to God. The incarnate Son is a human "I" and does encounter others and lay moral obligation on those whom he encounters. But the Spirit is as circumambient as the wind, blowing unpredictably as it wills and radiating "through" us. In that regard, it is radically "free from," and therewith "radically other" than, the creatures about whom the Spirit is circumambient. Correlatively, the Spirit is "radically close" to them, knowing them better than they can know themselves.

The second phrase of the Trinitarian formula, "sent by the 'Father,'" stresses, as it has in other contexts, the Triune God's ontological prevenience relative to creatures in each of the three strands of God's economy. That "priority" to creatures is the basis of God's "sovereignty." That in eschatological blessing the "Father" sends the *Spirit* in particular to draw creatures toward eschatological consummation underscores that the Trinity's sovereignty in eschatological blessing lies in God's self-regulating how God goes about relating to creatures preveniently in eschatological blessing, viz., in the Spirit's "circumambient" way of relating to creatures. We have seen that the Triune God's sovereignty in creative blessing, as an absolutely unconditioned "relating to" creatures, can not to be understood to imply God's absolute "control" of creatures that violates their ontological integrity. It cannot imply that precisely because it is the on-going steady-state condition of the very possibility of their concrete actuality and goodness in their own right in the first place. Nonetheless, we have also seen that taken as the *only* way in which God "sovereignly" relates to all else in the economy, God's creative blessing it is open to having that very inference drawn. The point being made here is that the Triune God's sovereignty in *eschatological* blessing is also an on-going steady-state condition of the possibility of something: it is the condition of the possibility of living creatures' actually beginning to undergo, in community, a transformation into the eschatological life that the already resurrected crucified Jesus lives, a transformation that is not yet fully actualized. As the condition of the possibility of a "now actually inaugurated, not yet fully actualized" eschatological life, the Triune God in the *taxis* the Spirit "sent by the 'Father'" relates, not "to" creatures but "circumambiently," around and radiantly through creatures in eschatological blessing. Characterizing the Triune God's relating to creatures in that fashion does not invite the inference that God's relating to creatures violates the integrity of their creaturely "otherness" to the Creator by "controlling" them and all that goes on among and within them. It serves to nuance the sense in which the Triune God is "sovereign" in such a way as to block any inference that to say "God is sovereign" means "God's power controls all creaturely interactions."

The third phrase in the Trinitarian formula for God's eschatological blessing, "Through the 'Son,'" significantly qualifies the triune God's "sovereignty" in eschatological rule in an additional way. That the Triune God draws creatures into eschatological life "through the 'Son'" underscores that God's "sovereignty" in eschatological blessing is exercised as the sovereignty of the self-same *pantocrator* in providence. Like the Triune God's sovereignty in providential care, God's sovereignty in eschatological blessing is a sovereignty in circumambiently "holding all things together" in "what goes on."

What distinguishes the sense in which God's eschatological rule as *pantocrator* is "sovereign" from the sense in which God's providential rule as *pantocrator* is "sovereign" is the particular "good" of creatures to which it is ordered: their eschatological "flourishing," blossoming, and thriving in their kinds, rather than their creaturely well-being. The Trinity's sovereignty in eschatological blessing "holds all things together" as *pantocrator* precisely in its drawing "all that is going on" toward eschatological consummation, beginning an ongoing transfiguration of creaturely human life in the direction of "eschatological life" here and now. That beginning of the fulfillment of a promise that is coeval with God relating in creative blessing was inaugurated by the resurrection of Jesus, the "Son" incarnate. But it was not entailed *by* creative blessing. It is a gift above and beyond the good to which creative blessing and providential care are ordered. It is in that sense "grace" that enhances created "nature." As scripturally narrated, God's exercise of eschatological sovereignty is faithful to the specific creaturely finitude of human beings in their interpersonal, social, and cultural inter-relationships with one another across time. Hence, although eschatological blessing is ordered to a flourishing that is above and beyond the good of creaturely existence and value, it is nonetheless consonant with the good of creation, not a negation, violation, or substitute for it. The good of eschatological blessing may be a "new creation," but it is a *creatio ex vetere*, (creation from the old) not a *creatio ex nihilo* (creation from nothing).

In drawing creatures toward eschatological consummation, the Triune God, with the Spirit in the lead position, exercises eschatological sovereignty as *pantocrator* "through the 'Son'" who is God's wisdom Incarnate. In eschatological blessing, it is wisdom about how to go about drawing particular creatures in particular situations into eschatological blessing in ways that are consonant with God's loving three-fold faithfulness: God's faithfulness to Godself, to God's own commitments, and to the creaturely integrity of all that with which God is actively relating.

"Sovereignty" characterized in that way blocks or weakens two types of theologically problematic inferences. It blocks any inference that God's "sovereignty" consists in God's "control of" or a "control over" what goes on. As the One who draws creatures into the actualization of eschatological blessing, the Trinity is sovereign in "working" with "what is going on" among and within creatures and not by controlling them extrinsically. Second, it fails to warrant any inference that the Trinity has a systematic "plan" generated by God's timeless theory about how the "drawing" into actualized eschatological blessing must happen, given some timeless fundamental blueprint God has for creation as a whole. As canonically narrated, the *Logos* through which the Spirit sent by the "Father" draws creation into actualized eschatological blessing is not that sort of "intelligence" or "mind." It may or may not be the case that the Triune God does have something analogous to a timeless theoretical blueprint for the entire "history" of creation as a whole. I am not arguing that it is false to claim that God does have such a "plan." I only argue that canonical Christian scriptural narratives do not adequately warrant analogical predication of such a "plan" to God.

To claim that, in eschatological blessing, the Spirit draws creatures into eschatological blessing "through the 'Son'" also reminds us that the Spirit is the "Spirit of the 'Son'" as much as it is the "Spirit of the 'Father.'" The Trinity relating circumambiently in eschatological blessing "in the power of the Spirit" gives human creatures new eschatological life that is nothing less than the Spirit's presence to their human interiority. That eschatological life is an interpersonal social life defined in terms of holy love: "God's love has been poured into our hearts through the Holy Spirit that has been given to us" (Romans 5:5). God's love "poured into our hearts" just *is* the Spirit shaping human creatures' subjectivities, "generating" eschatologically new life in community that is itself defined as human love for God and for others, especially for enemies. That love is concretely defined by the story of the Incarnate "Son's" life-trajectory. Just that love is the fundamental quality of the Triune God's sovereignty in relating to all else in eschatological blessing with the Spirit in the lead "through the Son," whose Spirit it is. It is just that love that is wise about how to draw particular creatures into eschatological blessing.

In eschatological blessing, the Triune God's "sovereignty" is the sovereignty of a love that is not only wise, but also holy. Its holiness is its persistent resistance of creatures' own resistance to being related to in eschatological blessing (in contradistinction to God's resistance to their resistance to God's creative blessing and providential care). It is an implacable resistance; but it is the resistance of God's *love,* where "love" is defined by the identity of the "Son" Incarnate. The eschatological life into which the Spirit draws creatures beginning here and now (and is ultimately fully actualized in a creaturely human sharing in the communion in love that is the Triune God's very life) is faithfully expressed in the "Son's" love for the "Father" and the "Father's" love for the "Son." The Triune God's "Sovereignty" in eschatological blessing is the "sovereignty" the Spirit exercises in drawing creatures "through the 'Son'" into that "new creation," the "eschatological kingdom." It is the "sovereignty" of that holy love.

In addition to warranting characterization of the Triune God's "sovereignty" in eschatological blessing as "good," "wise," and "holy" in distinctive senses of those terms, the way God relates in eschatological blessing, as narrated in canonical scripture, warrants ascription of hospitality and beauty. God's relating in eschatological blessing is freely and faithfully expressive of the Triune God's singular identity in a way that is conceptually different from the "generosity" of God's creative blessing. The generosity of the Triune God in creative blessing lies in God's giving creatures time and space to be themselves in their kinds as genuinely "other" than God. It does not lie in God's drawing them in their creaturely realities into the Triune God's life of community in joyous communion. In contrast, as God drawing all else into a participation in God's own life, God's eschatological blessing faithfully expresses God's intrinsic hospitality. However, coeval with creative blessing, and ordered to a good that goes above and beyond the good to which creative blessing is ordered, it nonetheless does in its own fashion also faithfully expresses God's intrinsic generosity.

In being ordered specifically to a good consisting of creatures' eschatological consummation, God relating to human creatures also faithfully expresses the overwhelming attractiveness of God's eschatological glory. That glory draws, indeed lures, human creatures to flourish in lives shaped by attitudes, dispositions, passions, and beliefs that are appropriate responses to that glory. Just as we have no cognitive access to the "causal link" between the Triune God and creatures in God's active relating to what is not God in creative blessing and providential care, so we have no cognitive access to the metaphysics of the Triune God's "drawing" creatures toward eschatological consummation. Perhaps the closest analogue to such "drawing" in human creaturely life is the power of various sorts of beauty to attract human beings, drawing them not merely to attend to what strikes them as beautiful but, beyond that, to love them in deep ways that, precisely by binding them to what they love, empower and free them to live more richly. This is not the place to outline a theological aesthetics. It is sufficient to recall that the analogy is fitting: Part I argued that the intrinsic glory of the living Trinity, which is the larger conceptual context within which we are analyzing the "sovereignty" of God and its qualities, is God's self-expressive radiance that is inherently attractive and warrants ascription of "beauty" to both the Triune God's intrinsic self-expressive self-relating and God's faithful self-expression *ad extra* in the economy. In particular, it is the beauty of the concrete way in which God inaugurates eschatological blessing, i.e., the beauty of the resurrection of the crucified Jesus of Nazareth.

* * * * *

Part of the strategy of this essay's effort to reconceive the power that is properly attributed to the Triune God is to reverse the traditional conceptual order of notions of God's power and notions of God's sovereignty. This chapter has proposed a reconception of the "sovereignty" attributed to God as the conceptual context and precondition within which to reconceive God's power. It has proposed a reconception of God's 'sovereignty,' not solely on the basis of God's way of relating to all else in creative blessing, but on the basis of an interplay between God's way of relating in providential care and God's way of relating in eschatological blessing. Doing the latter has led us to an unsystematic account of the sense in which the Triune God is "sovereign" in relating to all else. It is "unsystematic" in that it necessarily toggles back and forth between two different registers in which God's "sovereignty" must be described, two different vocabularies in which it must be characterized. In both, claims are made about the sense in which God is "sovereign" in the economy that are well-warranted by canonical Christian Scriptural accounts of how God goes about relating in providential care and in eschatological blessing. It is "unsystematic" in that those two sets of claims cannot be synthesized in a single systematic account of God's "sovereignty" without obscuring or minimizing features of each that distinguish it from the other, and thereby distorting it. We turn now to analyze the senses in which "power" may be ascribed to the triune God, also in two different registers, and in the conceptual context of this chapter's exploration of two registers of senses of God's "sovereignty."

6 | Excursus: Must God Have Only One Eternal Purpose?

An Objection and a Counter-Question

There is an important objection to the way my discussion of God's sovereignty has been framed. The objection comes from the perspective of the sorts of Christian theism that I have dubbed the "traditional" doctrine of God. This is an appropriate point in the development of an account of God's power to address the objection directly.

In brief, the objection is that the account promoted here of God's "glory" and "sovereignty" (and accordingly, the yet-to-be-developed account of God's "power" as well) rests on the thesis that each of the Trinity's three ways of relating to all else (viz., in creative blessing, in eschatological blessing, and in liberative promise making and promise keeping) has a different end or *telos* in a different sort of "good" for creatures. Against that stands a traditional claim that God's singular intrinsic reality necessarily entails that God can only be said to relate to all else in a way that has but one overall *telos* for the economy. It looks as though this proposal at least implicitly is "anti-teleological" in its account of the Triune God's way of relating to all else.

To be sure, the objection could acknowledge, the traditional view recognizes in regard to providential care that God relates to realities other than God in a multitude of ways to a multitude of proximate ends. However, it is traditional to say or assume that all of the ways in which the Triune God relates to all else are ordered to one and only one ultimate goal. God may have particular purposes in relating to

Eve or Abram or Moses or Mary or Jesus or Paul, or even to Balaam's ass, to actualize particular proximate goals. However, a single ultimate divine purpose must subsume all such proximate goals. It must order them to the realization of the single overarching ultimate goal of all of God's relating *ad extra*. In that way, God's ultimate purpose integrates God's more proximate goals within a single overarching movement. Any account of God's economy that does not do that fails to comport adequately with "what" God most fundamentally *is*, i.e., comport with the utter singularity of God's being.

As we have noted, God's economy has traditionally been understood to have four major moments: In the first, God relates to create; in the second, creatures fall out of communion with God and into estrangement from God, with all its consequences, viz., bondage to sin, evil, and death; in a third moment, God relates to reconcile estranged creatures through the ministry, crucifixion, resurrection, and ascension of Jesus Christ, the Incarnate Word of God; and in the final moment, God relates to consummate creation eschatologically. It is also traditional, the objection continues, to hold that God actualizes a single overall purpose through this four-moment movement. It is because the Triune God is singular or "One" that God's economy must be said to be a singular, if complex, whole teleologically ordered to a single *telos*.

Different theologians identify God's overall goal in importantly different ways. Each brings with it a different picture of the movement itself. For example, in the late second century Irenaeus seems to characterize the economy as a maturational process through which human beings, created immature and inexperienced, collectively and individually become fully actualized and capable of sharing eschatologically in Jesus Christ's unique fellowship with God, which is the goal of the entire movement. According to M. D. Chenu, OP,[1] in the thirteenth century Thomas Aquinas characterizes the overall

[1] "The Plan of St. Thomas Summa Theologiae," *Review Thomiste*, March, 1939.

economy in his *Summa Theologiae* as a cosmological movement of reality other than God in an *exitus* out of God through increasing differentiation and then increasing integration in an eschatological *reditus* to God, which is God's one goal for the whole movement. According to other traditions, notably among some Reformed theologians in the seventeenth century, God's glory is manifested in both God's justice in eternally decreeing the damnation of fallen creatures and God's mercy in decreeing the election of a few for salvation. In this approach, the entire economy is characterized as a soteriological movement. It is told as a salvation history whose every event executes God's eternal decree – including the Fall[2] itself and its (logically secondary) remedy in the crucifixion of the Incarnate Son of God, who is sent in response to the consequences of the "Fall" (Christological *infralapsarianism*). This movement unfolds in time the eternal decree that God's glory be manifested. For Karl Barth in the twentieth century, the overall goal of God's various ways of relating to all else is to actualize God's eternal decree to enter into covenant relation *ad extra* with a particular "other," the particular humanity of the eternal Son of God Incarnate, Jesus Christ. The overall movement to that goal – except for the impossible possibility of sin – is the unfolding of the logical implications of that one eternal decree: Because Christ's humanity is intrinsically social, the creation of fellow human beings is required. Because fellow human creatures are bodied, the creation of the physical world is required. Because God has eternally decreed to be in covenant fellowship with the Incarnate Son, Jesus Christ must be born into that world whether or not creatures have "fallen" (Christological *supralapsarianism)*. Because in the fall Jesus' fellow human creatures are estranged from God, Jesus' reconciling death is unavoidable. Because God eternally decrees that God's covenant fellowship with Jesus and his human covenant partners be actualized and manifested in an eschatological

---

[2] Cf., *The Book of Confessions*, "The Westminster Confession of Faith," (Louisville, KY: The Presbyterian Church (USA), 1999), ch. III and ch. V.4.

consummation, the resurrection of the crucified Jesus is required. This is a logical, not a chronological, sequence although it is played out in time as a "history." For Barth "the eternal covenant which God has decreed in Himself as the covenant of the Father with His Son as the Lord and Bearer of human nature"[3] is the "inner basis."[4] not only (as Barth explicitly has it) of creation, but of every other moment in the economy moving toward the actualization of God's eternal decree, except sin.

This variety shows that traditional insistence on the singularity of God's overall goal provides plenty of conceptual space within which identification of its single overall goal can be worked out in different ways. All of them assume that God's ways of relating to all else are purposive, i.e., are teleological. And they all assume that God's *telos* is and must be singular.

In contrast with that, the objection goes, it looks as though the proposal urged here would, if adopted, require Christian doctrine of God to abandon an internally consistent teleological understanding of God's economy as a single overall movement ordered to a single end. That violates a central traditional claim: there may be room for theological disagreements about how best to characterize that one end to which God's active relating *ad extra* is ordered; but, the objection goes, there is no room in a conceptually coherent Christian doctrine of God for disagreement about the claim that the one Triune God has but one ultimate *telos* to which and by which God's economy is ordered.

Meeting that objection requires challenging that basic assumption. Hence my counter-question is this: why *must* God be said to have only one eternal purpose? For what Christian *theological* reason must a Trinitarian doctrine of God hold that in the economy (in the broadest sense of that term) God can have only one overall goal or *telos*? This is not to challenge the traditional claim that

---

[3] *Church Dogmatics* (Edinburgh: T. & T. Clark, 1958, III/1), p. 97
[4] Ibid.

God's relations to all else are teleological. It is only to question the necessity of ascribing to God only a single *telos*.

A Roadmap of What Follows

I suggest that insistence on the singularity of God's overall goal in the economy generates serious systematic problems for Trinitarian Christian theology. I want then to urge that acknowledgement of the singularity of God's reality or "being" does not *necessarily* entail that God has only one overall goal. That, I suggest, opens conceptual space for this book's overall argument.

The following argument moves through three steps. First, we review theological reasons for insisting on the importance of a single overall *telos* for God's economy. Then, second, we review three sorts of ways in which warranting the claim that God (must) have but one overarching *telos* in the economy by appeal to canonical Christian Scripture ends up distorting other central Christian theological reality claims. This exhibits what is theologically problematic about identifying some one Scripturally warranted overall *telos* of God's economy. At the same time, it shows that the root of the problem does not lie in teleological patterns of thought just because they are "teleological." It lies rather in a theological over-reach that presumes to be able to make broader reality claims about God and God's ends than we are in a position to warrant. Rebuttal of theological reasons given to justify insistence on the singularity of God's *telos* in the economy concludes the chapter. The upshot of the chapter's overall argument is to commend an account of God's sovereignty that is significantly more modest in scope that most "traditional" accounts.

Three Reasons for the Traditional View

According to much of the Christian tradition, one rationale for the claim that God can have only one overarching goal for the various ways in which God relates to all else follows from the nature of God's intellect. The argument goes something like this (I take Thomas Aquinas' explanation of God's intellect in *Summa Theologiae* I, Qu. 14 to be paradigmatic of "traditional" theological doctrines of God): if we attribute to God any of a family of terms like "know" and "understand," we can only do so as names for acts of "intellect." So we attribute "intellect" to God.

But what is "intellect"? Begin with the premise that intrinsic to the soul of a bodied human being is the capacity to be inwardly "formed" by the nonmaterial "form" of another material creature. A human knower passively takes in the "form" of the known creature through the knower's bodily sensory experience. The knower's sense experience of the known object is made possible by the material bodiliness of the known creature. A human knower has the capacity actively to abstract that nonmaterial "form" (or "species") of the known creature from that sensory experience. Thereby the knower is itself so "in-formed" by the essence or form of the known creature as to know it for "what" it is (in different contexts call it the "form," "essence," or "nature" of the known). Because in human creatures intellect is a power of a nonmaterial soul that is united with a material body, however, it is a power whose openness to the world is constricted by the materiality of its body. Thomas holds it to be a universal, i.e., metaphysical, truth about reality that "the immateriality of a thing is the reason why it is cognitive" (Qu. 14, art. 1), i.e., has the power called "intellect." Accordingly, it is appropriate to attribute "intellect" to God as well as to human creatures: "Since ... God is the highest degree of immateriality, ... it follows that [God] occupies the highest place in knowledge" (Qu. 14, art. 1).

However, the sense in which God has "intellect" and thereby "knows" things is very different than the sense in which human creatures have "intellect" and "know" things. The difference follows from the claim that God's being is absolutely "pure" actuality. It is not a composite of "actuality" and "potentiality." Because "potentiality" is precisely the potentiality to undergo some sort of change, and God's substance is free of potentiality, God cannot undergo any sort of change. It follows that God is incapable of undergoing any change in the act of knowing.

More fundamentally, given God's pure actuality, it follows that there is no possibility of God undergoing the "change" from existence to nonexistence (cf. Qu. 4). Accordingly, to say that God's being is "pure actuality" is to say that God's "essence" is simply "to exist" *a se*. Hence, given God's absolute simplicity, in God "to exist" and "to know" are one and the same simple act (Qu. 14, art. 1, ad. 2). In God, "knowing" something is not the actualization of God's potentiality to know that thing. Thus God's "knowing" is not, as it is for human creatures, the actualization of the potential that intellect provides to know a particular thing. Rather in God, to know or to understand just *is* God's "substance and pure act" (Qu. 14, art.1, ad. 1; Qu. 14, art. 4). Furthermore, because time is the measure of change and there is no change of any sort possible in God's being, God's being, and therewith God's knowing (which is one and the same as God's being), is, unlike human creatures' knowing, time-less, i.e., it is eternal. It does not go through successive steps, which take time. It is not "discursive" (Qu. 14, art.7). The sense in which we may attribute "intellect" to God is best characterized as an all-at-once universally comprehensive vision (cf. Qu. 14, art. 12) of all creatures in every "time zone" of the universe from creation to eschaton.

Moreover the relation between God's knowing things and the things God knows is the opposite of the relation between human creatures' knowing things and the things they know. A human creature's act of knowing something presupposes that the thing known exists independent of its being known. The human knower's knowing is true when the in-"formation" of the knower con-"forms" to the "form" that makes the known thing to be what it is. But God does not know things insofar as they exist independently of God's knowing. Rather "God causes things *by* [(emphasis added)]

God's intellect, since [God's] being is [God's] act of understanding; and hence [God's] knowledge must be the cause of things insofar as [God's] will is joined to it. Hence the knowledge of God as the cause of things is usually called the *knowledge of approbation*" (Qu. 14, art. 8).

Finally, because God's intellect is absolutely immaterial, unlike human creatures' body-located intellects, it is absolutely unrestricted. Hence the scope of God's one simple act of knowing in eternal "vision" is absolutely universal. It simultaneously (Qu. 14, art. 13) knows actual things as actual and possible things as possible (Qu.14, art. 10 and ad 3); necessary things as necessary and contingent things as contingent (Qu. 14, art.13); what has been as past, what will be as future, what is present as present. Because it is eternal all this "knowing" is "simultaneously whole" in its "presentiality" to God's "sight" (cf. Qu. 14, art. 13).

It is this "simultaneous whole" that brings us back to our question of why God can have only one overarching goal for the various ways in which God relates to all else. The content of the cognitive "vision" that eternal God's intellect has of temporal creation is ordered as a coherent whole. For Thomas that ordering into a whole just *is* God's providence: "[T]he providence of God is nothing other than the notion of the *order* of all things towards an end" (Qu. 22, art.2; emphasis added). For Thomas, "providence" is God's comprehensive ordering of all creaturely change in time. All of the ways in which God relates to what is not God – in regard equally to creative blessing, eschatological blessing, and the making and keeping of liberative promises, all as witnessed in Christian scripture – are "providential." They are all moments in God's providence. As such, they are ordered to one another in a definite pattern within the overall movement of providence to a single (eschatological) *telos*.

It is God that causes all things and all changes in creation to be ordered into a whole by being ordered to a single end. Since, as we have just seen, "God causes things by [God's] intellect, since [God's] being is [God's] act of understanding; and hence [God's] knowledge must be the cause of things insofar as [God's] will is joined to it," it follows that the ordering must be said to be done by God's intellect. Given "that God knows all things, both universal and particular" (Qu. 22, art.2), it follows that in regard to providence we are dealing here with God as the "universal cause." Because God is the "universal cause," nothing whatever can escape God's providence (cf. Qu 22, art.2 ad 1). This is a prime example of God understood as the cosmic *arche*.

Thomas thinks the "universal cause/particular cause" distinction helps him to solve a sticky problem: "[O]ne who is in charge of a particular thing," Thomas writes, "excludes all defects from what is subject to his care as far as he can; whereas one who provides universally allows some little defect to remain, lest the *good of the whole* be hindered" (emphasis added). So precisely as creator self-committed to the providential care of creatures, God "allows" certain defects that damage some creatures to remain in the good creation. That addresses the age-old question of how come God's good creation includes "natural evils." "Hence, corruption and defects in natural things are said to be contrary to some particular nature, yet they are in harmony with the *plan of universal nature* [emphasis added], inasmuch as the defect in one thing yields to the good of another, or even to the universal good.... [F]or if all evil were prevented, much good would also be absent from the universe" (Qu. 22.2 ad 2). The "good of the *whole*" is the one *telos* toward which all of God's ways of relating to all else are ordered. God's "plan" describes both that "good" and how it will be actualized for creation as a whole. Note that the argument requires the notion that what God creates is the sort of "whole" that can have its own *singular* "good," and that God has a "plan" of that "whole" that is being worked out in God's "universal" providential causality.

Thomas is clear about at least two features of the "good of the whole," the perfection of the universe. It is, first, necessarily hierarchical in the order of being: the "good of the whole" "would not be [actualized], were not all grades of being found in things.

Whence it pertains to divine providence to produce every grade of being" (Qu. 22.4). Its good is diminished when that hierarchy is disrupted.

The second feature of the "good of the whole" is that the overall movement to which it is ordered has a definite profile. It is ordered as creation's *exitus* from God in creation and moving in *reditus* toward God eschatologically. It culminates in the beatific vision, human creatures' participation in their own way in God's own beautitude. The "good of the whole" would be diminished were the arc of that movement distorted in any way. That fulfilled *reditus* is not only the *telos* of creation; its singularity is also what makes providence itself a single overall cosmic movement. It makes all that is not God to be the coherent "whole" it *must* be if the God that is "pure act of being," whose "essence is to exist," is to be said to have a timeless "vision" of it. That defines the kind of "whole" that it is and its distinctive "good" as a whole.

Taken on its own terms, this argument provides a powerful support of the claim that God's economy in relating to all else must be said to have only one *telos*.

A second sort of argument for the claim that God can have only one overarching goal for the various ways in which God relates to all else also follows from the nature of God's will. In much of the Western Christian tradition, the argument goes something like this (here, too, I take St. Thomas Aquinas' explanation of God's will in his *Summa Theologiae* I, Qu. 19 to be paradigmatic): If we use any of a family of terms like "decree," "elect," "decide," "plan," "intend," and "love" in relation to God, we can only do so as names for acts of "will." So we attribute "will" to God in addition to "intellect."

So, what is "will"? Begin with the premise that every being is disposed to its own good. That is, every being is disposed to what makes and sustains it in being the kind-of-being it is. What counts as a being's "good" is relative to the "kind" of creature it is. In nonrational beings, this disposition to good is "natural appetite." But in intellectual beings, including God, a disposition to the good is called "will" (Qu. 19, art. 2). Only intellectual beings have will because their willing their own good depends on their knowing, or thinking they know, what their good is. Will is an intellectual being's natural disposition to rest in its good if it has it, or to seek it if it does not; "but also to diffuse [its] own good among others, as far as possible" (Qu 19, art. 2).

So, what is the good that God wills, i.e., that to which God is disposed? Given the doctrine of the absolute simplicity of God's being, there is no difference in reality between God's existence and God's goodness. There is a conceptual distinction between the two, but not an ontological difference. God simply is the Good itself. Creatures are good in their kinds only as their being reflects in some respect(s) the good Being that creates and sustains them. Because in God intellect, i.e., "to know," is identical with "to be," God knows God as the Good itself. Hence, "in God to will is really the same as to be" (Qu. 19, art. 2 ad 1).

So God's will is (a) God's disposition to rest in the good God knows God to be (namely, being God!) and (b) God' disposition to communicate God's goodness by willing creatures into being such that they reflect God's goodness in their kinds. Hence, "God wills things other than Himself only for the sake of the end, which is God's goodness" (Qu19. 2 ad 2).

Doubtless, then, God wills a great many particular agents and actions during the course of providence's movement. Some have creaturely intellect and will; some do not. But given God's absolute simplicity, that multiplicity cannot be an unordered assemblage of disparate "ends." Rather, the multiplicity must all be subsumed in a single internally coherent overall movement to the single goal of those active agents in a Good that just *is* God. So understood, God cannot have but one *telos* for creation as a "whole."

Consequently, God's ways of relating to all else must be seen as a single movement toward a single goal: the eschatological participation of creatures – as far as is allowed by their creaturely kinds in their finitude – in the goodness that just *is* God. In virtue of that single goal that entire movement, i.e., "providence," is a "whole" that necessarily has at least three general characteristics. (i) It moves in time as a single whole from God and back to God according to an eternal "plan." (ii) It is a whole that is ordered in every moment as an ontological hierarchy of beings that differ from one another in the degrees to which they "participate" as creatures in their Creator's "perfection" (in the case of intelligent creatures, such as human beings, that "participation" is the eschatological beatific vision). (iii) That ontological hierarchy is manifest empirically to human creatures in their experience of various sorts of hierarchical order – in the food chain, in gender relations, and in social, cultural, economic, and political power and authority – in their shared physical world. (iv) Each "level" or "status" in that ontological hierarchy has its own "good," i.e., to "rest in" and sustain the ontological "kind" or "status" that it is as created. The content of God's providence as a whole, however, has its own overarching "good" that *necessarily* includes certain "defects" (i.e. as opposed to "moral" evils) that do not necessarily cohere with the "good" of creaturely beings in their kinds.

Taken on its own terms, that amounts to a second powerful argument in support of the claim that God's economy in relating to all else must be said to have only one *telos*.

I have already signaled a third argument in support of the claim that God's "economy" can have only one *telos*. It arises from doctrine about the nature of Christian Holy Scripture as a single, internally coherent Canon. Christian theologians have traditionally acknowledged that Canonical Scripture is in some way a faithful expression of how God concretely relates to all else. It is definitively revelatory of God's ways of relating.

But how can it do that? The most casual reader of Scripture can see that it includes a large number of different literary genres. Such a reader can also easily see that Scripture tells quite a variety of stories about what human beings have done or what God has done. How can that jumble serve as theology's single norm? For that is what "canon for theology" means: a measuring rod by which to assess the relative adequacy and truth of contrasting theological proposals on the same topic. If Scripture is going to be a single Canon, it must be some sort of unity. Despite Scripture's great inner diversity, it must be possible to say what unifies it. But what is the unifying principle that makes the Bible's collection of disparate books to be one single "Canon"?

As we have already noted, from Irenaeus in the second century onward it has been customary to interpret the Biblical canon as unified by a single narrative that moves from Genesis to Revelation. It moves through four major moments that we have already identified: Creation, Fall, reconciliation by way of Incarnation, and eschatological consummation. That narrative is the armature around which are gathered all the other Scriptural texts of songs, prayers, laws, proverbs, letters, etc., all of which refer in one way or another to one element or another of a single extended narrative.

A narrative is single if it is moved by an internally coherent plot to its end. That end is what makes it a single narrative. Accordingly, if Biblical texts read in the context of the Scriptural Canon as a whole are indeed faithful expressions of how God relates to all else, then any theological account of God's economy (in the broad sense) must posit that God has but one overarching purpose in relating at all to reality other than God.

Given its premise, this too seems a strong argument in support of the claim that God's economy in relating to all else must be said to have only one *telos*. Furthermore, it coheres especially closely with the second sort of argument in support of that claim and offers Scriptural warrant for it.

Theological Objections to the "Single Telos" View

Despite these impressive theological reasons for framing God's ways of relating to all else as a single overall movement toward actualizing a single eternal purpose, I urge that doing so unavoidably generates serious problems for Christian theology. They are systemic problems.

The problems do not arise from characterizing God's ways of relating to all else in teleological ways. The objections I am raising are not objections to teleological ways of thinking in Christian theology. It is central to Christian discourse about God to attribute to God such mental acts as "decision," "intention," "election," "decree," "purpose," and "self-commitment." They all belong, explicitly or implicitly, to teleological accounts of God's active relating. The problems on which I wish to focus here do not arise from such ways of talking about God, simply because they are "teleological" (problematic as they may or may not be in other respects). Rather, they are rooted in the assumption that God's ways of relating to all else must be said to have only *one* identifiable overall goal that unifies God's ways of relating to all else into a movement that is single precisely because it is oriented to the actualization of a single ultimate goal.

I suggest that the critical question is this: what is the character of the overall *movement* of God's one way of relating to all else that can have only one *telos* to which all of God's ways of relating are ordered? That is not a question about what that the one goal is. Rather, it is a question about the "narrative logic" that plots the movement through the four Scripturally narrated "moments" in God's overall way of relating to all else. Different answers to that question generate systemic problems for the overall structure of Christian theology. There are in principle, I suggest, three types of answer to this question.

Recall that we have seen that the single overarching divine movement has traditionally been understood to have four moments: God relating to create, human beings estranging themselves from God, God relating to reconcile them to God, and God relating to draw creation to an eschatological consummation. Assuming that humankind's estrangement is not God's eternal intent, that leaves three types of ways in which God purposefully relates to all else. Each has its own goal:

(a) To create ex nihilo realities genuinely other than God that are, in their finite ways, good, true, and beautiful manifestations of God's glory;
(b) to reconcile creatures to God when they are estranged; and
(c) to glorify creatures eschatologically.

Note that the goal of each of these ways in which God relates to all else is the "good" for creatures to which it is ordered. And the "goods" are different.

In Christian doctrine, each of those three goals that God has in relating to all else correlates with, respectively, doctrines of creation, reconciliation, and eschatological consummation. As rendered in Scriptural narratives, God relates in importantly different ways in each of them. If God's ways of relating are to be unified in a single movement toward the actualization through time of a single eternally decreed goal, then that single goal must be the goal of just one of three sorts of ways named above in which God relates to all else. Call it the "privileged" moment in the one four-movement overall narrative that synthesizes all three ways in which God relates to all else.

In that case, the "narrative logic" that moves the particular way in which God goes about relating in the privileged moment must serve as the plot of the entire extended movement of God's way of relating to all else. Furthermore, the goal of the privileged moment will have to serve as the goal of the entire extended divine intentional action.

This will necessarily have theological consequences. The doctrine that explicates the nature and significance of the privileged "moment" and its goal will be given a certain privileged status in the overall explication of Christian teaching. It will become the conceptual context within which the doctrines that explicate the other two "moments" must be framed. The privileged goal will, in turn, govern the relations of different doctrines to one another. It will organize doctrines in one systemic way or another.

We may set aside the "moment" traditionally called the "Fall" of creation. It is not ordered to any type of "good" for creatures. It can hardly be explained as God's doing.

So, which of the remaining three ways in which God relates, with its distinct "good" for creatures, should be privileged? I submit that no matter which one we select, it inevitably leads to theologically unacceptable distortions of doctrine about the other two ways in which God relates and their "goods." It distorts them because it subordinates them to itself conceptually.

Each of the three moments has a "good" that is its own goal in its own right. It is irreducibly different than the other two. (I defend this claim in the subsection "The Scriptural Basis of Those Arguments Is Inadequate.") If one is selected as the single overall goal that makes a single movement out of God's ways of relating to all that is not God, then actualization of the goals of the other two moments are necessarily interpreted as something like steps in a developing process that is not completed or fully actualized until it reaches its single final eternally decreed goal. The subordinated goals are not interpreted as God's goals for particular ways in which God relates and are creatures' "goods" *in and of themselves.* Rather, they are interpreted as instruments God has chosen to use to move beyond them to realize the single ultimate goal. Because that leads to distortions of doctrine about the two subordinated goals, I am arguing, it inevitably leads systemically to distortions of doctrine about the Triune God who pursues those goals.

Consider the possibilities, each of which is theologically unacceptable. I present them schematically. This strategy means that, although I am confident it can be done, I do not attempt to identify theological projects that illustrate each of those problematic possibilities. I must warn you that when presented schematically, these possibilities are downright dizzying.

Reconciliation as God's One Ultimate Goal

One possibility is to privilege God's goal in relating to *reconcile estranged creatures to God* as the overall goal to be actualized by the entire single movement of God's relating to all else. Human creatures' reconciliation to God, and all that goes with it for sinfully estranged and "fallen" creatures, is its "good." In this framework God's goal in creating is to provide the context of, and possibility for, creaturely estrangement from God. After all, if there is no estrangement, there is no need for the "good" of reconciliation. In that case, creation is understood instrumentally as a necessary step toward that one ultimate goal of reconciliation. Its "goodness" is a function of its utility in the process of reconciliation.

However, a chiefly instrumentalist doctrine of creation distorts the doctrine because it cannot affirm God creating as a way in which God relates to reality other then God *for creatures' own sakes,* whether or not they are estranged from God.[5] An instrumentalist interpretation of creation does not bring with it conceptual resources adequate to resist exploitative attitudes toward at least nonhuman creatures as instruments that are needed for the actualization of a greater goal, viz., reconciliation. The theological inadequacy of such a doctrine of creation scarcely needs to be pointed out in a time such as ours, when there is heightened awareness of the importance of valuing the earth as precisely God's creation for

---

[5] This has been especially true of Western theology, in both Protestant and some Roman Catholic theologies. In this scheme God's goals, in relating to create and in relating to consummate creation eschatologically are, in one way or another, understood as ordered to and subordinated to the goal of reconciling estranged creatures. This scheme does not necessarily deny God's goal to create a community of finite creatures whose reality, goodness, powers, and beauty, although fragile and finite, are their own and genuinely "other" than God and delighted in by God. Both Thomas Aquinas in the *Summa Theologicae* (1a. 44–74) and John Calvin in the *Institutes* (Bk I., Chs. V, XV–XVII) take great care to make just those points. Without such care, their account of the overall movement of God's one way of relating to all else has been open to this sort of distortion. Not all their intellectual successors took such care.

its own sake, and the urgency of our taking on the discipleship of stewardship of the earth.

So, too, God's movement toward the goal of glorifying creatures eschatologically is distorted when it is subordinated to the actualization of the goal of reconciling them to God. Understood in that context, God's movement toward the actualization of the goal of eschatological consummation is seen chiefly as an extrinsic postscript to the movement toward reconciliation. Movement to the goal of reconciliation is completed in Jesus Christ's crucifixion; and then a movement to the goal of eschatological consummation – which begins with Jesus' resurrection and ascension – is a chronologically and logically discontinuous bonus above and beyond reconciliation.

Theologically interpreted in that context, however, doctrines of God's movement toward an eschatological glorification of creation inevitably become distorted. Understood as an extrinsic bonus following reconciliation, God's movement toward the goal of eschatological consummation cannot be seen as part of the proximate and creaturely context, the *here and now*, within which God's movement toward the goal of reconciliation takes place. It has to do only with something beyond reconciliation, e.g., either going to "heaven" or to "hell."

Hence, what happens in the history of the movement toward the goal of reconciliation cannot really be said to manifest God's work in the present toward eschatological transformation of the world's unjust and oppressive structures and dynamics of power. Reconciliation comes first, here and now; eschatological consummation comes only afterward. In this framework, eschatological consummation of creation can have no "now"; it can only be "not yet." Consequently, there can be no theological grounds for hope for occasional manifestations of God's movement toward eschatological transformation here and now.

One does not need to be an uncritical advocate of all types of Liberation and Political Theology to see that in some way God's movement toward an eschatological transformation of unjust and oppressive powers and principalities, with its preferential option for the poor, does ground hope that by the grace of God's eschatological blessing liberation from specific forms of oppression is possible here and now. Doctrines of eschatology are distorted when they fail to provide those grounds for such hope in and for our proximate contexts, distorted as they are in in multiple types of bondage. But that is what happens in theology when the goal of God's movement toward the eschatological consummation of creation is incorporated into a single, longer movement whose goal is reconciliation of estranged creatures. This is important enough to bring into question the traditional assumptions that the teleology of God's ways of relating to all else consists of a single movement to toward the single goal of reconciliation.

Eschatological Consummation as God's One Ultimate Goal

A second way to construe the economy as a single overall movement is to hold that *eschatological glorification of creatures* is the ultimate goal toward which all God's ways of relating to all else are ordered thus making them a single teleologically ordered movement. In such a theological framework, eschatological consummation is the goal to which all other divine goals are subordinated. Here, eschatological consummation is indeed intrinsic to the here and now and not an extrinsic bonus added to fully realized reconciliation. It is the goal what makes the here and now just what it is: Creatures en route to eschatological glory.

However, subordinating reconciliation to eschatological consummation tends to distort doctrines of reconciliation in either or both of two ways. When God's goal of reconciliation is subordinated to God's goal of eschatological consummation it requires accounts of the "Fall" and reconciliation that instrumentalize them by construing them as necessary steps in the process of actualizing the ultimate goal of eschatological consummation.

This ordering, too, is theologically problematic. Consider this: reconciliation is impossible unless creatures are actually "fallen" and estranged from God. So, if reconciliation itself is a necessary step in God's economy as oriented to eschatological consummation, this move would seem to be theologically problematic because, at least implicitly, it also makes the "Fall" itself one of God's subordinated goals. The problems of making such a theological account of the "Fall" coherent with affirmation of God's goodness seem insurmountable.

So too, accounts of God's movement toward the goal of creating are distorted when they are conceived as subordinate to the ultimate goal of full actualization of the ultimate goal of eschatological consummation. At the very least, that is the case with human creatures. In such a framework, creation as it is here and now seems implicitly to be judged to be something of a botched job, such that God needs to make a new, improved, eschatological version of it. Such a view of creation obviously is difficult to reconcile with the affirmation of creation as good, a genuine – if secondary – manifestation of God's glory.

Moreover, in such a framework God's creating is seen as a process that is fully actualized only at its future eschatological consummation. Creatures here and now are, to be sure, something in themselves. But, however one characterizes their ontological status, what is important about them is not what they actually are now, but what they are potentially; what they are now is only potentially what they shall be when eschatologically consummated. Only when they are fully consummated eschatologically can human beings be said to be fully actualized creatures, if what they are as eschatologically consummated is the *telos* of God's relating to them creatively. God's creativity is an extended process that does not reach its goal until the creatures are actually consummated eschatologically as creatures. They are not constituted by God's creativity as creatures that are in some way good in and for themselves as they are here and now, because what they are here and now is not yet "fully human" creatures. Here and now they are only potentialities of the fully actualized creatures they will become eschatologically.

This pattern of thought has very problematic entailments, especially for theological anthropology. It is fully actualized human beings that have the sort of dignity deemed worthy of unqualified respect for their own sakes. In that case, if human creatures are not yet fully actualized human creatures here and now, but are only the potentialities of such actualization, they cannot be said to deserve respect as ends in themselves here and now and never merely means to some further end. The theological problem with this is, I think, perfectly clear when we consider the horrors committed in the past couple of centuries on the basis of political theories that human beings as they are now are not yet fully human, but can be brought to full human actualization, whether by eugenics, or by certain economic programs from either the right or the left, or by inevitable social change for the better driven by the inner logic of a world-historical movement toward the actualization of truly human life.

Creation as God's One Ultimate Goal

The third possible way to frame the economy as a single teleologically ordered movement is to identify creating concretely actual, inter-relating and interdependent creatures as the as the ultimate goal of all of God's ways of relating to all else, the overarching *telos* toward which the entire movement of the economy is ordered. In such a theological framework, human creatures are indeed fully actualized here and now and demand respect for their dignity in and for themselves as God's creatures, to be treated as ends in themselves and never as means only.

This move also proves to be theologically problematic. If creation is the one ultimate goal of God's relating to all else and has now already been actualized, then the divine economy itself has already been fully actualized. God's *telos* has been achieved. In that case, doctrine about God's relating to reconcile or to draw creation to eschatological glory are simply alternative ways of talking about God's telos in creating a universe of actual creatures. That is theologically problematic because it deeply distorts doctrine about each of those alternative goals.

To speak of God relating to reconcile is then simply to speak of God's creativity "healing" the distortions and brokenness that may occur in and among creatures. God's power to reconcile is nothing other than the powers for "self-care" and "healing" that creatures are given by God's creativity. This is problematic because it drastically underestimates how profoundly the systemic and dynamic power of evil distorts creatures' own powers to "heal" their own distortions and brokenness. With a relatively superficial view of evil, it deeply distorts theological accounts of the way in which the "power of the cross" is required for reconciliation of human creatures to God. Here, when all is said and done doctrinally, "redemption" is equated with "self-realization" and "self-fulfillment."

So, too, in this framework to speak of God drawing creation to eschatological glory is simply to speak of creation's glorious beauty, perhaps in aesthetic language about our experience of creation as sublime, or in generically religious language about the spirituality of our oneness with creation. God's power to glorify creation eschatologically is fully actualized precisely in God's creating it. Eschatological consummation is wholly realized "now," and there is nothing "not yet" about it. Theologically, this notion is problematic because it too sentimentally overlooks the magnitude of the creaturely suffering and horrors and too complacently identifies grounds for hope already found within creation. Thus, it distorts theological accounts of eschatological consummation that ground hope, not in resources intrinsic to creaturely powers, but in God's power to transfigure creation that is not only at work "now," but is at the same time "not yet."

In short, taken together the arguments that defend the thesis that God must necessarily have only one *telos* for God's economy have consequences for theological explanations of how God goes about relating to all else in the economy that unavoidably distort those theological explanations systemically.

Why the Defenses of the Tradition Do Not Necessarily Stand

How shall we avoid these problematic theological consequences of insisting that God's economy can have only one ultimate *telos*? I have a programmatic proposal.

Assuming that a Christian doctrine of the Triune God comports with Canonical Christian Scripture's faithful witness to the economy (in the broadest sense of the term): (a) explore the implications of the irreducibility of any two strands of the economy to the third strand for claims about the qualities (or "attributes" or "perfections") that are traditionally ascribed to God in Christian doctrines of God; (b) identify what is at stake theologically in traditional arguments in support of the claim that God's economy logically must have a single *telos*; (c) show that the arguments (identified in this chapter) for that claim are "conceptual artifacts" of conceptual decisions that are not necessarily entailed by the specifically Christian theological issues that are at stake; and (d) show that the basis of those "traditional" arguments in canonical Scripture is inadequate. This book is devoted to doing (a) in regard to attribution to the Triune God of the qualities "glory," "sovereignty," and "power." Steps (b), (c), and (d) are outlined here.

What Is at Stake in "Traditional" Claims That God Must Have Only One Goal in the Economy?

The short answer is this: what is at stake is God's trustworthiness. One cannot praise a reality one cannot trust, much less lodge faith, hope, and love in it.

As we have seen, the first two sorts of argument defending the claim that God's economy must have only one *telos* turn on a particular definition of God's "providence." Why "providence"? Also, why that particular definition of "providence"?

Why is "providence" the crux of an argument in support of the claim that God's economy must have but one "end"? Recall Thomas' contention: "[T]he providence of God is nothing other than the notion of the order of all things towards an end" (Qu. 22, art.2). The "order" of all things toward an end makes God's economy a certain sort of "whole" that is constituted *as* a "whole" by being moved to only one ultimate, overarching *telos*. That end is the fundamental good of creatures. It consists in their eschatological *reditus* to God in the beatific vision. Because God's reality *as God* is unchanging and unchangeable, God's knowing and willing that one end for creatures, and therewith the overall order of the movement through time toward actualization of that end, is *unchangeable*. In that case, providence is unchangeable. Hence, it can be trusted to lead to the actualization of creatures' "goods." This brings us to what is at stake in the traditional theological stress on God's simple perfection. It is the basis in reality of the trustworthiness of the God who relates to all else in providential care of them. One can have faith in God only if God is trustworthy. Surely it is correct that the fundamental theological interest here is that an account of God's economy show that God is worthy of our trust.

Why treat an account of God's economy as an account of God's providence understood in this particular way? The answer the arguments give to that question turns on an analysis of what it means to ascribe "intellect" and "will" to God. Here, I continue to take Thomas Aquinas' *Summa Theologiae* as paradigmatic of major themes in many "traditional" Trinitarian doctrines of God.

As we have seen, the argument bases its accounts of God's intellect and will on logically prior claims that God's "being" is both "simple" and "perfect." As "simple," God's being is absolutely noncomposite (Qu. 3, art. 7). As "perfect," God's "being" is pure actuality (cf. Qu., 4, art. 1). That entails the positive claim that as "purely actual" God's being is "perfect" or complete, lacking nothing of what it is "to be" concretely actual. It is on that basis that Aquinas argues that God's acts of knowing and willing God's eternal providential plan are not the actualization of any cognitive and volitional potentialities in God "caused" by the single comprehensive *whole* of what God knows. Rather, that "whole" is created by God's eternally knowing and willing it. As their *arche* and creator, God's being (which is one and the same as God's "intellect") lacks no perfection of being that is found in creatures' beings (cf. Qu. 4, art. 2). That includes the perfection "goodness" (cf. Qu. 6, esp. arts. 1 and 4).

Here the argument turns on a particular definition of "good." Recall that a being's "good" is defined in general as whatever it is that makes it, and sustains it in being, the *kind* of being that it is. Every kind of being is inherently disposed to its own "good." Moreover, "will" is understood in terms of this definition of "good": will is an intellectual being's natural disposition to rest in its good if it has it, or to seek it if it does not; "but also to diffuse [its] own good among others, as far as possible" (Qu 19, art. 2). Because "intellect" may be ascribed to God analogically, "will" also may be ascribed to God. Because God's noncomposite or absolutely "simple" being entails that there is no difference in reality between God's "to know" and God's "to be," for the same reason God's "to will" must be said to be identical with God's "to know" and God's "to be." God simply *is* goodness itself. So, as we have seen, *God's* will is God's disposition (a) to rest in the good God knows God to be (i.e., simply to be God!), and (b) to communicate God's goodness by willing creatures into being such that in their kinds they variously reflect God's goodness. Hence, "God wills things other than Himself only for the sake of the end, which is God's goodness" (Qu19. 2 ad 2).

Because "God's knowledge must be the cause of things insofar as [God's] will is joined to it" (Qu 14, art. 8), and because "God wills things other than Himself only for the sake of the end, which is God's goodness" (Qu19. 2 ad 2), it follows that God's own goodness is the only possible end to which God's economy is ordered in

God's providence. Given the argument's way of defining "providence" and "goodness," the only coherent account of God's relating in the economy is that it is a single interiorly coherent "whole" because it is all ordered to a single overarching end: Godself.

That entire analysis, rooted in the fundamental claim that God's reality is pure and simple actuality, provides what is arguably a conceptually coherent and persuasive rationale for understanding "providence" as "nothing other than the notion of the order of all things towards an end" that is absolutely singular (Qu. 22, art. 2). Clearly, the claim that God's reality is pure actuality expresses a metaphysical belief. More exactly, it expresses an ontological belief, a belief about God's being.

Those Expressions of a Metaphysical Belief about God Are "Conceptual Artifacts" of Certain Conceptual Decisions

The force of this argument in support of the thesis that God's economy can have only one overall *telos* is an artifact of a decision about how to frame the argument. It is the decision to frame it in the conceptuality of a metaphysical analysis that is based on the systematic use of a binary conceptual distinction between "matter" and "form." If that decision is not made, the relevant definition of "providence" is not metaphysically warranted and the argument dissolves.

The arguments in support of the claim that God can have only one eternal purpose rest on a series of analogical uses of the conceptual binary "form and matter." Analogical use of the binary moves something like this:

> The most general thing – i.e., the basic metaphysical claim – that can be said about physical creatures is that the concretely actual being of each of them is formed matter. A physical creature's form is its "essence" that makes it be the kind of creature it is. Its matter makes it the particular individual instance it is of that "kind." To

cite a standard illustration: The "form" of being Fido is the family dog's essence, what makes it a "dog," and not a "squid," its "canine-ness," which is identical in all dogs; what makes Fido "Fido in particular," is Fido's allotment of (in this case) living matter. As such, a physical creature is a "substance," that of which other things may be predicated but which cannot itself be predicated of anything else. "Brown" and "fuzzy" may be predicated of Fido; but "Fido-ness" cannot be attributed of any other concretely actual being, organic, inorganic, or nonmaterial.

The form/matter binary is then used analogically in analysis of other aspects of creatures' substantial being. The analogy has some-times been expressed in the following formal manner: "$x : y :: a : b$" (read as "x is related to y as a is related to b"). For example, an actual creature's essence may be distinguished from its existence, for the two may separate. When they do separate, the concretely actual individual creaturely substance no longer exists, but the essence of which it was an individual instantiation continues to exist and may have many other instantiations. So we may say of a creaturely substance that "its existence is to its essence as its form is to its matter" (formalized as "its *existence* : its *essence* :: its *form* : its *matter*"). The formula is not an equation. Rather, it is intended to express an analogy between two otherwise different relations.

The analogy is then used *negatively* in a characterization of God's "manner of existence": because God is pure actuality and is devoid of potentiality, there is no way God's *existence* is related to God's *essence* in a fashion analogous to how God's *actuality* ("form") is related to God's *potentiality* ("*matter*"). A point is made about God's singular reality: because there is no difference in God between "existence" and "essence," there is no relation between the two to be understood on analogy with the relation between form and matter. God's "essence" just is to "exist." For the same reason, there is no difference between God's being and God's "intellect." Accordingly, there is no analogy between (a) the relation between God's knowing and God's being and (b) the relation between form and matter. God's "knowing" is not an actualization of potentialities resident in God's intellect, whose actualization is caused by the objects of God's knowledge. Rather, God's knowing of them is the universal cause of all that "goes on" among creatures. As their universal cause, God's knowing is itself an all-comprehending, timelessly simultaneous, "seeing." Its content is God's providence.

Moreover, the way in which God's act of knowing the content of God's providential care of creatures causes them to exist ex nihilo can also be explained by analogical use of the form/matter conceptual binary. What a cause "effects" is some sort of change in the substance that undergoes the change. Change of every sort (or, as the Scholastics usually refer to it, "motion") is an actualization of a potentiality in substances. A substance is actually what it is at this moment and potentially is what it is when it has undergone change in some respect. The key ontological claim about change of any sort in substances is that the cause of the change must itself already actually be what it is actualizing in another substance (e.g., if an iron poker is to actualize a potential for burning in something else, it must actually be hot itself). Four factors are involved in all "causal" interactions between creatures with intellect, as the causes, and other creatures (whether they have intellect or not) in which change is effected by the intelligent cause: formal factor (the relevant actuality of the causal agent that is to be actualized also in the effect – say, the heat of a torch's flame that is to actualize the potential for burning in kindling); final factor (the end to which a causal agent with intellect causes the change effected in another – say, so as to warm the room); efficient factor (the power the causal agent has to actualize the relevant potentiality in another – say the igniter's strong right arm); and material factor (the potentiality in another for the effected change – say, the flammable kindling). Although they are usually referred to as "four causes" it is probably less misleading to construe them as four factors in the metaphysics of change in "substances," where "substance" is understood in terms of the "form/matter" binary.

This metaphysical analysis of change, framed in terms of the form/matter binary used analogically, is then employed to explicate the Triune God's intellect's causality of all the changes in creation: God's intellect conjoined to God's will is the "final," "formal," "efficient" cause of all else. Each of those terms is used analogically in this context. Intellect and will conjoined in God's knowing has a single final *telos* or end (creatures' eschatological glorification in the beatific vision); the essences or forms of creatures are ideas in God's intellect; God's power in knowing and willing is the efficient cause of a single, complex, internally coherent movement of creaturely reality "out from" God and "back to" God. Given that God is *actus purus* and that creatures created ex nihilo are not created "out of" anything, there is no material factor in God's universal causality. Because it is caused by the singular God's intellect conjoined with God's will and is the content of God's timeless, synoptic and simultaneous knowledge of all reality other than God, that movement from *exitus* to *reditus* must be ordered to a single *telos* that the content of God's knowledge itself be a coherent whole. That "whole" is providence. It is the "whole" of God's economy. That is why this argument in support of the claim that God's economy must have but one *telos* hangs, not just on the notion of God's providence, but on *this* definition of providence: "[T]he providence of God is nothing other than the notion of the order of all things towards an end" (Qu. 22, art. 2).

Now, as we have seen, when the form/matter binary's use in analysis of God's providence is brought together with its use in analysis of the ontology it generates of the physical creatures, an understanding of creatures' "good" emerges that distinguishes between the "good" that is relative to each creature's "kind" of being, i.e., its "essence" or "form," on one hand, and the "good" of the "whole" of creation that is constituted as a whole by the one end to which it is ordered by God's providence. That distinction, in turn, is open to the inference that apparent "defects" that occur in creation's providential movement from *exitus* to *reditus*, such as the "defects" that cause some sorts of horrendous suffering by loved ones, are in fact "sent" by God's intentional "plan" as a means to the greater "good" of providence as a certain sort of "whole."

That inference is what warrants theologically the pastorally problematic, if well-intentioned, remarks that anger those who anguish over loved ones' suffering and prompt this entire proposal.

But the Way the Arguments Are Framed Is Not Theologically Essential

What opens this traditional argument that God's economy must have but one overall *telos* to this particular theologically problematic inference is, I suggest, an artifact of the argument's reliance on binary use of the form/matter distinction in the metaphysical conceptuality it employs to define both God's providence and the nature of the "good" for creatures to which providence is ultimately ordered. That reliance is not conceptually necessary.

The decision to rely on a systematic metaphysical conceptual scheme rooted in the form/matter conceptual binary is not necessarily entailed by the ways in which God relates to all else, as they are canonically narrated. Nor is it necessarily entailed by the theological claim that God's trustworthiness is rooted in God's intrinsic un-changeability *as God*. Nor is it necessarily entailed by theological claims that the sorts of "goods" for creatures to which God is self-committed in each of God's ways of relating to all else are themselves unchangeable, and are therefore trustworthy. Rather, the thesis that God's economy can have only one overall *telos* is warranted by the implications of a particular way of framing metaphysical analysis of "substance" and "change" in a binary use of the "form/matter" distinction. The warrant for that thesis is an artifact of that conceptual scheme that is chosen to express the thesis rather than by relevant theological reality claims backed by canonical accounts of God's economy.

What is at issue here is how best to explicate the Triune God's praise-worthiness in the sorts of ways in which God relates to all else in the economy. Central to a theological decision about such explication is the insistence that in the sorts of ways in which God relates *ad extra* in the economy God faithfully expresses God's *intrinsic* praise-worthiness. Indeed, it is the insistence that God is worthy of praise whether or not God relates to all else. God does as God is. That is the root of God's worthiness in the economy of human praise expressed not merely in words but in forms of life that are shaped by love for God, trust in God, and hope in God. Whatever the changes may be in what "goes on" among creatures, between creatures and God, and between God and creatures in all the strands of the economy broadly understood, God does not change in regard to being, precisely, "what" and "who" God is. So the central issue turns on the question how best to explicate "what" it is to be God.

The binary form/matter metaphysical conceptual scheme employed in the "traditional" sort of argument from the nature of God's intellect and God's will to the conclusion that the economy must have one and only one overarching final *telos* offers one answer to that question. What is argued here is that doing so has problematic theological consequences because (a) it systemically entails distortions either of the theological implications of canonical accounts of the Triune God relating in creative blessing, or of the theological implications of God relating in eschatological blessing, and (b) it – however unintentionally – entails theological warrants for the pastoral remarks about God's power to those anguished by others' deep suffering that we have seen are theologically problematic (argued in Part III).

To be clear: This critique of the argument under examination here does not amount to a wholesale rejection of teleological accounts of the Triune God's economy. It is obvious that the concrete and particular ways in which God relates to all else in the economy, as canonically narrated, cannot be adequately explicated apart from "agentic" and teleological ways of speaking. God is said to make promises, often very open-ended promises. God then said to "act" in concretely particular ways to actualize as identifiable "ends" toward which God's relating to all else in the economy is ordered. The issue is not whether the Triune God's three-stranded way of relating to all else is "teleological," i.e., action that is not random, arbitrary, or whimsical but "intentional" and "ordered to ends" for which, presumably, God has "reasons." Rather, the issue is whether there is any theologically necessary reason why the Triune God's relating to all else must be said to have but one "overall" and comprehensive end.

So, too, this critique of the argument under examination here does *not* amount to a quasi-Barthian polemic that metaphysics in theology is the anti-Christ. Nor is it a quasi-Wittgensteinian polemic that metaphysics as a branch of philosophy is always nothing more than a spinning of conceptual wheels, intellectual machinery running but in "idle." Theological claims that God's reality as God intrinsically does not undergo, and cannot be coherently claimed to undergo, change are metaphysical claims about God's intrinsic being. The theological issue is how best to frame the claims conceptually.

It is not self-evident, however, that a metaphysical *belief*, or a metaphysical claim expressing that belief, necessarily implies some one systematic metaphysical *theory*. Nor is it self-evident that it can only be formulated by systematic employment of such a theory. There are, after all, a number of systematic metaphysical theories on offer, old and new. Presumably, if the decision is made to employ one such theory systematically in Christian doctrine of God, the decision about which theory to employ needs to be made, among other considerations, on the basis of judgments about how well it comports with Christian theological beliefs on many other theological topics as well.

However, it is not obvious that such a decision must be made. A more modest alternative would be to make decisions about conceptualities to be used in an account of God's intrinsic trustworthiness in an ad hoc theological subtopic-by-subtopic fashion. The way that borrowed terms are used would, in the theological contexts within which they are used, shape how they mean in those theological contexts more decisively than would the body of systematic metaphysics that was their original home.

For example, the proposal promoted here brackets the entire logic of the traditional focus on the absolute simplicity of God's being and, what is the same thing, the simplicity of God's willing, insofar as they are framed in terms of analogical – but nonetheless systematic – use of the form/matter conceptual binary. Where, for example, Thomas privileges ontological simplicity as the perfection of God on which all other perfections ascribed to God *in se* are grounded, and by which what is said is about God's "attributes" is governed, the proposal developed here privileges God's glory. It proposes that glory is the sum-total of all God's perfections. God's glory is God's faithful self-expression, both *in se* in the eternal relations among the "Persons" of the Trinity, and in each of the three ways God relates *ad extra*. The proposal is that a doctrine of God that unfolds the content of God's glory avoids the problematic features of other ways of grounding doctrine of God if (a) it acknowledges the inseparability and radical differences among three purposes God has, as canonically narrated, and (b) grows out of theological reflection on the complex and asymmetrical relations to each other of the three strands of God's economy that are each ordered to a different on of those ends.

The proposal made here does not necessarily prohibit ascription of "absolute simplicity" to God. Nor does it question the wholly negative force of "simplicity." Like the traditional argument, it affirms the absolute trustworthiness of God's ways of relating to all else – in all three strands of the economy. It affirms that the three ways in which God relates to all else faithfully manifest the glory of

God that, in a three-fold way, expresses who and what God is. The proposal does, however, question the way the traditional argument for the simplicity of God rests on a metaphysical analysis framed in terms of the conceptual distinction between "form" and "matter," even if it is used only to deny its applicability to God.

The Scriptural Basis of Those Arguments Is Inadequate

The third sort of argument noted above in support of the claim that the Triune God's way of relating to all else in the economy must have only one end relied on a traditional way of defending the claim that Christian Scripture is enough of a "whole" that it can serve as the "Canon" by which the adequacy of theological proposals can be measured. That traditional approach grounds the "unity" or "wholeness" of the collection of disparate writings that comprise Christian Scripture in the claim that there is a single narrative running through the Christian Bible that renders God's economy as a single movement toward a single eternally decreed end. That way of grounding the "unity" of the biblical canon is very ancient in Christianity.

I have already laid out the counterargument to that account of the basis of canonical Christian Scripture's "wholeness." The counterargument is based on exegetical work by Claus Westermann, especially his commentary on *Genesis 1–11*,[6] and his two studies *Blessing*[7] and *Beginning and End in the Bible*.[8]

Recall that, on literary grounds, Westermann distinguishes two quite different sorts of narrative in the Pentateuch: (a) narratives of God's deeds of deliverance (e.g., Genesis 12–50 and the rest of the Pentateuch) and (b) narratives of God's creative blessing

---

[6] *Genesis 1–11: A Commentary*, translated by John J. Scullion S.J. (Minneapolis: Augsburg Publishing House, 1984).

[7] *Blessing*, translated by Keith Crim (Philadelphia: Fortress Press, 1974), p. 65.

[8] Philadelphia: Westminster Press, 1972.

(e.g., Genesis 1–3). In *Blessing* and *Beginning and End in the Bible* Westermann identifies a third type of Scriptural narrative of God relating to all else. He urges that canonical narratives of God drawing all else to eschatological consummation tell of that consummation as a blessing upon creation, blessing upon blessing. The three sorts of canonical narrative of different strands in God's economy are irreducibly different because each has a different "naratival logic" (my term, not Westermann's): narratives of God's deeds of deliverance are moved by a narrative logic of eventful and episodic deeds whose goal is to liberate and deliver God's covenant people from some sort of bondage that seems to threaten God's longstanding promise that God's people will flourish. The series of them is a "salvation history." For Christians, that history culminates in God's deed of deliverance in the crucifixion and resurrection of Jesus Christ. In regard to the Canon's witness to God's deeds of deliverance, Irenaeus got it right. Canonical accounts of God's creative blessing are moved by a narrative logic of an ongoing relation of God to creatures in virtue of which the creatures are always radically dependent on God for their very reality as beings "other" than God and for their intrinsic value. That blessing commits God to caring for creatures' well-being in their kinds, as long as they last, for their own sake in and of themselves. That creaturely well-being, and not anything beyond it, is God's eternal goal in relating to them in creative blessing. Narratives of God's creative blessing do not tell of punctiliar divine acts, episodes, or events. They do not even explain an "event" of creation. Narratives of God relating in eschatological blessing, like accounts of God relating in creative blessing, describe an ongoing steady-state relationship between God and creatures. That relating begins as a promise that is coeval with God relating in creative blessing and has yet to be fully actualized. However, canonical narratives of how God goes about drawing creatures to eschatological glory move from the promise to the concrete punctiliar event in which God's keeping the promise is inaugurated in the resurrection of the crucified Jesus, and from that toward the goal of the full actualization of the promise in eschatological consummation. In the relevant Christian canonical narratives, the fully actualized *inauguration* of the fulfillment of promises has occurred once and for all. However, the full actualization of that which has been inaugurated is "not yet."

Given their different narrative logics and different goals, those three types of canonical narratives of the movement of God's economy cannot be coherently synthesized in a single narrative moving to just one of the three goals. The three are inseparable strands of the economy. However, the inter-relations among them are complex and asymmetrical. On exegetical grounds, it seems that it is mistaken to think that the Canon is constituted a unity by having a single narrative of God's single movement toward God's single eternally decreed goal. If Westermann is correct (as I believe he is), this notion trumps the exegetical argument in support of the theological claim that God can have only one "eternal purpose." The unity of the Canon must be grounded in the complex and asymmetrical relations among these three distinct types of narrative in Canonical Christian Scripture, at once irreducible to one another and inseparable.

Note that none of this implies a positive thesis that the Triune God does *not* have a single overall end or *telos* for the three-stranded economy. Rather, it argues a far more modest thesis: if God does have such singular overall *telos*, it escapes our cognitive grasp. It is not made available to us by the concrete ways in which the Trinity goes about relating to all else in the three strands of the economy, as that is faithfully rendered in canonical Christian scriptural narratives and commentary on those narratives. Accordingly Christian theological accounts of "what" and "who" the Triune God is that relates to all else in the economy, and accounts of all else in its relation to God, overreach when they seek to present themselves as comprehensive conceptually systematic "wholes." What is proposed here is a more modest ad hoc approach, offering an account of some things that we are, arguably, warranted by the economy to say about "what" and "who" the Triune God that "does as God is and is as God does" in relating to all else in the economy, namely that the Triune God is the God of "glory," "sovereignty," and "power."

* * * * *

Back now from this excursus to the modest proposal. Grant that Christian doctrine of God is grounded in Canonical Christian Scripture's faithful witness to the economy, that is, to the ways in which God relates to all that is not God. Grant also that that witness gives three different kinds of narratives of God relating to all that is not God, each an account of God's movement toward actualizing a different goal. Then Christian doctrine of God must be rooted in the economy understood not as a single movement of God *ad extra* toward a single eternal purpose, but as three inseparable but irreducibly different movements toward three distinguishable but not incoherent goals. More exactly, because the relations among them are complex and asymmetrical, theological accounts of God's reality and qualities should be rooted in theological reflection on various kinds of interplay among the three strands in God's economy. Definitions of the perfections ascribed to God, such as goodness, holiness, wisdom, power, grace, freedom, and will, would be warranted by those interplays. The totality of those perfections could be called the "glory" of God, in which God is faithfully self-expressive. Such a doctrine of God would be framed teleologically, but in regard to three different, albeit inseparable, goals. I suggest that this would yield rich, albeit relatively "unsystematic," doctrine of God that does not distort its account of either the movement or the goal of any one of the three strands of God's economy. That is, it would avoid the problematic consequences we saw in every version of the economy understood as ordered to a single goal. The proof of this proposal, of course, lies in its execution. Part III aims to complete just that.

Part III | Power

7 | Assumptions about God's Power in Problematic Pastoral Remarks

Chapter 1 began with the observation that many conventional pastorally well-intentioned remarks meant to comfort people who anguish over others' suffering serve only to deepen their anguish. Telling those who anguish about another's suffering that God is in control of all that "goes on," that God sent the suffering for a purpose, that in such matters God has a plan, that God will not send the sufferer more pain than she can handle, etc., intensifies their anguish, often into a profound anger at God. This book has been developing an argument to support the claim that such pastoral remarks, however well-intentioned, are theologically problematic. It proposes a theological alternative to the theological assumptions that lie behind and justify such problematic pastoral comments.

It is important to keep clear just what my argument holds is "problematic" about such pastoral remarks. The thesis here is not that they are theologically problematic *because*, as pastoral remarks, they are remarkably insensitive emotionally (although they are that also!). That would be a non sequitur. There is no reason why a theological claim cannot be both a valid theological claim about someone and a psychologically insensitive claim to make to that person in the circumstances of their anguish over another's suffering. Nor is the thesis that those remarks are theologically problematic simply because they attribute power to God. To the contrary, the negative thesis of this essay is that such remarks are theologically problematic because they attribute to the Triune God a theologically simplistic, misleading, and univocal concept of power.

The positive argument of this essay assumes that God self-faithfully does as God is and is as God does. Therefore, what Christians have to say by way of characterizations of what God is as "powerful" must be warranted by what God "does." The sorts of things that "God does" is what canonical Scriptural narratives render in accounts of how God goes about relating to all that is not God. So Christians' claims about how God goes about doing what God "does" must be warranted by scriptural accounts of, in the broadest sense of the technical term, God's "economy." More exactly, my argument has claimed that there are three irreducible strands to scriptural accounts of God's economy. Each of the three strands of scriptural accounts of how God goes about "doing" what God does warrants theological accounts of "what" it is to be "God" and "who" the God is that relates to humankind (along with all else that is not God). Together they are also what warrant the essay's assumption that God is most aptly characterized in Trinitarian fashion.

Part I sketched a characterization of "what" and "who" the Triune God is in terms of God's intrinsic "glory." That laid out the first step in an argument supporting the proposal that an adequate account of the senses in which God is "powerful" needs to be rooted in an account of "what" and "who" God *intrinsically* is as One "powerfully" relating to all else: namely, that the "powerfully" living Triune God is the intrinsically "glorious" God.

Part II outlined a characterization of "what" and "who" the Triune God intrinsically is in terms of a characterization of one quality of God's intrinsic glory: sovereignty. The Triune God is "sovereign" in the self-faithful, self-expressive, generous self-giving-in-self-relating that just is the living Triune God's life. That intrinsic "sovereignty" consists of God's absolutely unconditioned initiative in God's self-regulation of the dynamic of God's self-relating. In such self-regulation of God's dynamic self-relating God is intrinsically "sovereign," whether or not God also "sovereignly" relates to realities other than God. That sovereignty is a quality of "what" and "who" God intrinsically is.

That intrinsic sovereignty is faithfully, if only partially, expressed in the three strands of God's economy in which the Triune God relates to all else to different ends: in the way in which God relates to all else in creative blessing; in the way in which God relates to all else in providential care; and in the way in which God relates to all else in eschatological blessing. Given that God "is" as God "does," those are ways in which God is "sovereign" in what God "does."

I privileged "sovereignty" as the quality of the Triune God that is the conceptual context in which God's power should be understood precisely because sovereignty is historically closely associated with discussion of God's power in ways that have indeed warranted just the sort of "pastoral" remarks we began by declaring theologically problematic. I have done so to show that when the term "sovereign" (and related terms like "king" and "lord") is attributed analogically to God on the basis of Scriptural narratives of how God goes about relating to all else, it does not imply but rather blocks the theological assumptions about God's power that justify the sort of pastoral remarks that we have identified as theologically problematic.

The negative argument developed in this chapter is that the theologically problematic ideas that warrant the pastorally problematic remarks assume that:

a) the Triune God's sovereignty is the sovereignty of God's power;
b) that God's power is what constitutes God's reality as "God," i.e., a certain sort of power is "what makes God *God*"; and that
c) that "power" is to be understood *only* in the sense of the unrestrained and unqualified power that is entailed by the claim that God creates all that is not God ex nihilo.

The negative argument to be developed here is that those assumptions about God's power are projected onto "traditional" accounts of God's power but are fundamentally inconsistent with "traditional" accounts of God's power.

A positive theological proposal, which is this book's counter-thesis, about God's power is developed in the next two chapters. It urges that:

a) the Triune God's power is the power of God's sovereignty in each of the senses of "sovereignty" sorted out in Part II;

b) what constitutes God's reality, i.e., "makes God *God*," is God's intrinsic glory, as outlined in Chapter 2, and is neither merely God's intrinsic sovereignty in that glory nor merely God's intrinsic power in that glory; and that

c) in consequence there are four different senses in which we are warranted in attributing "power" to God, not just one: a sense in which God is intrinsically powerful in God's sovereignty, and three inter-related but irreducibly different senses in which God's sovereignty may be said to be "powerful" in the economy, viz., respectively, in relating in creative blessing, in relating eschatological blessing, and in relating to reconcile estranged creatures to God.

So this chapter begins as a critique of the assumptions that God's intrinsic power is "power-as-such" that constitutes what it is to be God and warrants theologically problematic pastoral remarks. The critique has two major steps. The first is to outline what I stipulate are "traditional" Christian accounts of God's power. The "traditional" accounts of God's power can be shown to block inferences from them that might seem to warrant troubling and theologically problematic pastoral remarks. They nonetheless yield an account of God's power that, because it is so vague, invites the projection onto it of additional "conventional" modern ideas about power that seem to "clarify" it by making it somewhat more precise.

The second step is to outline what I stipulate are currently widely shared "conventional" notions of power that are projected onto the "traditional" account, serve as a lens through which it is misinterpreted in theologically misleading ways, and warrant troubling pastoral remarks that are theologically problematic.

The chapter then becomes a meditation on how the claim, *The Triune God is intrinsically "powerful"* is understood when God's "power" understood in the context of the senses in which "sovereignty" is attributed to God in each of the three strands of the economy – which themselves have been explained in the context of Part II's account of the sense in which the Triune God is "sovereign" in the self-giving self-relating, whose attractive self-expression just is God's *intrinsic* life and "glory," as was explained in Part I.

On Power

In its most general sense, "power" is a relational notion. It names a "something's" capacity to make a difference in some respect in relation to an "other." The qualifier "in some respect" is important because it points to the very broad range of ways in which *x* may be said to have the capacity to "make a difference" to any number of *y*s. Jane may be said to have the capacity to make a difference to *y*'s physical location, beliefs, emotions, economic situation, bodily health and well-being, *y*'s own capacity to solve some sort of problem, etc. The capacity to make each of those sorts of "difference" may be said to be a different sense in which Jane is in some degree "powerful." Each warrants our ascribing to her a different sort of "power": physical power, emotional power, social power, economic power, intellectual power, legal power, governmental power, etc. When talking about fellow creatures, we are accustomed to using the expression "power" in quite different senses in different contexts.

The sheer range of sorts of "difference" that *x* may make for *y* makes "power" a very vague term. We often have to rely on the context in which the word "power" is used to grasp in which sense it is being using. The variety of senses in which we ordinarily use the expression "power" is not entirely arbitrary, however. It is not merely a set of equivocal uses of the same word. There is something like a "family resemblance" among those different uses of the expression. They all have something to do with an agent's "making (some sort of) difference."

One thing they do not share is any implied particular explanation of *how* a given "difference" is effected or "caused." Our ascription of one sort or another "power" to Jane can be well-warranted without our having a clear understanding how she makes the specified "difference," what the "causal joint" is between her and the particular "difference" she makes. There are entire academic disciplines dedicated to investigating particular sorts of "power" and to developing explanatory theories of how their exercise "make," "cause," "effect," of "occasion" the differences they do.

In that very vague way, we may say that it is clear that relatively informal Christian talk about God assumes that God is "powerful," at least in relating to creatures. Such talk mostly consists of remarks about the sorts of "difference" God makes for creatures. One feature of such talk about God by many Christians and others shows that they assume that God is intrinsically "powerful" *whether or not* God relates to realities other than God. That is shown by the way in which even informal Christian talk about God regularly affirms that when God does "make a difference" of some specifiable sort, it is "grace": God does it "freely." God remains "God" even if God does not make the sort of difference that is in question.

This implies that God intrinsically "has" the power to make a given sort of difference even if God does not in fact relate to some particular situation to make just that difference. In such talk, God is not "powerful" merely in the events in which God does in fact make some sort of "difference." God is inherently "powerful," i.e., intrinsically capable of making those sorts of difference whether God in fact does so or not.

The usual warrants for those sorts of informal Christian remarks are canonical Christian scriptural accounts of how God has gone about relating to reality other than God so as to make certain sorts of "difference." They warrant remarks about ways in which God is "powerful" in what God "does." A question for doctrinal theology is whether those same accounts can warrant somewhat clearer and more precise characterizations of God's *intrinsic* power, the sense in which God is "powerful" in "what" and "who" God "is."

That is not an idle question. Its answer, if one can be persuasively formulated, would be a key guide to questions about what is fitting to hope for from God and what is not, what is fitting to ask for from God and what is not, what is fitting to ascribe to God and what is not, and what is fitting to say to others on God's behalf and what is not. These are very practical questions about the shape of life lived in faithful response to God's ways of relating to us. They can be existentially important questions.

The pastoral remarks made to people anguished by loved ones' suffering that this essay has labeled "theologically problematic" assume the validity of one kind of answer to those questions. That assumed theological "validity" is precisely what is theologically problematic about them. The goal of this book is to show why it is problematic and to outline a theologically more adequate answer.

To that end, I want to begin by distinguishing between what, for convenience sake, I have been calling the (a) "traditional" way of developing a more precise and clear (and quasi-technical) account of God's intrinsic power and what has become (b) the "conventional" version of such an account.

The "traditional" version, I shall argue, is well-warranted so far as it goes; but it limits its warranting of its account to canonical Scriptural accounts of God's relating in creative blessing and the implications of the theological claim that God creates ex nihilo. It holds that God "is" as God "does," but the only way in which God "does" that is relevant to understanding the sense in which God is "powerful" is God's relating to create all else ex nihilo. One consequence of that, I shall argue, is that, when all is said and done, its account of God's power is vague in a way that invites the projection onto it of a culturally familiar understanding of "power" deemed compatible with it and clearer than it.

The "conventional" version, I shall argue, is a modern cultural artifact deeply shaped by scientific and technological developments in the nineteenth and twentieth centuries, an understanding of "power-in-general" that is shared by those of us who, willy-nilly, are shaped by that culture. That familiar understanding of "power" is conventionally projected onto the "traditional" version of God's power to clarify the latter's final vagueness; or so the argument goes here.

"Traditional" Accounts of God's "Power"

"Traditional" theological explanations of God's power have their home in what is sometimes referred to as "Christian Theism." In its broad outlines, it is common to Roman Catholic and Protestant theological traditions. Its "classic" formulations in both Catholic and Protestant theology typically exhibit the hallmarks of theological "scholasticism."[1] On the Catholic side, it has been most influentially expressed in St. Thomas Aquinas' *Summa Theologiae*. On the Protestant side, it has been expressed in theological writings beginning in the seventeenth century that defended either the Lutheran or the Reformed[2] theological critiques of certain features of Roman Catholic theology (and defended either Lutheran

---

[1] As one commentator says of medieval scholastic philosophical writings, they are "hard and dry for much the same reason as a beetle is hard and dry: its skeleton is on the outside" (Introduction [unsigned], *The Cambridge Companion to Aquinas*, ed. Norman Kretzmann and Eleonore Stump [Cambridge: Cambridge University Press, 1993]), p. 6. So too in "scholastic" theologies: their "skeleton" is an explicit statement of the formal structure of the argument that is being made. Historically "scholastic" theological writings also typically formulate their arguments in the technical metaphysical conceptuality of some variation of "classical" philosophical traditions that trace back to "Hellenistic" Greco-Roman thinkers.

[2] Here "Reformed" is used in reference to the sixteenth-century reformation of the Church in various Swiss Cantons and its spread to France, the Netherlands, England, and Scotland.

theological formulations against Reformed critiques or Reformed formulations against Lutheran critiques). Protestant scholastics also explored the systematic implications of the positions they defended in those controversies for other traditional doctrines that earlier sixteenth-century Reformers had not much discussed. Perhaps the culturally most influential Protestant scholastic expression of the doctrine of God, and therewith God's power, in the United States up through the nineteenth century was that of the Reformed scholastic theologian Francis Turretin.[3] "Scholastic" theology is thus inherently controversial theology, written to defend one side or another in theological controversies.

The first question Thomas takes up in Part 1a of the *Summa* concerns the distinctive nature of theology or "sacred doctrine." There is a "science" whose subject matter is God, viz., "divine doctrine." What is distinctive about that "science" is that it argues from first principles that are scripturally revealed. Such "divine doctrine" is fundamentally different from the philosophical science of metaphysics whose subject matter is not God, but being-as-such. The first principles of metaphysics are discovered, not in revelation, but by rational analysis of the most general features of the concretely actual instances of "being" that human experience encounters. It can study God only indirectly as the "first cause" implied by the existential contingency of all concretely actual instances of "being"[4] that we experience. God does not fall under "being-as-such," i.e., is not one sort of "instantiation" among others of "being-as-such." That is why the science of metaphysics cannot study God directly. On the other hand, the questions about God that follow the first two questions in Part 1a of the *Summa* are directly about God,

---

[3] Francis Turretin, *Institutes of Elentic Theology*, Ed., James J. Dennison, tr., George Musgrave Geiger (Phillipsburg, NJ: P & R Publishing). An "elenchus" is an argument that refutes another argument.

[4] Cf. *Summa Theologica*, Ia. Q 1, 1–8.

i.e., are "divine doctrine" and not "metaphysics."[5] That holds true even though, based on scripturally revealed first principles, they nonetheless freely make analogical use of the conceptuality that is developed in the "science" of metaphysics to analyze "being-as-such."

Focusing here on the concept of power that is "traditionally" attributed to God, I shall take Thomas Aquinas' explanation of God's "power" in his *Summa Theologiae* to be representative of the "traditional" theological account of God's power. In Part Ia of his *Summa,* as elsewhere, Thomas expresses the *Summa's* "exo-skeleton" as a series of questions whose answers cumulatively add up to an explanation of the rationale for some basic Christian theological claim. The theological claim whose rationale is explained in Part 1a of the *Summa* is that God is One God in three Persons.

Thomas locates his explanation of "power" as a quality that is properly attributed to God in the next to last of a set of twenty-two questions about such qualities or "attributes" of God. It is placed just before Thomas' explanation of the attribution to God of "Beatitude," which Thomas arguably treats as the culmination and summary of all the other nineteen qualities that he has already argued comprise God's oneness; and it comes just before Thomas turns in Part 1a of the *Summa* from an account of the Triune God's "Oneness" to God's "Threeness."

I suggest that the full force of his explanation of the sense in which God is "powerful" is shaped, not simply by what he expressly says about that power, but just as importantly by where he places his explicit account of God's power in the larger context of his full account of the "manner of God's existence." By explaining "the manner of God's existence, in order that we may know its essence,"[6] the twenty-one qualities attributed to God before "power" is

---

[5] The most obvious sign of that is that it is an account, not of "what" and "who" generic "Divinity" or "God" is, but "what" and "who" the *Triune* God is.

[6] *Summa Theologica,* Ia Preface to Qu. 3.

explained tell us "what" it is to be the God who is "powerful." By the time he gets to "power," Thomas has pretty much told us all he thinks we can hope to know about the qualities that make God *God*. Indeed, he has placed "power" so far down (or back?) in the full list of divine qualities that, although undoubtedly traditional, his explicit account of God's "power" is basically redundant once the preceding twenty-one qualities have been explained. The explanation of God's quality of "Beatitude" that follows his account of God's "power" serves to sum up "what" and "who" the God is that is "powerful."

To show why I suggest interpreting Thomas' account of God's power in Part 1a of the *Summa* in the way outlined above, I shall proceed in the following fashion. First, we will consider what Thomas explicitly says about God's power. Then we will analyze the larger context within which he locates that account. That will involve, first, a very brief tour of the overall structure and movement of Thomas' account of the "manner of God's existence" in Part 1a of the *Summa* leading up to his explanation of God's "power." We will then be in a position to summarize the import of that context for interpretation of Thomas' account of the power of God.

Thomas' Explicit Account in the Summa of God's Power

Thomas' explicit account of God's power in Part 1a of the *Summa* begins with an article that explains the sense in which "power" is attributed to God and then continues with five articles that discuss the scope of God's power.

He makes two general points about "power" attributed to God. The first is a distinction between two senses of "power," only one of which may be attributed to God. "Active power" is the "principle of acting upon something else." "Passive power," on the other hand, is the "principle of being acted upon."[7] At the creaturely level, for example, something that is actively burning has the "active power"

[7] *Summa Theologica*, 1a 25, 1.

to make something else hot, perhaps even to ignite. That which it heats has the "passive power" to be heated, perhaps even the "power" to burst into flame. Given that "everything, according as it is in act and is perfect, is the active principle of something," and given that "God is pure act, absolutely and universally perfect, . . . it most fittingly belongs to [God] to be an active principle."[8] "Passive power," however, "exists not at all in God."[9]

Thomas' second general point about the sense in which "power" may be attributed to God concerns the relations among "active power," "act," and "effect." In general (i.e., metaphysically speaking), "active power" is "founded"[10] *on* act. That is, in regard to "active power," it is "acts" that are powerful. In God, "active power" is not an underlying "power" separate from God's acts and more basic than God's acts, which sometimes is "enacted" by God. Indeed, given the noncomposite simpleness of God's concrete actuality, "God's action is not distinct from [God's] power" because "both are [God's] essence"[11] and God's essence is identical with God's existence.[12] So God's "active power" cannot be conceived as something distinct from God's "manner of existence,"[13] something that God "owns" and lies "below" or "behind" God's acts, and is

---

[8] *Summa Theologica*, 1a 25, 1.

[9] *Summa Theologica*, 1a 25, 1.

[10] *Summa Theologica*, 1a 25, 1, ad. 1.

[11] *Summa Theologica*, 1a 25, 1, ad. 2.

[12] Cf. *Summa Theologica*, 1a 25, 1, ad. 2.

[13] The phrase "manner of existence" will be used frequently in this discussion. It comes from Aquinas' preface to *Summa Theologica* 1a Q 3, the beginning of his consideration of "what belongs to the divine substance," (which can only be described in terms of what it is *not*), which he distinguishes in Q 14 from "what belongs to God's operations." He distinguishes between operation that "proceeds to an exterior effect," which he sets aside until he turns to consideration of the economy, and operation that is "immanent." There are two "immanent" operations in God: knowledge and will. Although discussion of them does not seem to be limited to "what God is not," they do seem to be qualities of God's "manner of existence" that, like all of God's attributes, are distinguishable conceptually, are not different ontologically, and so are interchangeable "names" for God's one "manner of existence."

occasionally exercised by God in particular acts. Rather 'active power' is a quality of God's simple 'act of existing.' In the order of being the relation between God's 'active power,' God's 'acts,' and God's concrete actuality is that of identity.

That identity marks the basic difference between the way God's "active power" is related to God's "acts" and to God's "manner of existence", on one side, and the way creatures' – especially human creatures' – "active power" is related to their "acts" and to their "manner of existence." In creatures "power is the principle not only of action but likewise of the effect of action."[14] In a creature, some "power" of the creature is activated and "causes" both the creature's action and the effect of that action in another creature. The creature's sheer "manner of existence" does not of itself cause an effect

---

[14] *Summa Theologica*, 1a 25, 1, ad. 3. The term "principle" that is frequently used in this discussion is a technical term borrowed from pre-Christian Greco-Roman metaphysical theories. "Principle" is an explanatory concept. In general, a being's principle is the *source* of that of which it is the principle. The basic analogy for the relation of a "principle" to the thing of which it is the explanatory principle comes from biology. A living entity's principle is the "essence" or "nature" of its life, the source of its *kind* of life. (For the following discussion cf. *Summa Theologica*, Ia 33, 1 and ad 3.) Thomas draws a distinction between those "principles" that are "causes" and those that are not. All are "principles," i.e., "sources" of some sort of motion or change (including, for Thomas, the "change" consisting of the cosmos' coming into existence). "Causes" are a subset of "principles." They are distinguished in two ways. One is the *dependence* of an effect on a cause: "cause" connotes a diversity of substances and the dependence of one (the effect) on the other (the cause). "Principle" (e.g., in the case of a living creature) used without further qualification does not necessarily imply either a diversity of substances or dependence of one being (the substance in which a difference, the "effect," is made) on the substance that is the "cause" of that difference. The second distinction between "principle" and "cause" rests on the *priority* of causes to their effects, in being if not in time. Used unqualified, "principle" only implies origin, not necessarily the ontological or temporal priority of the principle to that of which it is the principle. Qualified as efficient cause, "principle" does imply such priority. It is "principle" as "cause." God is the "first principle" of all creatures as both "source" and "cause" of both "what" they are, i.e., of their individual particular "principles," and of the fact "that" they are, i.e., that they exist as parts of a creation that is an ordered cosmos and not a chaos.

in other creatures. But given the absolute simpleness of God's "manner of existence," there is no difference in the order of reality between God's "manner of existence" (which is nothing other than God's "act of existing"), any "act" of God, and "God's power." Therefore, "in God the idea of power is retained [*only*] in so far as it is the principle of an effect, not however, so far as it is a principle of action," because that principle "is the divine essence itself."[15] In short, what is "powerful" about God's "acts" is their effects, and not, strictly speaking, some "capacity" or passive potency "in" God that is the effects' "cause." God's singular "manner of existing," and not some element of some power-pack God "has," does the "acting"; and it is "powerfully" effective in making certain changes in some creature(s). The difference between God and creatures in this regard means that the "power" we attribute to creatures can only be predicated of God analogically to characterize the "effects" God has on creatures.

Following this analysis of the general sense in which "power" may be attributed to God Thomas addresses five issues concerning the scope of God's power:

a) God's active power is unrestricted in scope, i.e., infinite, because "active power exists in God according to the measure in which [God] is actual" and because God's being is "not limited by anything that receives it,"[16]; for the same reasons, however, no effect of God's power "agrees with [God] either in species or in genus"[17] and therefore "[I]t follows that [God's] effect is always less than [God's] power."[18]

b) God's active power can do all things "that are [logically] possible,"[19] the best evidence of which is that "God's

[15] *Summa Theologica*, 1a 25, 1, ad. 3.
[16] *Summa Theologica*, 1a 25, 2, ad. 1; emphasis added.
[17] *Summa Theologica*, 1a 25, 2, ad. 2.
[18] *Summa Theologica*, 1a 25, 2, ad. 2.
[19] *Summa Theologica*, 1a 25, 3.

omnipotence is particularly shown in *sharing and having mercy*, because in this it is made manifest that God has supreme power, namely, that [God] freely forgives sins... [It] is thus shown because by sparing and having mercy upon [us], [God] leads [us] to the participation in infinite good [i.e., "sharing" in God's "good"]; which is the ultimate effect of the divine power."[20]

c) Because "that the past should not have been implies a contradiction,"[21] it cannot be said that God's active power extends to making the past not to have been.

d) Because God's active power in creating and providentially governing "the present scheme of things" is caused by God's free will and not by "natural necessity," "we must say absolutely that God can do other things than those [God] has done."[22]

e) The scope of God's power to make creatures better is limited in one way and not in another. "Make better" has to do with creatures' good but is ambiguous. In one sense, the "good" of a creature is defined by its essence. Given, for example, that by the "ordained power" of God's creative will rationality is essential to human creatures, "as regards this good God cannot make a thing better than it is itself."[23] On the other hand, it is also the case that by God's "absolute power" the scope of *sorts* of good creatures that God could create is unlimited: So "God can make another thing [say, an angel] better than [say, a human creature]"[24] with regard to their "ontological good." That point can be extended from particular creatures to the created universe as a whole. "Given the

---

[20] *Summa Theologica*, 1a 25, 3 ad 3.

[21] *Summa Theologica*, 1a 25, 4.

[22] *Summa Theologica*, 1a 25, 5.

[23] *Summa Theologica*, 1a 25, 6.

[24] *Summa Theologica*, 1a 25, 6.

things which actually exist, the universe cannot be better, for the order which God has established in things [by the ordained power of God's will], and in which the good of the universe [as a whole] consists, befits things. For if any one thing were bettered, the proportion of order would be destroyed; ... Yet God could [by the "absolute power" of God's will] make other things, or add something to the present creation; and then there would be another and a better universe."[25] In a second sense of "good," the "good" of a human creature is "over and above the essence; thus the good of a [human creature] is to be virtuous or wise. As regard this sense of 'goodness,' God can make better the things [God] has made."[26]

The last two claims Thomas makes about the scope of God's power introduce an important distinction between two different senses in which "power" may be attributed to God. Because God's free will (in contradistinction to God's "nature" or "essence") creates a wise and just creation by active power, an important distinction is introduced between two senses in which active power may be attributed to God: "*absolute power*" and "*ordained power.*" Thomas bases that distinction on the claim that "nothing prevents there being something in the divine power which [God] does not will, and which is not included in the order that [God] established in things."[27] That claim itself follows, he argues, from the freedom of will by which God acts: "God does things because [God] so wills; yet [God] is able to do so, not because [God] so wills, but because [God] is such in [God's] nature."[28] "[I]n God, power, essence, will, intellect, wisdom and justice are one and the same. Whence, there can be found nothing in the divine power which cannot be found in

[25] *Summa Theologica*, 1a 25, 6 ad.3.

[26] *Summa Theologica*, 1a 25, 6.

[27] *Summa Theologica*, 1a 25, 5 ad. 1.

[28] *Summa Theologica*, 1a 25, 5, ad. 1.

[God's] just will or in [God's] wise intellect. Now, because [God's] will cannot be determined by necessity to this or that order of things, . . . and because the wisdom and justice of God are likewise restricted not to this present order,"[29] it follows that there may well be things within God's power that God nonetheless does not will and so are not included in the "present scheme of things" in this creation.

That, in turn, entails the distinction between two senses in which God is "powerful": "[B]ecause power is considered as *exercising*, will as *commanding*, and intellect and wisdom as *directing*, what is attributed to [God's] power considered in itself God is said to be able to do in accordance with [God's] *absolute power*."[30] It is "absolute" in that it is abstracted from what God does actually will and pertains only to what in the abstract is logically possible. It follows from the sense in which God is omnipotent: the scope of God's power extends to all noncontradictory possible projects. Nonetheless, it is an *abstract* claim, a conceptually coherent claim about logical possibility. It is not a reality claim, i.e., a claim about concrete actuality.

"On the other hand," Thomas continues, "what is attributed to the divine power, according as it carries into execution the command of a just will, God is said to be able to do by his *ordained power*."[31] It is "ordained" in that it is what God's causal willing does in fact "approve"[32] or "ordain." In the first question in which Thomas discusses God's will he argues that, unlike our creaturely acts of will, the will of God, and here we may add the "ordained power" of the will of God, "must needs always be fulfilled."[33] The reason is that God's power is the same as God's will, and God's will

---

[29] *Summa Theologica*, 1a 25, 5 ad. 1.

[30] *Summa Theologica*, 1a 25, 5 ad. 1. Emphasis original.

[31] *Summa Theologica*, 1a 25, 5 ad. 1. Emphasis original.

[32] Cf. Thomas' characterization of God's creating things by knowing them "knowledge of approbation," *Summa Theologica*, 1a 19, 5; cf. also 1a 19, 10.

[33] *Summa Theologica*, 1a 19, 6.

is the same as God's being which is creation's *arche* or the "agent cause" that is creation's "universal cause" and an "effect cannot possibly escape the order of the universal cause."[34]

It is important to interpret this distinction between God's "absolute power" and God's "ordained power" in the context of the second general point that Thomas makes about the sense in which "power" may be attributed to God[35]: because "active power" is "founded"[36] on act and "both are [God's] essence,"[37] God's "power" cannot be conceived as something distinct from God's "manner of existence," something God "owns" and that lies somehow "below" or "behind" God's acts, and is occasionally exercised by God in particular acts. Not only is God's "absolute power" not a potentiality God has; it does not have the ontological status of an actual "capability" for various "acts" that are independent of, and ontologically more basic than, the "acts" God does in fact do. Hence, God's "power" does not have a neutral "foundational" status, both prior to and independent of God's actual just and merciful "acts," such that it ("in principle") might just as well be the principle of unjust and cruel acts.

Thomas' explicit discussion of God's power makes it clear that the qualities of God's power are defined by "what" and "who" it is to be God. God's "power" is "active power" rather than "passive power" and it is "founded"[38] *on* God's acts, rather than God's "acts" being ontologically dependent on God's underlying unlimited supply of "power-in-general." God's singular "*a se* act of existence" is "what" God is, what makes God *God*, rather than God's power being what makes God *God*. Thomas' account identifies grammar-like rules governing how to talk (or how not to talk) about the scope

[34] *Summa Theologica*, 1a 19, 6.
[35] P. 13.
[36] *Summa Theologica*, 1a 25, 1, ad. 1.
[37] *Summa Theologica*, 1a 25, 1, ad. 2.
[38] *Summa Theologica*, 1a 25, 1, ad. 1.

of God's power considered either "absolutely" or "ordained." However, in his explicit discussion of God's power Thomas does not explain what the qualities of God's power are. Consequently, left at that, and read without reference to its context in Part 1a of the *Summa*, Thomas' account of God's "power" has little substantive conceptual content concerning the character of God's power. It is, I suggest, the context at the end of which Thomas places his account of God's power that provides that characterization. That in particular is what makes Thomas' account paradigmatic of "traditional" accounts of God's power. God does as God is. Because of God's con-composite simpleness, there is no distinction in the order of being between God's "manner of existing," i.e., God's "substance," and God's "power" in the effects of God's actively relating to what is not God. Accordingly, the qualities of God's "manner of existing" just are the qualities of God's power. We turn to that now.

Thomas' Explicit Account of God's Power in Its Larger Context

If, as Thomas argues, God's active power is "founded" *on* God's act and does not lie "behind" or "beneath" God's act as though it were a separate reality (God's "power-pack" or "power-as-such," perhaps analogous to a "faculty" or a "capability") that God may or may not exercise, then that "power" must have qualities that are not the qualities of some "power-as-such," but the distinctive qualities of the God that acts. The larger context in which Thomas places his account of God's power is precisely his account in Part 1 of the *Summa,* questions three to twenty-six of what can be said (or, better, cannot be said) about the qualities of "what" it is to be God and, in a certain way, "who" God is. It is that context that identifies the distinctive qualities of the "power" that may be attributed to God.

Questions three through twenty-six and questions twenty-seven through forty-one taken together offer an extended argument that develops cumulatively to explain the Christian claim that God is One God in three Persons by explaining, first, what "belongs to the unity of the divine essence," i.e., explaining "the manner of God's existence," (questions three through twenty-six) and then, second, "what belongs to the Trinity of the three persons in God" (questions twenty-seven through forty-three). Together they are the larger context in which Thomas' explicit account of God's power is set. It is located just before the transition from discussion of the unity of the divine essence to discussion of Trinity of three persons in God. Thus, the questions explaining "the manner of God's existence" (questions three through twenty-six) are the part of that larger context of Thomas' discussion of "what" and "who" God is that identifies qualities of God that are also qualities of God's power in the singular sense in which "active power" may be attributed to God.

So we focus here on questions three through twenty-six that culminate in an explanation in question twenty-six of the attribution to God of "Beatitude." They give a developing picture of God's intrinsic or "essential" qualities that moves through two clearly distinguished steps. The first step (questions three through eleven) lays out what can be said about the metaphysical singularity of God's "manner of existence." Its capstone is a discussion of God's unity in question 11, explaining the sense in which the Triune God is nonetheless one God. The qualities attributed to God in this step are abstract, metaphysical, and, to modern ears, largely "impersonal." The second step (questions fourteen through twenty-six) lays out what can be said about God's willing and knowing. The transition to it is marked by two questions (twelve and thirteen), not directly about God, but about the metaphysics of human capacity to know and to "name," i.e., talk about, God. The metaphysical analysis in those two questions is then used analogically in questions fourteen through twenty-six to explain attribution to God, as additional qualities of God's "manner of existence," "operations" of knowing and willing that are ways in which it is essential to God to be actively self-relating.[39] The qualities attributed to God in questions fourteen through twenty-six are somewhat more concrete and, to modern ears, more "personal." As we shall see, according to Thomas God's Beatitude (question twenty-six) sums up the entire series of Thomas' questions whose answers outline God's "manner of existence," not just in terms of "what" it is to be God but also in a certain way in terms of "who" God is.

We shall take a short tour through each of those two steps in Thomas' analysis of "God's manner of existence" to harvest the qualities of God's singular reality that are, therewith, necessarily also qualities of the sense of "power" that may be attributed to God. We shall be interested chiefly in getting clear just what those qualities are. We will usually not linger to analyze and assess Thomas' arguments in support of attribution of each of them.

"[B]cause we cannot know what God is, but rather what He is not, we have no means for considering how God is," *questions three through eleven* ask "how [God] is not."[40] Hence, the qualities Thomas ascribes to God in his explication of God's substance are not only highly abstract but also all negative: the Triune God is *non*composite (simpleness),[41] *lacking* potentiality (purely actual; perfect; good),[42] *without* extrinsic limits (infinite),[43] *un*restricted (ubiquity),[44] *in*capable of change (immutability),[45] time*less*

---

[39] That essential self-relating by God lays the basis for Thomas' later explanation of the sense in which God essentially can be One in *three* persons (questions twenty-seven through forty-three), because each "person" of the Trinity is constituted as the "person" it is by its unique relations to the other "persons" of the divine Trinity. Cf. especially Part Ia 40, "The Persons as Compared to the Relations or Properties."

[40] *Summa Theologica*, 1a, Preface to 3.

[41] *Summa Theologica*, 1a 3.

[42] *Summa Theologica*, 1a 4–6.

[43] *Summa Theologica*, 1a 7.

[44] *Summa Theologica*, 1a 8.

[45] *Summa Theologica*, 1a 9.

(eternal),[46] and *utterly singular* (unity).[47] Given the immutability of God's noncomposite "simpleness" it also follows that emotions that are inherently changeable and often fleeting cannot be attributed to God. In "traditional" accounts of God's power, such emotions are often called "passions." God is *impassive*. These are qualities that are unique to "what" it is to be God, qualities of God's "nature." They are sometimes described as "impersonal" or "metaphysical" qualities of what it is to be God. We have justifications (rooted in revelation) for attributing them to God even though we have no capacity to grasp conceptually how they positively mean when attributed to God.

Because Thomas argues that all the other qualities of God's "nature" follow from it, Brian Davies holds that Thomas' account of the quality of simpleness in the first of these questions (question three) is "a doctrine which forms the core of his teaching about God."[48]

God's "simplicity" entails that God's concretely actual "manner of existing" is utterly singular: God is so purely (i.e., noncompositely) "actual" that God cannot be thought to be a "composite" of an "essence" or "nature" on one hand (say the essence "divinity" or "being-as-such") and "existence" on the other hand. Nor can it be thought as a "composite" of some "species" of being, on one hand, and on the other hand whatever distinguishes that "species" from other "species" of beings that fall within the same "genus" of beings. God "manner of existing" is not an instance of any species or genus of beings.[49] It is not even an instance of being-as-such, which is the subject of the science of metaphysics. Furthermore, God's "simpleness" entails that, although qualities such as "pure actuality," "infinity,"

---

[46] *Summa Theologica,* 1a 10.

[47] *Summa Theologica,* 1a 11.

[48] *The Thought of Thomas Aquinas* (Oxford: Clarendon Press, 1992), p. 44.

[49] Cf. *Summa Theologica,* 1a 5–7.

"ubiquity," "eternity," and "unity" are indeed used to attribute conceptually distinguishable qualities to God, in the order of reality in God they do not constitute a "composite" of qualities in God. Rather, they are ontologically one and the same as God's "substance" or concretely actual "manner of existing."

The closest Thomas can get to characterizing God's "essence" by characterizing God's "manner of existing" is to hold that God's essence is just to exist *a se*. God's "essence" or "nature" simply *is* God's act of concretely existing.[50] That "act" does not depend on or otherwise entail any other reality. It simply, timelessly is. That singular "act" is "what" it is to be God.

Given that, as we have seen, for Thomas God's "active power" is "founded"[51] *on* God's "act" of existing, it follows that the singularity of God's "act of existence" entails the singularity of the sense in which "power" may be attributed to God. To claim, "God is powerful," is like claiming, "Each of us is powerful," in the general and very vague sense of "power" that, like our ways of relating to other beings, God's relating to other beings "makes a difference" for or in them. Indeed, as we have seen, Thomas insists, that "in God the idea of [active] power is retained in so far as it is the principle of an effect [in a creature], not however, so far as it is a principle of action."[52] An act's "effects" are the "differences" it makes. However, because the "principle" of God's active power "is the divine essence itself,"[53] that power is a quality that is simply the same as God's "act of existing." Consequently, it is as different from our creaturely "powers" as God's "manner of existence" is different from our creaturely "manner of existence." Hence God's power has the quality of "unity," i.e., not being part of a composite. Accordingly, we are also justified in ascribing to God's power such qualities as

---

[50] Cf. *Summa Theologica*, 1a 3, a 4; 1a 11.

[51] *Summa Theologica*, 1a 25. 1, ad. 1.

[52] *Summa Theologica*, 1a 25, 1, ad. 3.

[53] *Summa Theologica*, 1a 25, 1, ad. 3.

being "purely actual" (i.e., has no "passive power"), "infinite," "ubiquitous" (or, "omnipresent"), and "eternal."

The grammar-like rules Thomas outlines that govern what we may say about the scope of God's active power rule out some things we might otherwise think we have warrant for saying about God's power on the basis of revelation, and they may rule in things we might not otherwise say (we will return to that point). But they do not widen the extremely limited scope of our conceptual grasp of how "power" means when attributed to God.

The second step in Aquinas' explanation of what 'belongs to the unity of the divine essence," *questions fourteen through twenty-six,* lays out what can be said about God's willing and knowing. It is framed as a discussion of qualities of God's intrinsic *operations* rather than on qualities of God's substance.[54] God's "operations" turn out to be the dynamics of an active self-relating that are essential qualities of God's "manner of existence." Aquinas distinguishes between an operation that "is immanent" to a substance and an operation that "proceeds to an exterior effect." He postpones discussion of God's operations that proceed "to an exterior effect" until later in *Summa,* after he has completed his account of the qualities intrinsic to God's "nature." In questions fourteen through twenty-six he identifies two "immanent operations" and their implications that are essential to God's substance: God's knowing and God's willing. Thomas' account of God's operations is not a departure from his account of "what" it is to be God. It is an extension of it. Indeed, when Thomas turns from his account of God's "unity" in questions three through twenty-six to explain the Triune God's intrinsic (or "immanent") "three-ness" in questions twenty-seven through forty-three he builds his explanation on his analysis of the *dynamic* of the "operations" that he has already shown in questions fourteen through twenty-four are intrinsic to God's substance.

[54] Cf. Preface to *Summa Theologica,* Ia 14.

Where the qualities that Thomas attributes to God as qualities of God's "manner of existing" in what I dubbed the first "step" of nine questions about God's unity (questions three through eleven) were negative, highly abstract, and "impersonal," the qualities he attributes to God as qualities of God's "operations" of "knowing" and "willing" in the second "step" of thirteen questions (questions fourteen through twenty-six) are largely, like "knowing" and "willing" themselves, dynamic, somewhat more concrete, and somewhat closer to the modern sense of "personal qualities" than the negative remarks about God's substance in questions three through eleven. Thomas' explication of God's knowing and willing rests on analogical attribution to God of his analysis of the metaphysics of human knowing and willing in questions twelve and thirteen.

According to that analysis, in addition to having their own "form" or "nature" the substances of knowing beings are "naturally adapted to have... the form of some other thing, for the [form] of the thing known is in the knower."[55] The relative contraction of a form comes from matter.[56] "Therefore it is clear that the immateriality of a thing is the reason why it is cognitive, and according to the

---

[55] *Summa Theologica*, Ia 14. 1.

[56] "The relative contraction of a form comes from matter." On Thomas' terms, that maxim is not as arbitrary as it may seem. Only living creatures "know." What "knows" in a living creature is "principle of life," i.e., its soul, which is its "form" and not its "matter." "Vegetative" and "animal" forms of "life" have, respectively, "vegetative" and "animal" souls that "know" only in very restrictive senses of the term having to do with identifying the goals toward which the creature's changes and "movements" are inherently directed. A human creature's "form" is a "rational soul," capable of selecting the array of goals to which it will aim its changes and movements. The cognitive scope of such a "rational soul" is less restricted by a human creature's matter than the "vegetative" and "animal" souls of plants and animals are restricted by their matter in that, unlike them, it can itself be "in-formed" by the "forms" of a great array of other kinds of formed-matter creaturely substances. Thinking analogically along the same line, the cognitive scope of a reality (the Triune God) that is purely actual and therefore absolutely nonmaterial, would be unlimited.

mode of immateriality is the mode of cognition."[57] Whatever a given substance's "mode of cognition" may be, it is a dynamic "operation" that is an essential quality of that substance.

Attributed analogically to God, Thomas' analysis of the metaphysics of cognition warrants the claim that God's "is the most perfect *knowledge*," i.e., universally comprehensive, completely detailed, and absolutely accurate knowledge, precisely because, given God's noncomposite simpleness, God is pure act and hence is *absolutely* immaterial. Accordingly God must be said to know everything that is knowable.

Given the absolute simpleness of God's "mode of existence," not just God's "intellect," but God's dynamic operation of "knowing" must be said to be identical with God's pure act of existence. Accordingly, God's "knowing" must be said to have the same qualities as God's "manner of existing": God's knowing is fundamentally a cognitive self-relating[58] in which God is absolutely transparent to Godself.[59] Moreover, given that that God's "manner of existence" is noncomposite and that, therefore, God cannot undergo either substantial or accidental change, God knows all that God knows simultaneously and not discursively.[60]

---

[57] *Summa Theologica*, Ia 14, 1.

[58] Cf. *Summa Theologica*, 1a 14, 1.

[59] It is only in knowing Godself that God knows other things. God knows other things in their particularities precisely by God's act of knowing Godself: "God could not be said to know [Godself] perfectly unless [God] knew all the ways in which [God's] own perfection can be shared by others" (cf. *Summa Theologica*, 1a 14, 5). "Neither could [God] know the very nature of being perfectly, unless [God] knew all the ways of being. Hence it is manifest that God knows all things with a proper knowledge, according as they are distinguished from each other" (cf. *Summa Theologica*, 1a 14, 7), i.e., knows them in their particularities. The basis on which God knows them in their particularities, the condition of the possibility of that "knowing," is that God's substance is dynamically cognitively self-relating and in being absolutely self-transparent knows all the ways in which others can share in creaturely fashion in what God is.

[60] Cf. *Summa Theologica*, 1a 14, 7.

Then, moving through an analysis of concepts ordinarily related to "knowing" ("ideas"[61]; "truth"[62]; "falsity"[63]), Thomas argues that God's essential "operation" of knowing entails that God "lives." "[A] thing is said to live insofar as it operates of itself and not as moved by another," so "the more perfectly this power is found in anything, the more perfect is the life of that thing... [T]hat being whose act of understanding is its very nature, and which, in what it naturally possesses, is not determined by another, must have life in the most perfect degree. Such is God; and hence in [God] principally is life."[64]

Accordingly, because the qualities of God's "power" are identical with the qualities of God's "operation" of knowing, then God's power also must have the qualities of a living reality constituted by an absolutely self-transparent cognitive self-relating that is non-discursive, i.e., is not exercised by God through temporally extended stages of some process. For all of its radical differences than human "power," God's "power" is intrinsically "living," "intelligent," "knowing," and "mindful." In those regards, God's intrinsic "power" has "personal" qualities.

If a substance's "immateriality" implies that some "mode of cognition" is essential to it, it follows also that "*will*" and the operation of "willing" is essential to it. As we have seen, "will" is not an independent second "immanent operation." It is an entailment of "intellect." Cognitive substances are disposed to seek what they *think* will make for the full realization of "what" they are when they do not have it, and to rest in it when they do. Realization of the fullness of "what" they are in their kinds is their creaturely "good." Both the tending and the resting pertain to the will. Thomas defines cognitive creatures' essential "disposition" to seek what they think

---

[61] Q 15.
[62] Q 16.
[63] Q 17.
[64] *Summa Theologica*, 1a 18, 3.

makes for their "good" when they do not have it, and to rest in it when they do have it, as their "will."[65]

Attributed analogically to God, Thomas' analysis of the metaphysics of willing warrants the claim that God necessarily wills "to remain in" God's own perfectly simple actuality, i.e., in God's own good, for that is a tendency inherent in every being. In God's case, the transparency of God's cognitive self-knowing entails that God knows truly what is God's own good. Hence God is intrinsically and timelessly self-faithful. In God's active self-relating and relating to all else God is trustworthily faithful to Godself.

If the qualities of God's "power" are identical with the qualities of God's "operation" of "willing" (as they are identical with God's "knowing"), then God's intrinsic power must also be fundamentally a self-relating that in absolutely self-transparent cognition knows its own "good," knows that it has that "good," and "rests" timelessly and unchangingly in it. For all of its radical differences to human "power," God's "power" is intrinsically ordered to the "good." That is the basis in reality of all the "goods" that creatures seek and exhibit, and to which God is timelessly faithful. That self-faithfulness makes God's "power" both trustworthy and attractive of trust.

Thomas then argues that God's "operation" of willing justifies attribution of the qualities "love," "mercy," and "justice" to God's *a se* "manner of existing." Because "love is the first movement of the will" toward the good, we must assert that "in God there is *love*."[66] God's will is also at once *just* (in the sense of "distributive justice") in the way that it goes about God's disposition to rest in God's good and to share it, and *merciful* in the way God will goes about God's disposition to share the good that God is, viz., by dispelling misery and by perfecting the defects that cause the misery.[67]

---

[65] Cf. *Summa Theologica*, 1a 19, 1 and 2.
[66] *Summa Theologica*, 1a 20, 1.
[67] Cf. *Summa Theologica*, 1a 21, 3.

Accordingly, because the qualities of God's "power" are identical with the qualities of God's "operation" of willing, then God's power also must have the qualities of a living reality constituted by an absolutely self-transparent cognitive self-relating that is intrinsically "loving" in the sense that it nondiscursively knows God's own good and "rests" timelessly and unchangingly in it, and loving in ways that are at once intrinsically "just" and "merciful." In those regards also, God's "power" has "personal" qualities.

* * * * *

A brief digression: Although Thomas Aquinas is broadly paradigmatic of "traditional" Christian theism in attributing both "intellect" and "will" alongside each other to God, his way of relating will to intellect is not paradigmatic of that tradition. It is arguable that, strictly speaking, in regard to human creatures Thomas does not have a concept of "the will" as a faculty or power that is conceptually irreducibly distinct from "the intellect," in contrast, say, to the way in which "justice" and "mercy" are conceptually irreducible to each other even though both may be attributed God's love. It is as though, for Thomas, a human creature's power of "intellect" is intrinsically ordered to the truth about all sorts of things, and "will" is intellect's intrinsic orderedness in particular to judgments about the truth of its own goodness in its kind, its tendency to seek it if it does not have it, and to rest in it when it does have it. A generation later than Thomas, some theologians treat human creatures' will as a human power fundamentally distinct conceptually from intellect (John Duns Scotus is often cited as the theologian whose writings formulate this alternative to Thomas most effectively). Human intellect may be intrinsically ordered to knowing the truth about many matters; by contrast, a human will is intrinsically ordered to actualizing goals that a human creature has set for itself in and through its interactions with other creatures by "marshaling" all of its resources, focusing its energies, and intensifying its efforts. Here "willing x" is not simply "choosing" x as one's goal. It is also so fully committing one's other powers to its actualization that it is successfully realized.

This second sense of "will" in human creatures has no conceptual resources to block three problematic inferences from it. It is open to the inference that human "will" is intrinsically ordered to "domination," to having the power to "control" what goes on in one's interactions with other creatures such that one can actualize one's goals. "Will" is thus by definition "will-to-power." Second, it is open to the inference that "intellect's" (or, "reason's") primary function is to identify the most effective ways to go about gaining control over "what is going on." "Intellect" is thus instrumentalized. Third, it is open to the inference that human creatures' powers are themselves intrinsically morally neutral. They are not intrinsically ordered to the good. They are morally neutral "resources" that human "will" deploys in ways that "intellect" knows maximize the possibility of control over "what goes on" so as to actualize goals the "will" chooses. The "ways" in which human powers are used may or may not be moral; they are nonetheless powerful. The grounds for choosing just those goals cannot lie in "intellect" when intellect is understood as an instrument in aid of establishing control over "what is going on," except insofar as any given human creature's "intellect" can grasp what lies in that human creature's self-interest. These inferences from this conception of human "will" are possible, but not conceptually necessary. However, neither does anything in this understanding of "will" conceptually block these inferences.

When this second understanding of "will" is analogically attributed to God, it is open to five theologically problematic inferences. It is open to the inference that God's "will" is more fundamental to God's "manner of existence" than is God's "intellect." God unrestrictedly "wills" certain goals regarding reality other than God (in the economy) and therewith "wills" to exercise power "over" all else, exercising "domination" over them to realize those goals. In willing those goals God "decides" that they are "good." They are "good" only because God declares them "good."

Second, it is open to the inference that God chiefly relies on God's "intellect" to guide the *means* by which that domination is best exercised to realize those goals.

Third, it is open to the inference that the unrestricted power that God uses to realize God's willed goals by way of God's dominating control over all that goes on is itself, simply as "power," value-neutral. It is conceptually distinct from God's will. In the order of being, it is more basic than either God's will or God's intellect. In effect, this second understanding of "will," attributed analogically to God, is open to the inference that God's "absolute power" (*potentia absoluta*) is God's concretely actual power. In that case, the power God actually exercises in realizing God's willed goals is just a modification of value-neutral "absolute power" that is ordered to a goal God wills and declares "good," but is not itself intrinsically good (*potentia ordinata*).

That is open, fourth, to the inference that God's will is intrinsically ordered to exercising unrestricted power. God's will just *is* unrestricted will-to-power.

Furthermore, it is open to the inference, fifth, that "unrestricted, value-neutral power" is definitive of God's "manner of existence." It is the quality that makes God *God*.

All of these inferences from analogical attribution to God of this conception of human "will" are possible, but not conceptually necessary. However, nothing in the attribution to God of this understanding of "will" conceptually block these inferences. When they are not blocked and are drawn, these inferences make it difficult to show that God's freely "willed" ways of relating to all else are not intrinsically arbitrary, dominating, competitive with and in conflict with creatures' exercises of their creaturely powers, untrustworthy because the power they exercise is itself as easily hostile and unjust as it is compassionate and just.

End of digression.

* * * * *

We have seen that, although Thomas' explicit account of the sense in which God is powerful tells us little about the qualities of God's power, the location of that explicit discussion of power in Thomas' account of God's "manner of existence" and its intrinsic "operations" identifies a number of qualities of God's "manner of existence" that, because of the noncomposite simpleness of God's singular concrete actuality, must be said also to be qualities of God's power. That point, I suggest, is implicit in Thomas' discussion of the final quality he attributes to God, immediately after his explicit discussion of God's quality of "power": "Beatitude."[68]

"[N]othing else is understood by the term 'beatitude' than the perfect good of an intellectual nature which is capable of knowing that it has the plentitude of the good it possesses, and which is properly the subject of good and evil and hence master of its own actions."[69] "As to contemplative happiness, God possesses a continual and most certain contemplation of [Godself, i.e., in God's transparent self-knowledge,] and of all things else."[70] Thomas analyzes beatitude by analogically attributing to God's beatitude Boethius' analysis of "earthly happiness" into "pleasure, riches, power, dignity, and fame": God "possesses joy in [Godself] and all things else for [God's] pleasure; instead of riches, [God] has that complete self-sufficiency, which is promised by riches; in place of power [God] has omnipotence; for dignities, the governance of all things; and in place of fame, [God] possesses the admiration of all creatures."[71]

In short, God's Beatitude sums up the entire series of Thomas' questions, whose answers outline the dynamic self-relating in knowing and willing that is essential to God's "manner of existence." Beatitude is the state of an intelligent substance whose

[68] Cf. *Summa Theologica*, 1a 25 and 26.
[69] *Summa Theologica*, 1a 26, 1.
[70] *Summa Theologica*, 1a 26, 4.
[71] *Summa Theologica*, 1a 26, 4.

dynamic cognitive and volitional self-relating just is (a) the singular pure actuality of the act of existence *a se*, whose essential qualities are that it is self-sufficient, cognitive, free, loving, just and merciful, and joyous; (b) is the condition of the possibility of creaturely realities that are not God, but whose "goods" in their kinds are ordered to God, are providentially governed by God, and worship (i.e., "admire") God; and (c), significantly, is "omnipotent" *in place of* "power."

The point of that last clause, I take it, is that the sense in which God is "powerful" is that in the abstract God can do any thing that is logically possible (i.e., "omnipotent"), but that what God does actually do is what is in fact concretely actual and is done "beatifically," i.e., done *God's* way: "self-sufficiently, wisely, freely, lovingly, justly and mercifully, and joyously" rather than "dominatingly, arbitrarily, competitively, conflictually, untrustworthily." God does as God is. "Beatitude" sums up God's "attributes" for Thomas; therefore, it sums up the qualities of God's power.

Some "Conventional" Notions about Power

Contrast the "traditional" account of God's power as outlined with several notions about the nature of "power" that are conventional in modern American culture. In *A Theology of Power: Being Beyond Dominion*, Kyle Pasewark[72] makes a persuasive case for the thesis that they include the notions identified in this section in slightly

---

[72] What follows in the text is based on an analysis by Kyle Pasewark. I attempt to identify points at which I modify his analysis. Cf. *A Theology of Power: Being Beyond Dominion*, esp. pp. 1–3. Pasewark points out that Tillich uses "power" with three different connotations that are expressed in German by "Kraft," "Macht," and "Maechtigkeit." "Macht" is close to what are outlined below as features of a currently "conventional" notion of "power." "Maechtigkeit" is closer to human "personal" power and is expressed in Tillich's texts written in English as "power of being" (cf. Pasewark, p. 385).

modified form. It needs to be stressed at the outset that Pasewark does not claim to offer an "archaeology" of these notions, tracing them to common source in the development of "modernity." We might plausibly speculate that they arise from an amalgamation of nontechnical popular understandings of physicists' theories of the nature of "atomic power" and "critical" theories of social and cultural power; but the validity of that genetic speculation is irrelevant to the validity of Pasewark's generalizations. Nor does Pasewark claim that these conventional notions about power amount to a coherent "theory" of power. They are neither rigorously formulated nor defended by rigorous critical argument. Indeed, on close examination many of them may well turn out to be inconsistent with each other. None of that, of course, would necessarily keep those of us shaped by that culture from uncritically relying on all of them in our reflections on "big" questions such as, "How is God's power related to the horrendous suffering so many people undergo?"

Nine of those "conventional" notions about power are salient.

- First, there is such a thing as *power-as-such*. In itself, it is impersonal. Although it may be exercised by human persons, it also can "make differences" in the world through impersonal systems of organization of both matter and social groups.
- Second, the concept of power is *univocal*. It can be properly attributed to various agents only in one and the same sense. It means the same thing in every case. It is possible in principle to construct a single coherent systematic comprehensive theory of power understood in this sense[73] (although it is not clear that any such theory is persuasive).

---

[73] This is not one of Pasewark's characterizations of the conventional concept of power (at least in American culture). However, he devotes the last part of his book to developing a theory of the correct univocal meaning of "power" through a critical dialogue with Paul Tillich's ontology. Engaging Pasewark's constructive project goes well beyond the scope of this book.

- Third, power is a *possession* of whatever or whoever exercises power. That which "owns" it can lose it. That which possesses any degree of power-as-such in may be either personal or impersonal, but the "power-as-such" that it possesses is itself intrinsically impersonal.

- Fourth, power-as-such is a *measurable* possession. One may possess more or less of it. One may also gain or lose the "amount" of power-as-such that one has.

- Fifth, power-as-such is *limited*. Hence, yielding some of the power one possesses to another entails loss of power by its giver and gain of power by its receiver.

- Sixth, power-as-such is *applied* by its possessor externally to some object or objects. Power-as-such is never exercised by one who "owns" it to some object or objects from within them to make an "internal" difference in them. An apparent premise of this notion is that interactions between possessors of power-as-such in which power is gained and lost are always external relations.

- Seventh, power-as-such is *exercised occasionally* or eventfully. When it is not exercised it is a "capacity" or a "potentiality" of its possessor.

- Eighth, although exercise of power-as-such in its external application to some object or objects makes some sort of difference in such objects, it *has no intrinsic telos or purpose* of its own that it seeks to realize by making any particular difference in such objects. If the possessor of some power-as-such is itself a nonpersonal thing, the sort of difference its exercise of power makes in other objects when externally applied to them in an event on some occasion will be determined by the kind of thing the power-possessor is. If the possessor of some power-as-such is a person, that person's chosen purposes or ends will determine the sort of difference her exercise of power makes when externally applied to some object in an event on some occasion. Human persons may exercise power-as-such "personally," but the "power-as-such" that they exercise is itself intrinsically a-teleological, value free, and "impersonal."

- Ninth, interactions between possessors of power-as-such necessarily have the "logic" of zero-sum games. To venture to exercise the measure of power-as-such that one possesses by applying it externally to another object in a particular event on a particular occasion is necessarily to venture either to gain power from that object or to loose power to it.

Traditional Theological Accounts of God's Power and Theologically Problematic Pastoral Remarks

Comparing "traditional" theological accounts of God's power and current "conventional" notions of power, I suggest four things.

a) The sorts of well-intentioned but theologically problematic pastoral remarks that are often made to people who anguish over other persons' profound suffering tacitly *assume* the validity of some or all of those "conventional" notions about power as qualities of God's power.

b) That assumption is key. It is the assumption that "traditional" Christian theological accounts of God's qualities and the qualities of God's power can be clarified by means of those "conventional" notions about power.

However, some themes in "traditional" Christian accounts of God's power are inconsistent with attribution to God of those "conventional" notions about power. The "conventional" notions about God's power are not compatible with major themes in "traditional" theological accounts of God's qualities or attributes. In principle, some of the themes in "traditional" accounts of God's power serve to block efforts to clarify them in terms drawn from conventional notions of power.

c) However, there is a certain vagueness in "traditional" account of God's power that invites efforts to make them more precise. The sorts of theologically problematic pastoral remarks that we have been focusing on take up that invitation. They implicitly "clarify" the vagueness by projecting "conventional" notions of power onto the "vagueness" of "traditional" theological accounts of God's power.

d) There is a structural or systemic reason why "traditional" Christian theological accounts of God's power have the "vagueness" that invites such problematic – mostly implicit – theological "clarification" it.

In the context of Parts I and II, the remaining chapters of Part III propose a remedy to that structural problem. The "remedy" does not eliminate the vagueness concerning God's power. Rather, it clarifies theological reasons to block inferences from "traditional" accounts of God's power that might otherwise seem plausible, inferences that serve to warrant the theologically problematic pastoral comments with which we have been concerned. Blocking those inferences thus blocks projection of conventional notions about power onto Christians' accounts of the qualities of God's power.

Theologically Problematic Pastoral Remarks and "Conventional" Notions about Power

Consider a set of three pastoral remarks that are typically said to comfort people who are in anguish over the profound suffering of someone else:

God sent it (your spouse's cancer or stroke; your daughter's automobile accident that left her in coma; your newborn's congenital disease of the lungs; your best friend's advanced dementia, etc).
God sent it (the same) for a purpose.
God sent (the same) for a purpose that advances God's plan.

Those three remarks are interconnected by some assumptions about the qualities of God's power. Those assumptions, in turn, are warranted by the "conventional" notions about the qualities of "power" that have been outlined.

The claim that God "sent it" – whatever the "it" may be as long as it causes deep suffering that makes a profound "difference" in someone's life – clearly assumes that "it" occurred by God's power when it might not otherwise have occurred. For, generally speaking, to say that some reality is "powerful" in some particular way is to say that it can make some particular difference in some other reality.

The claim that God "sent it for a purpose" clearly assumes that "it" occurred because God intended for "it" to happen to actualize some particular "difference" in relation to the particularities of some human life or lives. If those particularities had been different, God might not have "sent" it. That assumes that, as attributed to God, "power" has the qualities "conventionally" ascribed to power as being (a) God's possession that (b) is externally applied to particular beings in particular circumstances (c) on the occasion of particular events.

The claim that God "sent it for a purpose" that advances God's "plan" seems to assume another "conventional" notion about the qualities of "power." The claim is usually made vaguely, leaving it unclear whether God's purpose is a purpose for the one who anguishes, or for the one who suffers, and unclear just what the "plan" is that God is thereby advancing. Nonetheless, the claim seems to assume that the power God possesses is itself value-neutral, having no intrinsic *telos* or purpose, and is only ordered extrinsically to God's purposes by God's "plan."

Note that whatever God's "plan" may be, no matter for what "purpose" the event that causes suffering is "sent" by God, and no matter to whom it is "sent," it seems clear that the intent of the three pastoral remarks taken together is to remind and reassure people in anguish that the One who "sends" the suffering-causing event is a God of love, mercy, and justice, whose purposes in sending the event are all good. However, it is also clear that taken together these three pastoral remarks assume – consistent with "conventional" notions about the qualities of power – that, precisely because it is God's possession, God can intentionally exercise power to make differences in people's lives for a good purpose by extrinsically applying that power to them in ways that damage them and cause them profound suffering.

That assumption is consistent with qualities that are conventionally deemed appropriate to ascribe to the "powers" that creatures exercise in their complex networks of interactions. Those qualities are the qualities of creaturely power-as-such. Creatures' powers are their capacities to make various sorts of differences in and for other creatures, often in ways that damage those "others." Those powers are, in a certain way, the creatures' possessions. They vary in extent, are measurable, and are limited. They are eventfully applied externally to other creatures in interactions on particular occasions in particular circumstances. Those interactions may strengthen and empower other creatures; or they may damage and weaken them. In either case, their interactive exercise of their powers generally has the logic of a zero-sum game: the more another creature gains power in such an interaction, the less power a given creature has, and vice versa.

The consistency between the qualities of creaturely power-as-such and the qualities assumed to be rightly attributed to God's power by the problematic pastoral remarks under consideration here rests on the pastoral remarks' univocal attribution to God of "conventional" notions about creaturely power-as-such. Its univocal attribution to God frames all accounts of how God goes about relating to creatures as though God were just one more agent interacting with creaturely agents on some shared "plane" or in some shared "space" in a zero-sum way that inherently includes competition and even violent conflict of power between creatures and God. This way of framing God–creatures relations follows from univocal attribution to God of "conventional" notions of power. As we have seen, assumption of the validity of univocal use of the term "power" is itself a feature of currently "conventional" notions of power.

Inconsistencies between "Traditional" Accounts of God's Power and "Conventional" Notions of Power

According to this analysis, the sorts of pastoral remarks that concern us here assume the validity of attributing to God some "conventional" notions about the qualities of power-as-such. Those assumptions make the pastoral remarks theologically problematic from the point of view of "traditional" Christian theological accounts of God's qualities because they are inconsistent with those "traditional" accounts.

As we have seen, "traditional" accounts of God's "manner of existence" stress qualities that characterize God's "manner of existence" as utterly singular. God does not fall within or, we may say, is not an "instance" of, any genus or species of being. Because of its singularity God's "manner of existing" is incomprehensible to human minds. It can only be characterized in negative terms: e.g., noncomposite, infinite, timeless, and the like. The "noncompositiveness" of God's manner of existence entails that, while they can be distinguished in the abstract, in concrete actuality God's "essence" ("what" it is to be God) and God's "existence" ("that" God is concretely actual) are the same. God's "essence" is simply "to be." God is *a se.* However, God's singular "manner of existence" can also be characterized in regard to its intrinsic "operations" of intellect and will. Those operations can be analyzed in terms of God's intrinsic dynamic self-relating in acts of self-knowing and self-willing. In those regards somewhat more "positive" qualities may be attributed to God, including life, love, justice, mercy, power, and beatitude.

The singularity of God's manner of existence blocks attribution to God of many of the qualities "conventional" notions ascribe to power.

- The singularity of God's "manner of existence" blocks univocal attribution to God of concepts of qualities conventionally attributed to creatures. But that is precisely what is done when it is assumed that qualities "conventionally" ascribed to the powers of creatures are also ascribed to God's power and serve as theological justification for problematic pastoral remarks.

- The singularity of God's "manner of existence" blocks attribution of power to God as a "possession" that God may or may not use on any particular occasion. Such an attribution would entail that "what" and "who" God is somehow different from the power God happens also to "have." But that entailment is precisely what is assumed when qualities "conventionally" ascribed to the powers of creatures are also ascribed to God's power and serve as theological justification for problematic pastoral remarks. This assumption is blocked by the radical "noncompositiveness" of God's "manner of existence" according to "traditional" account of God's qualities.

- The noncomposite singularity of God's "manner of existing" entails that God's power and God's concretely actual reality are the same. Hence, the sense in which "power" may properly be attributed to God is "active power." That blocks attribution to God of "passive power," i.e., "power understood as a "capability" or "potential," which might or might not be actualized to make a difference in and for other realities. But such "capability" is precisely what is assumed when "conventional" notions about power as a possession that God may or may not activate are attributed to God.

- Because the singularity of God's "manner of existence" entails that God's "to be" and God's "power" are the same, it follows that God's "power" is the same as the difference God's reality makes, i.e., God's power lies in the "effect" of God's singular reality, as God actively relates to other realities. That has several further entailments.

- One "difference" that God makes is creation ex nihilo. The "active power" of God's singular reality is rightly said to "cause" the existence of creatures. However, in the context of "traditional" accounts of God's power, "cause" is used to refer to a subset of metaphysical "principles" that are the "source" of what an inanimate substance is and what a living substance matures into. God's power is the "cause" of a difference for another substance, viz., it is the condition of the possibility of the "other" being's existence as "what" it is. As the "cause" of a "difference" it makes for another substance – e.g., that is actually concretely exists – it is a "cause" that is internal to the "other's" actual existence. That blocks the notion that God's creative power is externally applied to other realities. But that is precisely what is assumed when qualities "conventionally" ascribed to the powers of creatures are also ascribed to God's power and serve as theological justification for problematic pastoral remarks.
- Another sort of difference that God makes is a providential care of creatures that is ordered to their actualizing their creaturely "goods" in their kinds. The "active power" of God's singular reality is rightly said to "cause" goods in creatures that would not otherwise obtain. Two things follow from the conjunction of several features of "traditional" accounts of the "causality" of God's power in providence. Given that in those accounts:
  a) "cause" is used to characterize a subset of the ways in which a "principle" relates to that of which it is the principle – viz., it relates to an "other" entity internally as the principle of "what" sort of entity that "other" is,
  b) and God's "active power" thereby defines what counts as a 'good' for that 'other' substance,

c) and God's noncomposite "act" of existence is the same as God's "active power,"

d) and God's noncomposite "act" of existence is the same as God's intellect and God's will, it follows that:

i) God's "active power" is *intrinsically* "intentional," intrinsically ordered mindfully and voluntarily to certain ends;

ii) and furthermore the ends to which God's "active power" is intrinsically ordered are the actualizations of "*goods*" for living creatures.

Those two entailments block the notions (a) that the "active power" that God possesses is itself intrinsically value-neutral, lacks any intrinsic *telos* or purpose to which it is ordered, and that (b) it is only ordered to creatures' goods when God occasionally wills to order "use" of that possession by applying it eternally to particular creatures. But what is blocked is precisely what is positively assumed when qualities "conventionally" ascribed to the powers of creatures are also ascribed univocally to God's power and serve as theological justification for problematic pastoral remarks.

In short, certain kinds of pastoral comfort offered in the name of "traditional" Christian understandings of God and God's powers to people anguished by other's profound, intolerable, and unfair suffering are framed in "conventional" notions of power that are inconsistent with just those "traditional" theological accounts of God's qualities.

The point of identifying inconsistencies between "traditional" theologies of God's power and the theological assumptions of pastoral remarks deeply shaped by currently "conventional" notions about "power-as-such" is to show that those remarks are "problematic" by entirely traditional theological standards that a great many Protestant and Roman Catholic faithful take for granted. It is no part of my argument that such comments are theologically problematic simply *because* they are demonstrably inconsistent with "traditional" theological explanations of God's power. I shall argue that those "traditional" accounts are themselves inadequate, albeit in a different way.

What needs to be acknowledged here is that it is entirely understandable that comments by people of Christian faith, yearning to comfort in God's name anguished neighbors and friends, might be inconsistent with "traditional" Christian accounts of God's power. To some degree, the Christian formation of the people they seek to comfort has been shaped by the language of prayers, hymns, sermons, theological instruction, and pastoral care in times of crisis that express God's trustworthiness in terms of God's unrestricted power. They have come to have expectations of God that are disappointed in times of profound suffering. In responding positively to the invitation to trust that "powerful" God, they have been formed to expect that indeed that God will not allow loved ones to suffer more than they can handle, will make clear what God's plan was in "sending" any suffering at all, or will at least disclose the purpose God has in allowing that suffering. Above all, they have been "spiritually formed" to expect that the God whom they are invited to trust loves each and every creature and will exercise the unconditioned creative power that is definitive of God's "divinity" to protect from horrendous suffering the fellow creatures that they themselves have been given to love.

But they have been "theologically overpromised." When they do expect those things, their expectations can be disappointed. In their anger in that disappointment, they will once again be estranged from God, estranged from neighbors in communities of Christian faith who have been similarly "formed," but have not had their expectations disappointed by the unequal distribution of horrendous suffering, and estranged from those who seeks to speak of God in terms of what and who God is as rendered in Christian scripture. In pastoral concern for them, we seek to remind and reassure them that God does love those who suffer, and that God is faithful to God's own love-commitments to them and their "good," and to that end that God is involved the sufferer's life and in the circumstances from which they suffer. Here, God's own faithfulness to the sufferers is the core issue for faith.

Struggling to remain present to distraught friends and neighbors who are grieving, terrified, outraged, and feeling utterly helpless before their loved one's suffering, we are at a loss for words when we try to reassure them of God's faithfulness and stammer phrases we have heard others say. Those "others," exactly like ourselves, have been deeply shaped by our shared culture's values, "common sense," and "what everybody knows." What comes to speech in our stammering is framed in conventional ideas and clichés. In that turbulent emotional weather, one does not try – and would not be wise to try – to self-reflexively monitor the formal consistency of what one says to comfort another. But that weather does change. Later, it would be wise to reflect, retrospectively, to critique what had been said and, prospectively, to imagine and internalize alternative ways of speaking pastorally that are more faithful and less theologically problematic. There is no aspect of the virtues of faith, hope, and love to be found in talking one theological view in general and verbally enacting another inconsistent view in certain emotionally stressful situations.

Why Pastoral Remarks Assume That It Is Theologically Appropriate to Attribute to God "Conventional" Notions about Power-as-Such

The assumption that it is appropriate to frame pastoral remarks in "conventional" notions about "power-as-such" is entirely implicit in those pastoral remarks. It may be incoherent with "traditional" accounts of God's power but, being implicit, the incoherence is not often noticed. Indeed, there is a strong incentive to frame pastoral assurances of God's trustworthiness even in the midst of horrendous suffering in ways that assume that God's power in keeping promises to sustain creatures and nurture them is absolutely unrestricted. If God has absolutely unrestricted power, then it follows that, despite fellow creatures' horrendous suffering, it must have been "sent" by God for a "purpose" that brings them "goods" that could only be actualized in that way. That assumption is precisely what "conventional" notions of power offer when attributed to God. Attributed univocally to God, "conventional" notions about power underscore God's faithfulness in love toward sufferers. It does so by framing God's "involvement" in circumstances that cause deep suffering as *God's control* of all that goes on.

I suggest that what I have outlined as "traditional" accounts of God's power do not, on one side, adequately block use of those "conventional" notions in Christian discourse while, on the other side, they seem to invite such use. The inadequate "blocking" and the "invitation" are two sides of a certain vagueness at a key point in "traditional" accounts of God's power. That key point concerns how to describe the relation between God's power and the various sorts and degrees of powers that God gives to creatures. Traditional accounts of God's power are vague about that.

On one hand, "traditional" accounts of God's power provide rich intellectual resources by which to underscore the unchanging trust-worthiness of the unfailing faithfulness of God's commitments to creatures' well-being and flourishing while blocking assumptions that "conventional" notions of power can rightly be ascribed to God. As we have seen, two themes lie at the heart of those "intel-lectual resources."

The first is that because God's reality is utterly noncomposite, so God's "power" is the same as God's life, God's love, God's mercy and justice, and God's beatitude; and each of them is the same as God's substantial "manner of existence." Hence, in God's ways of relating to creatures, God's power is *intrinsically* (and not merely extrinsically and "occasionally") ordered in love, mercy, and justice to creatures' participation in God' beatitude. That affirmation underwrites the claim that God's faithfulness in relating powerfully to nurture creatures' well-being and flourishing is absolutely trust-worthy. It would seem to block any characterization of God's power that would imply that in it God relates to creatures' powers, and especially to human creatures' powers, in such a way as to intentionally damage or diminish them so as to "cause" or "send" horrendous suffering.

The second theme is that, for the same reason, God's concrete actuality is utterly singular. It does not fall within any genus or species of "being." Consequently, God cannot be said to "share" any common "plane" or "space" with creatures. God's creative and providential relating to creatures is the condition of the possibility of the concrete actuality of creation as a whole. Creation as a whole is the common "plane" or "space" in which creatures' powers interact. They "apply" their powers externally to one another in interactions that have a zero-sum "logic." God's power, however, is not "externally applied" to creatures on occasions in which God and creatures when creaturely powers and God's power interact on some shared "plane" or "context." God is not one of the entities whose powers interact within that "plane" or "space." That, it would seem, blocks the assumption that the "power" of God can be correctly described as competing with creaturely powers of various kinds and degrees. After all, there is no "plane," "field," or "space" on which or in which to compete.

It would also seem to block the assumption that the "power" of God can be correctly described by comparing it with certain creaturely "powers" as though the two could be placed at various points on a common scale or spectrum of degrees of power-as-such.

Blocking comparative ways of characterizing the relation between God's power and creatures' power underscores affirmation of God's trustworthy faithfulness. It would seem to emphasize that God's "omnipotence" cannot rightly be defined as God's having "more" of the powers that creatures have such that in all interactions with creaturely powers in their shared "plane" or "space" God's "extrinsic application' to them of power always overpowers and "controls" them. It would also seem to make clear that attribution of "omnipotence" to God does not imply that God has "power" that might self-consistently break God's commitments in love to the well-being and flourishing of creatures, violate their creaturely well-being and the possibilities of flourishing, "sending" horrendous suffering onto them or failing to "prevent" horrendous suffering from happening to realize the "purpose" of a "plan" that is and remains unknowable and whose connection to God's self-commitments to creatures remains unknowable.

At the same time, however, the combination of

a) the rule that God's power ought never to be characterized by measuring it in comparison to creaturely powers to affirm that it is always "more" than creaturely powers, and

b) exclusion of any picture of God and creatures interacting on the same "plane" also yield a vague account of God's power.

It is vague enough to leave open a question whether "traditional" accounts of God's power do adequately warrant the fundamental faith claim that God's promises to sustain creatures' existence and value and to nurture their well-being are trustworthy.

Consider: If it is a violation of the singularity of God's reality to compare God's power with creatures' powers and to characterize the relation of God's power to creatures' powers as an "interaction on a common plane," is it possible to characterize God's power at all in humanly understandable ways? And if not, then is it not also impossible to give reasons why God's power should not be characterized as capable of "sending" horrendous suffering?

Moreover, the reliance of "traditional" accounts of God's power on the metaphysically formulated claim that God's singular reality is noncomposite requires it to deny that "passions" like outrage, grief, sorrow, and compassion may be attributed to God analogically. Hence, it cannot be said that God "shares" either the pain of those whose suffering is horrendous or the anguish of those who care deeply for them. At the end of the day, according to "traditional" theological accounts, can it really be said that God's power and creatures' powers really do *engage* each other at all?

On the other hand, "traditional" accounts of God's power are typically framed in a binary way that *does* clearly affirm that God's power and creatures' powers really engage each other. They often frame the relation between God's power and creatures' powers in terms of the binary "transcendence/immanence." The binary trades metaphorically on two and three dimensional spaces to describe how God is related to creation as a "whole." God is either "inside" or "outside" the "two-dimensional field" or "three-dimensional volume" of creation-as-a-whole. The two poles of the continuum are inversely related: the more "outside/transcendent" God is of creation-as-a-whole, the less "inside/immanent" God is, and vice versa. Insofar as God is "immanent/inside" creation God's relations with creatures may be conceived as that of one more causal agent interacting with individual creaturely agents on the "plane" of creaturely reality. In that theological context, there is no question that God's power directly engages creaturely powers.

Insofar as God is "transcendent/outside" creation, God's relations with creatures may be conceived in two was. It may be conceived as that of a causal agent relating externally to "creation as a whole" to control creation's overall changes so that they move toward some overarching purpose God has. And it may be conceived as that of a causal agent occasionally "breaking into" the ordinary regularities (or "laws") governing the zero-sum interactions and exchanges of power among creatures to control them externally such that they have outcomes that differ from and in some ways "exceed" the "normal" consequences of those interactions.

When the engagement of God's power with creaturely powers is framed in terms of that binary, not only may the magnitude of God's and creatures' powers be compared. Framed in that fashion, God's interaction with creaturely agents in providential care may also be compared as competitive and even conflictual. It is itself a zero-sum engagement. God always "wins" because, according to "traditional" theological accounts, God's "transcendent" will is always fulfilled. The unconstrained power of God's will may overwhelm any creaturely resistance, even if that "overwhelming" involves violating its ontological integrity. Framed in terms of the "transcendence/immanence" binary God's "sovereignty" in creating and providential care is a function of God's absolute power, either as a causal agent on the same plane or within the same three-dimensional space as creatures, or as a an agent extrinsic to creation-as-a-whole.

I suggest that not only does traditional use of the "immanence/transcendence" binary to frame accounts of the relation between God's power and creatures' power not block the assumption that "conventional" notions of power are rightly projected onto "traditional" accounts of God's power, but that it is an *invitation* to do so.

It is an invitation to do so as a way making as emphatic as possible Christian claims about the trustworthiness of God's promises to sustain the existence and value of creatures creatively and to nurture their well-being and flourishing in the face of anguish at fellow human creatures' profound sufferings. "Conventional" notions about power can be understood as conceptually enhancing "traditional" theological accounts of God's power by reinforcing aspects of the "traditional" accounts that suggest that God's power not only genuinely engages with creatures undergoing horrific suffering, but "engages" them by *externally controlling* what goes on among creatures. Where reliance on the "transcendence/immanence" binary invites that projection, the vagueness of "traditional" accounts of God's power makes such a conceptual "projection" easy by weakening their ability firmly to block such "projection."

A Structural Problem in "Traditional" Accounts of God's Power

The vagueness of "traditional" theological accounts of God's power that not only fails to block projection on to it of "conventional" notions about the nature of "power-as-such" but actually invites it is rooted in the structure of those "traditional" accounts. It is theologically "structural." The problem is not that "traditional" theological accounts attribute unrestricted power to God and thereby permit us, and even invite us, to "clarify" and emphasize that "unrestricted power" by adding to it the "conventional" notion of a "power-as-such," which God owns as a possession and on occasion eventfully applies externally to creatures so as to override their powers and control them.

The theological claim that God's power is absolutely unrestricted is, after all, entirely consistent with canonical Christian Scriptural accounts of how God goes about creating all else ex nihilo. By definition, there is nothing other than God that could "restrict" God's power in creating ex nihilo. It is also consistent with canonical Christian Scriptural accounts of God promising providentially to sustain creatures' reality and value and to nurture their well-being, which is entailed by God's creating them. It is consistent with theological claims about providence in that God's making that promise is itself also unrestricted by any reality other than God's own self-commitment to them in creating them ex nihilo.

However, as canonically narrated, that is not the only way in which God actively relates to all else. Part II explored some theological implications of the differences among canonical narratives of how God goes about relating to create, how God goes about relating to draw creatures into a fully actualized eschatological consummation, and how God goes about relating to reconcile estranged creatures to God. They stressed that the three sorts of narrative were irreducibly different because they each had a different narrative "logic." Those chapters, and the following chapters of this Part III, also stress that, although the three sorts of ways in which God relates to all else, as canonically narrated, are asymmetrically related to one another in a definite pattern, they cannot be synthesized as the beginning, middle, and end of one extended narrative without distorting the narrative "logic," i.e., the narrative integrity, of two of the three sorts of narrative. Part II explored how two of the three sorts of narrative render God's sovereignty and the way in which each expresses a different aspect of God's intrinsic glory. In this part, we explore differences in the sense in which God's sovereignty in each of the ways God relates to all else is "powerful." The general upshot of that exploration is that the three different senses in which God is "powerful" each express aspects in which God's intrinsic glory is powerful but that (a) the three senses of "power" rightly attributed to God are irreducibly different conceptually, (b) no two of them can be correctly understood as merely versions or modifications of the third, (c) the three cannot be comprehended in some systematic "meta" account of "God's power," and (d) that neither all of them together nor any one of them alone is God's "essence," i.e., is what makes God *God.*

The point made here is that the vagueness of "traditional" theological accounts, which leaves it open to projection onto it of "conventional" notions of power, which, in turn, shape and justify theologically problematic pastoral remarks, is rooted in the "traditional" accounts' systematic privileging the unrestricted power of God's creating of all else as alone definitive of God's power. "Conventional" notions of "power-as-such" superficially seem to be compatible with "traditional" theological concepts of God's unrestricted creative and providential power. Privileging the unrestricted power of God's creating ex nihilo structurally requires that the power of God's relating to draw all else to eschatological consummation and God's relating to reconcile estranged creatures must also be understood as further instances of God exercising "power" in the same sense. The vagueness of "traditional" accounts of God's power leaves them incapable of blocking and, indeed, in some respects invites, projection onto God of "conventional" notions of "power-as-such." One consequence of that is that there is no theological basis that is conceptually independent of the acknowledgment that the power of God's creativity is unrestricted on which to block such projection.

The structural privileging of the unrestricted power of God's creating ex nihilo in "traditional" explanations of God's power is evident in Thomas' explanation, which I have taken as paradigmatic. Following the distinction Thomas draws in the first question of Part I of the *Summa* between the "science" of metaphysics and the "science" of Christian theology, and before his extended theological analysis of qualities that may be attributed to God's "manner of existence," Thomas offers five arguments demonstrating the existence of God in question 1a 2. Three features of all five of those arguments rely on privileging the Christian theological claim that God's power in creating and providential care is unrestricted power.

The first relevant feature of the five arguments is that they are framed as questions about the basis of order and intelligibility in a cosmos shot through with contingencies and changes of several sorts, rather than as a question about the causal dynamics of the origin of the cosmos. That is, they are framed as metaphysical questions about cosmology rather than cosmogeny. We touched on this point briefly. In framing his demonstrations of God's existence in this context, Thomas locates his entire subsequent account of God's "essence" in the context of a long tradition of Christian use the concept of a cosmic "first principle" or *arche* in pre-Christian Greco-Roman philosophical cosmology to explain YHWH's providential care of creation as rendered in Scriptural witness.

The second salient feature of Thomas' five arguments is that he ends each of them with some variant of the sentence, "That is what everyone understands to be God." Christians, Jews, pagans, and later Muslims – everyone! – once they understood the force of the concept of a cosmic *arche*, could say of it "we call that God." It is not that self-evident, however. "Everyone" might be persuaded that the cosmos has a "first principle," But why call it "god"? For example, not every Greco-Roman philosopher conceived the *arche* as a cause that is independent of and ontologically prior to that of which it is the "first principle." But Christians, Jews, and later

Muslims all did. Thomas' answer comes explicitly later in the *Summa* when he addresses the question whether the word "God" names a "nature" or an "essence." Thomas answers, in effect, "No, not exactly." He explains that "everyone" understands "God" the same way because the word "God" is "an operational word in that it is an operation of God that makes us use the word "God" – for the word is derived from [God's] universal providence."[74] The God who will later in the *Summa* be said to be "powerful" is initially identified as the cosmos' *arche* that exercises providential care of the cosmos by ordering it to its good.[75]

The third relevant general feature of Thomas' five arguments is that, for Thomas, the theologian they *necessarily* assume that God who "operationally" exercises universal providential care of the cosmos is even more basically the creator of the cosmos ex nihilo. To be sure, theological explanations of God's relating to all else in "providence" and God's relating to all else in "creation" are two distinctly different claims about two irreducibly different ways in which God relates to all else. They are irreducibly different in that God's relating to create ex nihilo by definition presupposes that apart from that relating there is "nothing" to relate to. Therefore, God's creative relating ex nihilo cannot itself be identical to God's relating to already extant creatures in providential care of them. Conversely, God's relating to already extant creatures in providential care of them cannot itself be identical to God's relating to create them ex nihilo. God's relating in providential care does not constitute God's creative blessing ex nihilo; rather, it presupposes it. For that same reason, although they are different claims, they cannot be

---

[74] Ia. 13, 8r.

[75] To call that first principle "God" is not to identify "providential caring" as "what" it is about God's "nature" or "essence' that makes God *God*. It is only to identify the cosmic function God fills and to show that it is rational to affirm God's reality. God's role or *function* in relation to the cosmos is not God's essence or nature; they are just God's job descriptors relative to the cosmos. For Thomas, "universal providence" is an "operational" use of the word "God."

separated. Theologically speaking, the claim about providence is necessarily entailed by the claim about creation. Accordingly, the "power" of God's providentially ordering creation is none other than the "power" of God's creating the cosmos ex nihilo.

As is typical of "traditional" accounts of God's qualities, and especially accounts of God's power, Thomas has framed his entire analysis of the qualities of God's "manner of existing" in a way that privileges God' relating in an absolutely unrestricted manner to create all else. That makes it definitive of how God goes about all the other ways in which God may be said to relate powerfully to creatures. In particular, the "power" of both God's way of relating to draw creatures to eschatological consummation and God's way of relating to reconcile estranged creatures to God are thus assumed to be simply further instances of the same sense of "power."

That is structurally key to "traditional" accounts of God's power. One consequence is that it undercuts how the peculiar ways in which God goes about relating to bless creatures eschatologically and to reconcile them to God can block ascription to God of theologically problematic "conventional" notions of "power-in-general." The next two chapters outline how, taken on their own terms and not reduced to additional instances of the power of God's creativity, they do block that move.

8 | The Triune God's Intrinsic Power

"Traditional" accounts of the power of God are theologically well-warranted as far as they go. They render the Triune God's power as "absolute power" in the sense that it is power unrestricted by anything other than God. Indeed, as we have noted, they tend to suggest that unrestricted power just is God's essence, that which makes God *God*. However, they do not describe God's power as sheer, morally neutral, a-teleological "brute force." Instead, they characterize it as the power of the Triune God's self-regulation. It is the power of the Triune God's intrinsic sovereignty. Traditional theological accounts characterize the power of God as the power of a generously and self-expressively self-giving in ways lovingly and rationally ordered to the good of the "other," both to "others" within God's intrinsic life (the "Persons" of the Trinity) and to creaturely "others." Such self-giving intrinsic to God just is the intrinsic glory that is God's Triune life. It is the power of a self-expressive ongoing self-giving that is at once radically "other than" that to which it relates and radically "close to" it. Its self-regulated (i.e., sovereign) self-giving is the condition of the possibility of the "other's" empowered reality and value, rather than something "applied" to the "other" externally in occasional events in which it competes with and may conflict with the "other's" more limited power.

This rejection of views of God's power that assimilate it to overwhelmingly coercive force is very ancient in Christian teaching. It is already explicit in the second or early third century in the

Epistle to Diognetus,[1] perhaps the earliest Christian denial that God's power is a tyrannical and oppressive force. Commenting on the Incarnation the author writes:

> Well, did [God] send him [Jesus] . . . to rule as a tyrant, to inspire terror and astonishment? No, [God] did not. No, [God} sent him in gentleness and mildness: as a king sending a royal son, he sent him as God: but he sent him as to [human beings], as saving them; as persuading, not exercising force (for force is no attribute of God).

In "traditional" accounts of God's power, force is not one of the intrinsic "ensemble" of attributes or qualities of God; but power is. Rejecting "force" as a quality of the triune God does not imply rejecting "power."

However, this essay has argued, "traditional" accounts of God's power do misleadingly suggest, or are conceptually open to the suggestion, that God's power can be assimilated to sheer force, a view of God's power that has "conventionally" developed, independent of any account of God's intrinsic sovereignty, as sheer power-as-such. This essay promotes as an alternative the proposal that Christian theological accounts of the power of the Triune God would be less likely to be formulated as sheer force if, instead of assuming that God's "sovereignty" is the sovereignty of God's intrinsic power understood as power-as-such, God's "power" were understood as the power of the intrinsic "sovereignty" of God which has a distinctive profile. As was argued in Chapter 4, "sovereignty" in this context is not the name of the exercise of absolute, unconditioned, unrestrained power over other powers. It denotes, rather, the distinctive way in which God self-regulates how God goes about relating, respectively, in creative blessing, in

---

[1] In Henry Bettenson, ed. and trans., *The Early Christian Fathers* (Oxford: Oxford University Press, 1956), p. 76. Emphasis added.

eschatological blessing, and in liberative promise making. Precisely because it is "self-regulating," it is intrinsic to God's life.

A distinguishing feature of that self-regulating is that in it God is self-binding by commitments God makes. That self-binding is the basis for part of an answer to the question, "Who is the Triune God?" God's self-binding does not constitute God's reality as God. It does not answer the question, "What is it to be God?" However, the ways in which God is self-binding in the economy do definitively express God's concrete identity, "who" God is. Such self-binding by God in each strand of the economy does not compromise God's intrinsic sovereignty. It faithfully expresses God's intrinsic sovereignty. In each strand of the economy God is "prevenient," coming before any creature in the order of being and acting before the creatures do anything. Such self-binding does not subject God's sovereignty to regulation by actions of other agents that are enacted before and independent of God's relating to them.

The qualities of God's self-binding in creative blessing are the qualities of God's sovereignty in the strands of the economy that faithfully express God's intrinsic glory (in "glory's" primary sort of reference) and are aspects of the glory of God (in its secondary sort of reference). For example, in regard to God's self-relating in relating to all else in creative blessing, God's identity is self-defined, as outlined in Chapter 4, as "One who, in blessing them creatively, is wisely (with all of the facets of 'wisdom' noted before: free, transcendental, ordered to the good, non-violent) self-binding to creatures" well-being in their kinds for as long as they last.

Accordingly, if the Triune God's power is understood as the power of God's sovereignty, it is understood as power that is intrinsically shaped by the same qualities that we have warrant to attribute to God's intrinsic sovereignty. Far from being sheer force, a-teleological, and value-neutral, in need of control, discipline, and wise guidance, God's power is intrinsically intentional in its orderedness. As God's self-regulated power, it intends (i.e., is "focused on") the creaturely "other" in its concrete particularity. It attends with a generous love that knows that "other" in its particularity. Its love for that "other" includes compassable knowledge of the other's affects. Those are qualities of the power of God's sovereignty that (in creative blessing) sustains the creaturely "other" in its concrete actuality and value, and (in providential care) intelligently provides for its creaturely well-being in its kind for as long as it lasts, all in ways that faithfully express the Triune God's intrinsic self-commitment to the mode of communion with each creaturely other that is appropriate to its kind.

The qualities, including power, that we may attribute as an ensemble to the Triune God are only knowable by us in God's ways of relating to all else as that is rendered in canonical Christian scriptures' accounts of God's economy, because those ways of relating faithfully express those qualities. What are expressed in God's ways of relating to all else are qualities that are intrinsic to the Triune God's reality, whether or not God relates to all else in any fashion whatsoever. That "ensemble" of qualities is "intrinsic" to the Trinity in that, although the qualities are "knowable" on the basis of the ways in which God relates to all that is not God, they are not merely functions of those ways of relating. In the order of reality they are qualities of the dynamic of the Triune God's life independent of and in that sense "prior" to God's relating. This chapter focuses only on the sense in which the Triune God's sovereignty is "powerful" in the strand of the economy consisting of creative blessing and the way that expresses God's intrinsic power. In Chapter 9, we turn to the senses in which God is "powerful" in the other two strands of the economy, i.e., relating in eschatological blessing and relating to reconcile estranged creatures to God.

The Power of the Triune God's Sovereignty in Creative Blessing

Christian theological claims about the senses in which God may be said to be intrinsically "powerful" can only be *definitively* warranted by appeal to canonical Christian scriptural accounts of how God goes about relating to all else. That does not imply that there are not also additional ways in Christian theology to warrant ascription of at least some intrinsic qualities to God, including warrants justified by metaphysical arguments. It is, however, to insist that in the sort of Christian theology of which this essay is an instance the qualities of God's ways of relating to all else that are exhibited by canonical scripture are "definitive" in this sense: any proposal to attribute an intrinsic quality to God on other grounds must at least cohere with those attributes that are warranted by canonical narratives of God relating to all else.

That is already illustrated by the passage quoted above from the *Epistle to Diognetus*. The *Epistle* blocks the attribution to God of the quality of tyrannical force. Presumably in his cultural context "Diognetus" assumes that when power is attributed to God "power" is conventionally used in a sense that was culturally commonplace, namely the "power-as-tyrannical-force" that is attributed to the Roman Emperor in political discourse. The *Epistle* blocks that assumption about the sense of "power" ascribed to God in specific-ally Christian discourse on the grounds that it is inconsistent with the qualities of the way in which God relates by way of Incarnation as canonically narrated: not tyrannically but gently, mildly, saving by persuasion and not by force.

We have seen that "traditional" accounts of God's power are warranted by canonical Scriptural accounts of how God goes about relating to create all that is not God and to care for creatures providentially. That they are -warranted in doing so is brought out by the following five exegetical remarks that build on Claus Westermann's reading of Genesis chapter 1.

To begin, the particularities of the canonical narratives of God relating in creative blessing justify the claim that, in relating in creative blessing, God is intrinsically radically free. In this regard the traditional conventional attribution of "absolute power" is cor-rect. The "Priestly" (P) editors' rejection of a medium out of which

God makes the world, or of sexual generation and birth of the world, or of a conflict between God and a resistant power whose outcome is the world as we know it, rules out any suggestion that God's relating to create is in any way constrained by any medium – material, sexual, or conflictual.

A second point: Westermann argues that, in regard to God's active creative relating to creatures. canonical narratives underscore the "utter transcendence of Creation over any . . . event."[2] Note that this is not the traditional claim that God is "transcendent" of all else in regard to God's being (nor is that denied). It is rather the claim that God's active relating to all else in creative blessing is itself "transcendental" of all particular events in that it is the condition of the possibility of there being any such events at all. It is not itself just one more "event" in cosmic history (or in "salvation history"). This ongoing transcendental creative relating by God is itself beyond comprehension by human minds and, therefore, is beyond further characterization. This point is brought out by the standard analysis of the history of the canonical editing of the text of Genesis, which Westermann generally accepts. The P editors received and modified older Sumerian, Babylonian, and Egyptian creation stories.[3] The narratives that the P editors received relied on one or another of four root metaphors to image the way in which God causes the world to be.[4] Westermann holds that the P editors effectively neutralized three of these images (viz., creation by action upon some medium; by sexual generation and birth; by conflict between God and a resistant power) and explicitly adopt the metaphor of creation through word ("God said . . . and it was so"). However, P effectively neutralizes that image also by making it

---

[2] 1974, p. 42.

[3] On Westermann's reading, the received narratives had a structure of eight days that the P editors conflated into six, to which they added a seventh culminating day in which God rests rather than creating; cf. Westermann, 1974, p. 41.

[4] Through a god's word. Cf. *ibid.* 1974, pp. 39–41.

clear that there is no addressee of the creative "word."[5] So none of
the received metaphors will serve to describe *how* God creates. The
contrast between the received creation stories and the particular
ways in which they were edited shows, Westermann argues, that the
function of the creation narratives in Genesis 1 is not to explain
the origin of the world. Rather, the editors intent is "to push the
Creation event back into the realm of the incomprehensible."[6] God,
in relating in creative blessing, is the incomprehensible ground of
the reality of all that is not God. In creative blessing, God does not
relate to creatures as one center of power among many interacting
on the same "plane" or in the same "field." Therefore, God's way of
relating in creative blessing cannot be likened to interactions that
are competitive and possibly conflictual.

A third point: Some of the particularities of the canonically
edited Genesis creation stories warrant the claim that God's relating
to create is the ground of the value and goodness of all that is not
God. Having created x, God declares that "x is good." The narrative
logic of the P editors' accounts focuses on the Creator' blessing: "Be
fruitful and multiply." Ordered to the rise of various forms of life
and to their nurture, the blessing is good for creatures. God's
creative relating empowers creatures rather than threatening to
disempower them.

A fourth point: The narrative logic of the P editors' account also
implies that in relating in creative blessing God may be said to be
"self-binding." God's relating in creative blessing is narrated as a
free relating in the sense that it is not "explained" as a logically
necessary consequence of God's own "nature," as though "relating
in creative blessing" were essential to God being *God*. It is "absolute," i.e., unconditioned, in that way too. It is not even "conditioned" by God's nature. Nonetheless, in creative blessing, God
binds Godself by God's self-commitment to relate to creatures only

[5] Cf. 1974, pp. 41–42.
[6] 1974, p. 42.

in ways that constitutes their reality and intrinsic goodness as long as they last. It is a self-commitment to which God is reliably faithful in the concrete ways in which God goes about relating in creative blessing and in the providential care of creatures that creative blessing entails.

A fifth point: Westermann points out that the P editors' rejection of violent conflict as a metaphor for the way God relates creatively implies that God's relating in creative blessing is intrinsically non-violent. Perhaps God's way of relating in providential care or in judgment is marked by violence. There are plenty of canonical Scriptural texts that image how God judges and punishes evildoers in violent ways and, in particular circumstances, commands God's people to do the same. However, as Westermann notes, the Genesis texts seem to make a point of eliminating such images from their account of how God goes about relating in creative blessing. To put the same point positively, in relating to create all else God is faithfully self-committed to honor the integrity of creatures in their kinds by relating to them in ways that do not violate what they are in their concrete particularity.

These five themes are underscored in the formula that tersely summarizes the traditional Christian claim about the Triune God's way of relating to create all else: "The 'Father' creates ex nihilo through the 'Son' in the power of the Spirit."

Placing the "First Person" of the Trinity in the lead position in God's relating to all else in creative blessing stresses several qualities of the power of God's "sovereignty" in creative blessing. Attribution of those features to God are warranted by some of the particular features Westermann's exegesis of Genesis 1 brings out in its account of how God goes about creating all that is not God, as noted.

The first three exegetical points about Genesis 1 based on Westermann's analysis warrant attribution of two qualities to the Triune God's power in creative blessing.

First, the Triune God's powerful sovereignty in creative blessing is a "free" relating in the sense that it is not constrained by any medium "through" which God accomplishes creation of all else. It is not creation "out of" or "by means" of anything. It is ex nihilo. Whatever the sense may be in which it is "powerful," it is a relating in which God alone is powerful. That is the respect in which it is indeed "unrestricted" power.

Second, focused on how God goes about *relating* to creatures in creating them rather than on the nature of the "causal joint" *by* which God creates them, what Genesis 1 describes is the active *relating* by God to creatures in creating them, rather than explaining the causal mechanism of creation. God's relating in creative blessing is not a singular "event" (although it arguably had a singular beginning "event").[7] Rather, it has the character of an ongoing blessing on finite creatures for as long as they last. It ongoingly constitutes the concretely actual reality of creatures in their kinds and the inherent value in their kinds given to them for as long as they last. As the power of the Triune God's sovereignty in creative blessing, God's power is to be understood as the power of God's self-regulated ongoing relating to all else to sustain it in actual reality and to ground its value, rather than uniquely the power of the one-off event that begins that active relating.

Placing the "Father" in the lead position in *taxis* or pattern of the Triune God's relating to all else in creative blessing stresses that, as the power of God's sovereignty (i.e., the power of God's singular self-regulating) in relating in that ongoing fashion, God's power in creative blessing faithfully expresses the character of the "Father's" ongoing generative relating to the "Son" and the Spirit. It

---

[7] Westermann emphatically rejects von Rad's characterization of creation narratives as accounts of the first moment in the Pentateuch's narrative of "salvation history." Creation narratives do not tell of the deliverance or salvation of anything. They tell of a different kind of relation God enters into with all that is not God. It has its own narrative logic. That, I suggest, is an abstract way of saying that it will not be possible for a reader to "follow" a narrative that conflates into one canonical accounts of God relating to all else in ongoing creative blessing and God relating to all else in punctiliar events of liberative and "saving" acts.

"expresses" the powerful, eternal, self-expressively generative, self-giving that is the Triune God's life; however, it does not replicate it. God's radical priority to creatures in creative blessing expresses a certain "priority" the "Father" has to the "Son" and Spirit. However, where the powerful generativity of the "Father's" relating to the "Son" and Spirit in their respective "processions" from the "Father" is so generously self-expressive that "Son" and Spirit are "of the same substance" as the "Father," genuine "others" to God that are creatures are not of the "same substance" as the Triune God. In creative blessing, the Triune God on one side and creatures on the other do not share a common "field" in which God relates to creatures on a common "plane." There is no "space" that creature and Creator share that is neither creature nor "of one substance" with the "Father."

That, in turn, entails claims about two additional qualities of the power of God's sovereignty in creative blessing that have far-reaching implications, some of which we have already encountered. Placing the "Father" in the lead position in the Trinity's *taxis* underscores that, because in creative blessing the Triune God and creatures do not share a common "field" in which God relates to creatures on a common "plane," the distinction between Creator and creature is the fundamental ontological distinction. Whatever else we may be warranted to claim theologically about the Triune God and God's ways of relating to all else, no claim about that relating is theologically valid that contradicts, or implies such a contradiction of, the fundamental distinction between Creator and creatures.

The second implication is that the Triune God's relating to all else in creative blessing is as singular as "what" God is. Because in creative blessing the Triune God and creatures do not share a common "field" in which God relates to creatures on a common "plane," God's relating to all else in creative blessing cannot be thought of as a singular "causal" action (much less "inter"-action) occurring on the some common plane with creatures or in a common "field" with them. The Triune God with the "Father" in the lead does not act powerfully with creatures on a common "plane" or in a shared "field" or "space." The Triune God's relating to creatures in creative blessing is not "powerful" in the same sense of "power" in which creatures are said to be more or less powerful than one another in their reciprocal and mutual interactions. Their various "powers" are relative to one another and comparable. Some have more, some less as measured on a common continuum or scale of power. God is "powerful" in creative blessing in an "absolute" sense in that it is not a "point" on any continuum of degrees of power shared with creatures, not even the "highest" point. The sense in which God's sovereignty in creative blessing is "powerful" cannot be explained by comparing it with the creaturely powers we regularly experience. That blocks any way of characterizing God's power that implies that its relation to creaturely powers is necessarily competitive and possibly conflictual. As nonviolating, God's power is intrinsically nonviolent.

That the Triune God and creatures cannot be thought to share a common "field" of creative blessing in which God relates to creatures on a common "plane" in creative blessing has a third implication. It presses our extended use of "relate" and "relating" to characterize God's creative blessing to the edge of unintelligibility. It implies that, in creative blessing, the Triune God is in some respects on both "sides" of the fundamental ontological distinction between Creator and creatures. In creative blessing, God is at once both radically "other" than creatures, prior to them in the order of being and utterly free in taking the initiative in creating them. God is also radically "close" to them, not simply as the condition of the possibility of their actual concrete existence and value, but as that "condition" in a way that is generously loving. God knows the creature in its particularity, is compassable with the creature's affects, and intelligently provides for its creaturely well-being in its kind for as long as it lasts. Indeed, God is closer to creatures than they can be to themselves in ways that faithfully express the

"Father's" intrinsic self-commitment to the dynamic communion in love with the other two "Persons" of the Trinity, which is God's own living reality. As we have noted, this "otherness" and "closeness" are correlative and not inversely related. It is not as though the more the Creator is "other" than creatures the less the Creator is "close" to them, or vice versa. In God's "relating" in creative blessing, each ("otherness" and "closeness") is the condition of the other.

However, it must be acknowledged that use of the word "relating" in this way and in this context stretches its intelligibility almost to the breaking point. It bears no close analogy to any mode of "relating" we experience with fellow creatures. Perhaps the closest analogy – and it is indeed a distant one – is the observation that, given that human creatures are profoundly social and "relational" beings, the "health" of intimate interpersonal relations depends on their keeping two factors in a correlative balance. Each partner must relate to the other in such ways as to be at once (i) emotionally maximally "open" to the other in giving and receiving their subjective interiority and (ii) maximally attentive to preserving the particularity of both their own identity and the other partner's identity in their own rights. The "health" of the relationship is said to depend on maintaining that "dialectic," because each of the two "poles" is the condition of the possibility of the vitality of the other. If one relates to another in a way that, in effect, tries to absorb the other into one's own identity, then to the extent that one succeeds one undermines the other's ability to share his own interiority; if one relates to another in ways that, in effect, try to lose oneself in the other's identity, then to the extent that one succeeds one undermines one's own ability to be open to share one's own interiority; if one relates to another in a way that, in effect, does not share one's interiority, one deprives one's partner of a genuinely "intimate" relationship; and if one relates to another in a way that, in effect, does not honor and engage the other's interiority, one deprives oneself of a partner in a genuinely "intimate" relationship. That, however, is only a very distant analogy to the Triune God's way of relating to creatures in creative blessing. It is confined to an aspect of human creatures' subjectivity and presupposes the dynamics of human psychology whereas the scope of the theological claim about the correlative "otherness" and "closeness" of Creator to creatures includes all kinds of creatures (some of whom may not have anything like human "interiority") and presupposes, not claims about psychological dynamics, but about ontology. For all of its analogical obscurity, however, the theme that, in creative blessing and in the providential care that is entailed by it, the Triune God is correlatively always on both "sides" of the relation serves at least as a "grammatical" rule governing what can and what cannot be intelligibly said about and inferred from the Christian theological claim that the Triune God relate to all else in creative blessing.

There is at least one more important theological point stressed by placing the "Father" in the lead position in *taxis* or pattern of the Triune God's relating to all else in creative blessing. It also stresses that the power of God's sovereignty in creative blessing is a power by which God binds Godself. That claim is explicitly warranted by the fourth and fifth exegetical points about Genesis 1 noted. In creative blessing, the Triune God's intrinsic self-regulating is self-binding (i.e., "sovereign"). Inasmuch as God's power in creative blessing faithfully expresses the character of the "Father's" ongoing eternal generative relating to the "Son" and the Spirit, it faithfully "expresses" the "Father's" self-binding by a self-commitment to the communion in love among the three "Persons" of the Trinity that is the intrinsically glorious life of the Triune God. Here, too, although the power of the "Father's" self-binding in self-commitment to the other two "Persons" of the Trinity in the communion that is their one life is expressed in God's sovereign self-binding in creative blessing, it does not replicate it. Where the first is the self binding of an eternal self-relating *a se* that constitutes the Triune God's life, the second is a self-relating that is self-bound to sustain creatures in their concrete actuality and value for as long as they last in ways that do not violate the ontological integrity of their "otherness" to God as creatures. It is a self-commitment to which God is also reliably faithful in the concrete ways in which God goes about relating in the providential care of creatures that creative blessing entails.

That means that the power of the Triune God's sovereignty in creative blessing is intrinsically ordered to the good of the creatures, i.e., to their concrete actuality and the value of their intrinsic dignity. That God's relating to all else in creative blessing is self-binding expresses that, far from separating God from creatures by hermetically sealing God off from creatures, God's self-faithfulness in unconditioned self-relating to all else binds God to them for as long as they last in a way that they can trust.

Move on now to the larger context in which the Trinitarian formula for God's relating in creative blessing places the "Father's" priority in creative blessing. Following the affirmation of the "Father's" lead in the pattern or *taxis* in which the Triune God relates in creative blessing, it adds that the "Father" creates "through the Son" and "in the power of the Spirit." This notion further nuances the sense in which God's self-regulating (i.e., "sovereignty") in creative blessing is "absolutely powerful." The eternal relation between the "First Person" of the Trinity and the other two "Persons" is generative. In the first case, it is the dynamically generous self-giving that eternally constitutes the "Second Person" as "only-begotten Son of the Father," and therewith also constitutes the "First Person" as "Father." In the second case, the relation is traditionally characterized, not on analogy with the way in which "like begets like," but on analogy with the way in which a life breathes itself in and out: the "Father" of the "Son" also "spirates" or breathes "out" the Spirit of the Triune God's own life in a self-relating that, by perfectly and generously expressing itself, constitutes the "Third Person" as a genuine "Other." Because, with the "Father" and "Son," that "Other" (the Spirit) "is worshipped together and glorified together,"[8] it is also deemed to be of "one substance" with the "Father."[9]

The "Son's" being begotten by the "Father" and the Spirit's "spiration" by the "Father" are both "traditionally" referred to as their "processions" from the "Father." However, "procession" and "proceeding" can be misleading. The use of two different analogies for these two senses in which the self-regulating dynamic that constitutes the Triune God's glorious life is intrinsically "generative" indicates that they are not two instances of some one and the same way – dubbed "processing" – of powerfully self-relating so as to "generate" a genuine "Other." One way in which they are intrinsically different is that, whereas the Spirit is said to be "spirated" by the "Father," Scriptural usage makes it clear that the Spirit is nonetheless as truly the Spirit of the "Son" as the Spirit of the "Father."

Because each sense in which the Triune God's intrinsic self-relating is powerfully "generative" is faithfully expressed in the "generatively" powerful ways in which God also goes about sovereignly (i.e., self-regulatingly) relating to all else in creative blessing, the differences in the two senses of God's intrinsic "generativity" nuance the sense in which God is also "powerfully generative" in creative blessing.

To add that the "Father" creates "*through* the 'Son'" is to attribute a quality to the power of the Triune God's relating in creative blessing that we have not noted before. The "Son" is not only identified in the Nicene Creed as the "eternally begotten Son of the Father" and "of one substance with the Father," but also as One who "for us . . . and our salvation came down from the heavens, and was made flesh." That is, the "Second Person" of the Triune God

---

[8] The phrase, of course, is from the Nicene Creed.

[9] In Medieval and early modern Western Scholastic theology, and in particular in Thomas Aquinas' account of the relations among the "Persons" of the Triune God, both the "Father" and the "Son" "spirate" the Spirit.

is identical with Jesus of Nazareth, whom the Gospel of John calls the "Word of God." Now, we have already seen that assimilation of "Word of God" (in the Fourth Gospel) to "Son of God" invokes the picture of God's Wisdom in Proverbs 8 and underscores (a) that the Triune God's sovereignty (i.e., self-regulating) in providential care and in drawing creatures to eschatological consummation has a quality more like the ad hoc practical wisdom celebrated in Proverbs than like the contemplative intellectual intuition that *logos* often connotes, and (b) that, intrinsic to God's sovereignty in creative blessing, is delight in the creation. What we have now is a different additional implication of the introduction of the phrase "through the Son." The "Second Person" of the Trinity is identified as God Incarnate in a particular human life that was crucified, suffered, was buried, and rose again on the third day. That is the concrete way in which the Triune God goes about relating to human creatures to "save" them. Because it faithfully expresses "what" and "who" God is intrinsically, the entire life-trajectory of the Word Incarnate, culminating in Jesus' death by crucifixion and resurrection, is "the image of the invisible God" (Colossians 1:15). For the Apostle Paul writing to the Corinthians, the ending of that life on a cross exhibits "the power of God and the wisdom of God. For God's foolishness is wiser than human wisdom, and God's weakness is stronger than human strength" (1 Corinthians 24b, 25). For Paul, writing to the Philippians and apparently quoting a Christian hymn earlier than Paul, the very beginning of that life exhibits at least one quality of God's intrinsic sovereignty, viz. the scope of God's self-regulating extends to self-restricting. For Jesus Christ,

> Who, though he was in the form of God,
> did not regard equality with God as something to be exploited,
> but *emptied* himself,
>> taking the form of a slave,
>> being born in human likeness.

(Philippians 2:6–7)

Although God's sovereignty is absolutely powerful in being unrestricted by any other reality, not only is it powerfully self-regulated to honor the ontological integrity of creatures in providential care of them, but more radically, it is also powerful in being self-restricting to the point of weakness and foolishness by the standards of "human wisdom."

This is not a maximum "degree" of divine self-restriction of what is otherwise "absolute" power. Rather, it warrants the claim that the power of the Triune God's sovereignty in creative blessing is the power to relate to creatures in a way that empowers them to be "other" than God in a way that in turn empowers them to respond to God as one of them living among them whom they can ignore or whose reality they may reject, denying their dependence on God, and denying the damage they do to themselves collectively by failing to respond appropriately to God's ways of relating to them. That is, the power of God's creative blessing, apparently "foolishly" gives them the power, and the permission to exercise it, radically to distort God's creative project and reject God's blessing on it, leaving the power of God's sovereignty in creative blessing to appear "weak" as it is thwarted by creatures' exercise of their creaturely powers. (Human wisdom's response: surely an all-powerful and all-knowing God could have created creatures that could not, or at least would never, exercise their creaturely powers in such a way as to reject God's blessing, distort God's creation, and thwart God's overall purposes in creating!)

To add further that the "Father" creates "through the 'Son' *in the power* of the Spirit" is to attribute yet another quality to the power of the Triune God's sovereignty in relating in creative blessing. In addition to being identified by its eternal dynamic relation of "proceeding" from the "Father," the Spirit is identified in the Nicene Creed by its relation to creatures as "the Lord and giver of life." That warrants the attribution to the power of God's sovereignty in creative blessing the quality of being intrinsically ordered not only generally to the concrete actuality and dignity of all creatures as such, but especially and particularly that of living creatures in their kinds. Given that, in creative blessing, as in every way in which the Triune God relates to all that is not God, God is concurrently and inseparably at once "radically other" than creatures and "radically close," "closer" to them than they can be to themselves, God's relating "in the power of the Spirit," which is intrinsically ordered the actuality and dignity of living creatures warrants the attribution to God of a power to that relating that does not violate the ontological integrity and well-being of creatures by being "interior" to the dynamics that constitute living creatures' life in their kinds.

As the condition of the possibility of the self-conscious aware-ness of at least some forms of creaturely life, the Triune God's relating in creative blessing "in the power of the Spirit" is a power relating "interiorly" to their consciousness without violating or threatening to violate the integrity of the complex sort of con-sciousness and mental powers that mark human creatures and their proper freedom. Such "interior" relating by God "in the power of the Spirit" in creative blessing is the condition of the possibility of the concrete actuality of human creatures whose life is distinguished by precisely that sort of complexity of conscious-ness and intellectual powers. God's "presence" to human mental life "in the power of the Spirit" in creative blessing is the condition of the possibility of that sort of life without being a "structural" feature of human creaturely life. As the power in which the "Father" relates creatively to human creatures, it is concurrently "radically other than" creaturely mental life as well as so "radically close" as to be "interior" to it. Because of that "radical otherness" it cannot be said to "engage" or "encounter" human creatures' "mental acts" in zero-sum interactions some shared "field" or on any common "plane." Such "otherness" rules out characterizations of then Triune God's way of relating to human creatures' consciousness that suggest it is somehow a "violation" of their creaturely integrity.

God is as God does and does as God is. The Triune God is "powerful" in God's own ways. God is "powerful" as "what" and "who" God is in God's self-regulating the ways in which God relates, i.e., in God's sovereignty in God's relating. Indeed, because God is self-bound by the commitments God makes in the ways God goes about relating, those commitment-laden ways of relating define "who" the God is that is powerful in relating. Hence the Triune God is "powerful" in different senses of the term in God's sovereignty in different ways of relating.

In regard to God's relating to all that is not God in creative blessing, the strand of the economy that has been in view thus far in this chapter, the power of the Triune God's sovereignty exhibits the qualities of free (unrestricted by any other power) ongoing (as opposed to a singular event) relating that "makes the difference" of sustaining creatures in concretely actual reality and value when that reality and value could in principle be annihilated. It is "power" intrinsically ordered to creatures' ontological integrity; power that empowers others rather than competing with them in zero-sum engagements; a power self-bound to honor creatures' ontological integrity in the ways in which it actively relates such that it is trustworthy power; indeed, power that is self-bound to relate in ways that look to human wisdom to be weak and foolish. It is "power" that is not comparable with the sort of power creatures have and does not interact with them on the same "plane" in competitive and possibly conflictual ways. Rather, it is always on both "sides" of the relation, correlatively at once radically "other" of creatures to which it relates and radically "close" to them.

The Triune God who relates in creative blessing is One who is wisely self-binding to creatures, i.e., One who is freely, transcendentally, and nonviolently ordered to the good in blessing them creatively. That is the "identity" of "who" the God is that is sovereign, i.e., self-regulating, in relating to create all else ex nihilo. Hence, the *power* of God's sovereignty, i.e., the power of God's self-binding self-regulating in relating, has the same qualities.

The Power of the Triune God's Intrinsic Sovereignty

Chapters 3 and 4 argued that the Triune God's ways of concretely relating to what is not God all consistently entail faithful expression of aspects of how the Triune God is intrinsically self-related. Particularly important is that God's ways of relating to all else always entail God's self-regulation by the self-commitments God makes in those ways of relating. The Trinity's self-regulating in the ways God relates *ad extra* to all else faithfully expresses God's self-regulation *ad intra* in the generative self-relating in love that is God's attractively glorious intrinsic life. That intrinsic self-regulating is the sense in which God is "sovereign" in God's own life. Aspects of that intrinsic sovereignty are faithfully expressed in qualities of God's sovereignty in the economy. In the first section, it was argued in particular that the unrestricted power of the Triune God's sovereignty in the creative blessing strand of God's economy expresses the sense in which the power of God's intrinsic sovereignty is unrestricted, viz., the power of "Father's" intrinsic sovereignty in eternally "generating" the "Son" and the Spirit. Thus far, this paragraph has been a recital of themes in those two chapters.

The point to be explored now is this: the senses in which God's sovereignty in the three strands of the economy is powerful faithfully express the sense in which the Triune God is powerful in God's intrinsic sovereignty in the self-relating that constitutes the Trinity's intrinsically glorious life, as discussed in Chapter 2. God's sovereignty is not God's "rule" or "self-regulation" *over* God's power. It is not as though God possesses a power that is a value-neutral force over which God's sovereign self-regulating exercises control, deciding whether or not to use it, on what particular occasions to use it, and, if using it in some particular circumstance, in what degree of force to use it and whether to order its use to the good. Rather, God's intrinsic power is simply the power of God's intrinsic self-regulation, i.e., God's intrinsic sovereignty itself.

The qualities of the power of that self-regulation are the qualities of "what" and "who" the Triune God is. It is the "God of Abraham" whose intrinsic self-regulating is powerful. The qualities of God's intrinsic sovereignty are the qualities of God's singular reality (i.e., qualities of "what" God is, some of which were noted in Chapter 2) and the qualities of God's eternal singular identity as that is defined by God's commitments in which God binds Godself in the three sorts of ways in which God goes about relating to all else in the economy (i.e., qualities of "who" God is, some of which were noted in 3 and 4). Accordingly, the qualities of the power of God's intrinsic sovereignty are simply intrinsic qualities of "what" and "who" the Triune God is.

However, we have a very limited basis on which to give content to the claim that God's intrinsic sovereignty is "powerful." As we noted in Chapter 4 in regard to God's intrinsic sovereignty, the language that is ordinarily used to characterize the dynamics of the self-relating in generous self-giving that comprises the Triune God's intrinsic *a se* life is largely drawn from what we consider to be human ways of relating "interpersonally" in faithful self-commitments to others and to shared projects. Interpersonal self-commitments, including private personal covenants, marriages, societies, and commercial transactions, are constituted by explicit and implicit promise making to which the promise makers commit themselves. Such interpersonal ways of relating share such qualities as intentionality, faithfulness, a certain limited knowledge of the "other" in her or his concrete particularity, orderedness to the good of the "other," love for the other, etc. They also share the quality of being powerful in various respects and in various degrees. Insofar as the dynamics and structures of such interpersonal relations also entail dynamics and structures of *intra*personal self-relating, they may also be used to characterize not only the ways in which God powerfully relates to all else, but also how God "self-relates" powerfully in God's self-commitments.

As was stressed in Chapter 3, such language must be used analogically when attributed to God's intrinsic dynamic self-relating. We may be able to offer warrants for using such language. However, we have no way to know just how such language means in relation to God's intrinsic reality. We have little grasp of the definition of those qualities when used in reference to God, little grasp of their boundaries and the limits to the range of further qualities that may be inferred from them when their attribution to God is accepted.

Then – as we did in Chapter 4 concerning the Triune God's intrinsic sovereignty – let us stammer boldly about the qualities of the intrinsic power of the Triune God's intrinsic sovereignty, power that is a quality of the Triune God, independent of whether or not God relates to any other realities.

Given the claim that in canonical Scriptural accounts of God's ways of relating to all else we have warrants for believing that there is some overlap between how the terms used to name some qualities mean when used to characterize human relationships and how they mean when used to characterize how God actively relates, we may venture to use them analogically to attribute certain qualities to the power of the Triune God's self-regulating in the self-binding self-commitments the Triune God makes in self-relating in the eternal and unrestrictedly generous self-giving of the "Father" to the "Son" and to the Spirit, which comprises the Triune God's attractive intrinsically glorious life.

As formulated in the Nicene–Constantinopolitan Creed, the Triune God's intrinsic generative self-relating is a perfect self-giving that constitutes the reality of each of the three divine "Persons" of the Trinity. Each "Person" has its own distinctive eternal identity in virtue of the character of the self-relating-by-self-giving that consti-tutes it as the "Person" it is. Furthermore, it is a self-relating in which "what" the three identically are (i.e., "divinity," "God's nature") is faithfully and fully expressed in each of them. Chapter 2 elaborated those points, and we build on them now.

The power intrinsic to the Triune God's singular reality, i.e., to God's intrinsically self-regulating life, is ordered to the good of each of the three "Persons" of the Trinity, i.e., to the integrity of each one's unique identity *vis á vis* the other two ("who" each is) and to the unity of their concrete actuality ("what" it is to be God). That orderedness to the good is intrinsic to God's power precisely because it is the power of God's intrinsic sovereignty (i.e., God's intrinsic self-regulation of God's active self-relating and relating in the economy) that is itself intrinsically ordered to the good. Its being ordered to that good is not an "end" to which the "Father" freely "chooses" to direct an otherwise a-teleological and value neutral unrestricted force at God's command. In particular, it is not the force of an efficient cause. Rather, it is power intrinsic to the dynamic of the intrinsic life of the Trinity that just *is* its singular *a se* reality. It is the power of the eternal "generation" of the "Son" and Spirit, but it is not their efficient cause. Nor does it itself require either an efficient cause or any other reality to be its "regulator."

The power intrinsic to the Triune God's singular reality is generously self-giving. It is "generous" in that the active self-relating among the three "Persons" that constitutes each of them as the "Person" it is does so in such a way that they are One in the *full* actuality of God. It is the power of a self-relating by self-giving that is perfectly self-expressive, such that the three "Persons" are "of one substance." It is power of the self-regulated dynamics of the inter-relations among the three "Persons" through which each is empowered noncompetitively to be "what" and "who" it is, for there is no further goal for which to compete. And, if noncompetitive and intrinsically empowering, it is intrinsically a power that does not threaten to conflict with that to which it is ordered. As intrinsically nonconflictual, it is an intrinsically nonviolent power.

As *intrinsically* ordered to the good of that to which it is related (viz., the "good" of each of the "Persons"), the Triune God's intrinsic power may be said to have the quality of intentionality. It *"intends"* the good of that to which it relates. That entails another quality: as intrinsically ordered to the good of that to which it relates, God's power is *cognizant* of the particularities of the good of the "other" relative to its concrete particularity. That is to say, the power of the three "Persons" perfectly self-expressive self-giving self-relating is not only generative, but also cognitive. In it the "Persons" of the Trinity may be said to *know* one another in their particular identity. Indeed, in the power of God's intrinsic sovereignty God is unqualifiedly transparent to Godself. Call the power of the Triune God's intrinsic sovereignty God's intrinsic *"self-omniscience."* The power of God's intrinsic sovereignty is *intelligently* self-regulating. Power that, in intelligent self-regulation, knows the "others" to which it relates in their concrete particularities, knows *compassively* the others' particular joys and sorrows.

Power that is intrinsically generative, relating to others at once as One "radically other than" and as One "radically close to" them, generously self-giving to them, faithful to the commitments to them by which it binds itself, ordered to the good of the "others" to which it relates, intending those others, knowing them in their concrete particularities, so fully self-knowing as to be transparent to itself, always relates in nonviolent ways, relating to others so radically closely as to be "internal" to them without violating their onto-logical integrity, knowing the others' passions, may fairly be called "loving" power. The intrinsic power of the Triune God is a *loving* power. It is tempting but seriously misleading to reverse the phrase and call it "the power of love." That phrase is misleading because it suggests that in every context of its use "love" names one and the same "thing" that is in some sense powerful. But in ordinary English "love" does not name some one thing. Nor is it evident that what it names in every one of the contexts in which it is used is in fact very powerful or, for that matter, intrinsically ordered to the good. The Triune God's intrinsic power is the power only of the love that constitutes the communion that is the intrinsic, attractively glorious life of God, God's singular concrete actuality.

* * * * *

This part of this project urges that God's power is best explained in the context of a logically independent and prior account of God's sovereignty or "self-regulating" self-relating such as the one outlined in Part II. There, God's sovereignty was explained in the context of a logically independent and prior account of God's concrete actuality understood as the intrinsic glory of God. This chapter has made proposals about how God's power, understood as the power of God's sovereignty, may be understood in two different contexts of God's sovereignty: God's sovereignty in creative blessing of all that is not God, and God's intrinsic sovereignty.

Chapter 9 urges that a theologically adequate account of the power of God's sovereignty should not be developed solely on the basis of some one strand of the economy, say, only on the basis of God relating to create ex nihilo. Rather, what can be said about the qualities of the power of God's sovereignty on the basis of canonical accounts of God relating in creative blessing must be nuanced by what must be said about it on the basis of canonical accounts of God relating in two additional ways: in providential care and in eschatological blessing. Each is a different register in which the power of God's "sovereignty" must also be understood. Each strand of the economy expresses an aspect of the "glory" of God in the secondary reference of that phrase. In each strand, God is faithfully self-expressive of aspects of God's own intrinsic glory and its power. The two strands of the economy examined in Chapter 9 define two additional different but coherent senses of the power of the Triune God's "sovereignty."

9 | The Triune God's Power in Two Registers

Certain sorts of well-intentioned pastoral remarks meant to comfort those who anguish over others' intense suffering are justified by theologically problematic assumptions about the phrase "the power of the God." One such assumption is that in Christian theology God's "power" should be defined solely by the unrestrained and unconditioned "absolute" power of God in creating ex nihilo, as that is rendered in canonical Scriptural accounts of God's creative blessing. A second assumption is that such power is properly understood as a morally neutral and a-teleological force that God employs as God "wills" in providential care of creatures. A third assumption is that God's sovereignty is the sovereignty of God's power in creating and in providentially caring for reality other than God by exercising that power to control all that goes on among creatures. A fourth assumption is that God exercises that power to realize an ultimate goal for each creature in particular and for creation as a whole according to a plan, one might say "a plan of action," that moves through a rationally ordered series of steps. A fifth assumption is that it is just that "absolute" power that constitutes God's infinite reality in contradistinction to the finite powers that constitute the sort of reality that creatures have. That absolute power is what makes God *God*. All of this sums up the diagnostic critical analysis that has woven through previous chapters regarding what is theologically problematic about a particular strand of conventional North American Christian pious talk.

Part I took the first step in developing an alternative account of the power of the Triune God that could clearly negate the validity of those assumptions. It outlined the conceptual context of an account of the Triune God's intrinsic sovereignty in an analysis of God's intrinsic glory. In that account God's "glory" is understood as the attractive radiance of the dynamics of the life of the Triune God in communion in love. The basic themes urged there are first: "what" and "who" the Triune God intrinsically is can be better limned in terms of an account of God's intrinsic glory than in terms either of God's intrinsic power or of God's intrinsic sovereignty; and second, God's intrinsic power can be more aptly explained as the power of God's intrinsic sovereignty in the dynamics of God's intrinsic glory than can God's intrinsic sovereignty be explained as the sovereignty of God's intrinsic power in the dynamics of God's glory. God's sovereignty in God's own life cannot be explained as the sovereignty of God's power over God's life. Such a line of thought would be open to the inference that the Triune God somehow has power from "outside" God's life by which God "shapes" or even "makes" God's Triune life.

What is at stake is the Triune God's trustworthiness grounded in God's self-faithfulness. If God can exercise a power that is not defined by "what" and "who" God is intrinsically to shape and perhaps change "what" and "who" God is, indeed to bring and keep God "into" existence, and if God's ways of relating to all else express aspects of such intrinsic power, then "what" and "who" God is would be intrinsically untrustworthy and faith in God entirely misplaced. For in that case it would be entirely consistent if, having committed Godself in the ways in which God relates to all else, God changed "what" and "who" God is and proceeded to relate to all else in ways contrary to God's initial ways of relating, leaving creatures unable to trust that God keeps promises and can be relied on.

Given the radical singularity of the Triune God's reality, "what" and "who" God is escapes comprehension by creaturely human minds. Because God's ways of relating to all else faithfully express aspects of God's intrinsic qualities, our ascription to the Triune God of any qualities, such as power and sovereignty, in the kind of theology being done here must be warranted by the ways in which God goes about relating to human creatures and to all else that is not God, as those ways of relating are faithfully rendered in canonical Christian Scripture. Part II introduced distinctions, borrowed from the exegetical work of the Old Testament scholar Claus Westermann, among three sorts of canonical narrative that are irreducibly different because they have different (in my phrase, not Westermann's) "narrative logics": narratives of creative blessing, narratives of punctiliar events or deeds of liberative and saving promise making and promise keeping, and narratives of eschatological blessing.

Each of the three strands of God's economy has qualities that faithfully express some aspects of God's intrinsic qualities. Part II then acknowledged that canonical accounts of God relating in creative blessing do indeed warrant an account of God's sovereignty in creative blessing as an "absolute," i.e., an unrestricted sovereignty that consists of God's self-regulation of how God goes about relating. Accordingly, they warrant attribution of unrestricted sovereignty to God as the sense in which God is intrinsically sovereign.

However, Part II then urged that, although God's creative blessing necessarily entails that God's providence be ordered to creatures' well-being, it also entails that the way God goes about providential care of creatures cannot be "unrestricted" because it is ordered to creatures in their concrete particularities which it honors. If the Triune God's way of relating in providential care is ordered to the well-being of creatures in their particularities, then it *is* restricted by so honoring those particularities as not to violate them. Thus, although God's providential care of creatures is entailed by God's creative blessing, God is "sovereign" in providential care in a quite different sense of "sovereign" than God is "sovereign" in creative blessing.

Finally, Part II argued that in the Triune God's ways of relating, respectively, in providential care and in eschatological blessing God is "sovereign" in two additional different but compatible senses of "sovereign," each of which faithfully expresses some aspects of

God's intrinsic sovereignty. There is no single sense of "sovereignty" that may be univocally attributed to the Triune God. The various senses in which God may be said to be "sovereign" cannot be understood simply as variations of some one sense of "sovereignty" that differ only in degree. Rather, they are compatible but irreducibly different than one another.

Thus far, Part III has promoted the general claim that the senses in which the Triune God is properly said to be "powerful" are all senses in which God's sovereignty is powerful. Accordingly, the senses in which the Triune God may be said to be "powerful" vary depending on whether the theological context of the claim is (a) an account of the sense in which the Triune God is properly said to be intrinsically "sovereign" or (b) the context of the claim is an account of the quite different sense in which God is properly said to be "sovereign," respectively, in each of the strands of God's economy. Chapter 8 explored the senses in which we are warranted to ascribe "power" to God's intrinsic sovereignty and the senses in which canonical Scriptural accounts of the ways in which God goes about relating to all else warrant our ascribing "power" to God's sovereignty in creative blessing and in providential care.

This chapter elaborates that last distinction by exploring differences between, and convergences of, the senses in which God is properly said to be "powerful" in God's sovereignty in the two strands of the economy that are distinct from creative blessing and its entailment, providential care: relating to bless eschatologically and relating to reconcile estranged creatures to God.

Thus, the chapters of Part III together map four distinguishable and irreducibly different senses in which God is properly said to be "powerful" in God's sovereignty. Each of three of the senses of "power" that we are warranted to ascribe to the Triune God in regard, respectively, to creative blessing, eschatological blessing, and reconciliation faithfully expresses some aspects of the sense in which the Triune God is intrinsically "powerful" in the Triune God's sovereignty in God's own life.

One consequence of the differences among senses of "power" that may properly be ascribed to the Triune God's sovereignty in different theological contexts is this: because those senses of "power" cannot be conflated as variations of some single sense of "power" even though they all express some aspect of God's intrinsic power, our account of God's power necessarily "stammers," shifting endlessly back and forth from one sense to another.

How Canonical Accounts of God Relating to Bless Eschatologically and to Reconcile Are Related to Each Other

We begin by noting what canonical Christian Scriptural accounts of how God relates, respectively, in eschatological blessing and to reconcile estranged creatures to God have in common and how they differ. We shall then reflect on the sense in which the Triune God's sovereignty in eschatological blessing may be said to be "powerful." That discussion will be followed by a reflection on the sense in which God's sovereignty in relating to reconcile the estranged to God may also be said to be "powerful."

We have already repeatedly noted that the Triune God's relating in creative blessing is prevenient, "coming before" any other way of relating to all else and thus "prior" to them in the order of reality, although not necessarily coming "before" them in the order of coming to know God. Hence, the relation between God's creative blessing and all other ways in which God relates to all else are asymmetrical. Absent God's creative blessing ex nihilo there is "nothing" there to care for providentially, to bless eschatologically, or to reconcile to God. The latter presuppose God's creative blessing; however, God's creative blessing ex nihilo presupposes precisely nothing other than God.

For their part, God's relating in eschatological blessing and to reconcile are themselves complexly and asymmetrically related to each other. On one hand, as the two are narrated in the New

Testament in the larger contexts of Old Testament accounts of God's hints and promises of an eschatological blessing of creatures and God's making and keeping of liberative promises, the two are clearly inseparable. New Testament accounts of how God begins to keep the promise to bless creatures eschatologically and of how God decisively keeps promises to liberate creatures bound by the consequences to themselves of their self-estrangement from God, are both "about" Jesus of Nazareth and the Holy Spirit, although "about them" in different ways. Their inseparability is manifest in the fact that the New Testament narratives of each way in which God relates (to bless eschatologically and to reconcile) all intersect in their references to the life-trajectory of Jesus of Nazareth as he relates to the One he calls "Father" and as he relates to the Spirit, and as the "Father" and the Spirit relate to him. In traditional theological terminology, they present Jesus of Nazareth as in some sense the "Incarnation" of God. They present God's concrete way of relating both to bless eschatologically and to reconcile in one and the same way: the way of Incarnation. Those canonical narratives, most explicitly in John and some of Paul's letters, present Jesus as the definitive expression of God's intrinsic "glory." So "glory" is to be definitively understood in terms of how God goes about blessing eschatologically and reconciling by way of Incarnation. As Daniel Migliore says, "This means that all of our images and names of God, however cherished, have to take on new and different meanings from what they previously had"[1] – and, we may add, were theologically warranted solely by canonical narrative of God relating to create ex nihilo.

However, although those two strands in canonical Christian Scriptures' narratives of how God relates to all else are inseparable, they are also irreducibly different and asymmetrically related to each other. The two are irreducibly different because they have

[1] *The Power of God and the Gods of Power* (Louisville, KY: Westminster John Knox, 2008), p. 41.

different "narrative logics." God's relating to reconcile estranged creatures to God by way Incarnation in and through Jesus' Spirit-empowered ministry, death by crucifixion, and resurrection in the power of the Spirit is narrated as the culminating episode of God relating in liberative deeds of deliverance that decisively keep God's promise to Abraham to make his descendants a blessing for all families. On this reading of New Testament accounts of Jesus' life-trajectory, it is the crucifixion of Jesus the Incarnation of the Word of God and Son of God that is the concrete way in which God goes about relating to reconcile estranged creatures to God. God's relating to reconcile is by way of the crucifixion of the Incarnate Word.

God's actively relating to bless creatures eschatologically, in contrast, is narrated as God's beginning to keep a promise of a steady-state ongoing transformative eschatological blessing on creatures, a promise that is coeval with God's creative blessing. On this reading of New Testament accounts of Jesus' life-trajectory it is the resurrection of the crucified Jesus that is the beginning of God's actualizing the promise of eschatological blessing of creatures. The concrete way in which God blesses eschatologically is by way of Incarnation of the "Son," who is raised from the dead as the "first fruits" of the general resurrection that marks the beginning – but only the beginning – of God's full actualization of eschatological blessing. Hence, eschatological blessing is at once now actually inaugurated and not yet fully actualized. By the power of the Spirit, other human creatures are drawn into beginning to participate in that eschatological transformation here and now, living in the tension of the "meantime" between the now actual inauguration of eschatological transformation and its ultimate full actualization that is not yet.

Irreducibly different yet inseparable, God's ways of relating to reconcile and to bless eschatologically are asymmetrically related to each other. In the order of reality, God's relating to reconcile presupposes God's relating to bless eschatologically. God's relating to bless eschatologically is coeval with and presupposes God's relating to bless creatively. It no more presupposes the reality of sin and creatures' estrangement from God than does God's relating in creative blessing. God's relating to bless eschatologically does not presuppose creatures' need to be reconciled to God. Because God's concrete way of going about blessing creatures eschatologically is by way of Incarnation, it follows that the Incarnation itself does not necessarily presuppose sin and creaturely estrangement.

Hence, in the order of reality, it is to realities to which God "already" relates in both creative and eschatological blessing that God also relates to reconcile creatures to God when they estrange themselves from God. It is the realities to which God relates in both creative and eschatological blessing that have inexplicably become *self*-estranged from God. God's relating to reconcile thus presupposes God's relating in both creative and eschatological blessing. Moreover, the concrete way in which God relates to reconcile presupposes the way in which God relates to bless eschatologically: the way of Incarnation. Thus, the two are asymmetrically related in the order of reality with God's relating in eschatological blessing being prior.

They are also asymmetrically related in the order of our coming to understand "who" God is. However, in that respect, the order is reversed. God's concrete way of relating to reconcile by way of Incarnation in which God Godself enters into solidarity with human creatures in the depths of the consequences to them of their self-estrangement from God to draw them into the relation that Jesus himself has with God, is the definitive expression *ad extra* of the covenant love that is the triune God's intrinsic glory and life: love whose powerful self-giving is so unrestricted as to embrace even enemies in a way that attracts and draws their love to God without violating the integrity of their finite creatureliness. Thus, in the order of coming to *understand* "who" God is, God's relating to reconcile is conceptually prior even to God's relating in eschatological blessing.

The triune God's sovereignty in relating by way of Incarnation is powerful both to bless eschatologically and to reconcile estranged creatures to God. However, given the differences in the sense in which God is "sovereign" in relating by way of Incarnation to bless eschatologically, on one hand, and the sense in which God is "sovereign" in relating to reconcile the estranged, on the other, the sense in which God's sovereignty "powerfully" makes a difference for God's genuinely "other" creatures is also importantly different in each case. Each expresses the intrinsic glory of the living Trinity in a different register. And the sense of "power" in each register blocks apparently possible inferences from canonical accounts of God's relating in creative blessing that could warrant the theological claim that "the power of God" is "absolutely unconditioned power"; that simply is what it is to be God.

Because it is prior in the order of reality ("ontologically prior") to God's relating to reconcile estranged creatures to God, we will explore first ("A") the way the phrase "the power of God" means theologically in relation to God's sovereignty in eschatological blessing by way of Incarnation. Against that background we will then turn ("B") to explore the way the phrase means theologically in relation to God's sovereignty in reconciling creatures to God by way of Incarnation.

As narrated in the Synoptic Gospels – and in Acts, on the assumption that it is Part 2 of Luke – the particular and peculiar way in which the Triune God begins to keep the promise of eschatological blessing turns on the inter-relations among Jesus, the One he calls "Father," and the Holy Spirit. Because we have already discussed in Part II the sense in which God is "sovereign" in eschatological blessing as that is canonically narrated, we can limit ourselves here to a sketch of some features of the structure of those narratives that bear on the sense in which God's sovereignty in eschatological blessing is "powerful."

"Sketch" is an important qualifier. In what follows, large generalizations are made about the overall movement of the narratives of the Synoptic Gospels and Acts without detailed exegetical support. Those generalizations neither deny nor seek to play down the important differences among those Gospel narratives, especially deep differences between the Synoptic Gospels and the Gospel of John. Nonetheless, the generalizations do urge commonalities among Gospels' narratives of God's particular ways of blessing eschatologically that are theologically important for any effort to tease out the narratives' implications for understanding the "power" of God's sovereignty in eschatological blessing.

One commonality of the movements of the Synoptic Gospels' narratives is the complex structure of the way in which Jesus and the Spirit are at once related to each other and in some tension with each other. They are each, in a different way, the focal center of the Gospels' narratives of God blessing eschatologically.

Jesus is their focal center in that the narratives are obviously about him, describing him in ways that identify him with the in-breaking of God's eschatological "reign" (in senses of "reign" or "sovereignty" that are discussed in Part II). He is described as the one sent by the "Father" in the power of the Spirit to proclaim the immanent in-breaking of God's eschatological "reign."[2] He is rendered throughout his ministry as one who relates to God in a unique closeness and as one to whom God relates in a uniquely close way. Accounts of Jesus' proclamation sometimes describe him as suggesting that God's eschatological "reign" is in-breaking there and then in Jesus' own person and acts of proclamation, including his healings and "casting out of evil spirits."

---

[2] It must be kept in mind that these remarks about the canonical Synoptic Gospels' narratival renderings of Jesus of Nazareth as proclaimer, and even "enactor," of the imminent in-breaking of God's eschatological "reign" are not made as historically warranted claims about what the "historical Jesus" said and did. Scholarly controversies about whether the historical Jesus had an eschatological message and how far, if at all, it can be characterized as "apocalyptic," are well-known, complex, fascinating, and ongoing. However, the "Jesus" in question in the theological argument developed here is the one whose identity is rendered by the canonically edited Gospels of the "New" Testament, bracketing for the purposes of this project the important question of the bearing on such theological proposals of the conclusions drawn by sundry historians about the "historical Jesus."

Against the background of contemporary forms of Jewish eschatological expectation, sometimes expressed in apocalyptic rhetoric that the Gospels echo and employ, it is Jesus' resurrection in particular that signifies that God's eschatological "reign" had indeed begun to break in then and there. In their religious contexts the Gospels' narratives of Jesus' resurrection describe the particular and odd way in which God goes about beginning to fulfill the long-standing promise of eschatological consummation of creation. However, what is actually begun, is not yet fully actualized.

On the other hand, although Jesus is clearly the subject of the Gospels' narratives, it is clear that both God's *inauguration* of the process of keeping the long-standing promise of eschatological blessing and God's *continuing blessing* moving toward the ultimate full actualization of that promise is accomplished by the power of the Spirit. In Matthew and Luke, it is by the power of the Spirit that Mary conceives Jesus. In all four Gospels. it is the "descent" of the Spirit onto Jesus at his baptism by John the Baptizer that Jesus is anointed by God (i.e., is made "messiah") for his ministry proclaiming the imminence of the eschatological kingdom of God by proclamation and by healing. In the Synoptics, it is by that power that he resists the temptations that immediately follow his baptism. The Spirit empowers Jesus' proclamation of the immanent in-breaking of God's eschatological "rule" by his acts of healing and casting out evil spirits. Understood against the background of at least some forms of contemporary eschatological expectations framed in apocalyptic terms, those healings and exorcisms signified that God's eschatological "reign" over powers of evil was indeed dawning. Finally, it is by the power of the Spirit that he is raised from the dead. In Luke–Acts it is by the power of the Spirit that there is continuity between what is inaugurated in the resurrection of Jesus, on one side, and the eschatological transformation after his resurrection of a congregation listening to Peter preach at Pentecost when the Spirit is "poured out" on all of them (cf., Luke 3:16 and Acts 2). Peter interprets the event as the fulfillment of God's eschatological promise through the prophet Joel that "[i]n the last days" God will "pour out [God's] Spirit upon all flesh, and your sons and daughters shall prophecy" (2:17). Against the background of eschatological expectations, the reference to the pouring out of the Spirit, not on individual prophets, kings or judges, but on "all flesh" is a sign that God's eschatological "rule" is in process of being actualized in the present. The narrative thereafter in Acts is an account of how, by the power of the Spirit, more and more people are drawn into what God had inaugurated in and through the resurrection of Jesus and the out-pouring of the Spirit. Luke–Acts frames the ongoing actualization of what was inaugurated in the resurrection of Jesus as the growth of the church. Paul, writing to rather different Christian communities earlier than Luke–Acts was written, frames an analogous story in terms of the power of the Spirit to draw those who were not contemporaries of Jesus into eschatological life with, through, and in the risen Jesus. In Jurgen Moltmann's favored phrase, the work of the Spirit in relation to Jesus is the *mission dei* in and through history. This *mission dei* is ongoing, far from self-evident, unpredictable, certainly nonlinear, not developmental, and perhaps incremental. Ultimately it will lead to a general resurrection by the power of the Spirit, a "Day" at once of judgment and of cosmic re-creation, that marks the full actualization of God's promised eschatological blessing of creation. This complex relation between Jesus and the Spirit is what moves the Gospels' narratives read as accounts of how God concretely goes about actualizing the promise of eschatological blessing.

The Power of the Triune God's Sovereignty in the Register of Eschatological Blessing

Part II suggested that the concrete way in which the Trinity goes about relating to all else in eschatological blessing can be summarized in the trinitarian formula, *"The Spirit, the Lord and giver of life, sent with the 'Son' by the 'Father,' draws creatures into eschatological consummation whose inauguration and 'first fruits' are the resurrection of Jesus from the dead."* The structure of that formula summarizes in short-hand fashion the distinctive register in which the Trinity's concrete way of relating to bless eschatologically expresses certain aspects of the intrinsic power of the Triune God's intrinsic sovereignty in the glorious life of the Trinity (see Chapter 8). The relation among the three "Persons" of the Trinity in the pattern or *taxis* in which the Triune God relates to all else in eschatological blessing nuances the sense in which God's sovereignty in eschatological blessing is powerful.

Some Implications of the Spirit's Location in the "Lead" Position

As was noted in Part II, canonical New Testament narratives of the Spirit and Jesus, read in the context of Old Testament accounts of God promising eschatological blessing as accounts of how God begins to keep that promise, employ a Spirit-specific vocabulary for the way the Spirit relates to creatures in the economy. Placing the Spirit in the "lead position" in the formula underscores ways in which that Spirit-specific rhetoric shapes an account of the "power" of the Triune God's sovereignty in eschatological blessing that has certain determinate features.[3]

For one, the Spirit that is in the "lead" role in the Trinitarian formula for God's eschatological blessing is the eternal "Person" of the Trinity identified by the Nicene Creed in terms of its relation to reality other than God as the "Lord and giver of life." That is to say, the way in which the Trinity relates to all else in eschatological blessing is a way that is, in creative blessing, the condition of the possibility of the concrete actuality of living creatures. Beyond that,

---

[3] I have developed the themes outlined in the next ten paragraphs more extensively in Part Two of *Eccentric Existence: A Theological Anthropology* (Louisville, KY: Westminster John Knox Press, 2009).

in eschatological blessing the Spirit is the condition of the possibility of creatures whose consciousness is complex enough for them to participate eschatologically in a creaturely fashion in the communion in love that is the Triune God's intrinsic life. The Spirit's sovereignty in the Triune God's creative blessing is its "sovereignty" in relation specifically to living, and especially living human, creatures. In creative blessing, in which the "Father" is in the lead position, the Spirit is notable for its freedom in circumambience, coming and going like the wind upon individual human creatures and particular events (cf. Jesus' analogy of the blowing of the wind for the presence of the Spirit in his conversation with Nicodemus, John 3:8; and Acts' metaphor of "the rush of a violent wind" for the outpouring of the Spirit at Pentecost, 2:2). However, after Jesus' resurrection, the Spirit is "poured out" on all members of the community of the church, not just on a few individuals. It retains its freedom and in that freedom is "radically other than" those to whom it comes. Its sovereignty lies in drawing them toward ultimate eschatological transformation. The circumambient Spirit draws human creatures into eschatological blessing in ways so free of the creatures that the latter can neither anticipate nor control the "drawing." Accordingly, the power of the Spirit's "sovereignty" in relating to them in eschatological blessing in principle cannot be characterized in any way that involves any violation of their ontological integrity. After all, in creative blessing, which is prior in the order of reality, the Spirit is already the "condition of the possibility" of human creatures' actual reality and value as living creatures with extraordinarily complex consciousness. The power of the Spirit's sovereignty to transform human creatures in eschatological blessing is both radically free of them, radically "other" than they and radically "interior" to them, "radically closer" to them than they can be to themselves in their self-awareness without being a heteronomous power that violates them.

A second respect in which the Spirit's way of relating in eschatological blessing determines the sense in which it is "powerful."

The Spirit's way of relating to creatures is typically characterized in canonical accounts in ways that are different from the ways in which God's relating, respectively, in creative blessing and to reconcile the estranged are characterized. At a high level of abstraction, we may say that in all three the Triune God always takes the initiative in relating, is always prevenient, always relating "before" creatures respond, and does so in ways that are the conditions of the possibility of the creatures' responding at all. At that level of abstraction, we may also say that in each of the three strands of the economy the Triune God's "sovereignty" in the ways in which God relates is correlatively "radically other than" creatures and "radically close to" them.

However, those commonalities among canonical accounts of the three strands of the economy are rendered in importantly different ways in those same accounts. As noted several times, because God's sovereignty in relating in creative blessing is utterly unrestricted, its "radical otherness" and "radical closeness" in creative blessing of creatures is best expressed ontologically as God's sovereignty in relating creatively "to" them as the condition of the possibility of their actual reality and value without their sharing any common plane or field within which the "relating" takes place. As we shall see, because the correlative "radical otherness than" and "radical closeness to" creatures of the Triune God's sovereignty in relating to reconcile estranged creatures to God is by way of Incarnation, it is best characterized as God's sovereignty in relating to creatures as "one among them" rather than simply as relating "to" them. And, as was urged in Part II, the correlative "radical otherness than" and "radical closeness to" creatures of the Triune God's sovereignty in relating in eschatological blessing is aptly characterized as God's sovereignty in relating to creatures "circumambiently."

Accordingly, the "power" of the Triune God's sovereignty in eschatological blessing can be characterized neither as the absolutely unrestricted power of God's sovereignty in relating in creative blessing nor as the power of God's sovereignty in relating by way of

Incarnation as one human creature to others, one among many, to reconcile them to God. Rather, it is most aptly characterized as the power of God's sovereignty in relating to creatures circumambi- ently. Although God's promise of eschatological blessing begins to be fulfilled in the singular event of the resurrection of the crucified Jesus, the Spirit's circumambience to creatures is not itself a one-off event. It is a blessing of eschatological transformation of creation coeval with creative blessing, initially in the form of a promise. Then, beginning with the singular event of Jesus' resurrection, it is an ongoing open-ended movement in the power of the Spirit here and now, neither an already fully accomplished transformation nor a purely future transformation.

The difference that the Spirit's "circumambience" makes is that it marks the Triune God's power in eschatological blessing as a "power" defined by being ordered to a distinctive end or good for creatures: eschatological blessing. It is a "good" compatible with the "goods" for creatures to which the Triune God's creative blessing and providential care are ordered; but it is a "good" in addition to them and exceeding them. It is good upon good. And because it is given freely by God it is, in one sense of the term, grace upon grace. Where the "good" to which the Trinity's way of relating in creative blessing is ordered is creatures' concrete reality and value as long as they last and living creatures' well-being in their kinds, the good to which the Triune God's eschatological blessing is ordered is the transformation of living creatures' proximate contexts, i.e., their lived-worlds, and along with that the transformation of their per- sonal identities, so that without ceasing to be finite and radically contingent creatures, they flourish eschatologically. It consists of their creaturely participation – whatever that may be, however that should be characterized – in the relation the eschatologically "glori- fied" risen Jesus of Nazareth has with the One he calls "Father." The Triune God's "sovereignty" in eschatological blessing is "powerful" in a determinate sense defined by its being intrinsically ordered to this good. Its being ordered to this good means that it makes a particular difference: that "difference" is traditionally called the creatures' eschatological "glory."

There is a third respect in which the Spirit's sovereignty in eschatological blessing determines even further the sense in which it is "powerful": God's eschatological blessing is determinately powerful in that it is intrinsically holy. The "good" to which its power is intrinsically ordered, i.e., the "difference" the Spirit's sovereignty makes in eschatological blessing, is at once a difference in the proximate social and cultural contexts in which creatures live and a difference in individual human creatures' interiorities. In both respects, the difference has both positive and negative aspects. Together, both aspects of both respects in which it makes a difference are particularly ordered to drawing creatures into eschatological "holiness." The movement toward full actualization of their holiness is traditionally called "sanctification."

The positive aspect of the difference the Spirit's sovereignty powerfully makes is both, on one hand, a difference in the proximate contexts in which creatures live and, on the other side, a difference in human creatures interiority.

In regard to the first "hand," the power of the Spirit's sovereignty in eschatological blessing is the difference it makes in an ongoing movement that takes place in and through the complex tangle of physical, social, cultural, and political dynamics that constitute human creatures' proximate creaturely contexts and in their particular individual lives. That "movement" has already been inaugurated in space and time in the resurrection of the crucified Jesus. It is not a "movement" that only begins with the ultimate full actualization of eschatological blessing. That is, it is not a "movement" that begins only after death. Rather, the transformation is an ongoing movement in time that marks human creatures' proximate here-and-now contexts with a triple tension. Human creatures live in proximate contexts marked by (a) a tension between an eschatological blessing that has actually been inaugurated and the open-ended reality of the *mission dei* that it has not been fully actualized.

(b) They live in proximate contexts marked by a tension between fully actualized creative blessing and its profound distortion by the consequences of creatures' self-estrangement from God, one another, and their proximate contexts. And (c) they live in proximate contexts at once creatively blessed and eschatologically blessed so that they are ordered toward two different, although compatible, sorts of "goods."

In regard to the positive difference made in human creatures' interiority by the Spirit in eschatological blessing, the power of the Spirit's sovereignty is the difference it makes in their individual lives. They undergo an interior transformation, beginning here and now, that consists of their lives being "formed," at once interpersonally and intrapersonally, as appropriate responses to those three tensions that structure their proximate contexts. The transformation comes as they learn more deeply and clearly to exhibit in their communal and individual practices and actions the hope – and the love and trust that such hope entails – that is appropriate response to the way in which the Trinity keeps concretely relating in eschatological blessing. The power of the Spirit's sovereignty in drawing them to ultimate and full actualization of eschatological blessing is a power particularly ordered to drawing them into creaturely participation in the covenant love that is the Trinity's life by sharing the way the risen Jesus lived it through his life-trajectory.

The positive difference the power of the Spirit's sovereignty in eschatological blessing makes both in creatures' shared proximate contexts and in human creatures' interiorities is the power of its expression of the attractiveness of God's intrinsic holiness. Part I argued that the Triune God's intrinsic holiness is the integrity of God's three-fold faithfulness. God is faithful to the promises God makes in the ways in which God is generously self-giving both in Godself and in the three strands of the economy. God is faithful to the integrity of that to which promises are made. And God is faithful to the integrity of "what" and "who" God is in the ways in which God concretely goes about keeping promises. That is to say that the Triune God's intrinsic holiness is the integrity of the attractive love that is the intrinsic glory of God, the communion in love among the three "Persons" of the Trinity that just is God's life *a se*. That attractive holy covenant love among the "Persons" of the Trinity is powerfully expressed positively in the way God goes about relating in eschatological blessing. Its attractiveness draws human creatures into sharing in creaturely fashion in the relation to God that the glorified Jesus has in virtue of his resurrection. It is the determinate character of the positive "power" of the Spirit's sovereignty in eschatological blessing.

There is a concurrent negative aspect of the power with which the Spirit's sovereignty in eschatological blessing makes a difference in creatures. It is inseparable from its positive aspect. It is the difference such blessing makes if and when human creatures resist eschatological blessing. It is a function of the intrinsic holiness of the Triune God who relates to creatures in eschatological blessing in a *taxis* in which the Spirit has the "lead" position. As expressed in the eschatological blessing strand of the economy, the intrinsic holiness of the Triune God's sovereignty entails that the Spirit "drawing" creatures into eschatological blessing will necessarily also be persistently and powerfully resistant of human creatures' resistance to acknowledging and receiving God's blessing them eschatologically. Human creatures who refuse to respond to the Triune God's eschatological blessing on them, actively or passively resisting it, may experience the "power" of the Spirit's persistent resistance to their resistance to it as both a condemnation of and as a counter pressure against, their resistance so intense as to be likened to an experience of fierce righteous anger.

The "power" of the Spirit's sovereignty in eschatological blessing is a determinately negative, as well as positive, "power" in the sense that it is ordered in definite ways that are intrinsic to the Trinity's way of relating in eschatological blessing. Neither its positive nor its negative aspects is an "accidental" constraint placed on some one underlying and otherwise unconstrained and indeterminate divine force by arbitrary self-commitments that God might make to "bless" some human creatures and "punish" others.

Thus, placing the Spirit in the "lead" position in the Trinitarian formula for the *taxis* in which the Triune God relates in eschatological blessing underscores that the "power" of God's sovereignty in eschatological blessing is not just one of several different expressions of an ontologically underlying indeterminate potency. It is not a "power-as-such" that God "owns" and can "apply" externally to creatures in various ways in different circumstances. Rather, as an expression of the Triune God's intrinsic holiness, it is the power (both positive and negative) of the sovereignty of God's intrinsically holy attractive love. Indeed, the Apostle Paul suggests that "God's love" which "has been poured into our hearts" just is the eschatological "Spirit that has been given to us" (Romans 5:5).

Some Implications of the "Son" in the Second Position as Sent "with" the Spirit

The Trinitarian formula for the *taxis* in which the Triune God relates to all else in eschatological blessing, after placing the Spirit in the "lead" position adds the phrase *"with the Son."* Doing so qualifies in at least three ways what is stressed about the character of the power of God's sovereignty by placing the "Spirit" in the lead position.

Adding "with the 'Son'" serves to stress that the Spirit is as much the Spirit of the Second eternal "Person" of the Triune God as it is the Spirit of the eternal First "Person." I have repeatedly urged that, as the eternal "Son" is traditionally identified with the eternal "Word" of God (following John 1:1–18), "Word" in John ought to be interpreted through the lens of the characterization of "Wisdom's" role in creation in Proverbs 8:22–31. In Proverbs as a whole, and in canonical Wisdom literature generally, Wisdom, and therewith God's "Wisdom," is characterized more as ad hoc concretely practical rationality than as an abstractly theoretical rationality.

The reminder that in eschatological blessing the Spirit is "sent" by the Father "with" the "Son," indeed as also the Spirit of the eternal "Son," stresses that the power of the Triune God's sovereignty in eschatological blessing needs to be talked about in a vocabulary that relies on analogies that liken it, (a) to an intrinsically "wise" and "canny" power that (b) makes differences in human creatures' lives in ad hoc and often unpredictable ways, rather than likening it to exercises of power that are ordered to an ultimate goal through a more or less extended series of steps or moments that are related to one another in a single, timeless overall "plan" whose rationality is demonstrable by a body of eternally true theory. The ad hoc wisdom of Triune God's powerful sovereignty in relating to human creatures in eschatological blessing entails God's focused attention on, cognizance of, and self-commitment to creatures' eschatological flourishing in their concrete particularities. Such attention is itself a sort of love for creatures intrinsic to God's sovereignty in eschatological blessing. As such, it is a love that is intrinsic to the power of that sovereignty, helping to make it attractive enough to draw creatures into God's eschatological blessing.

Adding "with the 'Son,'" the formula for the Triune God's way of relating in eschatological blessing also stresses, second, that the Spirit is the Spirit of the eternal Son Incarnate through the entire life-trajectory of Jesus of Nazareth that culminates in his resurrection from death by crucifixion. As narrated in the Synoptic Gospels' accounts of God relating in eschatological blessing, the Spirit and Jesus are inseparable but not identical. The resurrection of Jesus in particular defines what it is that the Spirit is actualizing, both by virtue of its being the resurrection of none other than Jesus in his unique relation to the One he called "Father," and because it is Jesus' eschatological resurrection. Explication of what the Spirit does in powerfully drawing human creatures into eschatological blessing and how it is done must be grounded in and be coherent with who Jesus is in his unsubstitutable concrete particularity. The particularities of the ways in which in his life-trajectory Jesus acts as one human creature among many human creatures in his particular circumstances, and particularly the ways in which he interacts with socially and culturally marginalized people, as variously narrated in the canonical Gospels, gives a profile of how the Triune God goes about so relating to human creatures to inaugurate the beginning of God's keeping of a long-standing promise of eschatological blessing. It profiles how the Triune God enacts both definitively and decisively love for them: namely, by fully identifying with them in their common lot in acts of compassionate love that are distinctive in embracing not merely those who respond to him positively, but also those who are his sworn and mortal enemies. This is a different, but not inconsistent, sense of "love" intrinsic to the Triune God's sovereignty in eschatological blessing than the sense of "love" that is intrinsic to the "Wisdom's" ad hoc practical rationality in eschatological blessing. It makes that sovereignty even more attractive and therewith more powerful.

Third, because by adding "with the 'Son,'" the formula for the Triune God's way of relating in eschatological blessing underscores that the life-trajectory of Jesus gives the definitive profile of God's love for human creatures, it also stresses that the appropriate human response to God's eschatological blessing is itself also the "glory" of God, here in its tertiary reference. The appropriate human response is, in Charles Wesley's phrase, communal "wonder, love, and praise"[4] of the God of Abraham. It is the wonder, love, and praise evoked by the attractiveness of the Triune God's intrinsic love as it is faithfully expressed by the way in which the Triune God goes about loving humankind in eschatological blessing. As the appropriate response to the Triune God's eschatological blessing, "wonder, love, and praise" of the Triune God does not merely characterize the shape of more or less formal acts of communal worship. More holistically, the phrase characterizes the shape of the entire way of life into which

---

[4] Cf. Wesley's hymn, "Love divine, all loves excelling."

human creatures are drawn by the Spirit with the "Son" in God's eschatological blessing. It characterizes what their personal identities are "formed" to be by the power of the Triune God relating in eschatological blessing with the Spirit in the "lead" position.

Some Implications of the "Father" in the Third Position as Sender of the Spirit

The Trinitarian formula for the *taxis* in which the Triune God relates to all else in eschatological blessing immediately follows its identification of the Spirit as the "lead Person" of the Trinity in eschatological blessing with the phrase, *"sent by the Father."* That serves to underscore that creatures are eschatologically blessed by the same One that blesses them creatively. Furthermore, it stresses that, like the way in which the Triune God goes about concretely relating in creative blessing, the way in which God goes about eschatological blessing faithfully expresses the singular reality of the dynamics of God's intrinsic self-relating in generous, generative, and attractive self-giving. It expresses the Triune God's intrinsic "glory" in the primary reference of that term, which consists of the communion in love among the three "Persons" of the Trinity that is God's *a se* life.

At the same time, the fact that it is the "Father" who sends the "Spirit" in the lead position in eschatological blessing underscores that the end to which God's power is ordered in eschatological blessing is different from the end to which God's power is ordered in creative blessing and providential care. The power of God's sovereignty in creative blessing is intrinsically ordered to the actual reality and value of creatures; and the power of God's sovereignty in the providential care of creatures that is entailed by creative blessing is intrinsically ordered to the well-being of creatures in their kinds for as long as they last. On the other hand, the power of God's sovereignty in eschatological blessing is intrinsically ordered to the eschatological flourishing of creatures.

Creatures' eschatological flourishing is the gift of the Spirit's sovereignty in the Trinity's eschatological blessing. It is a gift in addition to and beyond the gift of creative blessing and providential care. The Apostle Paul famously characterizes it as a "new creation" (Galatians 6:15; or "new life," Romans 7:6; 2 Corinthians, 5:17; cf. beyond Paul's writings, 2 Peter 3:13 and Revelation 21:1, 2, 5). In providential care the Trinity's actualization of creatures' well-being in their kinds works with and through resources of creaturely powers that are "already" available by virtue of God's creative blessing. In contrast with that, because eschatological blessing is "new" relative to creative blessing, the power to actualize it cannot be construed as available in resources and potentialities already integral to creatures' proximate contexts by virtue of God's creative blessing.

Nor can the "power" that actualizes that new creation be conceived as an extension, aspect, or entailment of the "power" of God's creative blessing, which is ordered to a different sort of good, viz., to creatures' actual reality and value. To borrow John Polkinghorn's distinction, the new creation arises "*ex vetere* [from the old], as redeemed transformation of the old creation, not as a second, totally new creation ex nihilo."[5] Just as God's faithfulness to God's self-commitments in relating in creative blessing entails that in providential care God will not violate the ontological integrity of creatures' finite concrete actuality in their kinds, so too God will not violate their creaturely ontological integrity in relating to them in eschatological blessing. The gift of eschatological blessing may be conceived as an "in-breaking" of a "new creation" upon creatures, but the creature that undergoes eschatological transformation is not transformed into something that is no longer a finite creature of the same kind. Eschatologically "glorified" human creatures do not become angels (angels are a different kind of finite creature). Nor

[5] "Eschatological Credibility: Emergent and Teleological Processes," in Ted Peters, Robert John Russell, and Michael Welker, eds., *Resurrection: Theological and Scientific Assessments* (Grand Rapids, MI: Eerdmans, 2002), p. 50.

do they cross over the creature/Creator distinction to become God or any aspect of God. Such transformations would entail a violation of human creatures' ontological integrity as creatures.

Accordingly the power of the Spirit's sovereignty in eschatological blessing is intrinsically ordered to a different order of "good" for creatures than is the power of the "Father's" sovereignty in creative blessing and providential care. We are warranted in saying that the Triune God is powerful in the economy; but we are only warranted in saying that the Triune God is powerful in different strands of the economy in different senses of "power."

Implications of This Taxis for the Way We Speak of the Power of the Trinity's Sovereignty in Eschatological Blessing

The particular sense in which the Triune God's sovereignty in eschatological blessing is *powerful* blocks attribution to God of several "conventional" notions about the nature of power. It reinforces how the "power" of God's sovereignty in providential care also blocks attribution of the same notions, but does so in its own and different way. Because the power of the Trinity's sovereignty in eschatological blessing, in a *taxis* in which the Spirit rather than the "Father" is in the lead position, is *intrinsically* ordered specifically to creatures' eschatological flourishing rather than to their creaturely well-being in their kinds, it cannot be conceived as value-neutral a-teleological force or "power-as-such."

For the same reason, the power of God's sovereignty in eschatological blessing cannot be conceived as a possession God has and may or may not employ in zero-sum interactions with creatures' powers. Rather, the "power" of the Triune God's sovereignty in eschatological blessing just is that sovereignty's faithful expression of some aspects of "who" God intrinsically is.

In addition, because the Triune God's sovereignty in eschatological blessing is powerful in a different sense of "power" than the sense in which God's sovereignty in providential care (and, as we shall see below, different from the sense in which God's sovereignty in relating to reconcile estranged creatures to God) while nonetheless being truly the power of God, this "power" cannot be conceived univocally, as conventional notions of power do.

There are "family similarities" among these senses of power, but they cannot be reduced to different degrees of some one underlying "power-as-such." Moreover, because the *taxis* of the Trinity's relating in eschatological blessing not only places the Spirit in the "lead" position but does so only as the Spirit is "with the 'Son'" understood as God's ad hoc practical Wisdom, the power of God's sovereignty in eschatological blessing cannot be conceived as a power that enacts a single comprehensive plan of action that moves through a rationally ordered series of steps, as conventional notions of power do.

In sum, placing the "Spirit" in the lead position in the *taxis* in which the Trinity relates to bless creatures eschatologically privileges a certain vocabulary as particularly appropriate, when used analogically, for characterizations of the "power" of the Triune God's sovereignty in the way in which God goes about blessing eschatologically. It is a vocabulary shaped by the conjunction of (i) the Spirit's intrinsic orientation to giving and nurturing both creaturely life and eschatological life and (ii) the Spirit's circumambience of creatures. The conjunction of those two has a paradoxical upshot.

On one side, it is a vocabulary appropriate to the "power" of the Triune God's correlative "radical closeness" to and "radical otherness" than, human creatures' subjectivities. It is a vocabulary of images for the "power" freely to "inspire" creatures' "insight," "wisdom," "discernment," and the like. It is a vocabulary of images for the "power" to elicit subjective states such as "love," "hope," and "faith." It is a vocabulary for the "power" to shape individual human creature's unique personal identities as holy. "Sent by the 'Father,'" the Spirit's exercising such power in creative blessing is the free giving of concretely actual life; exercised in eschatological blessing it is the free giving of "life more abundant." "Sent with the Son,'" it is the power to give such gifts wisely in ways that do not violate the creaturely integrity of the human creatures to whom they are given.

On the other side, paradoxically, there is another vocabulary appropriate for describing the power of the Triune God's circum-ambient sovereignty in eschatological blessing. The Spirit's "radical otherness" and "radical closeness" to human creatures is circumam-bient in the quotidian, in the every-dayness of human creatures' physical, cultural, and social proximate contexts. Its "power" to ground, nurture, and renew all dimensions of human creatures' lives is most adequately expressed in analogical use of images usually used to describe psychological, social, and cultural dynamics of the systems of power organization that constitute the proximate con-texts of human creatures' lives. Relating to human creatures circu-mambiently the Spirit has no "face." Unlike the "Son" Incarnate in the life-trajectory of Jesus, the Spirit has no stable uniquely identifi-able location or identity. Nor, because it is circumambient precisely in human creatures' proximate contexts, can it be "located" in negative ontological terms as can God the creator. Consequently, the vocabulary appropriate to describing the power of the Trinity's relating in eschatological blessing in the *taxis* that places the Spirit in the lead position relies on markedly impersonal terms used ana-logically, despite its also being a vocabulary especially focused on analogical use of terms usually used to describe ways human subjects have "power" in relation to one another's subjectivities.

The Power of the Triune God's Sovereignty in the Register of Reconciliation

The very same narratives in the canonical Gospels that tell of how God goes about relating in eschatological blessing also tell a second story. It is a story rendering how God concretely goes about relating to estranged creatures to reconcile them to God by way of Incarnation. Read as reconciliation narratives, the canonical Gospels are instances of scriptural narratives that Claus Westermann calls narratives of "deeds of deliverance." As such, they have yet a different "narrative logic" than canonical narratives of either creative or eschatological blessing. New Testament scriptural narratives read as accounts of God relating in eschatological blessing render an ongoing, steady-state way in which God relates through a movement in time toward an eschatological transformation of creatures that was promised long before and then was actually inaugurated in Jesus' resurrection, but is not yet fully actualized. The same New Testament narratives read as accounts of God relating to reconcile estranged creatures to God render the punctiliar event of Jesus' particular life, ending in his particular death by crucifixion, as the already fully actualized, once for all reconciliation of estranged creatures to God.

Both a narrative of eschatological blessing and a narrative of reconciliation are told by the same New Testament stories. Because Jesus, the Spirit, and the One Jesus called "Father" are central to both of them, the two narratives cannot be separated. Because they have different "narrative logics" they cannot be conflated into a single coherent and "followable" narrative even though they are told by using the same stories about Jesus, the Spirit, and the One Jesus called "Father." What allows them to be distinguished from one another is their different "narrative logics." The difference correlates with the fact that, although the Spirit is the "lead figure" in the narrative of eschatological blessing and the significance of Jesus' resurrection focuses what the "Father" is doing in that narrative, Jesus empowered by the Spirit is the "lead figure" in the narrative of reconciliation and the significance of Jesus' crucifixion focuses what the "Father" is doing in that same narrative.

As was noted in this chapter's first section, the relation between the Trinity's reconciling creatures to God and the Trinity blessing creatures eschatologically is complex and asymmetrical. Whereas theological claims about creative blessing presuppose nothing other than the reality of God, claims about eschatological blessing and reconciliation, both by way of Incarnation, presuppose God's creative blessing. Claims about eschatological blessing by way of Incarnation presuppose nothing beyond God's creative blessing with which it is coeval. They do not presuppose the reality of the sin that estranges creatures from God. Consequently, neither do they presuppose God's reconciliation of that estrangement. God's relating in eschatological blessing precisely by way of Incarnation is coeval with relating in creative blessing. God's relating in eschatological blessing is by way of Incarnation whether or not creatures are estranged from God. It is "Incarnation anyway."[6] However, claims about God relating to reconcile estranged creatures by way of Incarnation presuppose not only God's creative blessing, but also the reality of creatures' estrangement from God and the reality of God's eschatological blessing by way of Incarnation. Because it presupposes God's eschatological blessing, God's relating to reconcile also necessarily presupposes the concrete way in which God goes about blessing eschatologically: the way of Incarnation. Therefore, given

(a) that God's self-commitment to bless eschatologically is coeval with creative blessing; and

(b) that eschatological blessing does not presuppose that creatures are estranged; and

(c) that God's way of concretely fulfilling God's self-commitment to eschatological blessing is by way of Incarnation,

it follows that God's concrete way of going about reconciling estranged creatures to God by way of Incarnation is, as it were,

---

[6] See Edwin Chr. Van Driel, *Incarnation Anyway* (New York: Oxford University Press, 2008) for a helpful sorting out of several kinds of "supralapsarian" Christology, the theological issues they address, and the issues they generate.

"parasitic" on God's way of blessing eschatologically by Incarnation. The relation between God's relating to reconcile and relating to bless eschatologically is asymmetrical. Although God relating in eschatological blessing does not *necessarily* entail God relating to reconcile because it only presupposes creative blessing and does not presuppose that creatures are estranged from God, God relating to reconcile does necessarily presuppose God relating to bless eschatologically by way of Incarnation. The combination of that asymmetry and the differences in the "narrative logic" of canonical accounts of God's relating to reconcile and blessing eschatologically blocks any conflation of accounts of the Triune God relating in eschatological blessing and relating to reconcile the estranged to God into a single narrative. God's relating to reconcile is its own strand of the economy, having its own "narrative logic," and is not simply a logically necessary implication of, and hence a moment in, another strand, viz., eschatological blessing, in the absurd circumstance of creatures' self-estrangement from God.

Rebutting an Objection

Here we pause to take a detour. It follows from our discussion, I suggest, that God's ancient promise of eschatological blessing of creatures by way of Incarnation does *not* necessarily imply that, if those creatures do inexplicably and absurdly become estranged from God, God must necessarily *also* reconcile those creatures to God as the precondition of fully actualizing the logically independent promise of their eschatological blessing. That suggestion goes against long-standing traditional Christian theological teaching.

A traditional theological objection to that suggestion is that creatures' estrangement from God would by itself keep those creatures from being candidates for eschatological blessing. But, the objection continues, God's purposes cannot be thwarted. God's promises must be kept. Therefore, the objection goes on, overcoming human creatures' self-estrangement from God, i.e., reconciling them to God, is a logically necessary precondition of God's fully actualizing their eschatological blessing. Accordingly, the objection concludes, given that God's promise to creatures of eschatological blessing is coeval with God's blessing them creatively, God in all self-faithfulness *must* reconcile them to God if they estrange themselves from God.

There are at least two general ways to rebut this objection. One is methodological. Insofar as this theological objection claims to be warranted by canonical Christian Scripture (just as the proposal being made here also does), it is problematic because it overlooks the theological implications of the differences between the "narrative logic" of canonical accounts of God's relating in eschatological blessing and the "narrative logic" of canonical accounts of God's relating to reconcile the estranged that have been outlined here. One implication of the asymmetry between canonical accounts of God's way of relating to all else in eschatological blessing and relating to reconcile estranged creatures is that the Trinity's relating to reconcile, although it presupposes God's also relating in eschatological blessing, is a gift in addition to, and in some ways above and beyond, the Triune God's gift in covenant love of eschatological blessing.

A second line of rebuttal is doctrinal. It is central to traditional Christian theological claims about the Triune God's relating to reconcile estranged creatures to insist that it is not "entailed necessarily" by anything. In it, God acts in unexpected, undeserved, and astonishingly radical freedom. It is not done arbitrarily, because it is done in love that is intrinsic to "what" and "who" the Triune God is. In that it is done freely it is "grace." However, it is "grace" in a particular sense of the term defined by the particular sort of love with which it is done: *agape* love. It is not love for the worthy or for the deserving, but love for those who are functionally and persistently God's enemies. Just that specific free loving is compromised by the insistence that the Triune God's self-commitment to keep the promise of eschatological blessing *obliges* God first to reconcile creatures to God, if their self-estrangement from God breaks out between God's creative blessing on them and God's full actualization of the promise of eschatological blessing on them. Compromising that freedom has additional major theological consequences because, in traditional Christian theology, it is precisely that agapeic grace in the economy that definitively expresses "who" the Triune God most fundamentally is.

Perhaps a theological thought experiment can bring into focus how it is that God's eschatological blessing of creatures by way of Incarnation does not necessarily entail that God must necessarily *also* reconcile them to God *as the precondition* of fully actualizing their eschatological blessing if those creatures become estranged from God. Suppose counterfactually (assuming the faithfulness of canonical scripture's narratives of the three strands of the economy!) that creatures who are eschatologically blessed by God by way of Incarnation do become self-estranged from God and that God does not relate to reconcile them. The result would be that eschatological blessing, fully actualized, would include only Jesus of Nazareth and would not include any estranged human creatures. One creature, but only one (and perhaps also his mother Mary), would be blessed by fully actualized eschatological consummation.

That counterfactual possibility would be theologically internally consistent. It would also, for what it is worth, keep open the possibility that "anti-universalism" could be theologically correct, i.e., that not all human creatures are either reconciled to God or drawn to fully actualized eschatological blessing. Indeed, it keeps open at least two further theologically consistent possibilities: that all human creatures other than Jesus could pass into nonbeing as their creaturely well-being ontologically totally disintegrates in consequence of their estrangement from God; or that they do not pass into nonbeing, but rather pass into interminable estrangement from God and all the consequences to them of such estrangement, which may be as good a definition of hell as any.

However, those are abstract counterfactual conceptual possibilities and not concrete actualities. The canonical witness is that there is a third actual strand of God's economy: in addition to relating powerfully in creative blessing of creatures and in eschatological blessing of creatures by way of incarnation, God does also relate powerfully by the same way of Incarnation to reconcile estranged creatures to God. It is "powerful" in the difference it makes to estranged creatures. That is an irreducibly different narrative.

The Power of the Triune God's Sovereignty in Reconciling Estranged Creatures to God

Like the "power" of the Triune God's way of relating to bless eschatologically (and God's way of relating in providential care of creatures, for that matter) the "power" of the Trinity's way of relating to reconcile estranged creatures to God is the power of one sense of God's "sovereignty." The analysis in Part II proposed that the Triune God's *intrinsic* eternal sovereignty is God's self-regulation of the dynamics of the generative self-relating in love that constitutes God's intrinsic life. It also urged that aspects of that intrinsic sovereignty are faithfully expressed in the way in which the Triune God goes about relating to all else in two steady-state, ongoing relations to creatures in their kinds for as long as they last, i.e., to God's relating by blessing them *in the economy*. It teased out senses in which "sovereignty" or "rule" may be ascribed to God's way of relating in providential care and eschatological *blessing*.

Thus far this part has proposed senses in which such "sovereignty" may be said to be "powerful" in eschatological blessing. However, we have just emphasized that the Triune God's relating to reconcile is not an ongoing steady-state relating in blessing. Rather, it is a singular, eventful, punctiliar once-and-for-all relating that has already been accomplished. Hence, it would be inappropriate to attribute to it "sovereignty" in the senses of the term that are appropriate to God's relating to all else in blessings.

Accordingly, neither can "power" be appropriately attributed to God's sovereignty in relating to reconcile in the same senses as it is rightly attributed to God's sovereignty in creative and in eschatological blessings. Like the "power" of the "sovereignty" of the Trinity's relating in eschatological blessing, the "power" of God's way of relating to reconcile estranged creatures lies in the difference that relating makes. The sense in which "power" may be attributed to the Triune God's relating to reconcile will be shaped by the sense in which God may be said to be "sovereign" in that relating.

Like other senses in which the Triune God may be said to be "sovereign," the sense in which God is "sovereign" in way in which God goes about reconciling estranged creatures faithfully expresses God's intrinsic sovereignty. It faithfully expresses the Triune God's self-regulation of the dynamics of the generous generative self-relating in love that eternally constitutes the reality of the three "Persons" of the Trinity in the communion in love that is their intrinsic life. God's relating to reconcile estranged creatures to God is a punctiliar event that is now accomplished once and for all in a particular concrete way that is variously narrated in the canonical Gospels and, very briefly, in some canonical Epistles. God's sovereignty *in*, i.e., God's prevenient self-regulating *of*, that punctiliar "once-for-all-ness" is not the regulating of an ongoing dynamic blessing that moves toward creatures' well-being or flourishing. Rather, its "once-or-all-ness" expresses the Triune God's intrinsic sovereignty in the "once-for-all-ness of" of the Trinity's eternally fully actual life. The profile of that sense of "sovereignty" is the basis on which to sort out the sense in which that "sovereignty" is "powerful." We turn to that now.

The Trinitarian formula for this strand of the economy is: "*The 'Son,' sent by the 'Father' in the power of the Spirit reconciles estranged creatures to God.*" The formula summarizes in short-hand fashion the distinctive register in which the Trinity's concrete way of relating to reconcile expresses certain aspects of the intrinsic power of the Triune God's intrinsic sovereignty in the glorious life of the Trinity. I have suggested that when the Gospels' narratives are understood in terms of that formula, "Father" is understood as the God of Abraham, the One Jesus often called "Father." The "Father" is doubly identified in the Nicene Creed as (i) the One whose eternal self-giving generates the other two "Persons" of the Trinity and (ii) the One who with them creates all else ex nihilo; the "Son" is doubly identified as)i) the eternal second "Person" of the Trinity, the "Word" of God (*Logos*) in John 1 (which should in turn be understood in terms of Wisdom in Proverbs 8), and (ii) as one "made flesh" in the life-trajectory of Jesus of Nazareth that comes to its narratival climax in Jesus' crucifixion. The Spirit is doubly identified as (i) the eternal Spirit of both the first and the second "Person" of the Trinity and (ii) as the "Lord and giver of life" to living creatures in their kinds.

Some Implications of the "Son's" Location in the "Lead" Position

Placing the "Son" in the lead position in the formula for the *taxis* in which the Trinity relates to reconcile estranged creatures focuses the fundamental question about the Gospels' narratives of Jesus, the Spirit, and the "Father": what is God doing in and through Jesus' life-trajectory to reconcile estranged creatures? Placing the "Son" in the "lead position" in the formula also underscores ways in which a "Son-specific" vocabulary must shape any account of the "power" of the Triune God's sovereignty in what God is doing through Jesus' life-trajectory to reconcile estranged creatures.

As for what God is doing through Jesus' life-trajectory to reconcile estranged creatures, placing the "Son" in the lead position stresses the particular and most odd way in which the Triune God goes about reconciling estranged creatures to God. The Triune God "regulates" it to be enacted in this fashion: God reconciles estranged creatures by coming *among* them to live as a particular *one of* them interacting *with* them in their shared creaturely circumstances. The personal name of that human life is "Jesus," further identified as "of Nazareth." That is, God "regulates" the way in which to reconcile estranged creatures such that it is the way of Incarnation.

What is "reconciling" about the Incarnation is not simply the moment or "fact" of Jesus' birth. "Incarnation" signifies the entire trajectory of Jesus' life, which describes a narrative arc that moves inexorably to its horrendous climax in his death by crucifixion. Again, what is "reconciling" is no more the event of Jesus crucifixion abstracted from the overall trajectory of his life as a whole than it is the event of his birth abstracted from the overall trajectory of his life. In certain important respects, Jesus' crucifixion can be the part of the overall trajectory that brings into focus the import of the whole trajectory and so can serve as the part that stands for the whole. However, it is by that particular life-trajectory as a whole that God Godself enters into solidarity with human creatures in their shared circumstances, once and for all accomplishing their reconciliation with God. The Triune God's "regulating" the way in which to go about reconciling estranged creatures in just this fashion (i.e., precisely by entering into solidarity with them by way of Incarnation) just is God's "sovereignty" in this third strand of the economy. What we want to discern is the sense in which that sovereignty is "powerful" to actualize estranged creatures' reconciliation to God, and therewith to one another and to themselves.

The first step toward that discernment is to note what is going on in human creatures' estrangement from God. Estrangement is the human condition that results from human creatures' resisting God's ways of relating to them in the three-stranded economy. Appropriate human response to the Trinity's ways of relating to them to bless creatively, bless eschatologically, and to reconcile, would be human lives shaped and ordered by love, hope, and trust in God. Human resistance occurs when people order and shape their lives in ways that are inappropriate as responses to the ways in which the Trinity relates to them. The particular actions that express such resistance to responding appropriately to God's ways of relating to them are traditionally called "sins."

As a distortion of their ways of relating to God, human creatures' estrangement from God has the consequence of subverting the well-being of their lives. It distorts the dynamics that constitute human creatures' personal identities. That distortion is traditionally called the condition of "original sin," or "sin" in the singular. It is a distortion that shapes and characterizes all actions, however well-intentioned, by human agents whose personal identities are distorted in those ways. It leads individuals to profound forms of self-estrangement.

Such human creatures are in a certain way in bondage to those distortions of their personal identities. A sign of that bondage is that they find they cannot "un-distort" their personal identities, for the agents that would attempt such "un-distorting" would be none other than themselves in their already distorted identities, or their neighbors collectively in their already distorted personal identities. Correlatively, their self-estrangement from God distorts the dynamics that move and structure their common life in the societies and cultures that constitute their proximate contexts, making those contexts oppressive and unjust. Born into those distorted proximate contexts, their identities are "formed" as they mature in correspondingly distorted ways. The humanly distorting consequences of estrangement from God may admit of degrees. However, in any case they also incrementally move in a certain way progressively, or perhaps we should say "regressively," away from creaturely well-being. They move in the direction of distortions of human creatures' personal and social dynamics so extreme as to count as their dis-integration into "nonbeing" or ontological annihilation.

Placing the "Son" in the lead position in the formula for the *taxis* in which the Trinity concrete relates to reconcile estranged creatures by way of Incarnation underscores that God concretely reconciles by entering into solidarity with humankind in the consequences to themselves of their estrangement with God. It is an entering into solidarity with them not only in the inherent weakness, fragility, and vulnerability of the dynamics of their bodily creatureliness understood as sets of finite "energy systems," but also solidarity with them in their condition of bondage to the distortions of those dynamics that drive their ontological dis-integration toward annihilation.

The human personal name "Jesus" identifies the concrete way in which that solidarity takes place. It is not simply the name of the "facticity" of his existence or of a peculiar event (the "Christ event"). It is more basically the name of the entire trajectory of the concretely actual movement of Jesus' life, ministry, death, and resurrection. It is in and through the trajectory of that particular human life that God is Emmanuel, "God with us," as one among many, relating by way of Incarnation.

Certain patterns in the movement of that trajectory are fundamental to the way in which the Triune God's sovereignly goes about relating to reconcile is "powerful." One pattern is Jesus' faithfulness to the One he called "Father," and the "Father's" faithfulness to him. The canonical Gospels, read as narratives of God relating to reconcile, make clear that, in Jesus' faithfulness to his vocation to a ministry of proclamation of the immanence of God's eschatological "reign," which he pursues voluntarily, he lives a life of solidarity with others in their oppression by social and cultural powers, in their bondage under evil powers that are the consequences of human creatures' estrangement from God and generate new estrangement in every generation, and in their weakness in suffering.

Read that way, those narratives move inexorably toward Jesus' death. His solidarity with his neighbors is most complete at its most extreme: his execution. There he is one with estranged creatures' experiences of the absence of God. Beyond that, because death by crucifixion was understood as a cursed death, it signified Jesus' solidarity with human creatures utterly cut off from God's people. His crucifixion raises questions. It raises the question of whether God has been faithful to Jesus. And it raises the question, if God was not faithful to Jesus, can God be trusted to be faithful to us? Jesus' "cry of dereliction" on the cross ("My God, my God, why have you forsaken me?") may not be an expression of Jesus' loss of faithful relating to God; it is at least an expression of a Job-like lament to One to whom Jesus still relates.

The crucified Jesus' resurrection appearances answer those questions in the affirmative. The particular faithfulness of Jesus to God and God to Jesus expresses definitively the faithfulness of the communion in covenanted love that is the intrinsic life of the Trinity. The sense in which the "Son's" solidarity with humankind in the most horrific consequences of humankind's self-estrangement from God is "powerful" to reconcile is that it is the "power" of just that love.

A second pattern in the overall trajectory of the movement of the human life of the Incarnate "Son" is exhibited in the ways in which Jesus relates to fellow human creatures. Repeatedly, the Gospels' accounts of Jesus' interactions with his neighbors represent him as at once radically "other than" they, unconditioned by their expectations and claims on him, and radically "close to" them, sometimes knowing what they were feeling and thinking before they spoke or acted. He is represented at first as interacting that way with fellow human creatures in compassion for them in their suffering in body and mind because of their bondage to trans-individual oppressive and destructive powers.

A third closely related pattern is that Jesus' ways of relating to his neighbors in this correlatively radically "other than" and "close to" fashion is always intrinsically ordered to their creaturely well-being. The way in which the Triune God goes about relating to reconcile estranged creatures to God is not the announcement that God is ready to let bygones be bygones, forgetting all about their resistance to God's ways of relating to them, and declaring a general amnesty. The damage done to human creatures and their proximate social, cultural, and natural contexts is far too deep and serious to be ignored away. God's forgiving is not a forgetting because mere "forgetting" does nothing to repair what has become radically distorted about human creatures. Human creatures' well-being has been fundamentally undermined. The Triune God's relating to reconcile estranged creatures to God is not itself ordered to their eschatological flourishing. To the contrary, it presupposes God's relating in eschatological blessing to draw them into eschatological blessing. However, because creatures' well-being is in radical jeopardy because of their estrangement from God, God's powerful reconciling them to God is ordered to the "un-distorting" of the vital dynamics that constitute their creaturely reality's well-being. God's relating to reconcile is intrinsically ordered to the regeneration of what is fundamental to human creatures' creaturely well-being: their active relating to the Triune God and to one another that shapes their personal identities as appropriate responses to the ways in which God relates to them. Thus, in being intrinsically ordered to the regeneration of human creatures creaturely well-being, the power of God's sovereignty in relating in just this "way of Incarnation" faithfully expresses the Triune God's intrinsically generative self-relating.

A fourth pattern emerges in his life-trajectory as Jesus' preaching becomes more controversial. He is increasingly represented as interacting with hostile opponents in the same fashion marked by correlative "otherness" and "closeness." The accounts culminate in scenes of betrayal, torture, trial, and crucifixion during which that correlation is heightened as Jesus interacts with cruel enemies in forgiving love. The sense in which this way of relating to reconcile the estranged enacts an attractive "power" of love is more exactly qualified. It is the attractive power of a distinctive sense of "love": *agape* enacted by one human being to the many enemies among whom he lives.

A fifth pattern in the life-trajectory of Jesus is the paradoxical character of the "power" of the Triune God's in sovereignly reconciling estranged creatures. The Apostle Paul stresses it early in the first Epistle to the church in Corinth. Making the point that "the message of the cross" (3:18) is plain foolishness to "the wisdom of the world" (3:20), he remarks that it is precisely Christ crucified that is "the power of God and the wisdom of God" (3:24). Jesus' helpless weakness in being crucified is the culmination of God's concrete way of relating powerfully to reconcile estranged creatures by entering into solidarity with them, even in the utmost consequences of their estrangement from God. In that way, Jesus' crucifixion is rightly used as the part of Jesus' life-trajectory that can stand for the whole.

Paul's point is that Jesus' crucifixion is the point in his life-trajectory at which the "power" of God's sovereignty in relating to reconcile by way of Incarnation is, paradoxically, apparently most hidden and in another way most clearly expressed. In the crucifixion of Jesus, as Martin Luther writes in the *Heidelberg Disputations*, God's power is "hidden in suffering,"[7] hidden, we may add, in plain sight.

Acknowledging that point, however, simply raises the question: just what is the Triune God doing powerfully in and through the life-trajectory of Jesus to reconcile estranged creatures to God, in light of the fact that the arc of that trajectory seems to move inexorably to Jesus' powerlessness in crucifixion? Paul's terse aphorism that Christ crucified is "the power of God and the wisdom of God" is hardly self-explanatory. It is open to a range of theological interpretations that are, I suggest, underdetermined by Paul's text and theologically dubious.

One might read 1 Corinthians 3:24 as the revelation of a theological transvaluation of "power" such that, given the crucifixion, it is disclosed that weakness *as such*, absence of power or minimal power, just *is* God's "power." However the claim, "The power of God is in reality identical with powerlessness" sounds suspiciously like a self-contradiction. As such it is vacuous.

---

[7] *Luther's Works*, pp. 31, 52.

Or 1 Corinthians 3:24 might be taken to imply that it is Jesus' helpless powerlessness in suffering that somehow *of itself* reconciles estranged creatures to God. However, it is a dubious move to premise an interpretation of Paul's text on the generalized axiom that suffering as such is intrinsically salvific. Intense suffering can as easily destroy human creatures' personal resilience and disintegrate their identities as it can strengthen and "perfect" them. Valorizing suffering has had terrible spiritual and psychological consequences in religious contexts. The Trinity's powerful relating to reconcile estranged creatures to God does indeed culminate just where it is most hidden, in Jesus' weakness in crucifixion. However, that weakness in which it is hidden does not of itself reconcile estranged creatures.

Or Paul's text might be interpreted by postulating, as Luther[8] sometimes seemed to do, that Paul assumes that an absolutely and indeterminately powerful "hidden God" stands, as it were, "behind" God Incarnate in the life-trajectory of Jesus at its culmination in the weakness of the cross – and that that hidden God's absolute and indeterminate power is God's true power, albeit truly hidden. That would imply that God has a power that is *not* faithfully expressed in what we see of God's power in the crucifixion of Jesus. It would also rely on an a priori conception of the power of God that, I have been arguing, is inconsistent with canonical Christian Scriptural witness to the three-strandedness of God's economy and all too consistent with what are by now "conventional" and theologically problematic cultural notions of power. The postulation would directly warrant the sort of pastoral remarks that this essay has argued are themselves for that reason also theologically problematic.

More plausibly, Paul's point may simply be a negative claim about the character of the "power" of God's sovereignty in the way God goes about relating to reconcile estranged creatures.

---

[8] Cf. Brian Gerrish, "To the Unknown God: Luther and Calvin on the Hiddenness of God," *Journal of Religion*, 53 (1973), pp. 263–292.

It may simply be Paul's version of "Diognetus'" characterization of how God goes about relating to humankind in Jesus, which we cited in Chapter 9: God "sen[t] him as saving them; as persuading, not exercising force (for force is no attribute of God)." Although Jesus was inflicted by the most horrific violence, in and through it all he himself related to others in "gentleness and mildness." And that is what manifests the intrinsic quality of the power of God's sovereignty in reconciling creatures by way of Incarnate solidarity with them in the predicament of their estrangement from God.

Also more plausibly – but sufficiently underdetermined textually as to count as "exegetically speculative" – is the possibility that Paul is offering a very sophisticated "dialectical" analysis of God's power that goes something like this. Given that the power of evil is a distortion of good creatures' dynamics and thus is parasitic on their power, God directly engages "objective negative mystery" in the crucifixion of Jesus Christ in a wise fashion that, analogous to some Asian martial arts, it invites the opponent's apparently superior strength to overreach, so that working against itself it exhausts the finite energies it draws from creatures and defeats itself, thus exhibiting that God's apparent foolishness in engaging so strong an opponent in so weak a fashion as crucifixion is after all wiser and more powerful that the opponent's apparent power.

A sixth pattern in the life-trajectory of Jesus is fundamental to the way in which the Triune God is "powerful" in sovereignly going about reconciling estranged creatures. It is a pattern that manifests the end to which the power of the Triune God's sovereignty in relating to reconcile estranged creatures is ordered. It will take a bit longer to outline.

The Apostle Paul's Greek name for the end to which this power is ordered in usually translated in English as "justification." It is a juridical term. It connotes being made "just" when one has not been "just." It connotes being set into right relation with a judge who represents the entire system of norms that makes properly human life possible. "Judge" stands in for the basis and font of moral goodness. "To be justified" connotes being "relocated" from a wrong relation with the "judge" that defines one as an "outlaw," outside the law and the entire system of norms that make properly human life possible, to being "right" with the law. Other translations are "rectification" of one's relation with the "judge," or, in the English translation of Rudolf Bultmann's German name for this "relocation," being "rightwised" with God.

Characterization of what the Triune God is doing in and through the life-trajectory of Jesus as "justification" of the estranged calls attention to a theme that regularly appears in very brief references to that life-trajectory in canonical Epistles. They assert, imply, or assume that the power God's sovereignty in relating to reconcile estranged creatures by way of Incarnation is intrinsically *decisive*. There can no more be another instance of "justification," much less other "examples" of it, than there can be of God's creating this world ex nihilo.

Its intrinsic decisiveness is a function of the ways in which it is different than God's way of relating in creative and eschatological blessing. New Testament accounts of God relating to reconcile estranged human creatures in and through the entire trajectory of Jesus' life, ministry, passion, crucifixion, and resurrection are what Claus Westermann calls narratives of God relating to human creatures in liberative events. That includes, we may add, accounts of God promising to relate in future liberative events and God subsequently keeping such promises, such as narratives of God relating to Abraham and his descendants in Genesis 11–50. Such liberative events are concretely individual, particular and punctiliar in contradistinction to the steady-state and ongoing character of God's ways of relating in creative and eschatological blessing.

Across canonical Christian scripture from the Old Testament's "historical" books through the Prophets and the Psalms, the particulars of God's promises change. The scope of the population to be liberated also changes. As Paul interprets the Genesis accounts of God's promise making to Abraham through his Christocentric hermeneutic, they become promises of liberation not only for Abraham's lineal descendants, but for humankind as a whole; and that promise is fulfilled in and through the life-trajectory of the crucified Messiah Jesus: "And the scriptures, foreseeing that God would justify the Gentiles by faith, declared the gospel beforehand to Abraham, saying, 'All the Gentiles shall be blessed in you'" (Galatians 3:8). The context of Paul's remark in Galatians clearly implies that the promised blessing is kept by way of Abraham's lineal descendent Jesus Christ. On this reading, what God is doing in and through the overall movement of Jesus' life-trajectory that drives toward his crucifixion is keeping the promise to Abraham.

God's sovereignly relating Godself to humankind that way in Incarnate solidarity is powerful to "relocate" estranged humanity in its relating to God. It relocates estranged humanity from the destructive consequences of estrangement from God into the uniquely close relating to God that Jesus has in his human life. It is not merely a "powerful" illustration or visual aid to help us understand how God ongoingly relates to estranged creatures, offering the possibility of forgiveness and reconciliation everywhere all the time as a structural feature of the ultimate context in which they live. Rather, it is powerful to reconcile decisively in the once and for all punctiliar "event" of Jesus' life-trajectory that takes place within the context of two other ways the triune God does relate to them ongoingly: in creative blessing and in eschatological blessing. It is "decisive" in that having been a done it need not and in principle cannot be repeated.

It in principle liberates human lives into an astonishing crea-turely freedom. It liberates human creatures into a freedom to shape their lives, their interactions with their neighbors, their care for their physical and social contexts, and their care for the dynam-ics and structures of their common life in ways that are appropriate responses to the three-stranded way in which the Trinity has related to them. In such lives they find their creaturely well-being. It is also a freedom in which they may, among other things, deny their liberation and "relocation" in relating to God, may ignore it, may protest it, or may live in ways that are inappropriate to it. Nonetheless, God's relating to them by keeping God's liberative promise through the life-trajectory of Jesus does decisively change the ultimate context of their lives and defines their actual personal and social identities. Their estrangement no longer defines who they in fact are. The dynamics of their individual personal identities and their social and cultural projects no longer intrinsically move toward their annihilation. The same conditions, however, give them the freedom to continue living as though nothing had happened and as though they were still in bondage. They are at liberty to live at cross-grain to reality.

There are connotations of "justification," however, that make it a problematic analogy for the way God "reconciles" the estranged. It is especially problematic when it is assumed that "justice" should be understood as "retributive justice." In that case, those who have been "unjust" can only become "just" and entitled to be in "right relation" with the "judge" when a penalty has been paid that is adequate retribution for whatever it was they did that violated the norms of moral goodness. Accordingly, it can be argued that Incarnate "Son" of God's suffering and death on the cross "justify" unjust human creatures because (given his "divinity") it provides the infinite penalty that is appropriate retribution for creatures' unjust treatment of God in self-estranging themselves from God.

The term "justification" is undoubtedly open to that sort of theological interpretation. However, it is a theologically problematic interpretation for at least two reasons. First, to frame "what is going on" in the movement of Jesus' life-trajectory in that fashion suggests that the conflict that God resolves by way of the Incarnation's power to "justify" the unjust is a conflict internal to God. It suggests that it is a conflict between God's justice and God's merciful desire to forgive estranged human creatures the penalties their estrangement deserves. But is that really the conflict that drives the Gospels' narratives of how God goes about relating in the "deed of liberation" that reconciles estranged creatures? Is it not rather a conflict between creatures' resistance of God's ways of relating to them and God's resistance of that resistance? Second, a juridical analogy of that sort for what is going on in the movement of Jesus' life-trajectory assumes that God's merciful forgiveness is the precondition of reconciliation with God. God's merciful forgiveness, it is assumed in turn, is impossible unless, as a precondition, the demands of justice are satisfied. But New Testament accounts, especially by Paul, of the significance of Jesus' crucifixion as the symbol for the upshot of Jesus' life regularly represent "justification" as something God has already actualized once and for all "while we are yet sinners" (Romans 5:8; cf. the verse's immediate context in 5:1–11), and that "justification" is the context *within* which God forgives. It is not that forgiveness is the precondition of the justification that effects reconciliation. Rather, reconciliation of estranged creatures to God effected by way of Incarnation is prevenient and brings forgiveness with it.

Following more closely the dynamic force of Bultmann's participle "rightwising," I suggest that it is the relational dynamics of "justification" setting us "in right relationship" with the basis of creaturely human well-being in community that is analogous to the way the Triune God has gone about relating to estranged creatures to reconcile them to God: viz., by way of Incarnation. The analogy between "justification" and the "difference" the Triune God's way of relating to reconcile estranged creatures is powerful to make, lies more in the relational imagery involved in undergoing an "exchange of locations" in relation to God than in the calculus of distributive justice. The overall pattern of the movement of the conflict-driven life-trajectory of Jesus is a sort of exchange of "location" in relation to God. It is the Triune God's concrete way of resisting creatures' resistance to being related to by God, which consists of God's solidarity by way of Incarnation with estranged creatures in the utmost consequences to them of their estrangement, which is *also* by God's prevenient relating by way of

Incarnation the creatures' solidarity with Jesus in his uniquely close relation to God. By the "Son's" "locating himself" in creatures' unjust form of life (estrangement from God, fellow creatures, and themselves), the creatures are "relocated" into the Son's just form of life in Jesus' uniquely close relationship with the "Father." It is in that pattern of movement of exchange that the Triune God's sovereignty in relating by way of Incarnation is powerful to reconcile estranged creatures to God.

The difference that the exchange effects for creatures is its "power." It is a structural difference in human creatures' proximate contexts, rather than a subjective difference in their interiorities or consciousness, whether of guilt or forgiveness. Of course, it will be subjectively experienced as a series of changes in human creatures' subjectivities. However, the pattern of exchange between Jesus and estranged creatures objectively relocates estranged creatures into the context of Jesus' way of relating to God, which is the supremely appropriate way for human creatures to relate to God. As such, it relocates estranged creatures into a way of responding to God's ways of relating to them that makes for their well-being instead of making for their ultimate annihilation. Thus, that pattern in Jesus' life-trajectory shows that the "power" of Trinity's way of relating by incarnation to reconcile estranged creatures to God is determinately ordered to the good of the creatures and is not the sheer force of an indeterminate absolute power-as-such.

Those five "patterns" in Jesus' ways of relating to God and to fellow human creatures converge, I suggest, to nuance the sense in which the Triune God's sovereignty in God's way of relating to reconcile the estranged is "powerful." It has the distinctive concrete form, not of "relating *to*" the creaturely plane of creaturely interactions without being on it (as in creative blessing), nor of relating to living creatures "*circumambiently* (as in eschatological blessing)," but of one particular human creature set among many, interacting intersubjectively in agapeic love. The "power" of the agapeic love God sovereignly enacts in relating to reconcile not only expresses the "power" of the love between the "Persons" of the Trinity, it expresses that love definitively. Furthermore, it expresses that love in distinctive ways of being correlatively at once radically "other than" and radically "close to" creatures, viz., in ways in which in intersubjective human interactions a "Thou" and an "I" can be at once "radically other" and "radically close."

Placing the "Son" in the lead position of the *taxis* in which the Trinity relates to humankind to reconcile the estranged also stresses the *decisiveness* of the "once-and-for-all" way in which the Trinity goes about relating to reconcile the estranged to God. Its decisiveness makes it *definitive* of "who" the God is who relates in any way in the economy. That does not imply that the Triune God does not also relate in other ways to keep other promises. However, the decisiveness of God's powerful relating way of Incarnation to reconcile estranged creatures by *while they are still dynamically resisting* the Triune God's relating to them in creative and eschatological blessing is definitive of what counts as an instance of *God* relating to make and keep promises. No event that might be identified as a candidate for inclusion in the set of ways in which God relates to keep liberative promise (i.e., what Westermann calls "deeds of deliverance") can count as such if its "power" to keep such a promise is inconsistent with the profile of the "power" specific to God's relating to reconcile by way of Incarnation in and through the life-trajectory of Jesus of Nazareth. The decisiveness is intrinsic to the power of God's relating in this fashion. It nuances determinateness of the Trinity's way of relating to reconcile "powerful."

Some Implications of the "Father's" Location in the Second Position

Immediately after naming the "Son" to the lead position in the *taxis* in which the Trinity relates to reconcile estranged creatures to God the Trinitarian formula adds the phrase *"sent by the 'Father.'"* The life-trajectory of the eternal "Son" Incarnate, as rendered in canonical narratives, is the content of that "sending" by the "Father." Adding that just that content is "sent by the 'Father'" serves to emphasize that the One that relates to reconcile is the same as the One that relates in creative blessing and in eschatological blessing.

Accordingly, although the sense in which God's sovereignty in reconciling by way of Incarnation is "powerful" is different than the sense in which God's sovereignty in either creative blessing or eschatological blessing is "powerful," it may not be construed in ways that are mutually exclusive of those senses of "power." Overall, the senses in which the Triune God may be said to be "powerful" in the economy express various qualities of the intrinsic power of God's intrinsic sovereignty in God's intrinsic glory. In their differences, they have family resemblances to one another that serve as implicit "grammatical rules" governing the way they are used in characterizations of the Triune God. They rule out theological uses of canonical narratives of the three strands of the economy that play them off against one another as though contradictory of each other. Sentences ascribing contradictions to God are not profound "paradoxes." They are nonsense.

Adding "Sent by the 'Father.'" emphasizes that it is not Jesus' powerlessness in his torture and crucifixion alone that is "powerful" to reconcile estranged creatures to God. To be sure, Jesus' powerlessness in crucifixion is a part of Jesus' life-trajectory that can stand for the whole of it as the sign of what the Triune God was doing through the entirety of that life-trajectory: entering in a concrete way in the uniqueness of a particular human life into the deepest possible solidarity with human creatures in the context of the circumstances in which their self-estrangement from God has bound them. However, it is what the Triune God is doing in and through Incarnation in the *entire* life-trajectory of a particular first century Jewish man from Galilee named Jesus, whose life ends in horrendous unjust dishonor, that is powerful to reconcile the estranged. So too it is not the sheer "fact" of the Incarnation of the second "Person" of the Trinity in the life-trajectory of Jesus that is in itself and as such "powerful" to reconcile the estranged. It is what God is doing *by way* of God the eternal "Son's" Incarnation that is powerful to reconcile.

What is that? The rhetoric that the Apostle Paul sometimes uses to convey what God is powerfully doing in and through that life whose upshot is its death by crucifixion suggests an answer along the following lines.

By the eternal "Son's" Incarnation, estranged human creatures and their profoundly distorted creaturely proximate contexts have been objectively placed within the context of the relation Jesus has with the "Father." As one among many in the particular ways in which Jesus was among his neighbors during his ministry and during the last week of his life ("Passion week"), the Incarnate "Son" lived out his unique relation with the One he calls "Father," the God of Abraham. In doing so, the Incarnate "Son" makes his relation with the "Father" a third aspect of human creatures' ultimate and proximate contexts (in addition to the Triune God's relating to them in creative and eschatological blessings). In virtue of the Incarnation, his relationship to the "Father" in the power of the Spirit is, so to speak, an objective "given" about the embracing reality that they share and within which they all live whether or not they know or acknowledge it.

That is to say that in virtue of the Incarnation the "many" have been "relocated" into the unique close relation that Jesus has with the "Father" by the Triune God's prevenient relating to them by way of Incarnation in this concrete fashion. What now fundamentally defines their personal and communal identities is not their estrangement from God and its self-inflicted consequences, but God's way of relating to them by way of incarnation in the life-trajectory of Jesus. The risen crucified Jesus continues to be one among many by the power of the Spirit.

That is a theological reality claim. It is a claim, not about some human creatures' subjective experience, opinion, or interpretations of certain events – although it surely also expresses some or all of those – but about how things stand in the creation that humans share. The "way of Incarnation" is a way in which the Triune God goes about relating to estranged creatures that is as unilateral, prevenient, and "objective" as the way in which the Triune God relates to create them ex nihilo; and like God's creative relating, it makes a profound "objective" difference in the proximate and ultimate contexts of their lives. It is powerful.

Adding "sent by the Father" to "the 'Son'" also stresses that the Triune God's "sending" is "grace" in that term's basic theological sense. "Sent by the 'Father'" underlines that estranged creatures' reconciliation to God is not an inevitable out-working and achievement of dynamics and resources already present in human creatures and their proximate contexts. It is a powerful gift of the Triune God's intrinsic covenant love. God's relating by way of Incarnation to reconcile is irreducibly different than the Triune God's relating either to bless creatively or to bless eschatologically. Despite those differences, each strand of the economy is in its own way the Triune God's "grace." This is signaled by the formulas' stress that the "Father" is freely prevenient in each strand in a way that expresses the Trinity's intrinsically free self-relating in love. In each strand of the economy, God relates to all else freely and in love. However each strand is "grace" in a different though analogous sense.

The Triune God's relating powerfully to reconcile estranged creatures while they are still estranged is "grace" in that it is an utterly unconstrained prevenient gift that at once is faithfully expressive of God's intrinsic covenant love, honors the fundamental ontological distinction between Creator and creatures, and honors God's eschatological blessing of creatures. More than that, however, it is the *basic* sense of "grace," the definitive sense of "grace" to which the other two are called "grace" using the term analogously. It is "grace" in the strict Pauline sense of the word. Paul usually uses "grace" in reference to a gift God gives *despite* continuing creaturely resistance to God's relating. It is a sense of "grace" that necessarily presupposes that the recipient actively resists receiving God's way of relating to reconcile. It presupposes not only God's creative blessing and eschatological blessing, but also creatures' sin and evil.

The Triune God's relating powerfully in creative blessing ex nihilo is also "grace" in that it is an utterly unconstrained prevenient gift of space and time for creatures to be themselves and in which their well-being as creatures lies in their responding appropriately to God in trust in God alone to ground their concrete actuality and value. It is a gift that is faithfully expressive of God's covenant love and constitutes the fundamental ontological distinction between Creator and creatures.

The Trinity's relating powerfully in eschatological blessing is "grace" in that is too is an utterly unconstrained prevenient gift that at once is faithfully expressive of God's covenant love. It presupposes and honors the fundamental ontological distinction between Creator and creatures and is compatible with creative blessing. However, it is not necessarily entailed by the Trinity's way of relating in creative blessing. It is "grace" in a different sense than is God's creative blessing because it is intrinsically ordered to a different good for creatures, the full actualization of their eschatological blessing. It is a superabundance of the Trinity's covenant love's self-giving. It is grace upon grace.

Neither of these two senses of grace presupposes or addresses the reality of sin and evil. The Trinity's relating in creative and eschatological blessing expresses in two irreducibly different ways the attractive unconditional generosity of God's self-giving covenant love that makes it God's intrinsic glory. They are occasions for joy, celebration, and wonder. The Trinity's relating to reconcile, however, expresses the unconditional generosity of God's covenant love in a way that is not only wholly unexpected, but is utterly humbling and astonishing because it is love for enemies. It is attractive, but in a wholly different way, because it is such love hidden in the weakness and the ugliness of the crucifixion.

Some Implications of the Spirit's Location in the Third Position

The formula for the *taxis* in which the Triune God relates to reconcile adds that the "Son" is "sent by the 'Father'" to reconcile estranged creatures *"in the power of the Spirit."* We have already seen that the Nicene Creed identifies the Spirit in terms of its eternal relations to the other two "Persons" as the "Holy Spirit" deserving our worship, and in terms of its relation to creatures in the economy as "Lord and giver" of both creaturely life and eschatologically transformed and glorified life. To add that the "power" of the sovereignty of the Triune God's self-regulation of how God goes about doing this is the "power of the Spirit" underscores that it is "power" expressive of the generative power of God's intrinsic sovereignty in the dynamic self-relating in holy love that is the Triune God's life. God's life is intrinsically holy. Expressions of that holiness are made in each of the three strands of the economy as they are ordered to God's persistent resistance to creatures' resistance to God's relating to them. In regard to God's relating to reconcile in particular, it is power intrinsically ordered to resistance of creatures' resistance to being reconciled to God.

That holy resistance is manifest in the conflict that drives the movement of the canonical Gospels' accounts of Jesus' life-trajectory of Jesus. Unlike the movement of canonical accounts of God's relating in creative and eschatological blessing, which are not driven by conflict, canonical accounts of God's relating in liberative events of deliverance are usually driven by conflicts between estranged human creatures' resistance to being related to by God and God's resistance to that resistance.

In the case of God's relating to reconcile estranged creatures to God by way of Incarnate solidarity with estranged humankind, the human side of this conflict consists of communal and individual human lives that are lived estranged from God by resisting God's creative and eschatological blessings, as sketched in the explication of "estrangement" as given above. God's side of the conflict is simply God's relating to estranged creatures to reconcile them to God by God's entering into complete solidarity with human creatures in the life-trajectory of Jesus who, unlike his estranged neighbors, himself relates to God and is related to by God in a uniquely close way. Increasing resistance to Jesus' proclamation of the imminence of the "in-breaking" of God's eschatological rule generates conflict between Jesus and civil and religious authorities. Initially enthusiastic crowds of listeners to Jesus' proclamation fall away. The conflict comes to its climax in Jesus' crucifixion. The power of God's sovereignty in relating to reconcile estranged creatures to God by way of Incarnation is a power intrinsically ordered to their holiness, i.e., ordered to overcoming their resistance to God's relating to them and regenerating the self-destructively distorted dynamics that constitute their creaturely reality.

Adding that the "Son," "sent by the 'Father,'" reconciles estranged creatures *"in the power of the Spirit"* also underscores that the Triune God relates to reconcile estranged creatures, not only within the context of God's relating also in creative blessing, but also – because it presupposes both – within the context of God's relating in eschatological blessing. As we have seen, the Triune God goes about blessing creatures eschatologically also by the "way of incarnation." The life-trajectory of Jesus of Nazareth in and through which the Triune God relates to estranged humankind to reconcile them to God once and for all is not only crucified but is, by the power of the Spirit, risen and lives as "One among many" now.

The circumambient Spirit is integral to the Triune God's sovereignty in the "way of Incarnation." Accordingly, it is integral to the "power" of God's sovereignty in reconciliation. It is by the "power" of the circumambient Spirit that estranged human creatures come to recognize, acknowledge, and trust what it is that God was doing in and through Jesus' life-trajectory, *and* to recognize, acknowledge, and trust that the risen Incarnate One lives here and now, *and* to recognize, acknowledge *and* trust that the Spirit is, indeed, Jesus' Spirit. That recognition, acknowledgment, and trust shapes their personal and communal identities in new ways marked by trust in, hope in, and love to God. That recognition, acknowledgment, and trust express estranged human creatures' appropriate response to the way in which the Triune God relates to them to reconcile them to God. It expresses their subjective response to God's way of objectively reconciling them to God.

Implications of This Taxis for the Way We Speak of the Power of the Trinity's Sovereignty in Reconciling the Estranged

The particular sense in which the Triune God's sovereignty in reconciling estranged creatures to God is *powerful* is most aptly expressed in the analogical use of two quite different sorts of vocabulary: a vocabulary ordinarily used in description of the dynamics of certain interpersonal relations; and vocabulary ordinarily used in description of the structures and dynamics of social and cultural systems, their creation, their distortions, their changes, and their power to shape human creatures' identities. Analogical use of those vocabularies in accounts of the power of the Triune God's sovereignty reconciling estranged creatures to God helps to block attribution to God of several "conventional" notions about the nature of power.

On one hand, placing the "Son" in the lead position in the *taxis* in which the Trinity relates to reconcile estranged creatures to God privileges a vocabulary that is particularly appropriate, when used analogically, for characterizations of the "power" of the Triune God's sovereignty, although it is ordinarily used in describing what Martin Buber has called "I–Thou" relations.[9] Those are uncommonly close interpersonal relations between human creatures in their full concrete particularities. In particular placing the "Son" in the lead position of this *taxis* of the Trinity privileges use of a vocabulary ordinarily employed to describe an "I–Thou" relation with someone whose very existence, we want to say, of itself makes "our world" different, better than it would have been otherwise, no matter how well or slightly we have known her. Given the Incarnation of the eternal "Son" who is the "Word of God," God's way of relating to human creatures is as "one of them among them." In Jesus' correlatively "radically other" and "radically close" relations with his neighbors, as rendered in canonical Gospel accounts, God relates to them as "I" to "Thou."

The vocabulary invoked by the "I–Thou" analogy warrants a high degree of "anthropomorphism" in characterizing the Triune God. It allows description of God relating to human creatures in grief, anger, compassion, amusement, pain, and suffering. It warrants analogical use of terms like "inspire," "enliven," "stimulate imagination," "bring to light," and "nurture creativity" to characterize the power of a way in which the Triune God relates ("I to Thou") to human subjects interiorly without violation of their integrity as finitely free creatures. For exactly the same reason, it blocks characterizations of that relating as God's exercise of unrestricted power "over" creatures to "control" them.

---

[9] For a brief, clear, and theologically insightful proposal that relies heavily on analysis of the Incarnation and some of its theological implications framed in terms of the notion of "I–Thou" relations, see Emil Brunner, *The Divine Human Encounter,* translated by Amandus W. Loos (Philadelphia: Westminster Press; 1943). It is also a cautionary example of the theological consequences of construing Christian canonical Scripture as one extended narrative whose sole "narrative logic" is that of God's relating to reconcile estranged creatures to God.

Adding "in the power of the Spirit" underscores that in "I–Thou" encounters with Jesus some "others" found themselves drawn into God's inauguration of God's eschatological "new creation" in and through all that Jesus did and underwent. Because those "others" are estranged from God, their neighbors, and themselves, the dynamics of the social, cultural, economic, and political power arrangements that are their proximate contexts are profoundly distorted, unjust, and oppressive. God's inauguration of the "new creation" in the resurrection of the crucified Jesus means that estranged creatures who have been "justified" by the "exchange" effected by God's solidarity with them in their estrangement have been "relocated," not only into Jesus' own relationship with the "Father," but also into distorted proximate contexts actively under-going eschatological "renewal." In Paul's apocalyptic rhetoric, the "powers and principalities" that have distorted those contexts are being overcome. The vocabulary that is particularly apt to describe the power that makes such differences is quite different than the vocabulary appropriate to "I–Thou" encounters. That is because the Spirit, in the circumambient freedom of its correlative "radical otherness" and "radical closeness" to human consciousness, has no unique and identifiable "face." It is no identifiable "Thou" or "I."

The Triune God relates powerfully through the ways in which the "Son," Incarnate in the life-trajectory of Jesus who exercises his ministry in the power of the Spirit that is the Lord and giver of life, reconciles estranged human creatures. It is a power that, in recon-ciling them, restores their creaturely wholeness. Our efforts to characterize that "power" will unavoidably shift back and forth between using analogically a vocabulary ordinarily used to describe the differences made by especially close interpersonal relationships and an impersonal vocabulary ordinarily used to describe the differences made by cultural and social "forces."

The determinate character of the "power" of the Trinity's sover-eignty in relating to reconcile estranged creatures to God is different than the determinateness of "God's power" in the sovereignty of eschatological blessing. It is ordered to a different creaturely "good." A feature that differentiates the "power" of the Trinity's sovereignty in eschatological blessing is that it is intrinsically ordered toward making human creatures' proximate contexts and individual identities flourish eschatologically in ways we hardly know how to describe. In contrast, what differentiates the "power" of the Trinity's sovereignty in relating to reconcile the estranged to God is that it is intrinsically ordered to the "un-distorting" of the dynamics of human creatures' communal and individual lives and their liberation from their bondage to the consequences of those distortions. The "power" of God's sovereignty in relating to reconcile presupposes the "power" of God's sovereignty in eschatological blessing. However, it is not a mere extension or "progressive development," or "further evolution" of eschatological blessing because it is intrinsically ordered to a different end. The two are two different, albeit analogous, senses of "power."

Adding that it is the "Father" that "sends" the "Son" in the power of the Spirit that "proceeds" from the "Father" to reconcile estranged creatures to God associates the vocabulary of "sending" only with the Creed's identity descriptions of the three "Persons" of the Trinity that are framed in terms of their eternal relations. It does not associate the language of "sending" with the lives of human creatures to whom they are "sent." So, too, apocalyptic rhetoric used in canonical New Testament texts associates vocabulary related to the notion of God's "plan" with the concrete way in which God "intends" to go about relating to creatures in eschatological blessing. The "apocalypse" is the disclosure of that "plan," which has been a mystery until that disclosure. The disclosure is simply the concrete way in which God goes about beginning to relate in eschatological blessing: the resurrection of the crucified Incarnate "Word" of God, Jesus Christ. Once disclosed it is no longer "mystery." That "way" is also the concrete way in which God goes about relating to reconcile the estranged. Tying "send" and "plan," and vocabularies related to them, strictly to the

"Father's" eternal relating to the "Son" and the Spirit fails to warrant, thereby blocks, problematic generalized use of those vocabularies to describe God's way of relating powerfully to particular human creatures in their experiences of horrific evil and suffering.

* * * * *

In Chapter 7 I noted that, by the time a reader gets to Thomas Aquinas' explicit account of the power of God, which he locates far back in the series of "attributes" of God's One-ness that he chooses to discuss, the account is virtually redundant. Everything that can be said about the power of the One Triune God (except about its scope) has already been said independent of analysis of the concept of power and argued on other grounds. Theologically speaking, Thomas was, I think, partly correct in doing that. The "nature" of the Triune God's power is simply (!) the nature of God. That is, the qualities distinctive of God's power express distinctive qualities of the singular reality of "what" and "who" the Triune God is. It is, after all, *God's* power and, given God's singular *a se* reality and the fundamental ontological distinction between the reality of the Creator and the reality of creatures, that power could not be rightly conceptualized as some sort of instrument different from God, possessed by the Triune God, and occasionally used in singular events.

However, "traditional" Christian theological accounts of the power of the Triune God, and Thomas' account in particular, also assume that canonical Christian Scriptural accounts of the ways in which God goes about relating to all that is not God comprise a single, internally coherent, extended narrative that begins with God creating the world and culminates in God eschatologically transforming and transfiguring creation into a "new creation." That assumption conflates canonical accounts of how God relates to reconcile estranged creatures to God and how God relates to draw creatures to an eschatological consummation into its account of

346

how God relates in creative blessing. God relating in creative blessing entails the God also relate in providential care for the well-being of creatures, and God relating to reconcile and to bless eschatologically are both construed as major instances of God relating in providential care. Accordingly, there is only one sense in which God is powerful in the economy. It is the sense in which God is unrestrictedly powerful in creative blessing. Like every other quality that is attributed to God, it is attributed to God analogically. But it is the only sense of "power" that is attributed to God. It is, I argued, an account of God's power as absolutely unrestricted that, although not theologically invalid in itself, is so vague that it does not provide an adequate basis on which to block the projection onto it of "conventional" notions of power that directly warrant the sort of theologically problematic pastoral remarks to those anguished by others' intense and prolonged suffering that were identified in Chapter 1.

Given that, as Westermann's exegesis points out, canonical accounts of how God relates, respectively, to bless creatively, to bless eschatologically, and to reconcile the estranged have irreducibly different narrative "logics," those assumptions by "traditional" account of god's power seem incorrect. For a reader to be able to follow that one extended narrative, i.e., for it to be narratively intelligible, the "traditional" way of reading canonical accounts of God's economy as one extended narrative requires that the narrative "logics" of canonical accounts of God relating to reconcile and to bless eschatologically be the same as the narrative "logic" of canonical accounts of God relating in creative blessing. I have argued that equating the Triune God's intrinsic power and power in the economy with that one sense of power occludes other and irreducibly different senses of "power" that, were they included in an account of God's power, would help to make the account less vague by making it more nuanced and layered, firmly blocking projection of "conventional" notions of "power-as-such" onto that account.

On the basis of canonical accounts of how God goes about relating in each of three strands of the economy, Chapters 2 and 3 sought to sort out the sense in which intrinsic "sovereignty" may be attributed analogically to the Triune God as a quality of God's intrinsic glory, and different senses in which "sovereignty" may be attributed to God's relating self-expressively in the three strands of the economy. Chapters 9 and 10 have sought to sort out the sense in which the Triune God's intrinsic sovereignty is powerful, and different sense in which power may be attributed to God's relating self-expressively in the three strands of the economy.

That "sorting out," however, has a consequence that poses an important challenge to this entire project: When all is said and done, how do these multiple senses of "power" which, it is claimed here, may be attributed to the Triune God fit together? It may be that we are well-warranted in analogically attributing them to God. However, that resort to "analogy" brings with it the admission that, although we may speak correctly in making these attributions to God, we cannot explain how the term "power" means in God's case in any of the multiple senses that we have sorted out. If we cannot make those explanations, how can we tell whether those various senses of "power" do not, say, mutually exclude one another? And how can we tell what are valid or invalid inferences from attribution of to God of any particular sense of "power"? If we cannot do that, can this "sorting out" be any more effective than "traditional" accounts of God's power in blocking projection of "conventional" senses of power-as-such onto the account of God's power promoted here?

We turn to those questions in Chapter 10.

10 | The "Uselessness" of the Triune God

Two themes have woven through these chapters. They may not seem to fit together. We began in Chapter 1 with the anguished, angry, and terribly familiar cry, "Don't talk to me about a loving God! A God of love would not have let her suffer the way she did. And don't tell me that God knows better what is good for us than we do ourselves, or that God never gives more than we can handle, or that God sent this whole terrible thing for a reason, or that God has a plan for this!" Chapter 2 turned to reflect on implications of the injunction: "The God of Abraham praise." The outcry is an angry rejection of pastoral remarks that were intended to console someone's anguish at another's horrendous suffering. The remarks try to "explain" the suffering as signs of God's "presence." They are inferences presumed to follow from "traditional" theological accounts of the qualities of the power God exercises in "sending" such suffering. But if we ask "what" and "who" is that "God of Abraham?," the answer warranted by canonical Christian Scripture is, as the hymn says, the

> Ancient of everlasting days, and God of love;
> the Lord, the great I AM, by earth and heaven confessed;
> we bow and bless the sacred Name for ever blest.

Ill-considered "pastoral" consolation offered in God's name to people anguished by other's deep suffering does not fit with the God described in the hymn. How can intolerably profound suffering be "explained" coherently by reference to a "God of love; the Lord, the great I AM" who deliberately "sends" it? And if it *can* be explained that way, how dare we "bow and bless *that* sacred Name"?

349

Two "Mysteries"; Two Silences

Those questions arise at the intersection of two antithetical "mysteries" and our assumptions about how to respond to each of them appropriately. It is a commonplace in traditional English language theological accounts of the Triune God to declare God a "mystery" or a "holy mystery" to which the only adequate human response, at least initially, is reverent silence. It is also common in English-language theology to find the presence of evil and horrendous suffering in God's good creation declared a "mystery" to which the appropriate response, to defend God's honor, is to give an explanation of its presence in God's name. Such explanations are usually called "theodicies," rationally persuasive justifications of the good, loving, and omnipotent God's "permitting" or even intentionally "sending" natural and moral evils that cause profound suffering. Call God the "positive mystery" and evil the "negative mystery."

In ordinary English, "mystery" is said in many senses. Some of them invite a question asking for an explanation of the "mystery." Homicide detective stories are called "mysteries" because they begin with a murder that calls for an explanation to assign responsibility and guilt: "Who did it?" An unusual event in nature may be called a "mystery" because it is unclear what caused it. For example, calling an unexplained UFO sighting a "mystery" invites the question of "How did it happen?" Sometimes an extremely unusual event is called a "mystery," not so much because it seemingly cannot be explained, but because it is experienced as "uncanny." It cannot be "located" in our menu of types of possible experiences, and raises the question "What was *that*?" Some events, especially ones that cause deep suffering, are called "mysteries" because they raise the questions, "Why did that happen? Was it a punishment for bad behavior? Was it a warning to change behavior lest something worse be sent? Was it in some disguised way actually a blessing, or even a reward?" For all the differences among those "Who?"

"What caused it?" "How?" "What is it?" and "Why?" questions, they all have one thing in common. They all assume that the "mystery" is not terminally "mysterious," because there is in principle an answer to the question that will remove the grounds for classifying it as a "mystery." They assume that the "mystery" is not *intrinsically* mysterious to human knowers.

Silence and the Positive Mystery

Using the words "mystery" or "holy mystery" to characterize the Triune God is not an instance of any of those other uses of the words in ordinary English. It is unlike them because it does assume that God is *intrinsically* "mystery." So, unlike them, its use to characterize God does not raise a question about "what caused" God's reality or "the how" of God's reality, and does not assume that in principle such questions can be answered by us. This holds both for use of "mystery" to characterize human subjective experience of the Triune God and use of it to characterize God's "manner of existence," the Triune God's "objective" concrete actuality in and of itself, independent of human experience or knowledge of God.

Subjective "Positive" Mystery

As paradigmatically expressed in Canonical Christian Scripture, human beings experience the Trinity's gracious relating to them as a "holy mystery" in each of the three strands of God's economy. It is fundamental to such experiences of the graciousness of God's relating that it is experienced as love freely given and as "prevenient," coming before we do anything or "deserve" anything. In Rowan Williams' image, it is an experience of something unmanageable by us, something whose grace is "wild" beyond our capacities to "domesticate" it. In the midst of such an experience, the most appropriate initial response is silence: "And ultimately," Williams writes, "everybody is silent in the face of the utterly unmanageable, which is God."[1] That silence blocks any temptation to assume that calling such experiences "mysteries" implies that they can be and need to be "explained."

Rather, they need to be lived into, lived within, and lived out of. All *that*, no doubt, does call for a great deal of reflection and explaining. All efforts to "explain" how best to live in, and ongoingly to live on the basis of, the silence fitting that subjective "positive mystery" are chastened by reminders that such "mystery" cannot be managed. They are especially reminders that such "mystery" cannot be managed by talking about it. They require that such talk speak mostly of what the experience of the Triune God's gloriously love is not. That is, subjective "positive mysteries" require that talk about them be "apophatic" and provisional. In particular they require that things said by way of pastoral care of those anguished about others' profound suffering be chastened by acknowledgement that the wildness of experience of God's grace cannot be managed, least of all by being "explained."

Objective "Positive Mystery"

As traditionally expressed in theological accounts of the qualities of the Triune God's "manner of existence," to call God's concrete actuality "mystery" is to acknowledge some qualities of that "concrete actuality" in and of itself, independent of human creatures' experience of the three strands of God's economy. Two such qualities are especially relevant here.

For one thing, it is to acknowledge that the ontological singularity of the Triune God's concrete actuality excludes it from the entire enterprise of "explaining" what caused it, how it was caused, or why it was caused. That is because, as I urged in Chapter 2 on God's intrinsic glory, the singularity of the Triune God's objective reality

---

[1] "Silence in the Face of Mystery," *The Christian Century*, August 29, 2018, p. 29.

is that God's concrete actuality is *a se*. God's 'manner of existing' does not fall under any species or genus of "manners of existing" of which it happens to be the one and only instance.

In particular, God is not part of a shared "field" or "plane" of interactions with other beings that, unlike God, are existentially contingent. God's concrete actuality is ontologically prevenient, "before" creatures' concrete actuality in the order of reality. It is the basis of their contingent concrete actuality, the condition of its very possibility. Now, the enterprise of explaining causally the objective reality of any particular being requires that it share a common field in which it interacts with other beings in a multitude of ways. In the order of reality that "common field" is prior to all of them. But there is nothing "prior" to God in the order of reality that could be the "field" in which God and creatures interact. Furthermore, if in those interactions one entity, or a set of them, is the "cause" of "effects" in another, including the latter's "coming into existence," it must be possible to identify both the "cause(s)" and the "effect" independent of each other. In addition, we need a body of causal theory, along with its conceptual framework, that specifies just what counts as an "explanation" of the ways in which creatures cause effects in one another. Absent such a shared "field" or "space," any ability to identify both the "cause(s)" and the "effect" (i.e., God's concrete actuality, and the differences it makes to creatures), and any body of theory that specifies what can count as an "explanation" of "What caused it?" "How was it caused?" or "Why was it caused?" the very notion of a "causal explanation" of God's concrete actuality is meaningless.

Nor does the claim "The Triune God is *a se*" offer such an "explanation." It cannot be understood as the claim that somehow God alone "causes" God's objective reality, for it fails to identify "cause" and "effect" independent of one another. Instead, "*a se*" has negative force: the ontological singularity of the Triune God's object-ive reality means that one should not agree to discuss questions about "What caused God?" "How was God caused?" or "Why was God caused?" That is because (given the sort of Christian discourse about God that is in question here) such questions are so "ungrammatical" as to be meaningless. Here God is "mystery" in the sense that God's singular "manner of existing" is *inexplicable* by human knowers, not because of our current ignorance of things that in principle are discoverable and may be discovered in future, but *intrinsically*.

To call God's singular concrete actuality "mystery" is to acknowledge a second quality of that "concrete actuality" that is closely related to the first. It is a "mystery" in that it is conceptually incomprehensible. It cannot be "comprehended," globally "grasped" all-at-once in a single coherent skein of concepts.

That does not mean that true claims about aspects of the Triune God's singular "manner of existing" cannot be formulated in grammatical English sentences. Chapter 2 urged that aspects of God's intrinsic glory are faithfully expressed in features of the ways in which God goes about relating to all else in three strands of the economy. Those features of God's intrinsic glory that are expressed in the economy are themselves the "glory" of God in a secondary derivative sense of the term "glory." They are occasions of experience of God's "unmanageable" and "un-domesticateable" self-expressive love, before which the only appropriate initial response is reverent silence. Nonetheless, those expressions of God's intrinsic "glory' in the strands of the economy also warrant Christian reality claims about God's intrinsic glory.

Chapter 2 proposed that one such claim is that the Triune God's intrinsic glory just is the *attractiveness* of the communion in generously self-giving and self-expressive love that is God's intrinsic *a se* life. Making that claim involves using "love," "communion," "self-giving," "self-expressive," and "*a se*" in particular ways that are governed by grammar-like rules. They are specifically Christian theological concepts. They are used to make theological claims about God that are, Christians say, "true" in the sense of being well-warranted.

However, the dynamic of God's generous self-expressive self-giving is inexhaustibly rich. No set of theological reality claims about God, however precisely formulated and systematically coherent, can begin to "capture" or "grasp" it all. The Triune God's "manner of existence" is intrinsically "mystery," ontologically "mystery." It is not "mystery" because it is vacuously meaningless and, therefore, utterly unintelligible and totally inconceivable. It is "mystery" because it is too *richly* intelligible. Its attractive beauty "overflows," slips through, and eludes human cognitive and expressive capacities.[2] In its inexhaustible richness of being and meaning it is "positive mystery."

The inexplicability of the Triune God's "objective positive mystery" and its "incomprehensibility" require that talk about God's "manner of existence" be "apophatic" and provisional. In particular, they require that things said by way of pastoral care of those anguished about others' profound suffering be chastened by acknowledgement that God's "manner of existing" cannot be managed, least of all by "explaining" either how it can be concretely actual or how it can be comprehended conceptually.

Silence and "Negative Mystery"

By contrast, to call both the concrete actuality of natural and moral evils and human experiences of suffering those evils "mysteries" *does* involve asking for various sorts of explanations of them. Let us

---

[2] "Mystery" is used in the New Testament in a sense different than all of the senses sorted in the text above. In the New Testament, it is used to characterize two things: (a) the way God concretely goes about relating to all else in eschatological blessing and to reconcile estranged creatures to God and (b) the concrete way in which that is disclosed. The first is usually referred to as God's "purpose" in history, or as God's secret "plan of salvation" of the world. It is not necessarily a "plan" for everyone's life other than that of Jesus Christ. The second explicitly refers to Jesus Christ, the open "mystery" of the concrete way in which God goes about blessing eschatologically and reconciling the estranged, the "secret" in plain sight. It is striking that by and large Christian theologians have not generally used "mystery" often in the sense in which it is used in the New Testament.

define "evils" functionally: they are dynamics between or within creatures that damage their well-being in their kinds. Such damage is experienced, at least by human creatures, as suffering. Evils' concrete actuality is that they are *distortions* of creatures. As distortions of the dynamic powers proper to various kinds of creatures, evils are themselves dynamically powerful in varying degrees. The distortions both damage the well-being of the creatures they distort, without necessarily weakening them, and damage the well-being of other creatures with which they interact. To suffer evil is, among other things, to wish intensely that some painful bodily condition, psychological state, social circumstance, or the loss of some deep attachment, cease or somehow be undone. The concrete actuality of the huge range of types of "evil" in our proximate contexts, and fellow creatures' suffering from them, is obvious. Understood in this way, evil and suffering need no argument proving their objective reality.

The appropriate initial response to evils in themselves and to the suffering they cause is horrified, profoundly painful, outraged silence. In the moment neither the experience nor the evil that occasions it can be managed. Soon, however, the response also gives rise to verbal and nonverbal expressions of grief, lamentation, and anger at "the way things are." That, in turn, gives rise to questions that demand explanations for evils and suffering.

Subjective "Negative Mystery"

However, because experiences of horrendous suffering look different depending on whether the singularity of the Triune God's concrete actuality is acknowledged at the same time that the reality of evil and suffering are acknowledged, the sort of questions raised by horrendous evil are different.

Even if the singular reality of the Triune God is *not* given, it is reasonable to think that at least some of the conditions, states, circumstances, and types of events that cause profound suffering to oneself and one's neighbors can be mitigated, perhaps ended, and the suffering they cause can even be undone. Expressions of grief, lamentation, anger give way to problem solving that begins by asking certain sorts of questions: "What caused this dreadful loss/disease/famine/drought/violence/social injustice/etc.?" and "How did it happen?" The suffering is seen as a practical problem to be solved. Those questions need not assume that any morally responsible agent "planned" or "sent" the suffering. Rather, they assume that the suffering is a solvable physical, psychological, or social problem. They assume that there is in principle a discoverable impersonal explanation for everything that "goes on." Those explanations are in principle discoverable by various modern physical and social sciences. When the explanation for a particular type of suffering is identified, its cause can be removed or corrected, thus decreasing or eliminating the suffering it occasions. This sort of response to horrendous suffering can be called a "secular" response. When suffering is understood in this way, if it is called a "mystery" it is not thought to be intrinsically mysterious. Until it is discovered, the "mystery" is merely what caused the suffering and how it did so. Once that is discovered and eliminated, the "mystery" of suffering is past.

In contrast, if the prevenient singular reality of the Triune God *is* given, those same questions arise at the *intersection* of two antithetical "mysteries" – and the experience of suffering evil is changed. In that intersection both the "positive mystery" of the Triune God's concrete actuality and human experience of it are prior to the "negative mystery" of objective evils and the subjective suffering they cause. The "positive mystery" is the condition of the possibility of the creaturely proximate contexts (that is the force of calling them "creaturely"!) in which the "negative mystery" is experienced as both concretely actual and as the *distortion* of creaturely proximate contexts *as "creaturely."*

The "intersection" of the two "mysteries" means that sufferers themselves, and those who care for them, bring *to* those questions personal identities shaped more or less deeply by certain strong feelings and convictions shaped by their experience of the "positive mystery" of the singular reality of the Triune God. Those feelings and convictions can shape how they perceive the "negative mystery" of evil and profound suffering and how they respond them. The intersection can shape experience of suffering in two ways in particular.

One result is that the questions themselves become more nuanced. If the singular reality of the Triune God *is* given, deep suffering quite rightly continues to give rise to the same verbal and nonverbal expressions of grief, lamentation, anger at "the way things are" that arise in the face horrendous suffering for those for whom the concrete actuality of the Triune God is not acknowledged. Those feelings also quite rightly lead to problem solving that begins with asking questions about "What caused this dreadful disease/famine/ drought/violence/social injustice/etc.?" and "How did it happen?" When the singular reality of the Triune God is a given, the experience of suffering evil is still seen as a set of physical, psychological, or social problems, some of which may be solved with the help of various modern physical and social sciences. When the singular Triune God's relating to all else in the economy is the context within which the experience of suffering evil happens, that does not invalidate "secular" problem-solving questions asking for explanations of what causes some particular evil. On the contrary, it endorses them as acts of human resistance to such suffering that is a fundamental part of appropriate response to God's own resistance to evil.

However, when horrific suffering intersects with the experience of the prevenient and wildly unmanageable grace of the Triune God's glorious love, the experience of suffering is itself complexified. That complexity is reflected in the way the intersection leads to reframing the questions that the experience of suffering raises. Given that the Triune God relates to all else in the three strands of the economy, including relating *within* situations of intense suffering as exemplified by Jesus' crucifixion, we have warrant for saying that in the economy God actively resists horrendous suffering by entering into it fully. That means that such suffering is experienced not only as a "problem" we intensely dislike, wish were otherwise, and set out to solve. It is correlatively also experienced as something that makes a difference to God because God resists it by freely being closer to us *as we are experiencing such suffering* than we can be to ourselves in the experience of suffering.

Hence, experiencing the prevenience of the Triune God's unmanageable love in the particular concrete ways in which God goes about relating in the three strands of the economy reshapes the ways in which we *talk* about those questions about suffering. As Parts II and III urged, the three concrete ways in which the Triune God goes about relating in the economy rule out any vocabulary for characterizing God's way of relating to our experiences of profound suffering as "controlling what happens," "sending the suffering," "causing the suffering for God's good purposes" – and all as though God "does" those things by applying power externally to our lives and proximate contexts in interactions with our much weaker powers that have a zero-sum logic. The three-stranded way in which Good relates to all else rules out vocabulary for describing God's relation to profound sufferings as though God's concrete *ways* of relating were tools, or even weapons, that God uses to control and forcibly change creatures' behavior, emotions, and thought. It rules out any vocabulary that otherwise makes it entirely reasonable to attempt to answer definitively the question: "If God controls all that is 'going on' why doesn't God just put a stop to all these kinds of occasions for deep suffering once and for all?"

Rather, the intersection of the two mysteries means that the ways in which the Triune God goes about relating in the economy call for vocabularies that describe God's relating to creatures creatively, circumambient of creatures, and as one among them, at once radically free of them and closer to them than they can be to themselves. It calls for a vocabulary that describes the Triune God relating in those ways *within the context* of human creatures' horrendous suffering to the ends of sustaining creatures in being and value, nurturing their movement toward well-being, drawing them to eschatological flourishing, and reconciling them to God, their neighbors, and themselves without being in competition or possibly violent conflict with them. Such a vocabulary must be able to frame questions that assume God Godself is participating in the suffering in ways ordered to bringing some good out of them just because those sufferings are part of the creaturely particularity of "what is going on" and of what the Triune God graciously relates to. They are questions that seek to discern where in the situation of suffering God is sustaining the sufferers, strengthening them, and generating new life.

This discussion brings us to a second way in which the intersection of the two "mysteries" shapes experience of suffering. Experienced in the context of the "mystery" of Triune God's wild and prevenient love, profound suffering is experienced, not only as something we evaluate as undesirable by us and intensely want to be rid of, but indeed as something that normatively *ought not* to be at all. It is experienced as something that is objectively and intrinsically wrong, and not merely something we deeply dislike. It ought "not to be" because, in the three-fold way in which the Triune God relates to all else, God Godself unambiguously resists it. Evils are not a function, an "unintended side effect," or "collateral damage," of any of the strands of the economy. And yet they are most obviously "there" in the proximate contexts of our lives. Given the singular reality of the Triune God, that complexity gives rise to a new additional question: "*Why* is such terrible suffering here? Given that the glorious life of the Triune God powerfully relates to us to bless creatively, to bless eschatologically, and to reconcile estranged creatures to God, how can that even happen?" That "why" question only makes sense *given* the singular reality of the Triune God relating to all else in the economy.

It is a double-edged "why": "Why is there such suffering in a creation that God declares 'good'; and how is that even possible?"

and, "Does God have some 'purpose' for such suffering in relation to our creaturely well-being and eschatological flourishing?" I urge that we are warranted to say that God has no "purpose" for such suffering, which God neither created nor "sent." We do believe we are warranted to say that God freely places Godself in those experiences of deep suffering to bring some good out of them. It makes no sense that horrendous suffering could be part of God's good creation; but the "negative mystery" is most definitely "there." We cannot explain "how come" that is the case.

Given God's singular reality in relation to suffering's double "why" ("How is this possible?" and "Does God have a purpose in this?"), the concrete actuality of experienced suffering (surely that is a redundant phrase?) is itself an "intrinsic mystery," a subjective negative mystery that cannot be explained.

Objective "Negative Mystery"

It is not only experience of terrible suffering that is a subjective "negative mystery" that cannot in principle be explained. The concrete objective actuality of the evils that cause such suffering is also singular, a "negative mystery" into the midst of which the "positive mystery" of the singular concrete actuality of God has already freely gone in generous and self-expressive self-giving before we do or deserve anything.

It is theologically conventional to distinguish between natural and "moral" evils. The natural evils are events in "nature" that damage creatures and inflict profound suffering, such as diseases, famines, floods, fires, earthquakes, and physical accidents. No morally responsible agent causes them or can be held accountable for them. "Moral" evils are intentional actions by morally responsible human beings that damage other creatures. The qualifier "morally responsible" rules out actions done by small children, the severely emotionally ill, and any others who, although recognized as human beings, are considered not to be accountable for their own actions.

The distinction between natural and "moral" is rough. There can be cases, such as some famines, about which it is difficult to determine whether or how far human intentional actions "caused" the evil. Moreover, there are evils that are part of a society's structural arrangement of various sorts of power that systemically and unjustly damage some sorts of people more than others. They may not count as natural in that, unlike the movement of tectonic plates in earthquakes or the apparently random genetic "accidents" that set off the spread of a cancer in someone's body, those dynamic systems of social power are intentionally enacted by human beings in ways that are damaging to their neighbors. On the other hand, although individual human beings can change their own patterns of behavior, albeit often with great difficulty, changing unjust socially systemic arrangements of the distribution of the powers human beings exercise in their behaviors *without* generating new forms of systemic injustice proves to be even more profoundly difficult. Granted those ambiguities in the distinction between them, natural and "moral" evils and the suffering they occasion, they are all perceived to be "problems" that must be overcome.

They are "problems" in two senses of the word. They are subjective "personal" problems in the sense that, when an evil inflicts damage that causes us deep suffering, or causes suffering in those to whom we are attached, we intensely wish for the damage and the suffering to cease and for our worlds to be rid of it. We dislike them, fear them, and wish them gone. That personal reaction leads directly to problem solving that focuses on discovering the cause that explains a particular "evil" and the suffering that follows in its wake, and the steps that will be useful to take mitigate its effects or even eliminate it altogether. Evils and the suffering they bring would be perceived that way even if the "positive mystery" did not intersect with the "negative mysteries" in our lived experience.

Second, both sorts of evils and the suffering they cause are objective problems in the sense of moral problems: They just *ought not* to be. That is why so-called moral evils are called "moral." Even if no intersection of the two "mysteries" is acknowledged and only "negative mysteries" are recognized, "moral" evils may be judged to be objectively wrong.[3] To say that moral evils "ought not to be" is not merely to register one's subjective dislike of them.

When the "positive mystery" of the Triune God's "manner of existing" does intersect with "negative mysteries," however, the objective "ought not" covers both "moral" and natural evils. The concrete actuality of so-called natural evils in our proximate contexts is incoherent with singular concrete actuality of the Triune God whose three-fold way of relating to creatures is their ultimate context and expresses the intrinsic glory of the communion in covenant love that is the Trinity's life

The Relation between the Two "Mysteries"

Evils cannot be considered creatures of God. God does not relate to them in "creative blessing." In creative blessing, the Triune God commits Godself to sustain creatures in existence and in value in their kinds for as long as they last, and also commits to nurture their well-being in providential care. The ways in which God goes about doing that express the intrinsic glory of God in God's love and delight in creatures. God's faithfulness to God's self-commitments warrants rejection of any suggestion that evils are a certain *kind* of creature of God. Therein lies a major feature of the singularity of evils' concrete actuality. The abstract *possibility* of creatures becoming distorted in evil, the "conditions of the possibility" of such distortion, can perhaps be shown to lie in

---

[3] Arguably, absent acknowledgement of the "positive mystery" of God's singular "manner of existence," so-called evils are not objective "problems" in the sense of something that just ought not to be. Presumable our intense dislike of them would motivate our taking steps to mitigate or eradicate them, but they would have to be considered to be merely changeable features of the "way things are."

the most general features (i.e., in the metaphysics) of human creaturely finitude.

On the other hand, the concrete *actuality* of evils lies in their being distortions of creatures. Evils are indeed as concretely actual as creatures are because they are distortions of creatures that do not cease being creatures for all of their distortions. Yet evils, precisely as distortions of creatures, are not in and of themselves creatures of any kind. They are powerful as distortions of actual creatures' specific powers in their kinds.

The theological "mystery" lies in the actualizations of the abstract possibility of distortions of creatures' dynamics that are evils. How does that come about? An "explanation" of how evils come to be actual in God's creation would need to provide a theory about the rational structure of the transition from that abstract possibility to its actualization. The "real-ization" of that possibility in concretely actual distortions of creatures cannot be explained by any dynamic intrinsic to finite creaturely reality as such. To postulate such a dynamic would be inconsistent with the theological claim that the Triune God creates creatures, including their intrinsic dynamics, which are "good." Concretely actual creatures, some of whose essential dynamics move them inevitably toward inevitable self-distortion, could not be considered "good" creations.

Nor are evils distortions that God "causes," as it were, ad hoc. On the contrary, given the Trinity's self-commitment in love to creatures' well-being, God can only be said to be unambiguously, unqualifiedly, and persistently resistant of evil that distorts the creatures. Accounts of how the God goes about that "resistance" must, moreover, be framed in ways that make it clear that the Triune God's ways of resisting evils do not simply increase evils by violating the ontological integrity of the creatures and their creaturely powers in their kinds.

The actualization in creatures of the possibility of distortions of their creaturely powers is inherently a-rational. If so, no rationale for it is possible in principle. Evils' concrete actuality is an absurd feature of our proximate contexts. That makes the concrete actuality of evils "singular" in its own way. If so, the concrete actuality of evils is intrinsically "mystery," not in the sense that it is ontologically too "rich" to be grasped in a conceptually comprehensive way, but in the sense that it is inherently inexplicable – except, perhaps, by God to God.

So the relation between the "positive mystery" of the singular concrete actuality of the Triune God and the "negative mystery" of evils that cause horrendous suffering cannot be understood in terms of the relation between Creator and creatures.

On the other hand, given the concrete actuality of the Triune God who relates to all else in the three strands of the economy, the concrete actuality of "evil" cannot simply be paired with the concrete actuality of the good "God" in a binary ontological fashion: Two sorts of intrinsically powerful "reality" – the "good" and the "evil." Some versions of such pairing add the nuance that they are both ontologically "prior" to, more basic than, creaturely reality. Such a binary implies that, although the two are antithetical, they conflict with each other as two powers interacting on some shared "plane" or in some shared "space" of "reality." Although it is true that the Triune God is persistently fiercely resistant to evil's resistance of God, and also resists the suffering evil causes, that resistance can no more be properly understood in terms of God's zero-sum interactions with an "evil other" on a common plane or in a shared "space" than can God's relating to "creaturely others" in creative blessing be understood in that fashion.

The relation between the two "intrinsic mysteries" must be understood in terms of God's gracious prevenient initiative in relating to all else in the three strands of the economy in ways correlatively "radically other" than and "radically close" to "others." Understood theologically, the relation between the "positive mystery" of the Triune God and the "negative mystery" of horrific evil and horrendous suffering must be understood in terms of God's ways of relating to creatures on their own terms just as they are as creatures, and *therewith* – given the a-rational actuality of creatures' distortions – in terms of God's ways of relating to those evils and the horrific suffering they cause.

Understood in that fashion, the intentional prevenience of the glorious Triune God's relating in the economy's three strands is fundamental. That is, the three different ways in which the Triune God is powerfully "sovereign" in the economy, which faithfully express the sense in which God is intrinsically "sovereign," are fundamental in both the conceptual order and the order of reality. In both the order of reality and in the conceptual order God's intentional "prevenience" is prior both to creatures and to their distortions. It is the condition of the actuality of creatures and of the possibility that they may become distorted. And, as rendered in Canonical Scripture, the concrete ways in which the glorious Triune God relates in the economy is the basis of the most appropriate ways in which to "conceptualize" theologically how the Triune God goes about relating to the evils that distort creatures and cause horrendous suffering.

Because that relating has three strands that cannot be conflated into a set of variations on some one way God goes about relating to all else, the relation between the "positive mystery" of God and the "negative mystery" of evil and suffering cannot be characterized adequately in a systematic and comprehensive theoretical "explanation" of how evil comes to be. It can only be characterized adequately in terms of something like a "practical" explanation. It would need to be an explanation of what God is graciously *doing* in the midst of that suffering and evil about the presence of that suffering and evil in our lives.[4]

---

[4] For that reason, I suggest, it is a systematic mistake to frame Christian theology as a theodicy, i.e., as an attempt to provide a theoretical explanation of the presence of evil and suffering in creation by way of a justification of God's "allowing," "sending," much less God's "causing" them. Doing so systematically skews an account of the Triune God's good, just, and loving "manner of existence" into an explanatory hypothesis to account for the reality of evils such that God's concrete actuality is understood, at least implicitly, to *consist* of the way(s) in which God "permits," "sends," and "uses" evils to actualize God's one overarching goal or *telos* for creatures.

The Uselessness of the Triune God

"Practical" explanations of what the Triune God is doing about
evil distortions of creatures' social, cultural, and psychological
proximate contexts, distortions of the powers of creatures own
creaturely dynamics, and the suffering those evils cause will
image the Triune God as intrinsically "useless." Given the
Triune God's ontological and conceptual prevenience in relating
to creatures' evil distortions and suffering, such "practical"
explanations need to be described in ways that emphasize the
centrality of God's *freedom* in the ways in which God relates to
all else in the economy, i.e., the freedom of God's sovereign self-
regulating of how God goes about relating to all else. For it is that
freedom that marks God's love in the three strands of the economy as "grace." Accordingly, "practical" explanations of what
God is doing about evil and suffering need to be framed in terms
of God's *intrinsic glory* as that is expressed in each of the strands
of the economy. It is the intrinsically glorious life of the Triune
God that preveniently *freely* relates to all else in the economy.
That is "what" and "who" is relating powerfully to human creatures' distortions and suffering. The two distinctive qualities of
"what" and "who" that God is on which we have focused are
"sovereignty" and "power."

Every thing about an account of the "sovereignty" and "power" of
the Triune God depends on which of the two sorts of "mystery" is
assumed to be the context within which the other is to be
characterized.

If it is assumed at the outset that the singular reality of the
"negative mystery" of evils and horrendous suffering, and its
appropriate response in a horrified silence, define the conceptual
context *within* which we should discuss the theological implications of the "positive mystery" of the Triune God's singular and
unmanageable reality, and the reverent silence that is the appropriate initial response to it, then the qualities of the "positive

mystery" of God's singular reality, and the quality of God's power in particular, will necessarily be defined in terms of how they help to "explain" evils and suffering. In that context, a theological account of God is framed as an explanatory exercises in which the concept of God functions primarily as a causal hypothesis. In particular, it frames imaging "what" and "who" God's singular reality is *in terms of* the explanatory roles God fills in relation to "negative mysteries."

In particular, when the quality of God's *power* is understood in terms of its ability to "explain" evils and suffering in God's good world, then the Triune God's "manner of existing" will be imaged in terms of God's usefulness to creatures, especially creatures in need. God's power "explains" human creatures' evils and suffering because the power's goodness and love entail that the evils and suffering they "send" upon creatures have a loving and just goal that makes "sense" of their otherwise "mysterious" actuality in a "good" creation. It will be precisely that power which is understood to make God *God*. It is *that* power that constitutes God's singular "manner of existing." In which case, in all self-consistency, the good, just, and loving God *must* relate to creatures in ways that, when properly understood, show a rationale, a "plan" "behind" the evils and suffering that makes "sense" of them. Imaged in that fashion, God's "manner of existence" is understood to be intrinsically *necessarily useful* to creatures whose lives are distorted by evils and suffering from those distortions. In such accounts it is not so much the case that "God does as God is and is as God does," but rather that "God is *what* God does about evil."

"What God primarily does" can be imaged in various ways: *Control* all that "goes on," overpowering creaturely powers to "solve" the problem of evil, whether by "permitting" evils and suffering, or by "causing" and "sending" them; *revealing* that "negative mysteries" are the unintended but unavoidable consequences of creating the "best" possible finite physical cosmos; moving creation through a *developmental process* through which the evils and suffering will be eliminated by the time of its full actualization; *entering into* the "negative mysteries" so deeply as to take them onto Godself and release human creatures from them. God's "manner of existing" is identified with God's "doing" one of such problem-of-evil-solving things.

Each of those ways of solving the "problem" of evil is a way in which God is "useful" to creatures whose lived worlds are profoundly distorted by evils and the deep suffering they occasion. In each of them, God is the hypothesis that "explains" what God is doing about the presence of "negative mysteries" in God's good creation. The account in each of them about "what" God is doing about the "problem of evil" shapes in a different way what it has to say about the sense in which God is "powerful." In each of them, God's being powerfully "useful" to creatures afflicted by "negative mysteries" is essential to "what" it is to be God.

The general upshot of Parts II and III is that an account of "what" and "who" the Triune God is – which is formulated in terms of God's "usefulness' to otherwise suffering and distorted creatures – entails an account of the sense in which God is "powerful" that does not cohere with canonical Christian Scripture's narratives rendering how the Triune God goes about relating to all that is not God. The particular upshot of Parts II and III is that it is just such an account of God's power that underlies and warrants the theologically problematic sort of pastoral remarks that this book has been analyzing.

On the other hand, if it is assumed at the outset that the "positive mystery" of singular and unmanageable reality of God's "manner of existence," and the appropriate initial response to experience of it in reverent silence, defines the conceptual context *within* which we should discuss the sense in which the Triune God is *powerfully* sovereign and how in God's economy God's powerful sovereignty engages of the "negative mystery" of evil, then the focus of the discussion will fall on the sense in which God's intrinsic sovereignty is powerful as it is expressed in images used in canonical accounts of the Triune God's ways of concretely relating to all else in the economy. One theme that is central and constant in all three strands of those canonical accounts is that God's relating to creatures – especially to liberate, heal, and transform creatures as they are distorted by horrific evils and suffer horrendously – is a free relating. That is the point of characterizing the different ways in which God relates to all else in the economy as "grace." Such freedom faithfully expresses the freedom of God's intrinsic sovereignty and its power. It expresses that God's powerful sovereignty in relating to creatures in the economy is "free" because God does not "need" to relate to creatures in such "sovereign power" to be God. God's intrinsically powerful sovereignty is free. God does not "need" to be "useful" to creatures suffering from evil distortions to be *God*. Intrinsically, God is useless and, for that very reason, capable of being freely, "sovereignly," *graciously* "useful" to creatures in their suffering.

Given the Triune God's intrinsic "uselessness," the praise we are enjoined to give God must first of all be praise of God's intrinsic glory for its own sake. It is praise of the intrinsically attractive glory of the Triune God's own intrinsic life, as outlined in Part I, whether or not God relates to any other reality. The joy and gratitude of this sort of praise of God is rooted not in joy and gratitude for the ways in which God has been and is "useful" to us in our brokenness, bondage, and starvation, but rather in love toward God for God's own sake, adoration of God's glorious singular reality whether or not God relates to anything in the economy, and in response to God's love for us for our own sakes, whether or not we respond appropriately to God. It is love of the "useless" God. That sort of praise of God is expressed in Christocentric form in a verse of a hymn sometimes attributed to Francis Xavier:

Why, O blessed Jesus Christ, should I not love thee well?
Not for hope of winning heaven, or of escaping hell;
not with hope of gaining aught, nor seeing a reward;
but is Thyself hast loved me, O ever-loving Lord!
E'en so I love Thee, and will love. And in Thy praise will sing
solely because Thou art my God, and my eternal King.[5]

Such is praise of "what" and "who" the Triune God is in and of Godself who, it is secondarily true, does also freely bless us creatively and eschatologically and reconcile us to God when we are in bondage to the consequences of estrangement from God.

Praise of the glory of God that is rooted in love of the Triune God for God's own sake is at the core of a tradition of Christian "spirituality" that is frequently seen as antithetical to worship of God that is centered on proclaiming forgiveness of sin and condemnation, salvation from meaningless life, and "good news to the poor, . . . release to the captives and recovery of sight to the blind, to let the oppressed go free" (Luke 4:18). It is considered to be antithetical for two general sorts of reasons. Both are unwarranted.

The two are sometimes said to be psychologically antithetical on the grounds that such "spirituality" is focused on an individual's "spiritual" growth. The goal is to reach the point where she or he is so spiritually "formed" by a series of spiritual disciplines as to be capable, with the assistance of God's grace, of personal fulfillment in the vision of God. As such, it is praise that is self-focused on the actualization of the praiser's personhood, which is antithetical to praise that is other focused on sharing good news about others' liberation and fulfillment.

---

[5] In the 1933 Presbyterian (USA) *Hymnbook*, this hymn was identified as an English translation of a seventeenth-century Latin sonnet ascribed to Francis Xavier. The English translation renders it in fairly clunky verse. Clearly, the text relies on the resonances of feudal imagery still culturally powerful in the seventeenth century in the waning of medieval European culture. The hymn has not been included in more recent Presbyterian (USA) hymnals.

The two are also said to be theologically antithetical on the grounds that, although the reconciliation and blessings praised in proclamation of the good news of God's economy are relational realities properly imaged by relational metaphors and analogies, praise of God for God's own singular reality is properly expressed by analogical use of nonrelational ontological terms such as "essence," "existence," "substance," etc. The judgment that the two are antithetical is reflected most clearly in interminable controversies within and between communities of Christian faith about the relation between an emphasis in their common life on "systemic social justice" and an emphasis on "spirituality."

However, placing praise of God's mighty acts in the economy in the more basic context of praise of God's singular glorious reality for its own sake gives a definite and distinctive structure and movement to all Christian communal acts of worship, including acts offering pastoral care. It immediately locates proclamation of good news of God's glory in the larger context of a logically prior characterization of "what" and "who" the God intrinsically is who does freely relate in those ways but is not essentially "required" to do so in virtue of being God.

Such an identification of God implicitly sets limits to the range of images of ways of relating that may be attributed to God. Of some such attributions, for example, that God for some "reason" "sends" evils and horrendous suffering, it warrants immediate rejection on the grounds that, given "what" and "who" God is, God would not do a thing like that. In particular, because it glorifies God's singular intrinsic "manner of existing," independent of whether or not God relates to all else in the economy, it warrants immediate rejection of any inference from canonical accounts of the economy that God does not relate to all else freely. In short, it is only when the Church's worship of God by proclamation of the good news of the economy is enacted within the context of praise of God's intrinsically glorious life for its own sake, and not primarily for the sake of the economy, that the good news of the Gospel can consistently be proclaimed as *grace.*

What is required to keep proclamation of "salvation," "redemption," and "liberation" truly a proclamation of grace is the context of a spirituality focused on praise of the Triune God's singular intrinsic life *for its own sake.* The "negative mysteries" of evils and suffering must be acknowledged for what they are: horrific but "mysterious" distortions of creatures. They must be acknowledged in the context of the proclamation of the good news of the Triune God's gracious three-stranded economy. It is the "positive mystery" of God's grace that is the contrast term against which the depth of the "negative mystery" of evils and suffering comes clear. Proclamation of that good news clearly implies that the Triune God's ways of relating to all else in the economy *are* "powerful" to make differences in the lived world of our proximate contexts and that that "power," in some senses of the term, does "explain" the differences God makes. However, the proclamation of the good news of the economy needs itself to take place within the context of praise of a reality even more basic than it: the Triune God's own glorious life. Such praise explicitly images "who" and "what" God's singular "manner of existence" is, and in particular what the "power" of God's intrinsic sovereignty is, putting proclamation of the gospel of God's economy in its proper context.

As the context within which proclamation of the good news of God's economy takes place – including practices of pastoral care – praise of the Triune God's singular intrinsic life also implicitly undercuts the objections that such a spirituality is antithetical to praise of God by proclamation of the good news of God's economy. Spirituality that is focused on praise of God for God's sake is not necessarily psychologically oriented to the personal fulfillment of the ones who praise. Of course, it can be oriented that way. It may be oriented that way, for example, when praise of God for God's sake is integrated into a spirituality that consists of a series of steps or stages of disciplined spiritual "growth" that, if followed rigorously and incrementally, is said to lead to one's own fulfillment in an experience of union with God. However, nothing about the practice of loving praise of God solely as response to "what" and "who" the Triune God is in and of Godself entails such a spirituality with logical necessity.

Moreover, an account of the Triune God's singular reality does not necessarily rule out a "relational" account of God. As Part I sketched in outline, the Triune God's intrinsic self-relations in generous self-giving love – which just are the Trinity's intrinsic, attractive, glorious life – are precisely what constitute the One God as "who" and "what" the Triune God is. Because of the Triune God's intrinsic relationality God's relating to all else in three strands of the economy is not incoherent with God's singular "manner of existing" *a se*. At the same time, because the Triune God is intrinsically relational, God does not "need" to relate to reality other than God to be "what" and "who" the Triune God is. If God does relate to all else in the economy, God does that in ontological freedom.

Praise of the "Useless" Triune God as the "Glory of God"

We are to praise the God of Abraham. Reverent silence gives way to behavioral human responses to the intrinsic glory of the Triune God as that glory is expressed in the concrete ways in which God goes about relating to all else in the three strands of the economy. I noted in Chapter 2 that the primary referent of the phrase "the glory of God" as used in canonical Christian Scripture is the Triune God's intrinsic glory, and that a secondary and derivative referent of the phrase are the expressions of aspects of God's intrinsic glory in the concrete ways in which God relates to all else in the three strands of the economy. Here we come to the tertiary referent of the phrase, the way in which human acts of praise of the glory of God expressed in the economy are themselves in their own way also the "glory" of God.

Such praise is expressed in a large array of intentional human acts. A great many of those acts involve speaking. They include, for example, hymns sung, sacraments celebrated, acts of mercy and charity, communal and personal prayer, communal and personal moral discernment, preaching, work for social justice, personal testimony, catechesis, moral guidance, communal decision making (however controversy-laden!), etc. Such acts involve expressions to God of joy, lament, acknowledgment of sin, anger toward God, trust, repentance, acknowledgement of confusion, and petitions of all sorts. Collectively, such acts comprise worship of the Triune God by communities of Christian faith, in the broadest and most encompassing sense of "communal worship."

Such praise of the glory of God in the economy is the whole the point of the Church's core mission to "proclaim of the Gospel." In acts of proclamation broken, bound, and starving human creatures not only tell other broken, bound, and starving creatures the good news of where they have found healing, liberation, and food, but also seek to share with them an ongoing life undergoing healing, liberation, and sustenance. Part of such "speaking" takes the form of pastoral care of neighbors who suffer horrendously from horrific evils and pastoral care of those who love them and anguish at their suffering.

In a deeply fractured, distorted, and suffering world, it is an urgently important mission. Taken all together, those acts of worship seeks to be appropriate response to the Triune God's singular intrinsic glory and to the way that glory is expressed in the three strands of God's economy. Insofar as it is truly "appropriate" it is itself, in a tertiary reference of the phrase, the "glory" of God on earth.

However, those acts are not necessarily "appropriate." Communities of Christian faith need to be self-reflectively self-examining to test whether their acts of worship, including pastoral care, are in fact "appropriate" responses to God's intrinsic glory and the ways that glory is expressed in God's economy. It is urgent that acts of worship not be done in ways that, however unintentionally, simply deepen the fractures, distortions, and suffering in the communities' common life.

In particular, this book has focused on the upshot of generations of Christians being formed by worshiping using a conventional language in hymns, prayers, sermons, moral exhortation, bible interpretation, theological instruction, and pastoral care that implicitly images the "almighty" Triune God's power as "absolutely unrestricted power to control all that goes on"; namely, it "forms" them to assume that God's role in experiences of horrific suffering may rightly be characterized in ways that are theologically problematic and deepen the anguish such characterizations of God's role are meant to comfort. The whole point of the sort of theological reflection undertaking here is to engage communities of Christian faith in critical theological self-examination of the ways in which they image God in their acts of worship, in this case acts of pastoral care in particular.

I want to urge that, as the "glory of God" in it tertiary reference, acts of praise of the "useless" Triune God in general, and acts of praise of God in pastoral care in particular, must in all faithfulness to God's intrinsic glory intentionally *stammer* a good bit more than they conventionally have. We turn to that in Chapter 11.

Part IV | Stammering Praise

11 | Stammering in Praise of the Useless Triune God

We are to praise the God of Abraham. Reverent silence gives way to behavioral human responses to the intrinsic glory of the Triune God, as that glory is expressed in the concrete ways in which God goes about relating to all else in the three strands of the economy. I noted in Chapter 2 that, as used in Canonical Christian Scripture, the primary referent of the phrase "the glory of God" is God's intrinsic glory, and that a secondary and derivative referent of the phrase is the expression of aspects of God's intrinsic glory in the concrete ways in which God relates to all else in the three strands of the economy. Here we come to the tertiary referent of the phrase, the way in which human acts of praise of the glory of God expressed in the economy are themselves in their own way also the "glory" of God.

Such praise is expressed in a large array of intentional human acts. A great many of those acts involve speaking. They include, for example, hymns sung, sacraments celebrated, acts of mercy and charity to neighbors who do not join the community of faith in worship of God, communal and personal prayer, personal moral discernment, preaching, work for social justice, personal testimony, catechesis, moral guidance, communal decision making (however controversy laden!), etc. Such acts involve expressions to God of joy, lament, acknowledgment of sin against God, acknowledgment of evil done to others both intentionally and by silent complicity in systemic injustices, anger toward God, trust in God, repentance, acknowledgement of confusion, and petitions of all sorts. Collectively such acts comprise worship of the Triune God by

communities of Christian faith, in the broadest and most encompassing sense of "communal worship."

Praise of the glory of God in the economy is the whole point of
Church's core mission to "proclaim of the Gospel." In acts of
proclamation, broken, bound, and starving human creatures not
only tell other broken, bound, and starving creatures the good news
of where they have found healing, liberation, and food, but also seek
to share with them an ongoing life undergoing healing, liberation,
and sustenance by the power of the Spirit. I have pressed the point
that pastoral care of neighbors who suffer horrendously from horrific evils and pastoral care of those who love them and anguish at
their suffering is in its own way an integral part of such sharing. In a
deeply fractured, distorted, and suffering world, it is an urgently
important mission. Taken all together, those acts of worship seek to
be appropriate response to the Triune God's singular intrinsic glory.
Insofar as it is truly "appropriate" it is itself, in a tertiary reference
of the phrase, the "glory" of God on earth.

However, those acts are not always truly "appropriate" responses
to the ways in which the Triune God has related to humankind.
Communities of Christian faith need to be self-reflectively self-
examining to test whether their acts of worship, including pastoral
care, are in fact "appropriate" responses to God's intrinsic glory and
the ways that glory is expressed in God's economy. It is urgent that
acts of worship not be done in ways that, however unintentionally,
simply deepen the fractures, distortions, and suffering in humankind's common life.

In particular, this book has focused on the upshot of generations
of Christians being formed by communal worship that uses a
conventional language in hymns, prayers, sermons, moral exhortation, bible interpretation, theological instruction, and pastoral care
that implicitly images the "almighty" Triune God's power as absolutely unrestricted power to control all that goes on. The conventional language of practices of Christian worship "formed" them to
assume that God's role in experiences of horrific suffering may

rightly be characterized in ways that are theologically problematic and only deepen the anguish such characterizations of God's role are meant to comfort. The point of the sort theological reflection undertaking here is to engage communities of Christian faith in self-critical theological self-examination of the ways in which they image God in their acts of worship, in particular in acts of pastoral care.

I want to urge that as the "glory of God" in it tertiary reference, acts of praise of the "useless" Triune God in general, and acts of praise of God in pastoral care in particular, must in all faithfulness to God's intrinsic glory intentionally *stammer* a good bit more than they conventionally have. It is only as they are stammering acts of praise that they can also be the "glory of God" in the phrase's tertiary reference.

Stammering in Praise of the Triune God

Our acts of praise necessarily stammer. In general, when we stammer we start out to speak, abruptly interrupt ourselves, lapse into silence, begin all over again speaking in a new way, only to interrupt ourselves once more. Our speech about God in particular is rooted in praise of the Triune God that is appropriate response to the concrete actuality of the "positive mystery" of God's intrinsic glory. It is based on and guided by Canonical Christian Scripture's accounts of how God goes about relating to all else in three strands of the economy because the concrete ways in which God relates faithfully express aspects "what" and "who" God is intrinsically, i.e., they express God's intrinsic glory in and of Godself.

From themes that we have developed, we can garner several reasons why our efforts to praise the Triune God must stammer.

Most fundamentally, we must lapse into stammering silences when we praise the God of Abraham in pastoral care because it is speech that emerges out of an even more basic silence that is the only initial response that is appropriate to the singular reality of the "positive mystery" of God's love. We dare break that silence to speak in praise of God not because, as Rowan Williams puts it, "we have been shut up" by God's positive mystery and must resist being made invisible and inaudible, but "quite the opposite, . . . because we've been opened up by it."[1] Nonetheless, we must remain conscious that our speaking in "praise" of God's love toward us all too easily turns into an effort to domesticate it. Stammering in our praise, breaking it off, lapsing into silence, and trying to start over in more adequate forms of praise is necessary to ward that off the temptation to "manage" God's wildly unmanageable love.

Second, we have frequently had reason to remind ourselves that the terms we use to attribute qualities to the Triune God, such as "love," "wise," "just," "glory," "sovereign," and "power," are used analogically. Those terms are ordinarily used to attribute qualities to certain creatures. In learning to use them, we learn the range of their connotations and nuances. We know with some clarity how they mean when used in different contexts to attribute certain qualities to creatures, qualities that we also know more or less independently in other contexts. In part because we know how those creatures are and are not like one another, we have some grasp of how one and the same term, say "intelligent," "selfish," or "loving," means when used to attribute a quality to different sorts of creatures. Knowing how they are similar and different, we know how the term "means" when used of each one. However, because God's singular reality is incomprehensible to us, we are incapable of a cognitive grasp of how God's reality is different from our own and that of other creatures. As the Fourth Lateran Council put it in 1215, "Between the Creator and the creature there can be noted no similarity so great that a greater dissimilarity cannot be seen between them."[2] Accordingly, although we may have good reason

---

[1] "Silence in the Face of Mystery," *The Christian Century,* August 29, 2018, p. 29.
[2] Denzinger, *Enchiridion Symbolorum* (St Louis, MO: Herder, 1957) p. 806.

in praise of the God of Abraham to attribute "glory," "sovereignty," or "power" to God, we do not understand how those terms mean in regard to God. Therefore, each time we do so we must pause to qualify the ascription to rule out ascription to God of senses of each of those terms that we recognize are misleading in regard to God. At least implicitly, all our efforts to say something in praise of God must have built into them a final self-reflexive moment that say says, "*And all the foregoing is true but incomplete, inadequate and easily misleading.*" We say what we have to say and then, in Denys Turner's words, must fall back into "that silence which is found only on the other side of a general linguistic embarrassment."[3] Every such pause followed by a qualified reformulation of an ascription to God of a quality such as power is the momentary silence of a stammer.

A third reason why in praise our attribution to the Triune God of qualities such as "glory," "sovereignty," and "power" must stammer lies in the basis on which such qualities are identified. These chapters have repeatedly turned to Canonical Christian Scriptures' accounts of the ways in which God goes about relating to all else in God's economy as the basis on which to identify what can be said about the qualities "glory," "sovereignty," and "power" as attributable to God. They did that on the grounds that the "glory of God," in the phrase's secondary reference to the economy, as rendered in the canonical accounts of God's economy, does faithfully expresses aspects of God's intrinsic glory. Thus, the glory of God in the concrete particularities of each strand of the economy is what warrants identification of which qualities may correctly be attributed to the Triune God. Among those "aspects" of God's intrinsic glory are the Triune God's intrinsic "sovereignty" and "power."

However, Canonical Christian Scriptures render the concrete ways in which God goes about relating to all else in three

---

[3] *Darkness of God* (Cambridge, UK: Cambridge University Press, 1995), p. 23.

irreducibly different strands. Parts I, II, and III of this book show
how each of those strands of the economy warrants a different
vocabulary for characterizing, respectively, the Triune God's "sovereignty" and the "power" of that sovereignty in creative blessing
and providential care, in eschatological blessing, and in reconciling
estranged creatures to God. Because the three strands of the economy are irreducibly different the vocabularies that each warrants
for characterizing God's sovereignty and its power, although not
contradictory, are simply different and cannot be synthesized into a
single comprehensive systematic account. Accordingly, praise of the
Triune God's sovereignty and its power in providential care must
stammer. Having started off with an account of, say, God's "sovereignty" in reference to providential care it must break off to give an
account of God's sovereignty in eschatological blessing, only to
break that off to give an account of it in reconciliation. There is
no conceptually "meta" framework within which to synthesize
those accounts in a systematic way.

The differences between the vocabularies by which each sort of
canonical narrative characterizes how God goes about relating to all
else in each strand of the economy brings out two more reasons
why praise of the "useless" Triune God must stammer.

A fourth reason comes into view when we hold together (a) the
explicit prohibition of human imaging of God in canonical
accounts of God's liberative promise making and promise keeping
to Abraham and his descendants and (b) the explicit identification
of Jesus Christ as "the image of the invisible God," in Colossians
1:15. The second commandment of the Decalogue prohibits us from
picturing God. It reads, in the English of King James' translators,
"Thou shalt not make unto thee any graven image, or any likeness
of anything that is in heaven above, or is in the earth beneath, or is
in the water under the earth" (Exodus 20:4). The next injunction is:
"Thou shalt not bow down to them nor serve them" (20:5). In short:
You are not to picture the God you worship, nor worship a "god"
you can picture. Note that we are not told that we are incapable of

picturing God. We are simply forbidden to picture God to ourselves. Perhaps it is because human beings are incapable of making "graven images" as focal centers of acts of worship without slipping into idolatry. On the other hand, the author of the Epistle to the Colossians is equally clear that, although *we* are not free to picture God to ourselves, *God* is entirely free to picture God to us. Speaking of "our Lord Jesus Christ" (Colossians 1:3), the author writes "He [Jesus Christ] is the image of the invisible God" (1:15). Evidently, it is not inherently impossible to picture God. God can do it. According to Colossians, the picture God gives of God consists of one human life in all its first-century Galilean particularity: Jesus of Nazareth, crucified and raised from the dead.[4] Because we are to some degree capable of picturing human beings, we must be capable to some degree of imaging the one who is God's own picture of God. We are not forbidden to "image" the Triune God in terms of canonical Jesus stories, i.e., Christocentrically.

Put in theological terms, the key issue for this project has to do with how most adequately to characterize both "what" and "who" God is: because God's way of concretely going about relating to all else both to bless it eschatologically and to reconcile it to God when it is estranged from God is "by way of Incarnation" in the unsubstitutable personal identity of Jesus of Nazareth, Jesus Christ *in person* is the image of "who" God is.

We tell anecdotes about someone and say, "In interactions like that she was most truly her self." That is why we look to biographies, and not to clinical reports, to learn "who" someone was. The sheer complexity of a human being requires a variety of narratives to begin to convey "who she is." Indeed, sometimes it is clear that several quite different stories do genuinely capture "who she is,"

---

[4] Unlike the "picture" of God the Decalogue forbids us to make for ourselves, the "picture" of God that God gives is not a static "graven" image, carved and fixed in stone, wood, or metal. Rather, it is a dynamic, living "picture." It simply *is* the life of the human person, Jesus of Nazareth.

even when it is not clear how the stories all fit to together. Canonical narrative accounts of who Jesus is have privileged status as warrants for characterizing "who" God is. Personal identities are in general more adequately characterized in their concrete particularities by being "rendered" or "re-presented" in narrative accounts of their singular ways of inter-relating with others than by attribution of relatively abstract qualities. We do not know what stories about Jesus pictured his identity to the author of Colossians. However, Christians for whom Colossians is part of the Scriptural Canon also have in that same Canon the Synoptic Gospels' varying narrative descriptions of who Jesus is. Christians are free to apply to the one who is pictured in the Synoptic Gospels' narratives the comment in Colossians that he, Jesus, "is the image of the invisible God." So we, in turn, may ourselves "image" God if our efforts to do so are governed by God's own picture of God in the personal identity of Jesus as it is described in differing ways by the narratives of the canonical Synoptic Gospels.

Accordingly, we are also warranted to judge that some quality or action is attributed to God wrongly because "God wouldn't be like that or do that," given the identity descriptions we have of the one whom God "sends" as God's own image of God. Praise of the Triune God must stammer back and forth between characterizations of the intrinsic glory of "what and who" God is by way of analogical attribution to God of relatively abstract names for qualities of God's glory, on one side, and on the other characterizations that are framed in terms of narratives of how Jesus went about relating to fellow creatures.

A fifth reason why praise of the "useless" Triune God must stammer comes into view when the third and fourth reasons are taken together. It has to do with the notion of "meaning." It is common in murder mysteries to explain the significance of a given fact x (the violent assault on the victim broke and stopped his watch at 10:30 pm) by saying that "x means y" (that the murder happened at or about 10:30). "X means y" in the sense that x *implies* y and y

may be *inferred* from *x*. By extension, proposition *X* ("God is all powerful") can be said to *"mean"* proposition *Y* ("God had the power to prevent that murder but 'chose' not to do so") in the sense that proposition *X* implies proposition *Y*, and *Y* can rightly be inferred from *X*. Add to that the claim that "Proposition *J*" ('God is good') *means* "Proposition *K*" ("God always acts for creatures' well-being") in the sense that it implies *K* and *K* can be inferred from *J*, and one has exactly the sense in which the theologically problematic pastoral remark, "God 'sent' that murder for a reason" is reasonably believed to be part of what "God is almighty" *means.*

However, reasons three and four given for the necessity of our stammering in our praise of the Triune God's intrinsic glory combine to block the chain of inferences that leads to: "God is almighty *means* that God sent horrific evil *z*, and the suffering it caused, for a reason." Given that the three strands of God's economy call for the use of three different vocabularies to characterize appropriately the sense in which the Triune God's sovereignty is "powerful" in each of the strands of the economy, reasonable inferences from the sense in which God's sovereignty in eschatological blessing and/or God's sovereignty in reconciling estranged creature to God are "powerful" can block what might otherwise be reasonable inferences from the sense in which God's sovereignty is powerful in, say, creative blessing. Each such "blockage" requires our characterizations of God's power in relating to all else to stammer.

Nor can a canonical narrative of God "causing" a horrific "negative mystery" and the horrendous suffering it occasions to happen "for a good but thus far unknown reason," or commands some human creature to cause it, be said to *mean* that "God's will" is the ultimate explanation of all such negative mysteries so that their occurring may also be rightly be narrated as stories of God's "mighty deeds." Such an inference is blocked by the privileged status of canonical accounts of God's "way of Incarnation" in the life-trajectory of Jesus of Nazareth as the concrete way in which the Triune God goes about relating to bless eschatologically and reconcile the estranged. Such an inference is blocked by the judgment that the Triune One, as self-imaged in the Incarnation, "would not do a thing like that." Such inference blocking also requires our characterizations of God's power in relating to all else to stammer.

Stammering Opens Space for Anomie in Praise of God's Role

There is a growing literature of theological reflection focused specifically on the authors' experiences of receiving the sort of well-intentioned acts of pastoral care that I have been calling "theologically problematic." It is likely that the authors disagree about any number of theological questions. Nonetheless, their books all have five important things in common.

First, they are written out of the author's own suffering either in an intensely painful disease or in grief at the untimely death of a loved one. They do so as persons who explicitly self-identify with some community of Christian faith.

Second, they are at once theologically imaginative, psychologically perceptive, bluntly honest, and wonderfully well-written.

Third, they concur in the judgment that many of the well-intentioned pastoral remarks made to them about their suffering were deeply problematic theologically. Kate Bowler ends *Every Thing Happens for a Reason, and Other Lies I Have Loved*,[5] her account of her treatment for stage 4 colon cancer, with two appendices. The first lists eight things "Absolutely Never" to say "to People Experiencing Terrible Things."[6] (Appendix 2 offers a helpful set of six alternative things to say and do, "Give This A Go, See How It Works: A Short List."[7]) To the point being made here, however,

---

[5] New York: Random House, 2018.
[6] Pp. 169–172.
[7] Pp. 173–175.

she concludes her book with "A Final Public Service Announcement to Suffering People":

> Just remember that if cancer or divorce or tragedies of all kinds don't kill you, people's good intentions will. Take the phrase, "but they mean well. . . . as your cue to run screaming from the room. Or demand presents. You deserve a break.'

Fourth, although they do not use the term, they call for a lot more "stammering" in Christian's talk about God's role in horrific evils and the horrendous suffering they cause. It is not to my purpose to offer a comprehensive survey of that literature here. However, I shall cite several of them pretty much at random, just because they make so very well important points about those "pastoral remarks."

Fifth, they have a theme in common. Writing out of her own experience as a cancer survivor, Lutheran theologian Deanna Thompson states the theme that is to be found, at least implicitly, in all the other writers:

> What's needed in our theologies is more space in the tellings of the Christian story – as well as in communal enactments of that story and the living out of the story's call to care for those who suffer – for the anomie that comes from living with serious illness.[8]

and also, one may add, the anomie that comes from living with other causes of suffering such as the untimely death of a loved one.

"Anomie" is the feeling that our experience – in this case, experience of horrific suffering – does not make sense. It does not make sense because, in the experience of suffering, it is impossible to see that we live in a world that has the intelligible order or norm (*nomos)* that would make sense of the experience. Rather, experience of deep suffering is closer to an experience of random chaos.

---

[8] *Glimpsing Resurrection: Cancer, Trauma, and Ministry* (Louisville, KY: Westminster John Knox, 2018), p. 5.

"Anomie" is the feeling that goes with being unable to find any answer to the question, "Why is this suffering, and the evil that causes it, happening?" While testifying to their trust in God, the writers of the literature I review all also testify that, in their intense sufferings, conventional efforts at pastoral care that purport to offer explanatory answers to that "Why?" question completely failed to persuade. A result of that failure was anomie. They all also witness to finding the space for anomie *within* practices of praise glorifying God. They all express their anomie in a *faithful* agnosticism about allegedly satisfactory theological "explanations" of horrific suffering.

Those writers suggest that the "space" for anomie that is needed in our "tellings of the Christian story" is opened by participation in certain practices that comprise Christian communities' praise of God in acts of worship of God. The "space" that is needed to allow for anomie in Christian practices of praise of God is opened up when we can get free of a pressure to domesticate and manage the "wildness" of our experience of "negative mystery" by filling the horrified silence it initially evokes with a lot of "explanatory" talk. That pressure to "explain" is exerted by at least two things. It is exerted by a cultural anxiety with silence, an anxiety that is "outside" of us and presses us socially; and it is exerted by the version of that anxiety that we have internalized within ourselves.

Theologically speaking, release from that pressure comes when trust in God's power to sustain us in and throughout the suffering allows us to let go of two things at once:

> Let go of the fantasy that we can and, in all faithfulness to God, *must* "make sense" of the cause of the suffering by relying on our "religious" resources and intellectual gifts to articulate an "explanation"; and, second, to let go of the internal pressure of our anxiety that we actually aren't up to that task by honestly acknowledging that the anxiety is not a sign that our faith is "weak" but rather is well warranted because we simply do not and at present cannot know of any persuasive "explanation."

So, for example, in *Lament for a Son*,[9] Christian philosopher Nicholas Wolterstorff's cry of grief over his twenty-five-year-old son Eric's untimely death in a hiking accident in the Swiss Alps, he writes"

> I have no explanation. . . . I believe in God the Father Almighty, maker of heaven and earth and resurrecter of Jesus Christ. I also believe that my son's life was cut off in its prime. I cannot fit these pieces together. I am at a loss. I have read the theodicies produced to justify the ways of God to man. I find them unconvincing. To the most agonizing question I have ever asked I do not know the answer. I do not know why God would watch him fall. I do not know why God would watch me wounded. I cannot even guess. . . . I am not angry but baffled and hurt. My wound is an unanswered question. The wounds of humanity are an unanswered question.[10]

He describes the life of faith as an "enduring": "I cannot fit it all together. I can only, with Job, endure. I do not know why God did not prevent Eric's death. To live without the answer is precarious. It's hard to keep one's footing."[11] In a chapter in a memoir he published several years later, Wolterstorff developed that description of faith further: "Faith involves cognition of some sort, be it belief or something else; but faith, at its core, is not belief but trust. After Eric's death, my trust in God became more wary, more cautious, more guarded, more qualified. I pray God will protect the members of my family. But I had prayed that for Eric. I still trust God; but I no longer trust God to protect me and my family from harm and grief."[12] When one's affirmation that one trusts in God as creator and redeemer raises questions about "why," then,

[9] Grand Rapids, MI: Wm. B. Eerdmans, 1987.

[10] P. 68.

[11] P. 67.

[12] *In this World of Wonders: Memoir of a Life in Learning* (Grand Rapids, MI: Wm. B. Eerdmans, 2019), p. 207.

Eric died, one stammers. One begins the affirmation anew in ways that block some of the inferences the questioner implicitly drew from the initial affirmation. The wary, cautious, guarded, qualified character of the life of faith, in the context of suffering profound grief, is an expression, I suggest, of the anomie Deanna Thompson identifies. In his grief, Wolterstorff trusts God in a way that no longer *requires* either that his trust, or that God, must provide knowledge of any *nomos* that would explain Eric's untimely death.

In *Among the Ashes*,[13] William J. Abraham, Outler Professor of Wesley Studies and Altschuler Distinguished Teaching Professor at the Perkins School of Theology, Southern Methodist University, writes of his grief over the sudden death of his forty-two-year-old son Timothy in Houston, Texas. Timothy had gone to a routine visit with his doctor, who rushed him to the hospital, by which time his vital organs had completely collapsed. His condition was later diagnosed as hepatitis related. The "full resources of the hospital were immediately deployed and they were able to save him, at least in the short term. His death, nine days later, was to all of us in the family unexpected; we were not prepared for it."[14] William Abraham was in Scotland at the time of Timothy's collapse. He managed to get back to Houston two days later.

> To say that those two days were a nightmare would be a gross understatement. The swing from faint hope to deep anguish and despair ripped through every fiber of my existence ... Aside from continual prayer for healing (indeed for the miracle of healing) my last-resort prayer was that Timothy would be still alive when I got back. When this was answered, my next prayer was that at some stage he would wake up from the induced coma and I could tell him how much I loved him. That prayer too was answered; in retrospect the answer to that prayer was and is an incredible gift... Yet the

[13] Grand Rapids, MI: Wm. B. Eerdmans, 2017.
[14] P. 2.

bigger issue remains: despite a massive out pouring of prayer, my beloved Timothy was not healed.[15]

Abraham's image for his grief is as powerful as it is simple: "to lose Timothy was to fall precipitously into a deep black hole. It was a hole of darkness, numbness, despair, and waves of excruciating pain. I had lost a friend, a counselor, a soulmate, a fellow-traveler, a spiritual companion, and a conversation partner; and, above all else, I had lost my firstborn son."[16] "What is paradoxical about that experience is that everything around it was marked by an abundance of providence."[17] The answered prayers noted in the paragraph above are only two of the "marks" of an encompassing providence that Abraham names.[18] He develops the point:

> I know all the standard moves in theodicy and even endorse a robust and integrated set of those moves; I do not sense that these are somehow irrelevant to my situation; what I find is that they are intellectually incapable of doing any work in my life. What is at issue is that I have found every philosophical and theological move utterly empty in wrestling with the problem of the loss of my son. . . If these philosophical and theological proposals developed in theodicy are cogent, given that I can readily entertain them, surely they ought to have made a difference in my grieving and my terrible sense of loss. The reality is that they made no difference; on the contrary, entertaining them would have been entirely hollow and they would have come across as inappropriate or vacuous. Yet if they are cogent, and I think they indeed are, this should not have been the case.[19]

---

[15] Pp. 2, 3.
[16] P. 4.
[17] P. 6.
[18] Cf. pp. 6–8.
[19] Pp. 11–13.

A bit further on in his first chapter, he characterizes his experience of grief as "apophatic," i.e., "in this experience we are at a loss for words; we are reduced to rest and silence; we cannot say anything positive; the mystery involved is ineradicable."[20] This is the silence that is the appropriate initial response to the experience of "negative mystery."

Abraham summarizes his reflections in three points. "First there is no persuasive theological rationale for much of the suffering we have to endure. Initially, such suffering naturally leads to the overwhelming of our cognitive capacities so that neither our central beliefs nor our attempts at theological explanation offer any kind of direct consolation... [W]e suffer because we love; and when we lose a beloved child, the measure of our grief and our darkness is the measure if our love."[21]

"Second, it is natural given the riches of our faith and the ingenuity of our speculative intellects to look for more. For my part I remain a radically skeptical Christian theist who believes that the glories prepared for us in the life to come are ultimately beyond our comprehension. This is matched by the parallel conviction that the reasons for the range and depth of our suffering are equally beyond our comprehension."[22] "Negative mysteries" and the "positive mystery" are parallel in their incomprehensibility, albeit for different reasons. Abraham is emphatic that it does not follow from his "radical skepticism" that the intellectual enterprise of theodicy is pointless and should be abandoned. To the contrary, it is a valid and important philosophical and theological task.[23] In his view, it is inseparable from any theological account of God's providential care of creatures in which they are blessed by God's unmanageably

---

[20] P. 14.

[21] P. 105.

[22] P. 105.

[23] Cf. pp. 16–18; 105. On this point, Abraham's position disagrees with the theses promoted here.

"wild" love and, indeed, encounter God face to face. Nonetheless Abraham has space for a faithful agnosticism about "explanations" of both suffering and God's blessing.[24] When one's affirmation that one trusts in God as creator and redeemer raises questions about "why," then, Timothy died, one stammers. One begins the affirmation anew in ways that block some inferences the questioner implicitly drew from the initial affirmation.

I suggest two things about that "radical skepticism." The first is that it is a tacit acknowledgment of the anomie that comes with experiences of deep suffering. Abraham is emphatic that the grief he suffers "is not the loss of meaning; it is the loss of our beloved son."[25] If "anomie" is the feeling that there is no "meaning" in our suffering, it does not cover Abraham's grief at the loss of Timothy. However, the fact that in that grief the "sense-making" arguments provided by theodicy and doctrine of divine providence no longer worked to "make sense" of the experience of loss – so much so that Abraham finds himself skeptical of them – all of that does strongly suggest that he also experiences anomie. Clearly, the "crucial point is simple: like the women at the tomb [of Jesus], we have lost a dear one and are overwhelmed by grief. Loss of meaning is not the primary matter; it is a secondary issue."[26] Nonetheless, it too is real; and the experience of it is "anomie."

Second, I suggest that it is significant that Abraham finds space for that skepticism, not in the context of propositional "sense making" of either suffering or blessing, but in the context of participation in one of the traditional practices that comprise acts of worship of God by communities of Christian faith: entering meditatively into canonical Scriptural narratives. In the fourth chapter of his book he focuses on *Job*. He sees it as "essentially a book about

---

[24] *In this World of Wonders: Memoir of a Life in Learning* (Grand Rapids, MI: Wm. B. Eerdmans, 2019), p. 207.

[25] P. 96.

[26] P. 97.

faith," or perhaps more exactly a narrative about the practices that comprise the life of faith. It illuminates "the proper motivation for faith, its intense internal conflicts, its ultimate survival, and its fundamental logic and character."[27] In it Job is "a man committed to scrupulous religious practice."[28] In Abraham's reading the "logic' of Job's narrative turns on Job's ultimate confrontation with God that chastens Job in two ways. Job had demanded an explanation of why he had been unjustly afflicted with horrific suffering; and in his confrontation with God the creator he recognizes the severe limitations of his creaturely capacity to understanding the divine action in creation, in society, and in his own personal life. Job's demand for an explanation of why he had suffered is "answered" by God's showing him that he did not have the cognitive where-with-all to understand God's working in "what goes on." His cognitive chastening entails, Abraham suggests, a fundamental revision[29] of a central theme in the "Deuteronomic" theology in the Old Testament: "Choose God and his ways and you will live; reject God and his ways and you will surely die."[30] Job's confrontation with God in his confidence of his own innocence shows him that that is not in fact "the policy that governs all divine action in the world and in history."[31] Rather, "God acts uniformly in the lives of the good and the wicked; it is divine action all the way to the bottom. Job himself is the supreme counter-example"[32] to the traditional Deuteronomic theme. In his encounter with God, Job does not receive a revelation of an alternative causal "explanation" of his suffering. Rather, he learns that it is pointless to ask "why" about his suffering because there is no "explanation" he would be capable of understanding. *At the same time*, in that confrontation with God Job "has undergone a personal encounter

---

[27] P. 65.
[28] P. 65.
[29] Cf., p. 67.
[30] P. 72
[31] P. 71.
[32] P. 73.

with God that has moved beyond a third-person perspective on his faith" based on others' testimony "to a first person perspective."[33] It was a person-relative encounter, face to face with God. "In meeting God face to face, Job does not have an explanation, but he does know God now in a way he did not know God before."[34] On this front, Abraham urges, Job's 'faith is marked by a retrieval of a vital element in the faith of Israel, that of intimate experience of God, which provides vital assurance in a pilgrimage challenging the foundations of suffering."[35] Participation in practices of worship in which experience of personal encounter with God may occur creates a space in which it is appropriate for an initial response in silence to give way to articulate praise of God that acknowledges that both the experience of the "positive mystery" in an experience of the blessing of grace, and the experience of the "negative mystery" in a deep suffering, are inherently unintelligible, inherently inexplicable by us. It opens a space in which initial silence gives way to responses to experiences of the blessing of grace in acts of articulate worship of God. It opens space in those acts of worship that glorify God for an agnosticism about causal explanations of both suffering and blessing that is nonetheless faithful to God.

Third, "there is no going back on the crucial Christian claim that the life, death, and resurrection of Christ have a decisive bearing on our understanding of experience of the reality of death." For Abraham, it is important that the "death of Christ as an atoning sacrifice for the sins of the whole world is a precious truth that has significant ramifications for our lives and for our deaths."[36] I take it

---

[33] P. 67.

[34] P. 80.

[35] P. 68.

[36] P. 106. Abraham specifies that particular traditional soteriological theme because it lies at the core of his critique in chapter 5 of alternative theological construals of the significance of Jesus Christ's suffering and death for understanding our own experiences of suffering and death by, respectively, Marilyn McCord Adams and David Bentley Hart.

that his larger point is that Christian theological accounts of God's roles in both "negative mysteries" and the "positive mystery" must be framed conceptually in Christocentric ways because Christians' experiences of both "negative" and "positive" mysteries are Christocentrically framed.[37]

We will return to Abraham's attention to the *conceptual* centrality of Christology in Christian accounts of God's role in the context of the reality of "negative mysteries" in our lived words when we note ways in which all of these writers suggest that the "space" for anomie that is needed in "tellings of the Christian story" is conceptual in addition to being "practical."

Adam Lischer was a thirty-one-year-old, recently married attorney serving with distinction as an assistant district attorney in eastern North Carolina when he was first diagnosed with a stage two melanoma in his brain. Surgery removed all of the melanoma. His lymph nodes were cancer free. Adam elected to enter a clinical trial with interferon, an immunotherapy that increased his body's power to resist cancer. For the next sixteen months, the cancer seemed to be in remission. Recently married, he accepted a position in a law firm in Durham, North Carolina, where he and his wife Jenny moved and bought a house. He began preparing for confirmation in the Roman Catholic Church so that he and his Catholic bride could share the Eucharist together. They soon learned that Jenny was pregnant. Then, in a routine three-month checkup, his tests showed that melanoma had metastasized, was in stage four, and was innumerable and inoperable. He lived for thirteen and a half more weeks, during much of which time he

---

[37] That reading of Abraham's third point seems to be supported by the paragraph that follows it. There seems to be a bit of textual confusion at that point. Abraham had said he was closing with "three central claims" (p. 105). However, the text adds a fourth point that does not so much identify a fourth claim as elaborate on the third claim by locating the conceptual centrality in theological exposition of the "life, death, and resurrection of Christ" in the larger context of "the whole tory of creation, freedom, sin, providence, and redemption" (p. 106).

was treated with whole-brain radiation and chemotherapy, with all of the debilitation and suffering that is their intensely painful side effect. In *Stations of the Heart: Parting with a Son*,[38] Adam's father, Richard Lischer, Lutheran pastor and Cleland Professor Emeritus of Preaching at Duke Divinity School, gives a deeply moving and unsentimental account of Adam's dying. "Those who grieve," Lischer writes, "have no illusions about denying death or making it into a beautiful experience. We only want to remember in a saving way so that something whole and complete may come into view. To remember in this way is the work of God. My religious tradition calls it Resurrection."[39] After Adam's death, Richard and his wife Tracy reread Dietrich Bonhoeffer's *Letters and Papers from Prison*. "We read them in the same spirit with which Adam explored his own illness: not so much for help in coping, but for insight into God's role in our suffering."[40] Richard had come to see himself as "the interpreter"[41] of Adam's death. His interpretation of Adam's suffering, dying, and death is richly theological.

The theology is expressed, not abstractly and systematically, but in the way in which Richard structures the movement of a narrative that renders who Adam is, how Adam lived faithfully with the cancer, with its pain, and the pain of the side effect of its treatment, how Adam lived faithfully with the immanent prospect of death, and, by grace, of Adam's "godly dying"[42] in faith. As Adam begins cancer treatment, Richard sees him starting down two different paths concurrently: "one would take him through the maze of chemo and radiation to an uncertain end. The other, originating in his baptism and nurtured by the rituals of his newfound

---

[38] New York: Alfred A. Knopf, 2013.
[39] P. 7.
[40] P. 227.
[41] P. 238.
[42] P. 84.

community, would led him through the labyrinth to his true des-
tination."[43] Later he called them "two entangled histories: a scien-
tifically charted history of the disease; and an enchanted, uncharted
history of the person who bears it with grace."[44]

Richard comes to see the first as a path in and through "a secret
Zombie Church with low, leaded rooms, coffin-like scanners,
draughts of poison, and skeletal dancers. First you enter it; then it
enters you."[45] "The very word 'cancer'" infects our language and
imagination. If you want to say the worst about any crime, blight, or
prejudice, you will call it a 'cancer' on the body politic... The one
with the cancer *becomes* a cancer on the human community, a
byword, whose plight is whispered by all who pass by."[46] "Cancer
Church knows only two categories – dead and alive. Adam was
looking for another category and another path. This is the path that
ventures beyond survival (which is nothing to be sneezed at) and
promises blessedness... For just as good *health* is making its sloppy
exit in bursting tumors and failing organs, another claimant to the
title is arriving in the form of kindness, courage, and an inexplicable
wholeness of human spirit – what the Bible calls 'health.'"[47] The
first path is the context within which Adam also walks the
second path.

Adam was set onto his second path through no agency of his own
by his baptism by Richard. As his first step in walking it in the
context of "Cancer Church," he "got rid of his cell phone" and
"threw a clock off the back deck of his house into the creek
below...,"[48] showing that "he was through with billable hours and
consultations measured in minutes."[49] He and Jenny "went off the

[43] P. 83.
[44] P. 95
[45] P. 93.
[46] P. 93.
[47] P. 95.
[48] P. 75.
[49] P. 99.

clock in earnest and began to live in a different idiom. They began performing the small, repetitive actions by which clocktime is abolished and the eternal takes its place. Jenny was already at home in the world of Catholic devotion; Adam embraced it as if he had been looking for this sort of work all his life."[50] In one conversation, Adam and Richard agree that the act of dying is "like manual labor to be done in this life. It is a work and, as such, the mystery is much overrated."[51] It is not "labor" that, once it is completed, deserves some payment that is proportionate to how "long" one had labored. Rather, it is a case of doing of something for its own sake. "Now [Adam and Jenny's] days would be measured only by devotion to each other, kindness toward others, the rhythms of prayer, and the growth of her belly. Together they lit candles, said their prayers, recited the psalms, went to daily Mass, did the Stations, knelt at icons, watched old movies, ate pizza, and observed stars from their deck, all according to a new standard of time that wasn't really time at all."[52] "It doesn't do them justice to say that they were simply trying to bring some order into their lives.... What they were doing was more original and countercultural... As the prisoner Dietrich Bonhoeffer wrote, 'I think that even in this place we ought to live as if we had no wishes and no future, and just be our true selves.'"[53] The "work" they did together accomplished its intent. It communicated. Richard reports a conversation with a woman from Adam's church some time after Adam's funeral. Richard recalls, "I impulsively interrupted her. 'I wish you had known him the way I did, when he wasn't a victim.' All I meant to say was that she should have known him from his 'time of hope,' which was how I wanted to remember him.

---

[50] P. 102.
[51] P. 156.
[52] P. 102.
[53] P. 102

"She pounced on my carelessness. 'No *one* saw him as a victim. He was a *witness*.'"[54]

Richard, too, came to see that Adam lived in a "time of hope" throughout his path through Cancer Church, a hope to be, and to be even more so in future, one's "true self," a hope doubly symbolized for Adam by both Christian witness to the hope of resurrection and by the future of his as yet unborn daughter.

As Richard presents them, the two paths of Adam's life in dying can neither be separated nor conflated. They cannot be separated because each is a true "history" of one particular person. They are *Adam's* stories. They cannot be generalized as paradigms of how everyone's life in dying "ought" to go if they are genuinely faithful to God. Nobody else who dies of cancer goes through Cancer Church in just the way Adam did. For one thing, he was capable of exercising his own agency until relatively close to his death. Not all those passing through Cancer Church can do that. Nor can the paths be separated into a "real history" charted by medical science and a "sense-making story" framed theologically in terms of "religious symbols." The "history" of Adam's second "path" is the history of the one and only one human being who also walked the first path. It is an account of the personal identity of the one who lived with that particular cancer and its extended medical treatment in just the particular way in which Adam lived it. Pastoral care of Adam would have needed to be expressed in ways that both acknowledged the reality and honored the importance of both the "paths" Adam was walking concurrently while he was walking them.

That's Adam's story, but because the author writes what he saw in the first person, it is also the story of Richard's grief as he accompanies his son in his dying. The question both he and Adam ask in the face of Adam's cancer was how best to live:

[54] P. 107; emphasis in original.

"How can we know the way?" "Neither one of us ever got a straight answer," Richard writes, "but we were both shown a path. His was marked, 'To Blessedness.' Mine was a bit more obscure and over-grown, but it eventually took me to a better place as well. It led me from the bitter gall of losing him to something like settled sorrow. From 'It is a robbery' to 'He was my son, and I give thanks for him.'"[55] Part of what made Richard's path possible was his comfort with acknowledging to Adam that he had no explanation why horrific painful diseases happen and why some people die untimely deaths.

> When it came to spiritual life, Adam and I were moving in opposite directions. His faith was in the ascendancy, mine was losing ground...He had been seized by certainties about God that I couldn't match... Just as Adam was mastering the discipline of prayer, I was losing my ability to pray... It wasn't that I quit believing in God, only that I had apparently misunderstood the scope of God's responsibilities, the way a citizen might telephone the Department of Finance to complain about a broken water main when everyone knows, or should know, that the Department of Finance *never* fixes broken water mains. It was my mistake, not God's fault... I was following the writer Georges Bernanos' advice: "If you can't pray – at least say your prayers."[56]
>
> When we talked about sickness, death, and eternal life, Adam approached those topics with the confidence of a believer and the wrinkled brow of seeker... He complained to ... our Lutheran pastor ... that he never heard a preacher who was willing to admit, "I don't know." When he finally found one, it was only his dad.[57]

In the context of suffering profound grief, Lischer's faith found the space that allowed for the faithful agnosticism about theological

---

[55] P. 8.
[56] Pp. 112–113.
[57] P. 111.

"explanations" of horrendous suffering that we have seen in all of these accounts of profound suffering from disease or from the untimely death of a loved one, or both. He was able to find that "space" in a continuing engagement in practices that make up communities of Christian faith's common life of responding in praise to the "positive mystery" of the Triune God's wildly undomesticateable love.

His faithful agnosticism expresses the anomie Thompson cites. The *nomos* that was not exhibited by the world of Adam Lischer's fight with cancer would have been an abstract, God-given, law-like orderliness that would make it possible to explain theologically why Adam was afflicted by the just and loving God and, by doing so, "make sense" of the suffering of both Adam and his loved ones. When one's affirmation that one trusts in God as creator and redeemer raises questions about "why" Adam died, one stammers. One begins the affirmation anew in ways that block some inferences a questioner implicitly drew from the initial affirmation.

Richard Lischer found space to stammer by asking, not "Why is God doing, causing, or sending this?" but "What is God's role in this suffering?" Richard saw that the narrative arc of Adam's suffering could be mapped onto the narrative arc of the Gospels' accounts of God's role in "Holy Week," Jesus' last week from his arrest to his resurrection. He suggests that the Catholic traditional practice of praying the Stations of the Cross can serve as a kinesthetic and visual image of the overall movement of the entire Jesus narrative. It is a coherent narrative, one that can be "followed." In it God's role is that, "not of the supernatural escape from illness, but the faithful companion in the Valley. Not the restored flesh we had hoped for, but God in the flesh of those who suffer."[58]

This might be considered a "sense making" of a different sort, not the propositional "sense-making" of an explanatory argument, but

[58] P. 231.

the narratival "sense-making" of an excellent biography or a "realistic" novel, short story, or play. That too relies on a certain sort of *nomos*. The crucial difference between the two sorts of theological sense-making is that the second, unlike the first, does not begin with the premise that God's "role" in "what is going on" in situations of horrendous suffering is fundamentally, and perhaps exclusively, that of, systematic teleologically causal explanation of its existence. It assumes only that, given that a certain situation is the case, even a horrific situation, God will be playing some active role in it as companion to those involved, a companionship ordered to some good. Faith is fundamentally trust that that is the case. Richard Lischer's narrative powerfully renders Adam's way of living with cancer, its various medical treatments, and imminent death in just that trust.

In *Everything Happens For a Reason, and Other Lies I've Loved*, Kate Bowler writes of her own experience living both with treatments of stage 4 colon cancer and with the well-intentioned things church people said and did to comfort and console her, sometimes effectively and sometimes outrageously. She writes in righteous anger and righteous hilarity, and without a trace of self-righteousness.

Bowler had been suffering acute abdominal pains. Her doctor thought it might be caused by her gallbladder and corrected by surgery, but first there needed to be a test. The results were unexpected. Her first chapter, "Diagnosis," registers the shock of the absurd way in which she learned of her cancer: by phone from the doctor's office while she is in her own office at school pacing at her treadmill desk and flipping through her recent research. The rest of the book falls into two time spans. The next three chapters sketch Bowler's life before the diagnosis. The six chapters that follow track concurrently the treatment of her cancer and Bowler's struggles to live with immanent death as a person of faith.

The thirty-five-year-old Canadian woman who received the cancer diagnosis, an Associate Professor of the History of

Christianity at Duke Divinity School, is a practicing Christian. Although not from a Mennonite family, she grew up surrounded by communities of Mennonites, and in her twenties married Toban, a Mennonite man she had met when they were both fifteen. The Mennonites' way of living the Christian gospel has deeply formed her own faith. Following college she entered a doctoral program in American religious history and began work on a dissertation on the "prosperity gospel" movement. As she explains, "The prosperity gospel is a theodicy, an explanation for the problem of evil. It is an answer to the questions that take our lives apart: Why do some people get healed and some people don't?"[59] "The prosperity gospel has a very simple way of explaining why life as it is must be inherently just. As it is told, God established a set of principles that keep the world in order. Just as there are natural laws of gravity and thermodynamics, there are spiritual laws that steer the courses of lives and ensure that good things really do happen to good people... Spiritual laws offer an elegant solution to the problem of unfairness. They create a Newtonian universe in which the chaos of the world seems reducible to simple cause and effect. The stories of people's lives can be plotted by whether or not they follow the rules. In this world there is no such thing as undeserved pain."[60]

Her dissertation required extensive field research across several years during which she developed a "surreal limpness ... [that] extended," she writes, "from my shoulders to my fingertips."[61] She visited more than thirty-five doctors over the next six months, but none could diagnose it. The limpness made her an "object lesson"[62] in the prosperity gospel church she was studying, changing the congregants attitudes toward her: "In the spiritual world" of prosperity gospel "in which healing is a divine right, illness is a

---

[59] P. xiii.
[60] Pp. 25, 26.
[61] P. 14.
[62] P. 15.

symptom of unconfessed sin ... A suffering believer is a puzzle to be solved."[63] "I knew I was loved. I was prayed for. I was ministered to. But when, week by week, I returned with the same droop in my arms and weakness in my hands, I thought I saw their lips close and their arms cross, and I felt like faithlessness personified."[64]

And then another setback. She and her husband Toban had been hoping to start a family. As she was being prepared for a surgery that one doctor thought might correct her arm limpness, she was given a pregnancy test and to their astonishment and joy it was positive. The surgery was put off. But by the time she got home she felt something was very wrong. She miscarried.

Because of her arm limpness, she was referred to a physical therapist who specialized in working with dancers and musicians. "Our first meeting was a barrage of humiliations... 'You walk like a gorilla she said ... Knuckles forward. Slightly hunched.'"[65] "I had been born with overly loose joints and, with all the sitting and typing for my dissertation, my natural asymmetry had become exaggerated. My body responded ... by seizing up around my joints, trapping my nerves, ... *Presto!* Just like that. A dark chapter of my life closed."[66]

"It was," Bowler writes, "the beginning of a series of gains for me, ... I landed my dream job at a major university seminary teaching the big survey of American religion to do-gooders of all kinds. I secured a contract for my first book. The publisher even let me do my own reading for the audiobook version."[67] Undergoing fertility treatments she entered "a season of endless postpone-ment."[68] Once again to their joy she got pregnant, but her body's laxness made it a difficult pregnancy. Her labor was long and ended

[63] P. 16.
[64] Pp. 16, 17.
[65] P. 32.
[66] P. 33.
[67] P. 33.
[68] P. 44.

in a C-section. Having baby Zach in her arms was "the most bizarre feeling I had ever had. I felt like something had pushed the reset button and my life had only begun. I should have asked for a birth certificate for myself... What followed was a blissful year."[69] This is the woman who then received a cancer diagnosis and was told to go to the hospital immediately for surgery.

The remaining five chapters tell two stories concurrently. One story tracks the sequence of treatments of her cancer: She fears she won't survive the operation. The surgery removes the tumor. As she recovered from the surgery, a doctor tells her she has a 30% chance of survival, where survival means two years ("All I could think to say was, 'If you're going to say stuff like that to me, you'd better be holding my hand.' *Hold my hand,* I kept thinking. *Don't give up on me yet.*"[70]). A physician assistant (who "moves though the pleasantries with enough warmth to suggest that, at least on social occasions, she considers herself to be a nice person"[71]) checks her surgical stiches and asks "'How are you?" ... "'It's hard' I say, ... 'Well' she says, ... 'the sooner you get used to the idea of dying the better.'"[72] Tests show that she has a disorder, which only three percent of people have, that opens up new treatments for her. Clinical trials of one such treatment are about to begin at Emory University. Prohibitively expensive medical insurance threatens to block her participation in the trials. Her extended family plans to mortgage or sell all their homes to cover the expense, which would ruin the family financially. Two well-connected faculty friends "pull the right levers and know whom to ask; ... and within twenty-four hours I have multiple assurances ... that I will see only green lights from now on."[73] She begins the clinical trials at Emory. Tumors

[69] P. 50.
[70] P. 79.
[71] P. 79.
[72] P. 79.
[73] P. 97.

grow on her liver, for which she receives immunotherapy. Ten months after her diagnosis, those tumors are not shrinking, but neither do they grow. At that point she is into uncharted territory with the new drugs where there is no previous experience by which to forecast future outcomes. Her doctor judges it is necessary to take her off chemotherapy. Thereafter, the tumors are examined every two months. She publishes this book a few years later.

Interwoven with that story is another one tracing Bowler's reflections on her experience living through her medical story as a person of faith. Four themes that we have seen in other texts recur. For one, she is confirmed in a faithful agnosticism about theodicies' explanations of evils and suffering. Already in her twenties when her body failed her and her arms went numb she had "lost faith in the whole concept of things being fair."[74] As she went through the stages of treatment of her cancer, she recognized that the prosperity gospel was not limited to a particular religious movement. It is pervasive in American culture. "There is something so American about the 'show-and-tell' of our daily lives. The big house means you work hard. A pretty wife means you must be rich. A subscription to the *New York Times* shows you must be smart."[75] Moreover, she recognized, she tacitly shared it. She came to see that "no matter how many times I rolled my eyes at the creed's outrageous certainties, I craved them just the same. I had my own prosperity gospel."[76] "Married in my twenties, a baby in my thirties, I won a job at my alma mater straight out of graduate school. I felt breathless with the possibilities... I don't think it was anything as simple as pride. It was certainty, plain and simple, that God had a worthy plan for my life in which every setback would also be a step forward. I wanted God to make me good and make me faithful, with just a few shining accolades along the way.

[74] P. 24.
[75] P. 20.
[76] P. xiv.

Anything would do if hardships were only detours on my long life's journey. I believed God would make a way."

"I don't believe that anymore."[77] "Everything happens for a reason," is for her a lie she has loved and no longer believes. "I plead with a God of Maybe, who may or may not let me collect more years. It is a God I love, and a God that breaks my heart."[78]

Without ceasing to trust God, her disbelief expresses an experience of the loss of an order or "*nomos*" that was identified by a theodicy that purported to make sense of experiences of suffering. It is an "anomic" faithful agnosticism.

Part of what opens space for the acknowledgment of anomie within the life of faith is a second theme. *Theo*dicies by definition ground the sense-making *nomos* they promote in a received account of "what" God is. Agnosticism about a theodicy might mean the abandonment of any "belief" in God. It does not mean that, however, when the experience of suffering that led to the agnosticism has been joined by a face-to-face encounter with God analogous to Job's encounter. That encounter grounds trust in God whose presence is experienced precisely in the midst of a suffering that defies "explanation." Bowler has a distinctive image for her encounter: In the

> first few days after my diagnosis ... I couldn't say for certain that I would survive the year. But I felt as though I'd uncovered something like a secret about faith... At a time when I should have felt abandoned by God, I was not reduced to ashes. I felt like I was floating. Floating on the love and prayers of all those who hummed around me like worker bees, bringing notes and flowers and warm socks and quilts ... They came like priests and mirrored back to me the face of Jesus... That feeling stayed with me for months. In fact I had grown so accustomed to that floating feeling that I started to

[77] P. xiv.
[78] P. xv.

panic at the prospect of losing it. So I began to ask ... pastors I knew, and nuns I liked, *What am I going to do when it's gone?* ... But all said yes, it will go. The feeling will go. The sense of God's presence will go...There will be no formula for how to get it back... But they offered me this small bit of certainty, and I clung to it. When the feelings recede like the tides, they said, they will leave an imprint. I would somehow be marked by the presence of an unbidden God... It is not proof of anything. And there is nothing to boast about. It was simply a gift.[79]

It is striking that "floating," the image she uses for the experience of God's presence, is the same image she had used for dying. In conversation with Toban after her surgery she tries to explain that "flying away" is not an apt image for death. "I don't know how to explain it, Toban. It's like we are all floating on the ocean, holding on to our own inner tubes. We're all floating around, but people don't seem to know that we're all sinking. Some are sinking faster than others, but we're all sinking."[80]

That theme is closely connected to a third theme that Bowler's book shares with others. To return to the distinction between "positive mystery" and "negative mysteries" (my terminology, not Bowler's), she is clear that the "why" of the "negative mystery" she suffered can no more be "explained" than can the "why" of her "positive mystery" of the experience of God's presence: "I can't reconcile the way the world is jolted by events that are wonderful and terrible, the gorgeous and the tragic. Except I am beginning to believe that these opposites do not cancel each other out... The horror of cancer had made everything seem like it is painted in bright colors. I think the same thoughts again and again: Life is so beautiful. Life is so hard."[81]

---

[79] Pp. 121, 122.

[80] P. 65.

[81] P. 123.

That connects to a fourth theme common to these books. Faith in God involves beliefs, but it is basically trust in God. Responding to Job's words, "Though He slay me, yet will I trust Him," she writes, "*Yes, yes, yes. Yet I will trust in Him. I don't know what the word 'trust' means anymore, except there are moments when I realize that it feels a lot like love.*"[82] Space opens in which to express anomie in the very act of expressing trust in God by praising God when the trust is not based on the claim that God, or our concept of God, causally "explains" why things go they way they do; rather, it is based on the gift of God's love to us expressed in a direct experience of it that elicits our love to God.

A final theme is unique to Bowler's book. It concerns the shape of faith in God lived in suffering and in the shadow of death, which may arguably also be the shape of the life of faith in all circumstances. Just before the cancer surgery she had a conversation with her friend Frank. "I asked him about heaven. He knew what I was asking because he always knows. Will I be connected? Will I miss everything? Will I see my son sprout up and learn the rules of Canadian football? . . . These are the plans I have made. These are the hopes that are being ground into dust. . . . 'Don't skip to the end,' he said gently. 'Don't skip to the end.'"[83] "Plans are made. Plans come apart. . . And nothing human or divine will map out this life."[84] "I think I believed that I was living in the center, but I rarely let my feet rest on solid ground, rooting me in the present. . . [I]f I were to invent a sin to describe . . . how I lived – I would not say it was simply that I didn't stop to smell the flowers. It was the sin of arrogance, of being impervious to life itself. I failed to love what was present and decided to love what was possible instead."[85] If trust feels a lot like love, it is not only love to God in response to experience of God's present love to us, but also love to the quotidian as God's world. Bowler describes living that way in terms of one season of the Christian liturgical year: living in "Ordinary Time," which follows the Easter season.

Bowler doesn't map the seasons through which she lives between receiving the diagnosis of her cancer and going off the experimental chemotherapy onto the seasons of the liturgical year of Christian praise of God. Rather, she maps the seasons of the liturgical year onto the seasons of her treatment for cancer. Each of the liturgical seasons – Advent and Christmas, Lent and Holy Week, Easter, and Ordinary Time – gets its concrete character for her that year from what is going on then in her other story, the story of her medical care. To get to the point where she can really live in "Ordinary Time," she endures Advent's waiting: specifically waiting for the surgery, maybe for recovery from the surgery, maybe not. On Ash Wednesday she, facing death, is called "to stare it down. We are solid flesh, and we are ashes."[86] "There is no denying our finitude. It is plain and hard and true."[87] And not unique to her. She writes, "I've taken up cursing for Lent, the forty-day stretch before Easter in which those who want to understand Jesus' sacrifice choose one of their own."[88] "This season is beginning to spark something close to rage."[89] She had read that people in grief swear because they feel language has reached its limits in a time of inarticulate sorrow. "Or at least that is what I tell people when I am casually dropping f-bombs over lunch as I explain the mysteries of Lent."[90] "And then one Sunday brunch, like a fever, it breaks."[91] She is having lunch with her friend Blair, whose dad is suffering from early-onset Alzheimer's and Blair is agonizing about whether she should take

[86] P. 133.
[87] P. 128.
[88] P. 126.
[89] P. 127.
[90] P. 127.
[91] P. 138.

a genetic test to find out whether it might happen to her too. "She can't bear the answer, and I realize deep into the story that I am smiling ear to ear. I am the worst person in the world. . . 'I am so sorry,' I say. Blair starts to laugh. 'It's not that I would ever want this for you, but – I'm sorry for saying this – but you live here too.' 'What do you mean?' 'You live with an uncertain future. You live here too. And – I'm so sorry – but I'm so *fucking* grateful to have you here.' And as I start to cry over our upscale lunch, Blair starts to laugh even louder."[92] Those on whose love and prayers she had "floated" in her experience of the "positive mystery" of the presence of God's love, those who "came like priests and mirrored back to [her] the face of Jesus," are often those who also experience the "negative mysteries" of deep suffering. Next, Palm Sunday under-scores how the concurrence of positive and negative "mysteries" makes the world irreducibly ambiguous. Bowler has been in treat-ment for five months and they take two-year old Zach to church. The service commemorates Jesus' "triumphal" entry into Jerusalem riding on a donkey, "people waving their arms in the air, tattered coats thrown down before the One who marches to his death."[93] The church service begins with a procession around the church with everyone waving palm fronds. Palm fronds are a symbol of martyrdom. "But at every Palm Sunday service, the only whiff of martyrdom is the senses that very child is about three seconds from getting a palm frond in his eyeball."[94] "Zach is utterly still as he takes in the view."[95] The procession "is a celebration. It is a funeral procession. Holding Zach in my arms, fifteen days from my next scan, I wish I knew the difference."[96] Good Friday services in prosperity gospel churches underscore for Bowler the absolute

---

[92] Pp. 139, 140; emphasis original.
[93] P. 112.
[94] P. 110.
[95] P. 111.
[96] P. 112.

reality of Jesus suffering and death by absolutely minimizing it, and thereby minimizing the absolute reality of her suffering and uncertain future. She received innumerable "Happy Good Friday!" greetings. The preacher opened the Good Friday service commemorating Jesus' crucifixion with, "Isn't it great we serve a risen Lord!" Bowler notes that she "loudly skipped the moment in the tradition where Jesus is conspicuously absent."[97] Bowler is "livid about a Facebook post that read something like 'Just a little life in the midst of death!' and an accompanying video testimony about a celebrity who learned that, in trusting God, she could expand her self-esteem and her business."[98] "'Everyone is trying to Easter the crap out of my Lent,' I say to my friends through gritted teeth and tears."[99] The season of Ordinary Time, and the life of faith appropriate to it, only comes after the season of Easter and the "positive mystery" of Jesus' resurrection; but Easter only comes after the seasons of Advent and Christmas, Lent and Holy Week, each of which is what it is only because it is concurrently marked by "negative mysteries" of suffering and death as well as the "positive mystery" of God's presence.

Stammering in Anomie to Comfort the Anguished

Those accounts of experience of suffering "negative mysteries" in the context of experience of the "positive mystery" of God's gracious ways of relating to us in love, both of which defy "explanation," all stammer as they characterize both "mysteries." They stammer as efforts, at least implicitly, to praise the Triune God in the various acts that comprise communities of Christian faith's worship of God, in the broadest sense of "worship." They stammer

[97] P. 131.
[98] P. 132.
[99] P. 134.

because, as we have seen, in general all efforts to characterize "what" and "who" the God is that relates to us in a love expressive of the Triune God's intrinsic love must necessarily stammer. In these texts, we deal in particular with efforts to comfort and console those who anguish at others' profound suffering. They do so as enactments of a subset of the practices that make up Christian worship of God. They do so as enactments of practices in which, at least implicitly, the Triune God is praised. Moreover, they stammer because they enact practices of pastoral care of the anguished in an anomic way. They stammer because the Triune God that they implicitly praise is, so far as they are capable of knowing, "useless" to "explain" the suffering they seek to comfort; therefore, it lacks any theoretical *nomos* by which to causally "explain" it.

This has several implications for how acts of pastoral care of those caught up in a "negative mystery." Some of those texts focus, at least in part, on someone who is afflicted by a "negative mystery" (Adam Lischer; Kate Bowler). Others focus on someone anguished by another's suffering (William Abraham; Richard Lischer; Nicholas Wolterstorff). This book has focused narrowly on theologically problematic pastoral remarks made to those share the latter situation. Accordingly, I shall limit elaboration of the implications of the need to stammer in an anomic way to some suggestions about their bearing particularly on pastoral care of those anguished by another's suffering.

At a high level of generality, those implications can perhaps be summarized in two rules:

1) In pastoral care intended to comfort and console those anguished by others' terrible suffering, we should focus both what we say and what we do as much on the one who is anguished as we do on God.

2) In pastoral care intended to comfort and console those anguished by others' terrible suffering, we should frame what we say about God's relation to that suffering in terms of

remarks about *where* God is in "what is going on" and *how* God relates to the sufferer and to those who love her, rather than in terms of *why* this evil is happening and *why* this loved one is suffering.

Each of these general "rules" has both negative and positive applications in the way the Triune God is implicitly praised in the way we relate to console people anguished by others' horrendous suffering.

The first rule would seem to be so self-evident as to be trite, except for the fact that the commonplace pastoral remarks we have deemed theologically problematic so regularly violate it, choosing to enter a conversation about "why" this terrible evil happened to someone else rather than addressing the one who anguishes *in* her anguish. Negatively, the first rule blocks immediate recourse to explaining God and what God is up to in this horrible thing happening to someone else.

Instead, the first rule positively promotes being present to the one who is anguishing about that someone else's deep suffering. In Appendix 2 of her book, Kate Bowler makes several suggestions of truly helpful things to do and say in comforting someone suffering profoundly from a horrific evil that primarily acknowledge the reality of the suffering by being fully present to it. They apply equally well to pastoral care for people anguishing over another's suffering. Being "fully" present involves being physically present: "Some of my best moments with people have come with a hug or a hand on the arm. People who are suffering," and we may add who are anguished at another's suffering, 'often – not always – feel isolated and want to be touched. Hospitals and big institutions in general tend to treat people like cyborgs or throwaways. So ask if your friend feels like a hug and give her some sugar."[100] Being "present" also takes the form of physically bringing presents.

---

[100] P. 174.

Richard Lischer reflects in particular on the resonances of people bringing food or sharing a meal:

> As long as we continue to eat and drink in community, we will never plug up the gap that separates us from our son, for every meal reminds us of how little self-sufficiency we can claim for ourselves and how dependent we are on others for nourishment... All our meals belong to the open space in the gap, because we are never finished with eating. We are never so full of love for one another that we don't need to share a meal, and we are never so full of God that we don't need him to feed us with bread and wine... When I approach the altar for Communion, the many meals of our lives coalesce into one.[101]

In her suggestions of things to do and say in place of theologically problematic remarks, Kate Bowler expands the array of ways we can be truly present by bringing a present: Try saying "*I'd love to bring you a meal this week. Can I email you about it?*' Oh, thank goodness. I am starving, but mostly I can never figure out something to tell people that I need, even if I need it. But really, bring me anything. Chocolate. A potted plant. A set of weird erasers. I remember the first gift I got that wasn't about cancer and I was so happy I cried... Do something that suits your gifts. But most important, *bring me presents.*"[102]

When it is time to talk, the first rule urges that we talk initially about the one who is anguished about the horrific evil that causes another's profound suffering, and not about the one she anguishes *for*. Instead of launching into explanations of why her loved one suffers so horribly, let the first remarks be acknowledgment that what the anguished person is going through is so hard. "Be willing to stare down the ugliness and sadness," Bowler writes out of her own experience. "Life is absurdly hard, and pretending it isn't is exhausting."[103]

---

[101] P. 232.

[102] P. 172.

[103] P. 175.

It is so hard that, as William Abraham wrote in his account of the time of his son's death, "ordinary people" would say to him, "'I have no idea what you are going through because I can only begin to imagine what it is like. I do not know what it is like.'"[104]

Only after all that may we turn to conversation about the suffering of the anguished person's loved one, why it happened, and God's relation to it. And that must begin with a frank acknowledgment that we do not know why it happened. Further remarks about God's involvement in their experience of "negative mystery" must be bracketed by a declaration of a faithful agnosticism about causal "explanations" of it. As Nicholas Wolterstorff puts it: "God has not told us why there is natural and moral evil in the world, has not explained to us why we do not all flourish until full of years."[105]

Negatively, the second rule calls for taking control of conversation with such folk by steering the conversation away from the "Why?" question about horrific evils and the suffering they cause. The question, "Why did this terrible thing happen?" assumes that the horrible thing that "happened" is like someone's intentional act. That is, it assumes that it was something "done" ("sent") on "purpose" (intention) to actualize a particular goal (its *telos*) according to a "plan" that is specific to the particular person to whom it "happened." It further assumes that the "someone" who intentionally acted in this way is God who is at once all-powerful, good, and just. It is precisely because God's almighty-ness empowers God to control all that "happens" in the created realm that God is capable of "sending" this evil. Accordingly, given that God is both good and just, the "why" question also assumes that God's "purpose" in "sending" this terrible thing is to bring some good to the one to whom it happened. Therefore, the question also assumes that in sending that person this terrible evil God will not let it cause so high a degree of suffering that the person won't be able to handle it. For

---

[104] *Among the Ashes* (Grand Rapids, MI: Wm. B. Eerdmans, 2017), p. 14.
[105] P. 209.

the same reason, the question assumes that God also can and has sent good "happenings" into that person's life so he should "Count his blessings." "At least" he has them, no matter how much else he has lost to this horrific evil "happening." Against all of that, the negative implications of the first rule are that the invitation to talk about this "negative mystery" in terms of that vocabulary of "intentional causality," "sending," "purpose," "*telos*," "plan," the invitation to draw up a balance sheet of blessings enjoyed and suffering endured, and the invitation to construe the ability to endure the suffering as a blessing from the same hand that sent the evil, should all be gently and firmly declined.

Nicholas Wolterstorff makes the point passionately in connection with his son Eric's untimely death:

> Saint Paul calls death the last great enemy to be overcome. If death is God's enemy, how could Eric's death be something God did? God may have permitted Eric's foot to slip, but God did not make it slip. . . Some say that tragedy is part of God's strategy for soul-making . . . But Eric was dead. The tragedy of his untimely death did nothing for his soul. And as for the souls of those who loved him: I found the very idea repulsive, that God would use Eric's death as a device for making me, and the others who knew and loved him, better persons. . . Others [argue] that tragedy is God's way of punishing us for our wrongdoing. . . I joined Job in rejecting the idea that God used Eric's early death as a way of punishing me – or anyone else. Jesus healed the infirm and the raised the dead. He did not declare that infirmity and untimely death are God's just punishment for sin, and then walk on.[106]

I have been arguing that the vocabulary that describes the occurrence of "negative mysteries" in terms of "intentional action" by God is intrinsically a vocabulary of theodicy that fails to

---

[106] *In This World of Wonders* (Grand Rapids, MI: Wm. B. Eerdmans, 2019), p. 208.

acknowledge that both "negative mysteries" and "the positive mystery" are not, albeit it for different reasons, subject to causal "explanation." This vocabulary relies on an assumption that "what" the Triune God is, what "makes God *God*," is the absolutely unqualified power of God's relating to all else in creative blessing *ex nihilo*. That sense of "the power of God" defines God's power in terms of an account of how God is "useful" to all that is not God: bringing it into existence, sustaining it in existence, ordering it to a single over-all *telos* that is its ultimate "good," by the unrestricted power to control all that "goes on" in creation. When that is "what" it is to be God, God's "usefulness" is intrinsic to God's concrete actuality. Conceived in that fashion, God is essentially "useful." That entire line of argument, however, is theologically problematic, because the Triune God's relating to all else in the economy has three strands, not just creative blessing; and God's sovereignty in each is powerful in a different sense of the term. Consequently, the argument here goes, our efforts to speak about "what" and "who" the Triune God is must stammer. When, on the other hand, occurrences of "negative mystery" are described in terms of "intentional action," the goal is to avoid stammering and explain the occurrence of a horrific evil in God's good creation with some precision and certainty.

The demand for certainty in "explaining" horrific evils is intrinsic to theodicies. An example: During the course of her treatment, Kate Bowler writes sardonically, "my in-box is full of strangers giving reasons... [Most] everyone I meet is dying to make me certain... Even when I was still in the hospital, a neighbor came to the door and told my husband that everything happens for a reason... 'I'd love to hear it,' he replied. 'Pardon?' she said, startled. 'The reason my wife is dying,' he said ... effectively ending the conversation as the neighbor stammered something and handed him a casserole."[107]

<hr/>

[107] Pp. 112, 113.

Bowler notes later that there "are three life lessons people try to teach me that, frankly, sometimes feel worse than cancer itself. The first is that I shouldn't be so upset, because the significance of death is relative." "It doesn't matter, in the End, whether we are here or 'there.' Its all the same,' writes a woman in the prime of her youth." Variations of this come from "believers" and "atheists." "But the message is the same: stop complaining and accept the world as it is." These Bowler calls the "Minimizers." "The second lesson comes from the Teachers, who focus on how this experience is supposed to be an education in mind, body and spirit… 'I hope you have a "Job" experience,' writes one man bluntly, and I can't think of anything worse to wish on someone. … The harder lessons come from Solution People, who are already a little disappointed that I am not saving myself. 'Keep smiling! Your attitude determines your destiny!' says Jane from Idaho, and I am immediately worn out by the tyranny of prescriptive joy."[108] "Most of their explanations," Bowler observes, "were assurances that even this [cancer] is a secret plan to improve me. 'God has a better plan.'"[109] "Apparently God is also busy going around closing doors and opening windows. He can't get enough of that."[110] "I became certain that when I died some beautiful moron would tell my husband that 'God needed an angel,' because God is sadistic like that." "There is a trite cruelty in the logic of the perfectly certain. Those letter writers are not simply trying to give me something. They are also, always, tallying up the sum of my life, sometimes for clues, sometimes for answers, always to pronounce a verdict. But I am not on trial."[111]

The second rule also has positive implications: Let what we say about God's relation to horrific evils and the horrendous sufferings they cause be framed in terms of remarks about *where* God is in

[108] Pp. 116–118.
[109] P. xvi.
[110] P. *xv*.
[111] P. 119.

422

what is going on and *how* God relates to the sufferer and to those who love her. Those remarks should emerge out of the silence that follows a frank acknowledgment of our faithful agnosticism about all the certainties that are routinely offered as pieces of a theoretical explanation of the of the presence of "negative mysteries" in God's good creation. Kate Bowler: "[T]ake the advice of one man who wrote to me with his policy: Show up and shut up."[112] Nicholas Wolterstorff describes his book *Lament for a Son* as a collection of "fragments – with lots of space between the fragments… I think of the white space between the fragments as silence. In the face of death we should not talk much."[113] Let pastoral remarks be framed in terms an affirmation of God's presence in the midst of the horrific distortion of creatures' dynamics that is the evil they undergo and the suffering in which they experience it. Together they are an inexplicable "negative mystery" in the midst of which is present the "positive mystery," also inexplicably. Framed in terms of that affirmation, pastoral remarks address questions about what God is doing in what is "going on," and not in terms of "why" it is going on. Those pastoral conversations around questions about how God goes about relating to the entire network of the one undergoing horrendous suffering, those who care for him, those who love him, those that care about those who love him. Framed in that fashion, pastoral remarks made to those who anguish over another's horrendous suffering will need to move freely back and forth between the different vocabularies that are appropriate to each of the three strands of the way in which the Triune God does relate concurrently to this situation in particular, inasmuch as God relates in those three ways to all else as rendered in the three strands of Canonical Scripture's accounts of God's economy. For that reason, pastoral remarks framed in that way will necessarily always stammer. And slip back into silence.

[112] P. 175.
[113] P. 198.

Bibliography

Abbott-Smith, G. (1937). *Manual Greek Lexicon of the New Testament.* Edinburgh: T & T Clark.

Abraham, William (2017). *Among the Ashes.* Grand Rapids, MI: William B. Eerdmans.

Adams, Marilyn McCord (2006). *Christ and Horrors: The Coherence of Christology.* Cambridge: Cambridge University Press.

(1999). *Horrendous Evils and the Goodness of God.* Ithaca, NY: Cornell University Press.

Agamben, Giorgio (2011). *The Kingdom and the Glory.* Stanford, CA: Stanford University Press.

Aquinas, Thomas (1945). *Basic Writings of Saint Thomas Aquinas.* Edited and annotated by Anton C. Pegis. New York: Random House.

(1964). *Summa Theologiae,* Vol. 1–7. New York: McGraw-Hill Book Co.

Barth, K. (1936). *Church Dogmatics,* I/1. Translated by G. T. Thomson. Edinburgh: T & T Clark.

(1957). *Church Dogmatics,* II/1. Edited by G. W. Bromiley and T. F. Torrance. Translated by T. H. L. Parker et al. Edinburgh: T & T Clark.

(1960). *Church Dogmatics,* III/3. Translated by G. W. Bromiley and R. J. Ehrlich. Edinburgh: T & T Clark.

Batut, Jean-Pierre (1999). 'God the Father Almighty': Thoughts on a Disputed Term. *Communio,* 26, 278–294. Cf. Batut, *Dieu le pere tout-puissant* (Paris: Parole et Silence, 1998).

Behr, John (2018). One God Father Almighty. *Modern Theology,* 34(3), 315–320.

Beker, J. Christian (1990). *The Triumph of God: The Essence of Paul's Thought.* Translated by Loren T. Stuckenbruck. Minneapolis, MN: Fortress Press.

Bettenson, Henry (1943). *Documents of the Christian Church.* London: Oxford University Press.

Bonhoeffer, Dietrich (2013). *Letters and Papers from Prison.* New York: Alfred A. Knopf.

Bowler, Kate (2018). *Everything Happens for a Reason, and Other Lies I've Loved.* New York: Random House.

Brunner, Emil (1943). *The Divine Human Encounter.* Translated by Amandus W. Loos. Philadelphia: Westminster Press.

Buber, Martin (1937). *I and Thou.* Translated by Ronald Gregor Smith. Edinburgh: T &T Clark.

Calvin, John (1960). *Institutes of the Christian Religion.* Edited by John T. McNeill. Translated and indexed by Ford Lewis Battles. Philadelphia: Westminster Press.

Case-Winters, Anna (1990). *God's Power: Traditional Understandings and Contemporary Challenges.* Louisville, KY: Westminster John Knox.

Chalamet, Christophe (2018). Immutability or Faithfulness? *Modern Theology*, 34(3), 457–469.

Chalamet, Christophe, Mariel Mazzocco, and Marc Vial (eds.) (2018). *Modern Theology*, 34(3). Special Themed Issue: Naming God Today: Contemporary Approaches to the Divine Attributes.

Chenu, M. D., OP (1939). The Plan of St. Thomas' Summa Theologiae. *Review Thomiste,* March.

Cobb, John B. (1964). *A Christian Natural Theology.* Philadelphia: Westminster Press.

Cobb, John B., and Griffin, David Ray (1976). *Process Theology: An Introductory Exposition.* Philadelphia: Westminster Press.

Cremer, Hermann (2016). *The Christian Doctrine of the Divine Attributes.* Foreword by Matthias Gockel. Edited by Helmut Burkhardt. Translated by Robert B. Price. Eugene. OR: Pickwick Publications.

Davies, Brian (1992). *The Thought of Thomas Aquinas.* Oxford: Clarendon Press.

Denzinger, Heinrich (1957). *Enchiridion Symbolorum,* 30th edition. Translated by Roy J. Defferici. St Louis, MO: Herder.

Doehring, Carrie (2015). *The Practice of Pastoral Care: A Postmodern Approach.* Louisville, KY: Westminster John Knox Press.

Evans, Donald (1963). *The Logic of Self-Involvement.* London: SCM Press.

Farley, Edward (1996). *Divine Empathy*. Minneapolis, MN: Fortress Press.

Farrer, Austin (1967). *Faith and Speculation*. New York: New York University Press.

Fergusson, David (2018). *The Providence of God: A Polyphonic Approach*. Cambridge: Cambridge University Press.

Gavrilyuk, Paul L. (2004). *The Suffering of the Impassible God: The Dialectics of Patristic Thought*. Oxford: Oxford University Press.

Gerrish, Brian (1973). To the Unknown God: Luther and Calvin on the Hiddenness of God. *Journal of Religion*, 53.

Hartshorne, Charles (1948). *Divine Relativity: A Social Conception of God*. New Haven, CT: Yale University Press.

Hodge, Charles (1872). *Systematic Theology*, 3 vols. New York: Scribner, Armstrong, and Co.

Holmes, R. J. (2007). *Revisiting the Doctrine of the Divine Attributes: In Dialogue with Karl Barth, Eberhard Juengle, and Wolf Kroetke*. New York: Peter Lang.

Jenson, Robert W. (1997). *Systematic Theology I*. New York: Oxford University Press.

Johnson, Keith L. (2019). Karl Barth and the Purification of Divine Simplicity. *Modern Theology*, 35(3), 531–542.

Johnson, William Stacy (1997). *The Mystery of God: Karl Barth and the Postmodern Foundations of Theology*. Louisville, KY: Westminster Press.

Kasemann, Ernst (1969). *New Testament Questions for Today*. Translated by W. J. Montague. Philadelphia: Fortress Press.

Kelley, Melissa M. (2010). *Grief: Contemporary Theory and the Practice of Ministry*. Minneapolis, MN: Fortress Press.

Kelsey, David H. (2009). *Eccentric Existence*. Louisville, KY: Westminster John Knox.

Levering, Matthew, and Kalantzis, George (2019). *Modern Theology*, 35(3). Special Themed Issue: Catholics and Evangelicals on Divine Simplicity.

Lischer, Richard (2013). *Stations of the Heart: Parting with a Son*. New York: Alfred A. Knopf.

Lohman, Freidrich (2018). God's Freedom to be Bound. *Modern Theology*, 34(3), 368–386.

Long, D. Stephen (2019). Thomas Aquinas' Divine Simplicity as Biblical Hermeneutic. *Modern Theology*, 35(3), 496–507.

Luther, Martin (1955–1986). *Luther's Works*. Edited by Jaroslav Pelikan. St. Louis, MO: Concordia Publishing House.

McCabe, Herbert (1987). *God Matters*. London: Continuum Books.

McFarland, Ian A. (2019). The Gift of the *Non aliud*: Creation from Nothing as a Metaphysics of Abundance. *International Journal of Systematic Theology*, 21(1), 44–58.

Mackey, James P. (1994). *Power and Christian Ethics*. Cambridge: Cambridge University Press.

Martyn, J. Louis (1997). *Theological Issues in the Letters of Paul*. Nashville, TN: Abingdon.

Mazzocco, Mariel (2018). The Secret Dynamism of Divine Simplicity. *Modern Theology*, 34(3), 434–444.

Migliore, Daniel (2008). *The Power of God and the Gods of Power*. Louisville, KY: Westminster John Knox.

Moltmann, Juergen (1974). *The Crucified God*. Translated by R. M. Wilson and John Bowden. New York: Harper & Row.

(1993). *God in Creation*. Minneapolis. MN: Fortress Press.

(1983). *Power of the Powerless*. Translated by Margaret Kohl. San Francisco: Harper & Row.

(1991). *Theology of Hope*. Translated by James W. Leitch. San Francisco: Harper & Row.

(1981). *Trinity and the Kingdom*. Translated by Margaret Kohl. New York: Harper & Row.

Pannenberg, Wolfhart (1971). *Basic Questions in Theology*, Vol. II. Translated by George H. Kehm. Philadelphia: Fortress Press.

(1973). *The Idea of God and Human Freedom*. Translated by R. A. Wilson. Philadelphia: Westminster Press.

(1990). *Metaphysics & the Idea of God*. Translated by Philip Clayton. Grand Rapids, MI: William B. Eerdmans.

(1991). *Systematic Theology*, 3 vols. Translated by Geoffrey W. Bromiley. Grand Rapids, MI: William B. Eerdmans.

Pasewark, Kyle (1993). *A Theology of Power: Being beyond Dominium*. Minneapolis, MN: Fortress Press.

Plantinga, Alvin (1980). *Does God Have a Nature?* Milwaukee, WI: Marquette University Press.

Polkinghorn, John (2002). Eschatological Credibility: Emergent and Teleological Processes, in Ted Peters, Robert John Russell, and Michael Welker, eds., *Resurrection: Theological and Scientific Assessments*. Grand Rapids, MI: William B. Eerdmans.

The Presbyterian Church (USA) (1999). *The Book of Confessions. The Westminster Confession of Faith*. Louisville: The Presbyterian Church (USA).

Price, Robert B. (2011). *Letter of the Divine Word*. London: Bloomsbury T & T Clark.

Rahner, Karl (1970). *The Trinity*. Translated by Joseph Donceel. New York: Herder & Herder.

Schwoebel, Christoph (2018). The Eternity of the Triune God: Preliminary Considerations on the Relationship between the Trinity and the Time of Creation. *Modern Theology*, 34(3), 345–356.

Sonderegger, Katherine (2015). *Systematic Theology Vol. 1: The Doctrine of God*. Minneapolis, MN: Fortress Press.

Soskice, Janet Martin (1985). *Metaphor and Religious Language*. Oxford: Oxford University Press.

Stevenson, Kenneth W. (2004). *The Lord's Prayer: A Text in Tradition*. Minneapolis, MN: Fortress Press.

Taylor, John (1972). *The Go-between God: The Holy Spirit and the Christian Mission*. Oxford: Oxford University Press.

Tanner, Kathryn (2010). *Christ the Key*. Cambridge: Cambridge University Press.

(2000). Creation and Providence. *The Cambridge Companion to Karl Barth*, Chapter 7. Edited by John Webster. Cambridge: Cambridge University Press.

(1988). *God and Creation in Christian Theology*. Oxford: Basil Blackwell.

(2001). *Jesus, Humanity, and the Trinity*. Minneapolis, MN: Fortress Press.

Thomas, Debie (2018). My Daughter's Wall. *The Christian Century*, p. 1.

Thompson, Deanna (2018). *Glimpsing Resurrection: Cancer, Trauma, and Ministry*. Louisville, KY: Westminster John Knox.

(2012). *Hoping for More*. Eugene: Cascade Press.

Tonstad, Linn Marie (2016). *God and Difference: The Trinity, Sexuality, and the Transformation of Finitude.* New York: Routledge.

Tillich, Paul (1954). *Love, Power, and Justice.* Oxford: Oxford University Press.

 (1951). *Systematic Theology, I.* Chicago: University of Chicago Press.

Torrance, Alan (2000). The Trinity. *The Cambridge Companion to Karl Barth*, Chapter 5. Edited by John Webster. Cambridge: Cambridge University Press.

Turner, Denys (1995). *Darkness of God.* Cambridge: Cambridge University Press.

Turretin, Francis (1992–1997). *Institutes of Elentic Theology.* Edited by James J. Dennison. Translated by George Musgrave Geiger. Phillipsburg, NJ: P & R Publishing.

Van Driel, Edwin (2008). *Incarnation Anyway.* New York: Oxford University Press.

Vial, Marc (2018). God's Almightiness and the Limits of Theological Discourse. *Modern Theology*, 34(3), 444–457.

Wartenberg, Thomas E. (ed.) (1992). *Rethinking Power.* Albany: State University of New York Press.

Westermann, Claus (1972). *Beginning and End in the Bible.* Philadelphia: Westminster Press.

 (1974). *Blessing.* Translated by Keith Crim. Philadelphia: Fortress Press.

 (1984). *Genesis 1–11: A Commentary.* Minneapolis, MN: Augsburg.

White, Thomas Joseph, OP (ed.) (2011). *The Analogy of Being: Invention of the Antichrist or the Wisdom of God?* Grand Rapids, MI: William B. Eerdmans.

Williams, Rowan (2018). *Being Human: Bodies, Minds, Persons.* Grand Rapids, MI: William B. Eerdmans. An edited version of Ch. Five was published in *The Christian Century,* August 29, 2018, as "Silence in the Face of Mystery."

 (2018). *Christ the Heart of Creation.* London: Bloomsbury Continuum.

Wittman, Tyler (2018). On the Unity of the Trinity's External Works: Archeology and Grammar. *International Journal f Systematic Theology*, 20(3), 359–380.

Wolff, Pierre (1979). *May I Hate God?* Mahwah, NJ: Paulist Press.

Wolterstorff, Nicholas (1987). *Lament for a Son*. Grand Rapids, MI: William B. Eerdmans.

(2019). *In this World of Wonders: Memoir of a Life in Learning*. Grand Rapids, MI: William B. Eerdmans.

Wood, Charles (2008). *The Question of Providence*. Louisville, KY: Westminster John Knox Press.

Index

Books of the Bible